LIVE & WORK IN

SCANDINAVIA

André de Vries

SERIES EDITORS VICTORIA PYBUS & DAVID WOODWORTH

Published by Vacation Work, 9 Park End Street, Oxford
www.vacationwork.co.uk

LIVE AND WORK IN SCANDINAVIA

First Edition 1995 Victoria Pybus & Susan Dunne
Second Edition 2002 André de Vries

Copyright © Vacation Work 2002

ISBN 1-85458-289-5

Cover design by
Miller, Craig and Cocking Design Partnership

Publicity: Roger Musker

Text design and typesetting by Brendan Cole

Printed and bound in Italy by Legoprint, SpA, Trento

CONTENTS

DENMARK

– SECTION 1 –
LIVING IN DENMARK

– SECTION II –
WORKING IN DENMARK

STARTING A BUSINESS

THE EURO

On January 1st 2002 the Euro became the legal currency in Finland (but not Denmark, Norway or Sweden), replacing the marka at the unromantic rate of 5.94573 marka to the Euro. The value of the Euro against the UK £ and the US $ varies from day to day: at the time of going to press one Euro is worth UK £0.62 or US $0.87.

FINLAND

– SECTION I –
LIVING IN FINLAND

– SECTION II –
WORKING IN FINLAND

NORWAY

– SECTION 1 –
LIVING IN NORWAY

– SECTION II –
WORKING IN NORWAY

SWEDEN

– SECTION I –
LIVING IN SWEDEN

– SECTION II –
WORKING IN SWEDEN

FOREWORD

Mention Scandinavia to most people and they think of wide empty spaces, unpolluted cities populated by leggy blondes of both sexes, the highest standard of living (and the highest taxes) in Europe, cradle-to-grave welfare that is the envy of many Europeans, true democracy, sexual freedom, liberal attitudes, a class-free society, midnight sun, forests, long white winters, cross-country skiing, reindeer, the Arctic Circle, saunas and wonderful food based around the *smörgåsbord*. Although these images reflect some truth, they do not really do justice to these complex societies.

The Scandinavian nations of Denmark, Sweden and Norway are linked by geography and a common Norse heritage giving them history, culture and customs in common, yet there are noticeable variations and more than a little rivalry between these related nations. Finland is the odd one out and furthest from the Scandinavian stereotype. The Finnish language is unrelated to the other Scandinavian languages and its people are not Nordics. Denmark and Norway were united under a single monarchy for several centuries and then Sweden became the dominant power. Norway broke away from Sweden in 1905 and became an independent state. Finland was part of Sweden for more than six hundred years, then, for nearly a hundred years until the Bolshevik revolution, it was a Russian Grand Duchy. Scandinavia in 2002 comprises two republics (Finland and Iceland) and three low-key monarchies (Denmark, Norway and Sweden).

The Scandinavian countries have shown no less individualistic tendencies in their approach to the European Union. Denmark was the first, and seemingly the only Scandinavian country willing to join the European Community back in 1972. Norway flirted with the EC and then shied away from full union in 1972 after a negative national referendum of which there was a repeat performance in 1994. Sweden and Finland joined the EU on January 1st 1995 (widely regarded as an impossibility considering the complexity of various issues, including Sweden's neutrality, which had to be resolved in the run-up period). Norway and Iceland are however, members of the European Economic Area (EEA), thus giving them access to the EU's vast market, which boosted their economies almost immediately.

The relevance of all this to the foreigner considering living and working in Scandinavia is that if he or she is an EU national it is possible to go to any Scandinavian country to look for work without prior permission or the need to obtain a work permit, or in some cases even a residence permit. The previous restrictions on working and duration of stays still apply to non-EU nationals, but with the increasing opening up of the Nordic economies, foreign expertise generally will be welcomed and prospects are much better also for non-EU nationals.

This book aims to provide a more complete picture of the different countries that make up Scandinavia and to provide insights into many aspects of daily life that will help the non-Scandinavian who wants to live and work amongst the Nordics and the Finns to settle in with as much ease as possible despite the different languages, customs, laws and attitudes that would otherwise hamper their progress. The fact that the small populations of these countries reveal their ability to speak English with alacrity and often with impressive fluency, means that even non-linguists may consider them places to exercise their entrepreneurial flair.

Each of the country sections in the book is divided into two sections *Living* and *Working* which between them cover all areas of these subjects from opening a bank account, finding accommodation and a job, employment regulations, advice on setting up a small business, not to mention the aesthetics of Scandinavian social mores, language, education and culture.

Much has been written of the reserve of Scandinavians and for the outsider this contrasts strikingly with, say, the peoples of Mediterranean countries and can be the basis of profound loneliness amongst foreigners initially. It takes perseverance to break the ice, which like the Scandinavian winters can seem unendurable at times. Those who have stayed long enough to do so usually find it impossible to leave Scandinavia permanently. There is no time like the present for discovering the extraordinary beauty of and the opportunities for living and working in Scandinavia.

André de Vries
April 2002

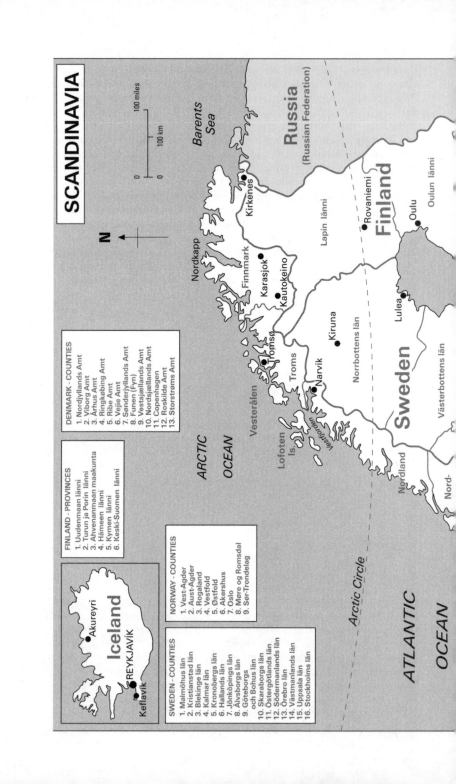

SCANDINAVIA

N

0 ├──────┤ 100 km
0 ├──────┤ 100 miles

SWEDEN - COUNTIES
1. Malmöhus län
2. Kristianstad län
3. Blekinge län
4. Kalmar län
5. Kronobergs län
6. Hallands län
7. Jönköpings län
8. Älvsborgs län
9. Göteborgs och Bohus län
10. Skaraborgs län
11. Östergötlands län
12. Södermanlands län
13. Örebro län
14. Västmanlands län
15. Uppsala län
16. Stockholms län

NORWAY - COUNTIES
1. Vest-Agder
2. Aust-Agder
3. Rogaland
4. Vestfold
5. Østfold
6. Akershus
7. Oslo
8. Møre og Romsdal
9. Sør-Trøndelag

FINLAND - PROVINCES
1. Uudenmaan läani
2. Turun ja Porin läani
3. Ahvenanmaan maakunta
4. Hämeen läani
5. Kymen läani
6. Keski-Suomen läani

DENMARK - COUNTIES
1. Nordjyllands Amt
2. Viborg Amt
3. Århus Amt
4. Ringkøbing Amt
5. Ribe Amt
6. Vejle Amt
7. Sønderjyllands Amt
8. Funen (Fyn)
9. Vestsjællands Amt
10. Nordsjællands Amt
11. Copenhagen
12. Roskilde Amt
13. Storstrøms Amt

Iceland
REYKJAVIK
Keflavik
Akureyri

ATLANTIC OCEAN

ARCTIC OCEAN

Arctic Circle

Nordkapp
Barents Sea

Finnmark
Kirkenes
Karasjok
Kautokeino
Tromsø
Troms
Vesterålen
Lofoten Is
Vestfjorden
Narvik
Kiruna
Nordland
Nord-

Russia
(Russian Federation)

Finland
Rovaniemi
Lapin läani
Oulu
Oulun läani

Sweden
Luleå
Norrbottens län
Västerbottens län

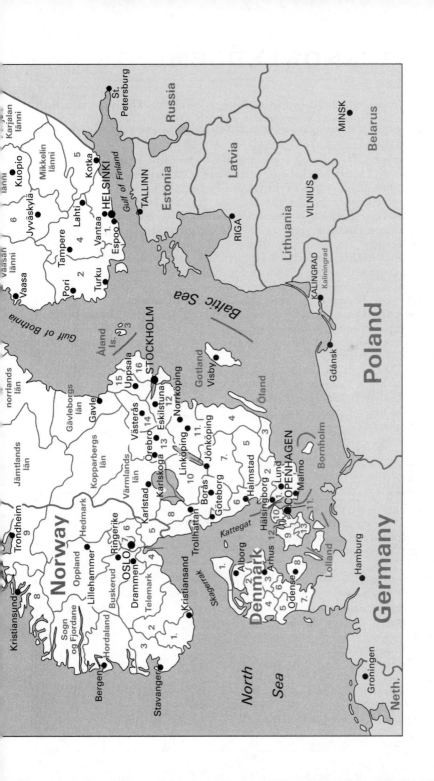

ACKNOWLEDGEMENTS

This is the second edition of *Live & Work in Scandinavia*. The first was written by Victoria Pybus and Susan Dunne and this edition has been fully revised by André de Vries. In addition we would like to thank the following for their invaluable help in compiling this book:

Denmark: James Gray for his account of life in Denmark, Julian Isherwood for his case history, Henrik Munkebo Christiansen for invaluable assistance, and the staff of the information office of the Danish Embassy in London.

Sweden: Christopher Fowler for his case history, Katarina Bjurstedt for translations, Peter Jacobi and Helga Zimmermann for hospitality in Sweden, A[ob]se Lofgren-Gunsten (Europatria) and Magnus Hammar (International Union of Tenants) for generously sharing their specialist knowledge, the staff of the Swedish Embassy information department, the Swedish institute and the national employment service of Sweden for their help in providing statistics and information on Swedish life and employment.

Norway: Ian Bryceson for his case history, Alexander Krivokapic for translations, the British Embassy in Norway and the Norwegian Tourist Board in London for prompt information, Jim Hoskin of Kvaerner Professional Services for employment data, and the tireless help of the Norwegian Embassy staff information department.

Finland: Nic Mepham for his case history and insights into Finnish daily life, Tom and Liz Paavelainen (Transite.fi) for generously sharing their time in Helsinki, Mike Baker, Marieke Saher and Timo Tapani for answering many questions on life in Finland, and the staff of the information department of the Finnish Embassy.

TELEPHONE NUMBERS

Please note that the telephone numbers in this book are written as needed to call that number from inside the same country. To call these numbers from outside the country you will need to know the relevant international access code; these are currently 00 from the UK, Denmark, Finland, Norway and Sweden and 011 from the USA.

To call Denmark: dial the international access code + 45 + the complete number as given in this book.

To call Finland: dial the international access code + 358 + the number as given in this book but omitting the first 0.

To call Norway: dial the international access code + 47 + the complete number as given in this book.

To call Sweden: dial the international access code + 46 + the number as given in this book but omitting the first 0.

To call the UK: international access code +44 + the complete number as given in this book – *but omitting the first 0 in the British number.*

To call the USA: international access code +1 + the complete number as given in this book.

Denmark

SECTION I

LIVING IN DENMARK

GENERAL INTRODUCTION

RESIDENCE AND ENTRY REGULATIONS

SETTING UP HOME

DAILY LIFE

RETIREMENT

GENERAL INTRODUCTION

DESTINATION DENMARK

AT ONE AND THE SAME TIME occupying the northern extremity of continental Europe and the most southerly part of Scandinavia, it is perhaps not surprising that Denmark (Danmark to the Danes), being the physical and cultural bridge between the two, was the first Nordic country to join what was then called the European Community (now known as the European Union) following a national referendum in 1972.

The golden age of Denmark can well be said to have been during the reign of the Danish King Knud (Canute) who, from 1016 to 1042, ruled a northern empire that stretched from England through Scandinavia as far as the Baltics. During the Middle Ages the power of Denmark was in decline as conflicts between church and state split the country. This in turn allowed the area to be dominated by Sweden and the nearby German states. Until the last quarter of the 18th century, German was the official language of the Danish court. Despite various military defeats, Denmark continued to enhance its reputation as a great trading and seafaring nation, as befits the descendants of the Vikings.

The Napoleonic Wars, in which Denmark unwisely allied herself to the French, ultimately led to defeat and bankruptcy for the Danes. In the ensuing Treaty of Kiel, Denmark was forced to surrender Holstein to the Confederation of German States. By 1848 Denmark was on the way to industrial prosperity when a series of constitutional reforms made it one of the most democratic nations of Europe. Novelties for the time included a code of civil liberties, free speech, and a new parliament, the *Rigsdag*, with an upper (*Landsting*) and a lower (*Folketing*) chamber; the latter elected by popular vote. Further military disasters led to the ceding of Schleswig to the German Confederation. At this point, Denmark became the smallest it had been for centuries.

Danish politics, as elsewhere in northern Europe, was a hotbed of radical ideas by the 1870s. These ideas accompanied the industrial and agricultural revolutions which were progressively transforming political and cultural life and increasing the expectations of the population. Proposals for reform included the outline of a welfare state including sick pay, maximum working hours and old age pensions. Such proposals were championed mainly by the 'United Left', a party whose manifesto also included demands for universal suffrage and equal taxation. Their demands led to a backlash from the rightist parties and eventually a compromise. Full parliamentary democracy was not instituted until 1901. At the onset of the First World War, Denmark, which had good relations with both Britain and Germany, declared itself neutral. In the ensuing peace settlement (Treaty of Versailles) Denmark regained northern Schleswig but not the southern part, which voted to remain part of Germany. The new Danish-German border was fixed just north of Flensborg. In the years between the two World Wars, Denmark became progressively more enlightened and liberal, notably in the removal of discrimination against illegitimacy and in the legalisation of abortion. National engineering achievements included the building of the bridge linking Jutland and Funen Island.

As the price for remaining neutral during the Second World War, Denmark conceded to inevitable Nazi occupation. The Germans wanted to use Denmark as a base for an invasion of Norway and, after threats that refusal would result in a German bombardment of Denmark, the Danes allowed the Germans in. Resistance came later when it was obvious the Germans were losing. For the duration of the occupation normal parliamentary government was replaced by a national coalition and German currency replaced the Danish krone. Despite the fact that Denmark had escaped the devastation wrought on much of Europe, the economy had collapsed and needed a generous infusion from the Marshall Plan funds. Denmark became a member of the United Nations in 1945. Aware of a fast developing polarisation of Europe into east and west, and notwithstanding a consistent policy of neutrality, the Danes joined NATO in 1948, albeit with an anti-nuclear proviso which it still maintains today.

Modern Denmark

The post-war years were marked by political upheavals as the various parties including the main ones, the Social Democrats and Conservatives, struggled to gain the upper hand and fell in and out of coalitions with smaller parties. Meanwhile the liberal ethos of Denmark continued to evolve. This has been a mixed blessing, admirable in its equal treatment of all citizens – for instance homosexuals can enter into a kind of legalised marriage and the equality of women has gone further in Denmark than in many other European nations – but perhaps less successful in other respects where an element of exploitation has crept in. Having abandoned all forms of censorship in the sixties, Denmark generally, and Copenhagen in particular, is considered the porn centre of Europe. Copenhagen even has its own museum of erotica, the top floors of which are devoted to the most extreme varieties.

Denmark's other well publicised but less lurid products include Hans Christian Andersen (who emanated from Odense), Lego, and its eponymous offshoot Legoland (an entire model village made from Lego at Billund), Bang and Olufsen high-tech consumer durables, Carlsberg-Tuborg lager, Danish bacon and blue cheese, the 'bog people' – 2,000-year-old human remains found perfectly preserved in peat bogs –, contemporary furniture, and (arguably) Hamlet.

PROS AND CONS OF MOVING TO DENMARK

TO SUMMARISE: Denmark is well-organised and efficiently run and typical of the Scandinavian countries, where small, well-disciplined populations facilitate administration. In addition, Danes are generally politically aware and contemporary in outlook, with a practical approach to everyday life and a talent for attention to detail. Underlying this pragmatism is a strong sense of history reaching back beyond the Vikings to antiquity, and an ability to incorporate the past in their lives without living in it. The Danes have, for instance, successfully modernised the monarchy, which is reduced and democratised but still an important part of their national identity. The Danes are proud of the way that their country has adjusted from being a state with an empire to what it is today, and believe that other countries would be wise to emulate them.

Pros:
- Rates of pay are higher than in the UK.
- Denmark is a well-organised country with a reasonably unobtrusive bureaucracy.
- The state provides womb-to-tomb care for all citizens.
- Standards of medicine and public health are amongst the highest in Europe.
- The Danes are very good linguists, so no problems communicating.
- The standard of living in Denmark is higher than in the UK, but at a higher cost.
- The business sector is diversified and well-developed offering plenty of opportunities for entrepreneurs.

Cons:
- There is a high rate of unemployment, so jobs are not easy to find.
- Prime holiday time mid-June to mid-August is virtually a write-off for anyone wanting to do business.
- Winters are much longer than in UK or US.
- An appreciation of Danish history and culture is essential as social life revolves around them.
- Although everyday relations are easy, Danes take time to open up and may seem withdrawn and cold.

It would be wrong to portray Denmark or any other Nordic country as Utopian. While on the one hand individual freedom and the right of all citizens to be cared for by the state are seen as paramount, there is also a seedy underside of social problems and delinquency, not just in the capital and large cities but in the remoter communities. Denmark also has one of the highest suicide rates in the world. About one per cent of the population are Inuit (Eskimo) immigrants from Denmark's other territory of Greenland. Greenlanders are widely regarded as second-rate citizens by even the liberal Danes and alcoholism and social problems are rife among them. The high level of immigration and many years of high unemployment have put a strain on the welfare state such that Denmark may find it difficult to maintain such exemplary standards indefinitely.

Another perceived ill is that there is a growing rationale among young people that employment is no longer a priority or even a necessity. In other words, those who have become used to relying on the state no longer see earning a living and paying taxes as their part of a social contract

POLITICAL AND ECONOMIC STRUCTURE

Government and Politics

Denmark is divided into eighteen major regions each of which elects representatives for the national parliament (*Folketing*). Each major region is broken down into smaller units.

The parliament is unicameral with 179 seats. In addition, frequent referendums provide the population with a direct say on major issues. Elections are held every four years. Each of the 18 regions elects its representatives to the *Folketing* and supplementary seats are allocated on the basis of the percentage of votes gained overall by the political parties. A minimum of 2% of all votes is needed in order to get into parliament. This system of proportional representation ensures a more accurate representation of the wishes of the electorate but inevitably leads to no one party governing the country. Over the past couple of decades Denmark has been ruled by coalitions made up of varying parties. The highest number of parties in parliament has so far been 11.

The Danes are strongly attached to their independence and historical traditions, much like the British, and feel great disquiet about the increasing control of the European Union over their affairs. Denmark experienced a major crisis over the EU when the Maastricht Treaty was rejected in 1992. A suitably revised version with negotiated opt-outs relating to common defence, common currency, union citizenship and pan-EU legal directives was put to the electorate in May 1993, when it was accepted. A referendum on the Amsterdam Treaty in 1998 was easily won by the Yes vote, but in September 2000 the Danes again showed their dislike of European integration by rejecting membership of the European single currency by 53% to 47%, in spite of a strong Yes campaign backed by the government. It is, however, likely that the next referendum will result in a Yes vote.

Political Parties

The 11 parties represented in parliament at the beginning of 2002 are: *Venstre* (the Liberal Party) and *det Konservative Folkeparti* (Conservative People's Party), who form the government, supported by the *Danske Folkeparti* (Danish People's Party), who have no ministers. The opposition is made up of the *Socialdemokraterne* (Social Democrats), the *Socialistisk Folkeparti* (Socialist People's Party) and the *Enhedslisten* (Red-Green Unity List); other minor parties are *det Radikale Venstre* (Radical Liberals), *Kristeligt Folkeparti* (Christian People's Party) as well as three parties representing Greenland and the Faroe Islands.

Historically the Social Democrats were the largest party and held the balance of power the longest. However from 1983 to 1993 there was a liberal minority government led by a Conservative Prime Minister, Poul Schlüter. In 1993 the Social Democrats again formed a coalition government headed by Poul Nyrup Rasmussen. This continued as a basic two-party coalition of Social Democrats and the Socialist People's Party after the election of March 1998. Poul Nyrup Rasmussen called early elections in November 2001 and saw his coalition soundly defeated. For the first time since 1920 the Liberals (*Venstre*) form the largest party in the *Folketing*. Their leader Anders Fogh Rasmussen is now Prime Minister. The Danish People's Party made big gains, while the extreme right parties failed to gain any seats at all.

Some 30% of those elected to the parliament and local councils are female. Some 750,000 people are members of political parties. The Danes are generally politically aware and involved in the democratic process; surveys show that 90% of the population are satisfied with the political system. National turnout of voters at parliamentary elections is always very high, ranging from 82% to 89%. They do not have a high opinion of politicians, however, who are poorly paid by European standards.

The Economy

The Danish economy is based largely on agriculture and light industry, including electronics, techno-chemicals, pharmaceuticals, furniture-making, paper and printing, textiles and cement. Food-processing and drinks, especially beer, are also important. This is supported by a high level of agricultural output which needs little introduction: bacon, butter and cheese being some of the most well-known products.

The lack of indigenous raw materials means that these have to be imported which leaves the Danish economy vulnerable to price fluctuations and supply. The discovery of offshore oil in the 1980s has helped to offset what was previously a large drain on the economy. Natural gas is another resource that has had an economic benefit. Denmark produces enough for its own use and also manages to export the surplus.

According to the Gross National Product per head of the population, Denmark ranks as the world's sixth richest country, and second after Luxembourg in the EU.

GEOGRAPHICAL INFORMATION

Area and Main Physical Features

Denmark is the smallest of the Scandinavian countries at 43,093 sq km (16,638 sq miles). Of the countries in the European Union only Belgium, the Netherlands (just) and Luxembourg are smaller. Denmark consists of the province of Jutland, which projects from northern Germany, and the Danish archipelago, made up of over 400 islands, many of them tiny and uninhabited, while one of the two largest, Zealand, contains the capital Copenhagen (København) and most of the commercial and industrial activity. Copenhagen is on the coast and is separated by the Øresund strait from Sweden, a mere half hour away by ferry. A 10-mile long bridge has been constructed across the Sound, linking Denmark and Sweden. Its completion is intended to bring greater prosperity to Copenhagen as well as to Malmö on the other side. A bridge and tunnel linking Zealand and Funen opened in 1997. The so-called 'Great Belt' bridge includes the world's second largest suspension bridge with a free span of a mile. The project cost £3.5 billion; as a result of all the bridge-building one can now take a train or drive directly from mainland Europe to Sweden.

Other important islands are Funen, the nearest large island to Jutland to which it is physically linked by road and rail; Lolland, and Falster, two artificially linked islands off the south of Zealand; and the isolated island of Bornholm which lies far to the east in the middle of the Baltic Sea between Poland and Sweden.

Denmark is a low-lying country, its highest point, the Uding Skovhoej, reaching only 550 feet (173 metres). The landscapes are open, and offer a great expanse to the eye especially the coastline, of which there is 7,000km. The stretch of coast from the Skaw to Blaavands Huk is the longest sand beach in Europe. Nowhere in Denmark is more than a 52km (32 miles) from the sea.

Greenland and the Faroe Islands

The predominantly Arctic island of Greenland, which is bigger than all of Scandinavia and has a population of 55,117, has belonged to Denmark since 1380, and still comes under Danish sovereignty, as do the 17 remote Faroe Islands (population 47,287), which are situated in the Atlantic between Scotland and Norway. Both are self-governing but have two seats each in the Danish parliament. Neither area belongs to the EU; Greenland was a member of the EC until 1985, when it voted in a referendum to secede. The Faroe Islands are negotiating for complete independence from Denmark, which would result in the generous Danish subsidy being phased out.

Most of Greenland lies permanently under an icecap; this immense island has some of the earth's most stunning scenery, especially if you like icebergs. In the short Arctic summer the coastal areas undergo a transformation as they explode into a mass of wild flowers and teeming wildlife. Iceland has invested much money in Greenland, bringing its tourist facilities up to date and the islanders' housing would not look out of place in a modern city suburb. The tourist potential, fishing grounds and probable mineral resources are Greenland's biggest assets.

The Faroe Islands on the other hand are a twitcher's paradise offering an unrivalled range of seabirds in quantities which make you wonder why Hitchcock didn't film *The Birds* there. Unfortunately the islanders' annual, bloodthirsty tradition of hacking to death a school of migratory whales has upset many tour operators, not to mention their clients, which has led to an almost total tourist boycott. The Faroese derive their income from fishing and whaling rather than tourism so they are not likely to change their ways.

Internal Organisation

For administrative purposes Denmark is divided into 14 districts plus the two cities of Copenhagen and Frederiksberg. These *amter* are the equivalent of counties. The smaller units into which the *amter* are divided are the municipalities (*kommuner*) of which there are 275. Both these entities have a small amount of autonomy in their localities but federalism is much less well-developed than in Germany or Spain.

Population

The population of Denmark received additions during the Middle Ages from German, French, Dutch and Polish stock. Until the 60s, the only 'foreign' population was the 20,000 strong German contingent in North Slesvig. In common with many other countries, so-called guest workers, mainly from Turkey, Asian countries and Yugoslavia were invited to Denmark as a source of cheap labour for the growing economy. Many have now settled there. In addition, several thousand asylum seekers, mainly from Iran, Sri Lanka and Vietnam were taken in by Denmark during the past couple of decades. Most recently, some thousands of refugees from ex-Yugoslavia have been granted asylum in Denmark. The immigrant population of Denmark is rising rapidly, and has gone up from about 2.4% in 1984 to over 5% today or 7% if you count the immigrants' children. Out of the total population of some 5.4 million, at least a quarter are based in the capital, Copenhagen, where the majority of immigrants are to be found.

Climatic Zones

Being more southerly, Denmark has a continental climate rather than the typical Scandinavian one of extreme and long winters. In fact Danish winters can be very wet. Long-lasting frosts tend to be a bigger feature of the cold months than snow. However the difference between summer and winter temperatures rarely exceeds 20°C. The average January temperature for Copenhagen (which is on the same latitude as Edinburgh or Newfoundland) is 0.4°C and July 17°C. The coldest month is generally February.

Spring and autumn can be very mild but the windswept agricultural plains of the Jutland peninsula can be a trial to farmers at sowing time; the seeds are literally tossed to the wind and may never reach the furrow.

REGIONAL GUIDE

Information Facilities

Most major towns have a tourist office. Outside Denmark you can contact the nearest embassy, if there is no tourist office.

National Tourist Offices:
   Danish Tourist Board, 55 Sloane St, London SW1; 020-7259 5958; www.visitdenmark.dk.
   Scandinavian Tourist Board, 655 3rd Ave, New York, NY 10017; ☎212-885-9700; www.visitdenmark.dk.

JUTLAND (JYLLAND)

The largest part of Denmark is the peninsula of Jutland which projects 250 miles (400kms) from the 42-mile (68kms) land border with Germany into the North Sea. Although appearing to be named for its jutting appearance, it actually takes its name from the Jutes, a tribe originally quite separate from the bloodthirsty Danes, who overran and absorbed them some time in the ninth century. Modern-day Jutland is highly cultivated, indeed the south is known as the breadbasket of Denmark, but with more variations of landscape than may be found anywhere else in Denmark. Schleswig in the south is home to 20,000 ethnic German, but Danish citizens. The town of Ribe, once a medieval port, has long silted up, but the ancient town has been lovingly preserved and is a great tourist attraction. The main southern city is Esbjerg mainly known as the docking place for Scandinavian Seaways ferries and fish-oil processing. The after-effects of the latter hang heavily on the air.

The eastern side of Jutland is hilly and in many parts wooded, unlike the windswept western side. Just south of the city of Fredericia is the bridge that links Jutland to Funen Island. Fredericia is also one of the country's main railway termini. Just north of Fredericia is the more attractive harbour town of Vejle whose prime industry is sausage-making. Anyone who harbours fond memories of interlocking little plastic bricks to create cars, castles, boats and the like, may indulge in the ecstasy of viewing over 43 million of them clamped together to form both fantastic and familiar structures at the Legoland Park at Billund, to the west of Vejle. The name Lego is derived from the Danish *Leg Godt* (good play).

Further north, but still in the east, is the area known as the Danish Lake District extending roughly as far north as Viborg. The area is characterised by gentle, wooded hills, some rather diminutive lakes, and is a popular camping area in summer. It contains the towns of Skanderborg, Silkeborg and the undisputed cultural gem of Århus. Århus is a lively university city and port of 200,000 residents that has its origins in the Viking era; one may catch the ferry from here to Kalundborg in Zealand. Note that the university still uses the old spelling of Aarhus.

The medieval heart of the city is the cathedral from which radiate narrow twisting streets. In contrast, impressive architecture from recent decades is much in evidence in the outer part of the city. Musikhuset, the concert hall/opera house complex, dates from the 1980s, and comprises the first phase of the new Scandinavian Congress Centre which opened in 1995. Its completion is expected to make Århus the leading conference centre of northern Europe. In addition to this architectural wealth is the collection of about 75 original buildings from the 16th to the 19th centuries brought from around the country and re-erected on a special site *Den Gamle By* (the Old Town), to recreate the atmosphere of market town life through the centuries. The entire city provides an atmospheric backdrop for The Århus Festival, a week-long arts extravaganza which takes place annually at the beginning of September.

Yet further north is the town of Randers and, almost in the centre of Jutland, the city of Viborg. As befits such an importantly sited city, Viborg was the coronation place of successive Danish kings, but only until 1655. Viborg has continued to decline in importance: 200 years ago it was the provincial administrative centre. These days its chief importance is as a market centre for the surrounding agricultural district.

The northern part of Jutland is actually an island, separated from the rest of the peninsula by the Limfjord. The northwest (known as *Limfjordslandet*) is a popular holiday area attracting the masses during the summer months with its expanse of excellent beaches and sea sailing on what is virtually a vast inland lake. However it is only for those who like their sea air fortissimo, as the area is generally blasted by the wind coming off the North Sea.

The northwest of Jutland is dominated by Denmark's fourth largest city, Aalborg, which is situated on the southern bank of the Limfjord. Beyond Aalborg, on the northern side of the Limfjord reached by the Limfjord bridge, the landscape is windswept, bleak and fairly uninviting. Aalborg has a rich mercantile past from which its wealth and importance sprang. It is also the home of the Danish Worldwide Archives whose records (a vast collection of them) detail the migration of every Dane who has moved overseas. The archives can be used by the public to trace the emigration of individuals. The grim northern port of Frederikshavn is principally known for being overrun by other Nordics who come to drink alcohol in life-threatening quantities, thanks to the less stringent drinking laws of Denmark and the ferry companies which dock there. The dramatically sited Skagen however, on the narrow projection of land that is the most northerly point of Jutland, is a magical place with inspiring light effects much favoured by indigenous painters in the 19th century. Some of their resulting canvases can be seen in the local museum.

Main tourist offices

Aalborg Turistbureau, Østergade 8, 9000 Aalborg; ☎98 12 60 22; fax 98 16 69 22; www.aalborg-tourist.dk, www.visitnord.dk.

Tourist Århus/Convention, Rådhuspladsen 2, Rådhuset, 8000 Århus C; ☎89 40 67 00; fax 86 12 95 90; www.aarhus-tourist.dk.

Fredericia Turistbureau, Danmarksgade 2A, 7000 Fredericia; ☎75 92 13 77; fax 75 93 03 77; www.sej.dk.

FUNEN (FYN)

The second largest of the islands, Funen, which lies between Jutland and the largest island of Zealand is known as the 'the garden of Denmark'. Typical of Danish cultivation is the symmetry and orderliness of the fields on Funen from which a vast quantity of fruit and vegetables is produced. The main city, and third largest in Denmark is Odense, which was also the birthplace of Hans Christian Andersen, though there is nothing very fairytale-like in the city's appearance today. Its famous son has generated a large tourist industry, high hotel prices and a week-long festival celebrating his life and works every July. Odense has a pleasant old centre away from which modern industrial development has sprawled along the canal bank. In the 19th century, the canal brought increased prosperity to the city by connecting Odense to the sea and facilitating export of the island's produce.

Denmark's largest engineering project to date is the 18km-long road and rail link (a bridge and a tunnel) between Funen and Zealand, over the Store Bælt (Great Belt).

Funen is a busy holiday area and the many harbours and marinas in the south attract a large number of the yachting fraternity, principally Danes and Germans. The hub town of the south is Svendborg from where you can also get ferries to the smaller islands such as Ærø or take the road bridge across to the island of Langeland. There is a host of small islands in this region and numerous ferries to reach them. Another southern town, Fåborg, is also popular with tourists, but tends to be less frenetic than Svendborg. The museum of the Funen painters is a major attraction of the town.

Main tourist office
Odense Turist Bureau, Vestergade 2, 5000 Odense C; ☎66 12 75 20; fax 66 12 75 86; www.visitfyn.dk/gb.

ZEALAND (SJÆLLAND)

Zealand is the largest of the Danish islands (roughly the same area and shape as Northern Ireland), and also the site of the capital, Copenhagen (København), which acquired this honour in 1443. Inevitably Zealand is where most of the population, production and commercial activity of Denmark are located.

Copenhagen: The founding of Copenhagen can be dated from the building of a castle in the 12th century, of which only ruins remain on the site of Christiansborg, the parliament complex of modern Denmark. Major construction of the capital's landmark buildings began in the 16th century under the auspices of Christian IV; the royal palace of Amalienborg is a 17th century edifice.

Modern Copenhagen is considered one of the friendliest capitals of Europe and certainly the most welcoming in Scandinavia. It is also one of the most pleasing, due thought having been given to the requirements of pedestrians over motor vehicles and corporate interests. The old city fortifications have been re-sculpted into parks and small lakes and the wharves and quaysides of the old 'merchants' harbour' have become public walkways. The general atmosphere has the reputation of being one of the most laid-back and Bacchanalian (especially the nightlife) in Europe. The Christiania area of the city has been largely taken over by those who prefer an alternative lifestyle. The first hippies arrived there in the 1960s and there is a commune of about 1,000 people now living there. They pay no taxes, build without permission and deal openly in soft drugs. The Danish government is not entirely happy about this situation, especially the drug dealing, which it is trying to limit by interrupting supplies as much as possible.

Surprisingly, Copenhagen is not one of the most expensive capitals in which to live, although in Denmark generally the cost of living is extremely high. Despite its reputation for the uninhibited pursuit of pleasure, the city is not without its moments of reflection: the red and white Danish flag (*Dannebrog*) flies at half mast on the morning of the 9th April, the anniversary of the German occupation.

Copenhagen is separated from Sweden by the Øresund, a narrow strip of water 16.8km wide across which a road/rail tunnel and bridge link was recently built. It is now possible to drive from Germany to Sweden without taking a ferry as the bridge/tunnel links between the main Danish islands are complete. Even so, many people still like to take the so-called 'Flying Boats' or *Flyvebådene,* which go directly from Copenhagen to Malmö, Landskrona and Helsingborg in Sweden. The original settlement on the site of Copenhagen grew rich from the levying of tolls on ships which passed through the Øresund. With the bridge/tunnel link, the so-called Øresund region will be truly common to both Denmark and

Sweden, and is destined to be one of the fastest growing commercial areas of Europe, with a combined population of over 2½ million.

Main tourist offices
Danish Tourist Board, Vesterbrogade 6D, 1620 Copenhagen V; ☎33 11 14 15; fax 33 93 14 16; www.visitdenmark.dk.
Wonderful Copenhagen Tourist Info, Bernstorffsgade 1, 157 Copenhagen V; ☎70 22 224 42; fax 33 93 49 69; www.woco.dk.
Roskilde Egnens Turistbureau, Gullandsstræde 15, 4000 Roskilde; ☎46 33 27 00; fax 46 35 14 74; www.destination-roskilde.dk.

GETTING TO DENMARK

Air

Both British Airways and Scandinavian Air Systems (SAS) operate regular daily flights between London and Copenhagen. BA also fly London to Billund, and Newcastle to Copenhagen. SAS have services from London to Århus, and Manchester to Copenhagen. British Airways franchise partner Maersk Air Ltd operates daily direct scheduled services to Copenhagen from Birmingham International Airport. There is also the Danish-based Maersk Air, Denmark's main private airline, which operates flights between London Gatwick and Copenhagen and Billund. From Billund there are connections (by air) to Aalborg, and (by coach) to Århus, Odense, Herning, and Holstebro an Struer. The cheapest flights are operated by the Irish airline Ryanair, with two departures a day to Esbjerg and Århus. Seats can be booked from anywhere in the world by internet. Destinations can change; the website www.ebookers.com will give you up-to-date information about destinations and prices.

From North America, SAS operates direct flights from New York, Chicago, Washington DC and Seattle to Copenhagen. With other airlines you will need to change at the national hub.
British Airways, ☎0845-77 333 77 *or* 0845-606 0747; www.british-airways.com. London/Manchester/Glasgow/Aberdeen to Copenhagen; London to Billund.
Maersk Air, ☎020 7333 0066; www.maersk-air.com. London to Copenhagen/ Billund.
Maersk Air Ltd, 0845 77 333 77; website at www.british-airways.com. Birmingham to Copenhagen.
Ryanair, ☎08701-569 569; www.ryanair.com. London to Esbjerg/Århus.
SAS, 52-53 Conduit Street, London W1; ☎0845-807 2772; www.flysas.co.uk. London/Manchester/Glasgow/Aberdeen to Copenhagen; London to Århus.
SAS (USA), ☎800-221-2350; www.scandinavian.net. New York/Washington DC/Chicago/Seattle to Copenhagen.

Ferries

Scandinavian ferries tend to set the standards comfort on ferries anywhere in the world. You can take a Scandinavian Seaways ferry (☎08705-333 000; www.scansea.com *or* www.dfds.co.uk) from Harwich or Newcastle in the UK to

Esbjerg. The overnight journey takes about 19 to 20 hours.

Rail

It is now possible to take a train to Copenhagen from London. One would start with the Eurostar to Brussels, then take the overnight train to Hamburg and change again for Copenhagen. There are also direct trains from Cologne to Copenhagen. The length (it takes about 24 hours) and expense of the journey would only make this attractive to someone with a phobia of flying or perhaps an InterRail Pass. See www.raileurope.com or www.europeanrail.com for further information on rail passes. Under-26s can get special deals on rail passes; STA Travel also specialise in under-26 travel to Scandinavia.

Rail Europe, 179 Piccadilly, London W1V 0BA; ☎08705-848 848; www.raileurope.com.

STA Travel, 86 Old Brompton Rd, London NW1 2SX; www.statravel.co.uk.

Bus

Eurolines runs a twice-weekly service from London to Copenhagen. The journey takes as long as by rail – about 25 hours – but is much cheaper: Eurolines charges £104 for a round-trip to Copenhagen (£94 for anyone under 26).

Eurolines (UK), 4 Cardiff Rd, Luton, Beds LU1 1PP; ☎08705-143219; e-mail welcome@eurolines.co.uk; www.eurolines.co.uk.

RESIDENCE AND ENTRY REGULATIONS

THE CURRENT POSITION

Denmark is a member of the European Union which guarantees free movement of goods, services and labour anywhere within the Union. This chapter may therefore seem superfluous for EU nationals. Unfortunately this is far from the case; despite the EU, Denmark still has its own regulations which govern other EU nationals taking up residence there. The simplest regulations are for citizens of other Nordic countries (Sweden, Norway, Iceland and Finland), who have rights identical to those of Danish citizens. For citizens of countries belonging to the EU (see below), there are registration procedures to be followed on arrival for stays of longer than three months. Nationals of countries outside the EU are the most restricted and normally need to apply before departure from the home country. Danish embassy websites are quite informative.

EU and EEA Nationality

Nationals of other EU countries namely Belgium, Britain, The Netherlands, Germany, France, Ireland, Luxembourg, Italy, Spain, Portugal, Austria and Greece have the right to work, and if they wish, settle permanently in Denmark. The European Economic Area includes the EU, Norway, Iceland and Liechtenstein. Norwegians and Icelanders are treated the same as Danish citizens.

Entry for EU citizens

Nationals of the above countries are free to go to Denmark to look for work for up to three months with no prior permission. In other words, there is no difference at this stage whether someone is entering Denmark as a tourist or as a potential resident. It is necessary to register with the labour exchange (*Arbejdsformidlingen* or *AF*), within seven days of arrival. Although this may not necessarily be the best way to find a job (see *Employment* chapter) it is a formality which should nonetheless be fulfilled as it shows the authorities that your intentions to find work are genuine. In order to look for work in Denmark you should be able to prove that you have sufficient funds to support yourself, which may include entitlement to unemployment benefit in the UK at the time of your departure (see *Employment* chapter). Once you have obtained a job it must fulfil minimum conditions as regards working hours and remuneration.

The Danish Ministry of Labour also stipulates that foreigners (only other Nordics are not counted as foreigners) must contribute to the social security fund of Denmark. Exempted from this regulation are foreigners who have paid into a Danish unemployment fund (*arbejdsloshedskasser*) for two consecutive years previously, those who are working in Denmark as au pairs, foreigners born in Denmark or married to a citizen of that country, or foreigners who are self-employed or carrying out services in Denmark.

In the case of Greenland and the Faroe Islands, British and other EU citizens do not require a visa to enter as tourists for up to three months. If you intend to work in these territories, you will require a work permit which you have to obtain before going to take up your job. It is not possible to extend a stay as a tourist to take up work, other than in exceptional circumstances. US citizens are subject to the same regulations.

Residence Permit

EU citizens who find employment within three months of arrival should apply for a residence permit (*opholdsbevis*) to the Copenhagen Overpraesidium or to their local town hall, or Rådhus, ideally two weeks before the three-month period is up; non-EU citizens are dealt with by the Utlændingestyrelse (Directorate for Aliens). Applicants will need to take the approved form (which may be obtained by post), their national identity card or passport, two passport photographs and confirmation that they have a job and have joined an unemployment fund. The job must pay a living wage. The Youth Information service Usit states that this could be as little as kr45,000 (approx. £3,650/US$5,2650) a year before tax, although this would hardly be a living wage in such an expensive country.

Personal Code Number

Anyone who is staying in Denmark to live and work, rather than as a tourist, must have a *personnummer* (personal code number) made up of their date of birth plus a selection of other digits. This is an indispensable part of the life of any Danish citizen or foreign resident. You need it for opening a bank account, joining a library, moving house, paying taxes, going to the doctor etc. Danes are given a personal code number (or CPR number) at birth, and foreigners have to apply for one as part of the residency procedure. You are often asked for your personal code number before you are asked to give your names, which can seem somewhat impersonal.

In order to be given a CPR number certificate you must have obtained the residence permit and have a permanent address (poste restante addresses are not acceptable, nor is a youth hostel or hotel). If you change your address, you are obliged to register details of your new abode within five days. Note that not all employers are aware of the procedures involved in registering foreigners; Danish bureaucracy can seem frustratingly slow, and without a knowledge of Danish you are inevitably hampered in your search for a job.

The personal code number certificate (*personnummerbevis*) is issued by the Folkeregisteret (National Register). Once you are registered there you also get a social security certificate (*sygesikringsbevis*) which entitles the holder to use the free national health service of Denmark. The *sygesikringsbevis* is compulsory in the sense that you are given one when you are put on the National Register; without it you cannot get basic services or medical treatment. A CPR number is also necessary to obtain subsidised Danish lessons. The card gives the name of your physician; it is yellow in colour. When you leave Denmark you should return it to the authorities.

Identity Cards

Danish citizens may voluntarily carry national identity cards with all the information mentioned above on them. The card has a magnetic strip containing the information. There were proposals to put a person's entire medical history on the card, which have been shelved. In practice, most only carry the social security card, which is virtually the same thing as an identity card, except that it cannot be used as a substitute for a passport abroad.

Entry For Non-EU Nationals

Denmark joined the Schengen area, along with the other Nordic countries, in March 2001. US and Canadian citizens landing in Denmark will, under usual circumstances, receive a Schengen visa which allows them to spend up to 90 days out of six months in one of the Schengen countries. They do not need to apply for a visa before they leave home. Nationals of countries other than Nordic ones and the EU are not allowed to do paid or unpaid work during their stay unless they have arranged a work and residence permit in advance with the Danish Embassy or Consulate in their home country, or the country in which they have had legal residence for the previous six months. Permits are in no way automatically forthcoming and will only be granted in specific circumstances, and only if there is no one available on the Danish labour market to do the job. For details of employment possibilities, see the *Employment* chapter.

Danish Citizenship

The minimum period of residency required to apply for Danish citizenship is four years for anyone who has been through legal marriage to a Dane, or seven years for a single person. Other essential requirements are an ability to speak Danish and an exemplary record of good conduct. For non-EU nationals, the citizenship requirements are theoretically the same, but it is more difficult to enter Denmark to live and work in the first place.

EU Citizenship

Following the Edinburgh Summit in 1993, Denmark finally accepted the Maastricht Treaty of the European Union, with certain opt-outs, one of them relating to union citizenship which was accepted by all other member states. Under the Maastricht Treaty, all EU countries, including Denmark agreed measures allowing the 5 million EU citizens living in countries other than their own to vote in the European Elections (from 1994) and local elections (from 1995) held in their adopted country.

Useful Addresses:

Royal Danish Embassy in London, 55 Sloane Street, London SW1X 9SR; ☎020-7333 0200; fax 020-7333 0270; e-mail dkembassyuk@compuserve.com; www.denmarkemb.org.

Royal Danish Embassy in the USA, 3200 Whitehaven Street, NW, Washington DC 20008-3683; ☎202-797-5300; fax 202-328-1470; e-mail wasamb@wasamb.um.dk; www.denmarkemb.org.

Royal Danish Embassy in Canada, 47 Clarence St, Site 450, Ottawa, Ontario K1N 9K1; ☎613-562-1811; fax 613-562-1812; e-mail danemb@cyberus.ca; www.danishembassy-canada.com.

British Embassy, 36-40 Kastelsvej, 2100 Copenhagen Ø; ☎35 44 52 00; fax 35 44 52 93; www.britishembassy.dk.

United States Embassy, Dag Hammarskjølds Allé 24, 2100 K benhavn Ø; ☎35 55 31 44; fax 35 43 02 23; www.usembassy.dk.

Udlændingstyrelsen (The Directorate for Aliens), Ryesgade 53, 2100 Copenhagen Ø; ☎35 36 66 00; www.udlst.dk. Non-EU nationals have their paperwork dealt with at this directorate.

Copenhagen Overpraesidium, Hammerensgade 1, 1267 Copenhagen K; ☎33 12 23 80; EU citizens apply to this Directorate for a residence permit.

Gentofte Rådhus, Bernstorffsvej 161, 2920 Charlottenlund; 39 98 00 00. City hall for Gentofte.

Folkeregisteret (Public Registration Office), Dahlerupsgade 6, 1640 Copenhagen V. Open Monday to Wednesday, 9.30am-2.30pm; Thursdays 9.30am-5.30pm; Fridays 9.30am-1.30pm; ☎33 66 33 66.

Use It, Youth Information Copenhagen, Rådhusstræde 13, 1466 Copenhagen K; ☎33 73 06 50; fax 33 73 06 49; www.ui.dk. Advice centre for low-budget travellers.

SETTING UP HOME

HOW DO THE DANES LIVE?

On paper, Denmark does not have a housing shortage, however, a lot of the housing stock is old and in need of renovation; about 37% of units were built before 1945. Because rents are kept artificially low not much new housing is built for the private rental sector. Every Dane would like to own their own home; about 55% of dwellings are owner-occupied, the most typical form being a bungalow on a small piece of land, a so-called *parcelhus*. About 30% live in apartments. Another uniquely Danish institution is the *andelsbolig*, a sort of commune where members buy shares in an estate, and take it in turns to cook and do other chores.

The Danes take great care of their homes; one will notice that their gardens are immaculately maintained and so are their houses. Danes are great antique lovers and try to decorate their dwellings in the best possible taste, as far as their means permit. Even the most down-market apartment has well-designed furniture and artistic posters or bric-a-brac to make it look homely. Danes are very skilled at DIY or *gør-det-selv*. No Dane worth his or her salt would call out a plumber or electrician if they can help it; many have professionally equipped workshops next to their houses. This is understandable considering the excessive wear and tear on buildings caused by the long hard winters.

RENTING PROPERTY

Most newcomers will, at least initially, rent rather than buy. Rents are strictly controlled by the state, with the result that there is a general shortage of rented accommodation. About half of all tenants receive rent support, something that works against newcomers. While the municipality has a legal obligation to house people, you will have to have a job and somewhere to live before you can be considered. Finding somewhere to stay that is not too expensive or inconvenient requires a lot of hard work – one English teacher describes it as 'a nightmare'. It is a question of trying everything: newspaper adverts, noticeboards in pubs and supermarkets etc. Information centres can also be helpful, as can the district housing office which may have non-profit housing at its disposal. The twice-weekly paper, *Den Blå Avis,* has many adverts for rented accommodation; look under the headings *bolig & have* and then *lejligheder* on the website: www.dba.dk.

Other useful websites include: www.boligsiden.dk; www.boligmangel.dk; www.bolig-guide.dk; and www.boligguiden.dk. It is also possible to advertise on the website www.lejeboliger.dk. Potential tenants pay kr549 (approx. £45/US$65) for the service; they are guaranteed to get their money back if they have not found a place to live within a year.

You may need a Dane to help you place an ad, or to interpret ads. Words like 'steady job' (*fast arbejd*), 'not noisy' (*ikke ryger*), 'peaceful' (*rolig*), and 'serious' (*seriøs*) frequently crop up. Apartments are advertised by the number of rooms (*værelse, vær.* or *v.*) and by floor area (*kvm*). You will also notice adverts offering *fremleje* or sub-letting, sometimes for only a month or two. If the tenant lives in a housing association property or accommodation subsidised by the state, they will require permission to sub-let. This can only be done for two years at most, and the sub-lessor will have to give some reason for sub-letting: i.e. they are moving away to study, to travel, or for a short-term contract.

If you are coming from abroad to work for a Danish company, then your employer will help you to find accommodation. If you are at the lower end of the food chain, then you may well have to sub-let to begin with. A useful address for short-term accommodation (private rooms and communes) is Use It (13 Rådhusstræde 13, 1466 Copenhagen K; ☎33 73 06 20; fax 33 73 06 49; useit@ui.dk; www.useit.dk). Use It is a tourist information office for travellers on a low budget. There is also a Youth Information Centre at the same address: ☎33 73 06 50; www.ui.dk.

Rental Prices

It is difficult to be precise about monthly rents, but you should expect to pay at least kr4,000 (approx. £325 or $470) per month for a two-room flat in the Copenhagen area. As a general rule of thumb rents for houses and flats in the capital are between kr100 and kr150 per square metre per month on the free market. The bigger the house the cheaper it tends to be in proportion to the floor area. Outside the capital, rents range from kr50 to kr100 per square metre per month, depending on the condition of the property. Danish residents can benefit from rent support. About 500,000 households receive rent allowances or live in subsidised dwellings; the average annual payment is kr17,500 (approx £1,420/US$2,050).

The Legal Aspects of Renting

Tenancy Agreements. According to lawyers at the Danish Ministry of Housing in Copenhagen (www.bm.dk), the laws governing Danish property are probably the most complex in Europe. Suffice it to say that when you rent a property, strictly speaking, a written tenancy agreement is not required as all such arrangements automatically come under the law of tenancy. However it is not a bad idea to have a written agreement just to avoid misunderstandings. Under the law, if either party insists on a written contract then it is obligatory to draw one up. A standard type of contract can be bought from stationers and bookshops. It is important to realise that while such special contracts exist and may be duly signed by both parties, the tenant still has statutory rights which cannot be superseded.

Deposit and Receipts. The landlord also has statutory rights: he or she can charge a pre-paid deposit of up to six months' rent before you move in, but two to three months rent is more usual. The tenant should always obtain a receipt for any money paid as a deposit and for the monthly rent payments. Rent automatically falls due on the first working day of each month and if the tenant fails to pay on time, the landlord is entitled to cancel the tenancy as the failure to pay is interpreted under the law as giving a notice to quit.

Notice to Quit. A landlord and tenant are both obliged to give notice to quit a minimum of one month in advance. A longer period may be agreed by both parties if a special contract is drawn up. Notice to quit should always be given on the last day of the month otherwise you cannot quit until the end of the subsequent month; i.e. if you give notice to quit on December 1st, the moving out date would be February 1st.

Moving Out. When you leave your accommodation it should be in the same state as when you moved in. It is a sensible idea to take a series of photographs (preferably with a camera that dates the photos), when you move in, especially of items or decor that are in a dilapidated state. Then if there is a dispute you will have evidence to support your argument.

Tenants' Associations. Denmark has a national network of tenants' associations which come under the umbrella organisation *Lejernes Landsorganisation* (LLO). For further details of your local one you can contact the LLO's Secretariat (Reventlowsgade 14, 4. 1651 København 5; ☎31 86 09 10; www.llo.dk). As a member of this organisation you are entitled to professional advice with any problems relating to your tenancy.

Unfair Rents. Under Danish tenancy law you can only be charged what the room is worth. If you wish to appeal against what seems to be an excessive rent you should contact the rent arbitrators (*Huslejenævnet*) in your locality. Not all municipalities have these, so if there is not one available contact the nearest advice centre instead.

TABLE 1	USEFUL TERMS
altan	balcony
brutto/netto	gross and net mortgage payment
fjv./fjernvarme	district heating
husdyrtill.	permission for pets
hybrid	cable TV
indret./indretning	decoration
køkken	kitchen
m./med	with
Netto	name of a supermarket
plankegulve	wooden flooring
sovevær.	bedroom
stue	living room
udbet./udbetaling	deposit
v./vær./værelse	room

HOME EXCHANGE

As a way of giving yourself time to find somewhere to buy or rent you might like to consider arranging a home exchange. Normally these occur between families, rather than individuals. The following organisations specialise in home exchanges for short periods:

Intervac Denmark, v/Bækkelund Hansen, Abildhøj 1, 7600 Stuer; ☎97 84 16 33; www.intervac.org/denmark.

Apollo Home Exchange, Tulipanlunden 2, 4593 Eskebjerg; ☎59 29 16 30; fax 59 29 1630; e-mail home@worldonline.dk.

RELOCATORS

Relocators generally work with businesses sending employees to foreign locations, helping to deal with bureaucracy, finding accommodation and schooling for their children, and preparing newcomers to deal with a new culture. Such services do not come cheap, and are only likely to be affordable for large corporations or the very well-off.

Copenhagen Relocations, e-mail contact@relocate.dk; www.relocate.dk.

Home from Home Relocation Services, e-mail info@hfh-relocations.dk; www.hfh-relocations.dk.

House of Relocation, e-mail enquiry@house-of-relocation.dk; www.house-of-relocation.

BUYING PROPERTY

Laws on buying property have changed in recent years as regards foreigners. An EU or EEA citizen who comes to Denmark with a job or to set up a business can buy a home without requiring special permission. If you are in any doubt then you should contact the Civilkontor of the Justice Ministry (Justitsministeriet, Slotsholmsgade 10, 1216 Copenhagen K; ☎33 92 33 40; fax 33 93 35 10; e-mail jm@jm.dk; www.jm.dk) in advance. Non-EEA citizens will first need a residence permit before they can receive permission to buy a home. There are still restrictions on the purchase of second or holiday homes by EEA citizens, which mainly affect Germans, Swedes and Norwegians. Unless a foreigner has lived in Denmark for five years they cannot buy a holiday home there, with few exceptions.

Property prices in Denmark are somewhat lower than in the UK, but at least 30% higher than in the USA. A small flat can still be found for as little as kr330,000 (approx £26,750/US$38,600) in Copenhagen. A disincentive to the buying and selling of property are the high fees charged by banks and real estate agents. A transaction that might cost £1,500 in the UK could cost you £5,000-£6,000 on a far cheaper property. The fees involved are given in advertisements; see the websites given above.

The main mortgage credit banks, given below, have useful websites which can help you to find a property to buy. In particular Nykredit's website, www.nykredit.dk, has a *Findbolig* (Housefinder) and *Boligguide* (House Guide) search facility. You could also look at the Housing Ministry website – www.bm.dk – and the house-building information website: www.byggeinfo.dk.

Loans from Mortgage Credit Institutions

The Danish Mortgage Credit System differs from systems in many other countries which tend to be based on an assessment of the individual borrower's financial circumstances. In Denmark the granting of loans is solely against mortgage in real estate, a system which has several advantages. There are limits on the proportion which can be lent and, in addition, if a change of ownership occurs it is not normally necessary to re-assess earlier loans. Mortgage rights in individual properties are protected by a national registration system.

Financial terms for buying property are easier than in many countries in the EU. The Danes are consequently the most heavily indebted borrowers in the EU; house loans total 70% of annual GDP. It is a peculiarity of the Danish property-purchasing system that the mortgage or mortgages are left with the property, so that whoever buys the property also gets the mortgage(s), usually on quite favourable terms. Every time the property is sold, the new owner will take out a new mortgage to cover the rise in price of property, so that there can be multiple mortgages on one property. It is not advantageous to consolidate all the mortgages into one loan.

As in other countries there are specialised mortgage credit institutions whose principal activity is to grant long-term loans for the purchase of real estate. The way in which these funds are traditionally raised is unique to Denmark, in that they are raised purely from the issue of bonds on the Copenhagen Stock Exchange. These have long been the staple of both the stock exchange and the non-speculative investor as they provide rock-solid investments regarded as gilt-edged stock along with government issued bonds. The practice of issuing such credit bonds arose out of a need to rebuild Copenhagen following two disastrous fires which consumed much of city in the 18th century. A balance between the volume of loans granted and the volume of bonds issued is carefully maintained so the interest risk to mortgage credit institutions is minimal. Borrowers can obtain loans for all the usual range of buildings and renovations. Lending limits are prescribed by law at 80% maximum of the value of residential property and repayments take place over 10 to 35 years. There are several types of mortgage loan with varying methods of repayment:

- *Serial.* Repayments by equal capital instalments, and reducing interest instalments.
- *Annuity.* Repayments are constant throughout the loan period.
- *Bullet.* Interest repayments only, with all the capital being repaid at the end of the loan.
- *Index.* (for new construction only). Variable instalments depending on the changes in the price index.

Loans from Banks

Those who obtain a mortgage from a bank are subject to fewer restrictions than someone who borrows from a mortgage credit institution, as the terms of the loan are based on the bank's assessment of the borrower's ability to repay, rather than on legalities. It may thus be possible to get a 100% mortgage if the bank deems the risk acceptable. Alternatively it might be possible to obtain the maximum 80% from a mortgage credit institution and the balance from a bank.

Repayment periods and rates of interest vary depending on the bank and the amount of the loan. Long-term (i.e. up to 30 years) loans are generally possible.

Useful Addresses

Danish Mortgage Institutions:
Byggeriets Realkreditfond (The Building Mortgage Fund), Klampenborgvej 205, 2800 Lyngby; www.brf.dk.
Realkredit Danmark (Mortgage Credit Association), Jarmers Plads 2, 1551 Copenhagen V; www.rd.dk *or* www.rd-almen.dk.
Nykredit (New Credit), Otto Mønsteds Plads 2, 1780 Copenhagen V; ☎70 10 80 08; www.nykredit.dk.
Dansk Landbrugs Realkreditfond (Danish Agricultural Mortgage Fund), Nyropsgade 21, 1780 Copenhagen V; www.dlr.dk.
Industriens Realkreditfond, Bredgade 40, 1260 Copenhagen K (specialists in industrial mortgages).

UTILITIES

Electricity & Gas

The electric current is 220 Volt AC (50 Hz), and plugs are of the two-pin variety, so bring continental adaptors if you don't want to change them. American equipment with a 50/60 label should work satisfactorily as long as you use a transformer with the right wattage.

For a small country, Denmark has a lot of electricity companies. Furthermore each community is free to choose its own sources. Many automatically opt for ecologically sound ones, which in Denmark often means wind. Thanks to a long North Sea coastline and an average windspeed of 7 to 8 m/sec throughout the year, this is a very practical option. Wind power is now a highly developed industry and the technology has become a valuable export. It is not unusual for an electricity supplier to utilise more than one source of power. For instance one small community in Jutland uses natural gas, biodiesel and over 200 wind turbines. Denmark is self-sufficient in oil and natural gas, and is a net exporter of refined energy products. There are no nuclear power stations. The coolant from power stations is used for domestic heating. Some power stations have been adapted to burn biomass or household waste.

Energy companies are listed under *energi* in the Yellow Pages. The main electricity supplier in Copenhagen and North Zealand is NESA: contact NESA Kundecenter, Hagedornsvej 4, 2820 Gentofte; ☎72 10 20 30; fax 72 10 20 30; e-mail kunder@nesa.dk; www.nesa.dk. For oil, gas, water and sewers, the company to contact is: Københavns Energi, Kongens Nytorv 3, Copenhagen;

☎33 95 23 01; e-mail kundeservice@ke.kk.dk. Meters are read once or twice a year; the charges are evened out over the year and paid monthly.

REMOVALS

Anyone who chooses not to transport their belongings to Denmark will certainly save money on removal expenses, but one should take into consideration that some goods are much cheaper in the UK and USA than in designer-conscious Denmark, and it may therefore be worth transporting them anyway. Always start with a list of 'essential items'. Then try to cut it down to a minimum. Electrical items and gadgets are expensive in Denmark and it may be worth taking them if they are compatible. However, repairs may cause difficulties if they are of makes not normally sold in Denmark.

If you are paying a removal company then choose a company experienced in overseas removals which can readily provide a quotation for any destination. The British Association of Removers (BAR, 3 Churchill Court, 58 Station Road, North Harrow, Middx; ☎020-8861 3331) will provide a list of firms and general information on moving possessions overseas. Individuals normally have to pay the removal company up-front for the removal. For anyone who is worried about the removal company going bust, or what will happen if their most precious items are damaged or lost, BAR has set up International Movers Mutual Insurance so that clients of any of the companies belonging to BAR will be compensated for loss or damage, or in the case of bankruptcy the removal will be taken over by another member company.

There are several websites giving lists of removal companies around the world:
Direct Moving, www.directmoving.com.
Household Goods Forwarders Association of America, www.hhgfaa.org.
Overseas Moving Network International (OMNI), www.omnimoving.com.

IMPORTING CARS

Cars are extremely expensive to buy in Denmark, but you will still be subject to high taxes if you bring in your own. In the case of cars registered in the EU, these can be imported free of duty and VAT as long as you have owned the car for at least six months outside Denmark and it has run 6,000km. For cars registered outside the EU, duty of 10% and VAT of 25% are normally payable, but you may be exempt from this if the car is imported as part of removal goods. All cars from abroad, whether from the EU or not, are subject to a registration tax which can actually exceed the new value of the car in Denmark. There is a sliding scale depending on the age of the car. It is essential to contact the customs authorities before trying to import your car if you intend to stay in Denmark for more than a year. If you stay for less than a year, you only become liable for tax if you have a 'home' in Denmark; the decision lies with the police *motorkontor.* But if you lend, hire out or sell your car then you will have to pay the full tax.

The customs house will give you their provisional assessment of the tax payable on your car, and send you a copy of form 21.009 to fill in. Once in Denmark you will need to register the car with customs within two weeks of arrival. Registration papers from your home country, invoices and tax receipts are required; also a certificate of road-worthiness from the *Statens Bilinspektion* (car inspectorate). You will need to take a letter from your employer stating that you are remaining in Denmark for more than a year and less than three years, as well as your passport. You will be asked for a deposit on the tax which is payable at the rate of 1% a month for up to three years. After this period you have to pay the remainder of the tax; it would naturally be advisable to export your car again before the three-year period is up. If you sell the car in Denmark then you have to pay all the outstanding duty. The main customs house address is: Told og Skat, Strandgade 100, 1016 Copenhagen K; ☎32 88 93 00; www.toldskat.dk.

Once you have completed all the above formalities, you can exchange your foreign licence plates for Danish ones at a *motorkontor,* run by the police. Note that there is also a twice-yearly road tax, the *vægtafgift,* to be paid at the *motorkontor,* which varies according to the weight of your car. There is a helpline concerning the road tax on 36 48 10 10; do not press any of the numbers but wait to be connected to a live operator.

IMPORTING PETS

Denmark is not officially rabies-free. If you are bringing a cat or dog from the UK, there are several conditions that have to be fulfilled: the animal must be identified with a tattoo or microchip; it should have a health certificate from a vet; and it should be vaccinated in accordance with current regulations. Airlines and shipping companies will have information about the necessary documentation; your veterinary surgeon will know which shots are necessary. Unaccompanied animals must enter Denmark at one of the frontier points where there is a veterinary surgeon authorised to inspect animals. These are: Billund, Copenhagen, Elsinore, Esbjerg, Frederikshavn, Padborg, Rødby and Rønne. In general it is easier to ship an animal as air cargo; indeed many airlines will only ship animals as cargo. There is information in English on the Danish Veterinary and Food Administration website: www.foedevaredirektoratet.dk, or one can e-mail fdir@fdir.dk or call +45 3395 6000 from abroad.

The Independent Pet and Animal Transportation Association International Inc members around the world can arrange for transportation of animals and advise on local rules; their website is www.ipata.com. IATA rules on animal transport can be found at: www.iata.org/cargo/live.htm. If you are bringing a pet from the United States, then vaccination against rabies is necessary, unless it is under three months old. See the above websites for further details. There is a club for US residents who want to take their pets abroad: www.takeyourpet.com.

If you intend to bring your pet back with you from Denmark to the UK, or you acquire a pet in Denmark and wish to bring it back with you, it may no longer be necessary to put your animal in quarantine, as long as you follow the right procedures. For information on the Pets Travel Scheme look at the UK Department of the Environment, Food and Rural Affairs website: www.defra.gov.uk, or call 0870-241 1710.

DAILY LIFE

Anyone who goes to live in a foreign country will find that many daily rituals, previously taken for granted, become far more challenging than at home. Admittedly in the small, well-organised country of Denmark this is likely to be less of a problem than in some other countries; moreover many of its citizens speak English very proficiently. There are estimated to be over 30,000 nationals of other EU countries living and working in Denmark, which, considering its small size and population is a significant number. The intention of this chapter is to provide as much as possible of the practical information required to cope with daily aspects of Danish life. If you have already experienced living or working in another Scandinavian country, much of the information will probably seem familiar.

THE DANISH LANGUAGE

Danish has some similarities with German, which many Danes also speak, and is related to Swedish and Norwegian. Many Low German words entered the language in the Middle Ages from Denmark's connection with the Hanseatic Traders. Swedish and Danish are mutually intelligible as both languages are rooted in East Norse, a language of the Viking period. Norwegians and Danes can also understand each other (more or less). Although Norwegian evolved from the slightly different West Norse, Danish was the official written language in Norway until the 19th century. A 'purification' of Danish took place in the 18th century when many French words in common usage were replaced with newly created Danish ones. As recently as 1948 the spelling of Danish was reformed to more closely resemble that of related languages (Norwegian and Swedish). Helpful as this may have been to other Scandinavians it has little effect on the ability of foreigners to understand spoken Danish. As with some other languages (notably English!) the pronunciation is frequently wildly at odds with the written appearance of the word, as consonants are often replaced with a glottal stop in the middle or at the end of a word, and many sounds are unvoiced. Danish has three extra letters: å (written aa before 1948), ø and æ which come at the end of the alphabet. In general, it would be true to say that Danish is the easiest Scandinavian language to read, and the most difficult to speak.

Is it essential to learn Danish?

On the whole you might wonder why you should bother. Most Danes speak English, and Danish is a difficult language to master. Many foreigners give up and lapse into English. However, if you are planning to live and work or stay in Denmark for any length of time it would be advisable to make a serious attempt to get to grips with it, although you will almost certainly find your efforts to practise thwarted by Danes who will inevitably reply in English. One good reason for acquiring a basic knowledge of Danish, is that if you are job-hunting, you will need to be able to understand the situations vacant adverts, which are invariably in Danish. If you are going to start a business, then a knowledge of Danish is absolutely necessary. Your social life will also benefit if you learn Danish.

Most people will be starting from scratch as Scandinavian languages are not taught in schools. There are various ways to go about learning the language which are dealt with below.

Self-Study Courses

You are fairly unlikely to find an evening course in Danish, which means that you will probably have to resort to a self-study programme, backed up by, if you are lucky, a private tutor. The main possibilities are the American company Audio-Forum, which has a UK distributor, and Linguaphone whose Danish starter course costs about £250. There are Danish courses on CD-ROM available from www.eDREAM.co.uk. The Routledge course, *Colloquial Danish,* with a book and cassettes is available in some British public libraries. There are free on-line Danish dictionaries at www.yourdictionary.com.

Useful Addresses

Audio-Forum, c/o Jeffrey Norton Publishers, 96 Broad St, Guildford, CT 06437, USA; ☎203-453 9794; e-mail info@audioforum.com; www.audioforum.com. UK Distributor: Audio Forum, Microworld House, 4 Foscote Mews, London W9 2HH; ☎020-7266 2202.
Linguaphone Institute Ltd, 111 Upper Richmond Road, London SW15 2TJ; ☎020-8333 4898; www.linguaphone.co.uk, www.linguaphone.com/usa.

Language Courses Abroad

You may be lucky enough to live near a university that has a Scandinavian department where you can attend a course in Danish language and culture on a part-time basis. If this is not the case, a possible alternative would be attending a course at a commercial language school:
The Berlitz School of Languages, 321 Oxford Street, London W1A 3BZ; ☎020-7408 2474; www.berlitz.com. This is an international organisation that offers language tuition specifically tailored to the individual's requirements. In the UK and USA Berlitz can arrange one-to-one Danish courses with native speakers. The cost varies but this is generally the most expensive way to learn a language. One advantage of the Berlitz schools is that courses begun in one

country can be completed in another. In the UK there are Berlitz schools in
Birmingham, Manchester, Leeds and Edinburgh. Danish courses may not be
available in all these localities because of the comparative rarity of Danish
teachers. The Linguarama organisation can also offer courses in Danish (see
www.linguarama.com).

The Danish Cultural Institute (3 Doune Terrace, Edinburgh EH3 6DY; ☎0131-225
7189; e-mail dci.dancult@dancult.demon.co.uk) can advise on Danish courses
in Scotland. Facilities for studying Danish in the USA are shown on the University of Minnesota website: http://carla.acad.umn.edu/lctl/access.html.

Private Tutors

If you live outside London or away from big cities, you could try to find a private
tutor. You can post a 'Danish Tutor Wanted' advertisement on suitable notice
boards in schools, sports centres, supermarkets, colleges and universities or in a
local paper. It is advisable to try to teach yourself some Danish before you begin
looking so that you are not starting completely from scratch.

Language Courses in Denmark

The good news is that if you don't have time to learn Danish before you depart,
then there are courses for foreigners in most towns in Denmark. As in most
countries, the cheapest courses are those which are connected to the state
education system; in Denmark they are heavily subsidised, so the cost to the
student is minimal. However, to be eligible for enrolment you have to have a
personnummerbevis or personal code number (see *Residence and Entry Regulations*
chapter). Another possibility is to attend a course in Danish at the local Folk High
School, a kind of community and adult education centre, of which there are about
100 throughout Denmark. Courses are residential and last one week to 10 months.
Private schools offering courses can be found under *sprogundervisning* in the Yellow
Pages, but these are generally very expensive.

Useful Addresses

Højskolernes Sekretariat, Nytorv 7, 1450 Copenhagen K; ☎33 13 98 22; e-mail
hs@grundtvig.dk; www.folkehojskoler.dk. Can supply a list of all the Danish
Folk Schools and the courses available.

The Danish Club, 40 Dover St, London W1X 3RB; ☎020-7794 4711;
www.denmarkemb.org.uk. Potential members have to be approved, but the
Club is for all ages and there is a special youth subscription rate. The Club
may be able to help with finding contacts or private tutors through newsletters,
noticeboard etc.

Anglo-Danish Society, 25 New Street Square, London EC4A 3LN. Membership
Secretary, 'Danewood', 4 Daleside, Gerrards Cross, Bucks SL9 7JF; ☎01753-
884846.

SCHOOLS AND EDUCATION

Education in Denmark

There are nine years of compulsory schooling between the ages of 6 and 16 with additional years: a one-year pre-school class and also a 10th school year. Children begin formal schooling at the age of 6 or 7. Nearly three-quarters of children aged 3 to 6 years go to pre-school kindergartens and other child-minding concerns.

Parents can choose to send their children to a municipal school which is free, or to a private elementary school where they have to pay 15% of the tuition fees; about 10% of pupils go to the latter. The emphasis in Danish education is making sure that all students get the most appropriate education for their needs and abilities. Thus slow learners are offered special education in smaller classes so that they do not lose out by not acquiring basic numeracy and literacy skills. Over the years the educational system has adapted to take account of the diversity of the pupils themselves. Children can, in the 8th or 10th years choose an extended syllabus in a range of subjects. In the 10th form there are a range of highly practical options as an alternative to the more academic subjects.

The school year normally lasts about 200 days. The overall framework of basic schooling is defined by legislation and administrative regulations but within this framework schools can work out their own curriculum. Teachers enjoy a lot of freedom with regard to the planning and organisation of their classes within this framework.

Upper Secondary Schooling. After completing basic schooling, students may go on to the 3-year academic and general cycle at the *Gymnasium* which culminates in the *Studentereksamen* (the upper secondary school leaving examination) that qualifies the holders for admission to universities and other higher education. About 33% of pupils qualify for the *Gymnasium*, which is open to those who have passed the leaving examination of the *Folkeskole*, which includes Danish, arithmetic/mathematics, and languages (English and German) or physics/chemistry.

The *Gymnasium* syllabus can either have a mathematics or a languages bias. In addition to these core subjects of the syllabus, students select three or four elective subjects. There was a major education reform in 1988, which aimed at increasing historical awareness in students, promoting languages and an international viewpoint, while strengthening science and incorporating new subjects such as computer science, business economics and technology. Most of the *Gymnasia* are publicly funded and run by the counties, but roughly 6% of gymnasium students are at private institutions governed by private boards which receive state grants for most of their operational costs.

It is also possible to attend a two-year course leading to the Higher Preparatory Examination (HF), which also qualifies students for entrance to higher education.

Vocational Education and Training. More than half of young people enrol on a vocational education and training course which may be technical, commercial or a health education course. The last is normally oversubscribed. The basic vocational education and training comprises a combination of on-the-job training and theoretical and practical training in college. In addition to the vocational subjects, general subjects are also taught. This kind of education allows for a great deal of flexibility of content, duration and structure. Courses last two to four and a half years; the college attendance element is six months to two years.

Courses are regularly updated to take into account the current job market and, in the area of advanced technology particularly, there are plans to double the capacity over the next few years.

Agricultural Training, also contains an element of theoretical instruction and practical training. There are approximately 30 agricultural colleges whose course content is regulated by the farming organisations, with very limited input from the Ministry of Education.

Further Technical and Commercial Education. Such courses usually come after vocational and educational training have been completed and are primarily theoretical advanced courses lasting one to three years. In combination with the Vocational Education and Training, they are a preparation for jobs in production, marketing, service and other sectors, such as health.

Higher Education

Danish higher education is yet another area of Danish life governed democratically. Most institutes of higher education are autonomous under Danish law. Students, through various student organisations, have joint voting rights with staff in the governing bodies of such institutions on integral matters concerning curricula, syllabuses and the distribution of financial resources.

About 15% of young people enrol in higher education in one of Denmark's five universities or other higher education institutions like the Royal Dental College of Copenhagen and the School of Architecture in Århus, all of which institutions are financed by the state. Only business schools are private foundations while some teacher-training colleges, engineering and social work colleges may be private or state foundations. The annual quota on an individual course is fixed by the Ministry of Education, the so-called *numerus clausus.* There are not always sufficient places to meet demand in some areas, notably health education.

There has been a tendency in recent years for universities to adapt courses to the needs of the private business sector and to restrict those oriented towards the public sector. Before 1988 most university courses lasted for five or six years. From that year bachelor programmes lasting three or four years were finally introduced.

General Adult Education

It is estimated that about 1 million Danes a year participate in leisure-time education. A special feature are the *Folkehøjskoler* (Danish Folk High Schools), created in the 19th century as an integral part of the socio-cultural political movements of the time. There are about 100 Folk Schools which are free, residential and which offer a range of subjects from general to practical. Certain schools run courses for specific groups, for instance retired people, while others are suitable for sports and physical education courses. Courses can last up to an academic year, but there are many short courses lasting one to four weeks. Those on the longer courses tend to be the young unemployed. Anyone can attend a Folk

High School provided they are over 17½ years old; there are no entrance or exit examinations.

In addition, all lectures at Danish universities and institutes of higher education are open to members of the public and students alike, the only limitation on access being the space available. All universities and other higher education institutions allow anyone to follow single-subject courses, but it is not possible to piece together a degree from such studies.

The 1990 Act on Open Education

A few years ago Denmark took steps to promote continuing further education and training for adults already in the workplace in order to keep up with new technology and an expanding marketplace, with particular emphasis on the type of skills required by export and import companies. Such courses not only benefit the nation as a whole by improving companies' performances, they also benefit employees by giving them the opportunity to be promoted through acquiring additional qualifications. Some firms run their own staff training courses but at least half of the courses are publicly run and 80% funded by the state; the participants pay the remaining 20% of the operational costs. Training courses are normally attended on a part-time basis and must be available out of working hours.

The admission rules for part-time students are normally the same as for full-time students but these can be waived if the candidate has real-life qualifications, i.e. those learned at work.

In addition to part-time training courses a new scheme allows those in employment to take a sabbatical year off to study, on 80% of their normal full employment pay. This is part of a government scheme to bring down unemployment. Another is to offer the long-term unemployed the opportunity to attend a course of up to one and a half years' duration, and to receive education benefit for this in place of unemployment benefit.

State Educational Support

The Danish state scheme for educational grants is the *Statens Uddannelsesstøtte* which provides grants to students over 18 as support towards living costs. The grants are means-tested and may be available for study periods abroad.

Foreigners in Higher Education in Denmark

Students from other EU countries wishing to study at a Danish university or other higher education institution should bear in mind that a knowledge of Danish is essential. Some institutions require prospective students to take a Danish test before acceptance. Foreign students who wish to study at a Danish university for one or two terms can participate in a Guest Student scheme if their studies are already well-advanced in their own countries, but they will need at least a working knowledge of Danish. The American-Scandinavian Foundation arranges summer courses for US residents in Denmark, and provides assistance with residence permits.

There are special university courses conducted in English through Denmark's

International Study Programme (DIS) for which American, Canadian or Australian students can apply through affiliated universities in their own countries. The Anglo-Danish Society offers scholarships for British students to study at the universities of Copenhagen, Aarhus and Odense; applications are made between 1 October and 31 December.

Useful Publications

The Royal Danish Ministry for Foreign Affairs produces a leaflet called *Studying in Denmark,* obtainable from the Danish Embassy.

The European Commission Information Office, Jean Monnet House, 8 Storey's Gate, London SW1P 3AT; ☎ 020-7973 1992, publishes a free booklet *Higher Education in the European Community* which describes courses and qualifications and gives advice on scholarships, insurance and living costs.

Useful Addresses

Anglo-Danish Society, 'Danewood', 4 Daleside, Gerrards Cross, Bucks SL9 7JF; ☎ 01753-884846.

Central Bureau for Educational Visits and Exchanges, British Council, 10 Spring Gardens, London SW1A 2BN. ☎ 020-7389 4157; fax 020 7389 4426; e-mail socrates@britishcouncil.org; www.centralbureau.org.uk/socrates. Arranges many types of European exchanges for a range of ages and qualifications.

Commission for Educational Exchange between Denmark and the United States of America, (The Fulbright Commission), Rådhusstræde 3, 1466 Copenhagen K.

American-Scandinavian Foundation, Scandinavia House, 58 Park Avenue, New York, NY 10016; ☎ 212-879-9779; e-mail info@amscan.org; www.amscan.org.

National Union of Danish Students, Danske Studerendes Fællesråd, DSF, Knabrostræde 25, 1210 København K; ☎ 33 11 82 60; fax 33 14 30 76.

Denmark's International Study Programme

(DIS), University of Copenhagen, Vestergade 7, 1456 Copenhagen K; ☎ 35 32 26 26; e-mail dis@disp.dk; www.disp.dk.

Eurydice, Eurydice unit for England, Wales & Northern Ireland, National Foundation for Educational Research, The Mere, Upton Park, Slough, Berkshire SL1 2DQ; ☎ 01753-574123; fax 01753-531458; e-mail eurydice@nfer.ac.uk; www.nfer.ac.uk/eurydice. Eurydice distributes information on all aspects of education and training in the European Union.

Erasmus UK, Socrates Erasmus Council, R&D Building, The University, Canterbury, Kent CT2 7PD; ☎ 01227-762712; fax 01227 762711; erasmus@ukc.ac.uk; www.erasmus.ac.uk. Distributes grants for students from the UK who want to conduct part of their studies at a university in another EU country.

Socrates UK, see Central Bureau address above. Embraces inter-EU exchanges at school level.

THE MEDIA, POST AND TELECOMMUNICATIONS

Television and Radio

Television in Denmark is far from inspiring. There are two national non-commercial channels, Channel 1 and DR 2, and the commercial Channel 2. The main cable channel is Channel 3. If you own a television you are obliged to obtain a television licence from the state TV company, Danmark Radio (see www.radiodanmark.dk). Alongside national TV and radio there are numerous local TV and radio stations. Denmark Radio 1 broadcasts a daily news in English at 8.30am on 93.8MHz. There is also an internet radio service where you can listen to the recorded mid-day news in English at any time of day, and to a weekly report: www.banns.com.

Books and Newspapers

Traditionally, the Scandinavians watch less television and read more than other Europeans. Denmark claims annual book publications of about 10,000 titles and publishes 48 daily newspapers of which Danes are avid readers. The main newspapers are *Politiken* and *Berlingske Tidende*. British newspapers are generally on sale by 10am, as are *International Herald Tribune* and the *Wall Street Journal*. For adverts and listings, *Den Blå Avisen* (meaning 'blue opinion' but entirely innocuous) is essential in Copenhagen. There is a weekly English newspaper, *The Copenhagen Post*, which comes out on Fridays and costs kr15 (approx. £1.20/US$1.75); see www.cphpost.dk. As in most of Scandinavia the public libraries are excellent, and have free internet access, although you will probably have to queue up.

Post

Post offices are open 9 or 10am to 5 or 5.30pm, Monday-Friday, and 9am to 1pm Saturdays. The central post office in Copenhagen is behind the Central Station at Tietgensgade 37, 1500 Copenhagen. There is also a branch office in the central station that opens 8am to 9pm Monday to Friday, 9am to 4pm Saturday and 10am to 4pm on Sundays. Postboxes are emptied on Saturdays but not on Sundays.

The correct way to address mail is; name, then street (name, then number), then town, preceded by a four-figure code (which is in turn preceded by the country code DK- if writing from abroad). The Danish post office has a useful website where you can calculate the price of postage for different weights: www.postdanmark.dk. Foreign post is divided into A Prioritaire and B Ordinary post; there is a small difference in the price. Prioritaire requires a sticker.

Telephone

The important thing to remember is that in Denmark telephone number area prefixes must be used even if you are dialling inside the prefix area. Copenhagen numbers are prefixed with a number between 31 and 39 or 42 and 49. Other codes are listed in all directories. The international access code is 00. For the UK dial 00 44 followed by UK area code (minus initial 0) and the local number; for US and Canada dial 00 1. The international country code for Denmark is 45.

Public phones take kr1, kr5, kr10 and kr20 coins. A local call costs kr2. With older phones, you put the money in before dialling, but no coins are returned even if you fail to make your connection, so insert only the minimum. On the other hand, you're allowed more than one call for your money, if the time hasn't run out. With newer coin boxes you don't have to insert money until there is an answer. All public telephones permit international calls. For collect (reverse charge) calls dial 144 for the operator; from some payphones you may need to insert kr1 first. Cardphones are replacing coin phones; cards come in kr30, 50 and 100 denominations. Phone 118 for national directory enquiries, 113 for international enquiries; calls to directory enquiries are very expensive and cost at least kr5. The emergency number to call for the fire brigade, police or an ambulance is 112.

All public telephones should have a directory, which comes in the usual two parts – personal and commercial. The letters Æ, Ø and Å come at the end of the alphabet. The Copenhagen private directory is in two parts: A-K and L-Å. There is some information in English and German. Both white and yellow pages can be consulted on-line at www.krak.dk, or www.degulesider.dk. For business numbers www.krak.dk (Kraks Business Directory) may be a better bet. This site also has complete maps for all of Denmark to locate any street address. It also allows searching on business categories.

For telephone installation call Tele Danmark on 80 80 80 80 (www.teledanmark.dk). Installation costs about kr1,000 (approx. £81/US$115) and there is a quarterly charge of some kr350. The main mobile phone companies are: Tele Danmark Mobil, Sonofon, Mobilix and Telia.

Telegrams. Are sent from telegram offices and post offices. In Copenhagen, the office at Kobmagergade 37 (☎33 12 09 03) is open 24 hours. Telegrams can also be sent by phone – dial 122.

CARS AND MOTORING

Driving Licence

Visitors to Denmark can drive on a licence issued by any EU or EEA country, without any further formalities. An international permit is neither required, nor recommended. However, provisional driving licences are not acceptable. The minimum age for driving is 18 years and for car hire 20 years. US visitors may wish to obtain an International Driving Licence, although there is nothing to stop them from driving on a US licence. It is compulsory to have a red warning triangle; you are also strongly advised to have your headlamps adjusted if you are coming from the UK.

Registration

If you are bringing a car (*bil* in Danish) from abroad and plan to live in Denmark, it is essential to contact the customs authorities beforehand. See Importing a Car section, in *Setting Up Home* chapter.

Registration tax is payable when you buy a car, to the Tax and Customs service;

see the site www.toldskat.dk for more information. The tax amounts to 180% on new cars, somewhat less on older cars, plus 25% VAT. In addition, every six months you pay a road users' tax called the *vægtafgift* on a graded scale depending on the size of your car; typically £550 annually for a medium-size four-door car. You also need to have your car checked annually for roadworthiness by the *Statens Bilinspektion* (cost: about kr370). Number plates (*nummerplader*) are issued by the police at a *motorkontor*. While the basic price of a car is quite low, and petrol cheaper than in the UK, overall, Danish motorists are probably the worst-off in Europe because of the excessively high taxes.

Roads

The road system in Denmark is modern and extensive. Needless to say anyone travelling widely in Denmark will need to make use of the excellent car ferries, and the bridges linking the major islands. Danish drivers have a reasonable safety record, although not as good as in the UK: the number of fatalities averages about 600 a year.

Parking. Parking is controlled by discs, available from police stations, post offices, banks and petrol stations. In Copenhagen, the time limit is shown on signs. Meters (limit: 3 hours) are also in operation in Copenhagen and in some other towns, and take kr 1, 5, and 10 coins. The sign *stopforbud* means no waiting; *parkering forbud* no parking.

Touring Club. The Danish motoring organisation is Forenede Danske Motoreje (FDM): Firskovvej 32, Postboks 500, 2800 Lyngby; ☎70 13 30 40; fax 45 27 09 93; e-mail fdm@fdm.dk; www.fdm.dk. The annual cost of membership was kr475 in 2001.

Accidents & Breakdowns. There are emergency telephones on motorways and emergency road patrols on all the main highways. A national rescue towing service run by the *Falck Organisation* can be called out 24 hours a day. Contact: Falck Redningskorps, Falck Huset, Polititorvet 1780 Copenhagen K. For help call 70 10 20 30; for customer service; 70 10 20 31, for general enquiries, 33 15 83 20.

In cases of accidents involving injury or material damage, the police must be called (☎112).

Rules of the Road

As in all Scandinavian countries, it is compulsory to drive, or motorcycle, with dipped headlights during the day, regardless of the brilliance or otherwise of the prevailing weather conditions, outside built-up areas. The speed limits are 31mph/50kph in built-up areas, 50mph/80kph outside built-up areas and 68mph/110kph on motorways. Town limits are indicated by a town silhouette on a white background. Children aged from three to seven years are legally required to have a properly fitted safety seat when travelling in the front of a vehicle.

The penalties for drinking and driving are severe. The blood/alcohol limit is 0.5 promille and there is random breath-testing of drivers. For more information on driving in Denmark see the website www.trafikken.dk.

TRANSPORT

Air

SAS runs Denmark's domestic network. In such a small country it takes under an hour to fly to all destinations within the Danish peninsula and archipelago. As the overland public transport is efficient and fast, there is not much need to use domestic air services. However, for certain age groups such as under-26s and over-60s as well as for families, it is possible to get substantial reductions on standby tickets. The details can be obtained from any SAS or Tourist office. If you book a return flight with SAS from the UK or USA, you can get a Visit Scandinavia Air Pass which consists of discount coupons for flights within Denmark, Norway, Sweden and Finland. With these coupons you can take internal flights for around $75 to $145; you can buy a maximum of eight coupons at a time, and they have to be used up within three months.

Fares come in three categories: The two cheaper ones are Red Departures (*røde afange*) which are return tickets for use on weekdays and Green Departures (*grønne afange*) for weekend returns. The most expensive are Blue Departures which are valid anytime.

Rail/Bus

Denmark has an excellent railway system. Trains are run by Danske Statsbaner (DSB), the Danish State Railways, who have information points at all major rail stations (in Copenhagen, call 33 14 88 00). The website www.dsb.dk allows you to plan your journey and calculate the cost. In the past, trains spent much of their time being transported across water. These days trains can travel directly from Copenhagen to Germany over the Store Bælt bridge.

A few areas are not covered by the rail network, for instance the remote northeast of Jutland and the island of Funen. In these areas there are bus services often linked to the train timetables. Supplements are payable for *Lyntog* (lightning) express trains, on which reservations are compulsory. Other types of train are the ICB and IC3 intercity trains for which seat reservations are also obligatory. The IC3s are the newest addition to the network and connect all four major cities.

Regionaltog are the slower trains that link the small towns, while *S-tog* are integrated bus and train transport in cities. It is possible to buy tickets on board a *Regionaltog* without a surcharge but not on other trains.

Fares are based on a zone system and are priced according to the number of zones the journey covers. Some examples of adult, single fares in 2002: Copenhagen-Vejle (213km/30 zones) kr246 (approx. £20/US$28.80); Odense-Esbjerg (137km/18 zones) kr151; Copenhagen-Frederikshavn (443km/62 zones) kr310.

Cheap Deals. The best deal in Scandinavia, where good deals are virtually non-existent, is undoubtedly the Scanrail Pass, which comes in several forms. The most popular allows you to travel on five days out of 21 and is valid all over Denmark, Norway, Sweden and Finland. It also includes discounts on some ferries, bus services and museums. It is available in Scandinavia; the only restriction is that you can only travel on three days within one country. See www.europeanrail.com

for more information. The Euro Domino pass is a holiday pass valid in one European country, sold by Rail Europe; see www.raileurope.com. In Denmark itself, there are reductions of up to 50% for students and anyone over 65 years old on Danish railways. Children under 4 years travel free and those aged 4-12 years pay half. Young people aged 12-25 can get a youth card which entitles the holder to discounted tickets all year round. There is a nationwide discount card valid for 3, 6 or 12 months which entitles the holder to discounted tickets on any day.

Long-Distance Buses

In some instances it may be easier to take a bus than struggle with complicated train connections; in some areas there are no train services. The best way to plan your journey is to use the website: www.rejseplanen.dk which shows you all the connections between buses and trains and ferries. The main long-distance services are from Copenhagen to Århus and Esbjerg to Frederikshavn. The new Danish Greyhound Bus company runs buses to Malmö Airport in Sweden, allowing you to make a connection with the cheap Ryanair flights from London Stansted.

Useful Addresses

Abildskous Rutebiler, ☎70 210 888; www.abildskou.dk. Århus to Copenhagen/Kastrup.
Fjernbusrute-SYD, ☎7465 0505; www.fjernbusrute.dk. Toender to Copenhagen.
Gråhundbus, ☎44 68 44 00; www.graahundbus.dk. Copenhagen to Rönne; Copenhagen to Malmö/

Lund (Sweden).
Hurtigbusser, ☎57 87 27 27; www.hurtigbussen.dk. Buses in Zealand.
X-busser, ☎98 900 900; www.xbus.dk. Jutland services, inc. Esbjerg to Århus/Aalborg, and to German border.

Sea

The peninsula and islands of Denmark are linked predominantly by ferries and the occasional bridge/tunnel. The old train-bearing ferries linking Zealand, Funen and Jutland have been scrapped; these days ferries serve routes other than those where there is a bridge.

Copenhagen is linked to Malmö in Sweden by the Øresund bridge and tunnel and also by hydrofoil (hourly from 6am to midnight: dial 33 12 80 88 for information). The main link from Denmark to Sweden is the ferry from Helsingør (Elsinore) to Helsingborg, which runs every 15 minutes from 5am to 2am for about Kr40 (approx. £3.20/US$4.70) each way. The ferries between Sweden and Denmark are popular with Swedes who go to Denmark to buy crates of beer; it is not unusual to see Swedes with three or four crates of empty beer bottles wending their way to a ferry terminal on the Swedish side in the early hours of the morning. To Germany, the Rødbyhavn to Puttgarden ferry costs the same and runs hourly. There are numerous other ferries linking Jutland and the islands of Denmark to Iceland, the Faroe Islands, Scotland, Norway and Poland.

City Transport

Bus/S-tog. Transport around main cities is normally by bus. Buses are one-person operated; board at the front and buy tickets from the driver. Copenhagen has both buses and electric trains. The whole of Denmark is divided into zones, on the Dutch model; zone 1 being central Copenhagen. The minimum ticket price in Copenhagen is kr13 (approx. £1/US1.40) to travel in 2 zones within one hour on all buses and the S-Bahn; add on kr6.50 per zone extra. You can buy discount cards, now called *klippekort*, worth ten 2-zone fares or *klips* for kr85; a 3-zone card costs kr115. A card valid for 30 days' travel over two zones costs kr235. The bus company HT has a customer service office in the centre of Copenhagen on Rådhuspladsen or see their website: www.ht.dk. The tourist office will have details of the discount day card which is valid for unlimited travel on urban transport for 24 hours.

Tickets are stamped with the date and time of issue. S-Bahn tickets are only valid if stamped in the machines on station platforms. There are fines (called a 'surcharge') for travelling without a valid time-stamped ticket of some kr250.

Bicycle

The flat terrain of Denmark (highest point 531 feet) is ideal for cycling holidays or excursions and also for getting about in towns. This is evidenced by the fact that there are over two and a half million bicycles in Denmark. Cycles can be hired from main railway stations for about kr50 (approx. £4/US5.80) a day, but if you are living and working in Denmark it would certainly be worth bringing your bicycle or buying one either to get to work or for recreation. If you wish to buy one in Denmark, it is worth considering the police auctions of unclaimed lost property. Details are published in local papers and you can inspect the goods before making a bid. Danes are very keen on cycling holidays and organised tours are run by various tourist offices, affiliated to the *Dansk Cyklist Forbund* (Rømersgade 7, 1362 Copenhagen K; ☎33 32 31 21; fax 33 32 76 83; e-mail dcf@dcf.dk; www.dcf.dk), a helpful organisation that can answer any particular queries about cycling in Denmark. Funen Island is a popular area for cycling holidays. The Danish Tourist Office produces a useful leaflet entitled 'On a Bike in Denmark'.

If you get tired of cycling, it is a simple matter to take your bike on most kinds of public transport. Trains and long-distance buses make a small charge, kr100 is charged for flights, while ferries usually take bikes for free.

Hitch-Hiking

It is the general wisdom that hitch-hiking in Denmark is extremely difficult. It certainly will be if you try to hitch on motorways as this is illegal. If you are dropped off in a lay-by or car park you can approach parked motorists. Otherwise try to hitch from somewhere the traffic has to slow down, like a slip road.

BANKING AND FINANCE

The three main banks are Den Danske Bank, Unibank, and the savings bank, Sparekassen Bikuben. Following the recession of the early 90s many smaller and medium-sized provincial banks got into financial trouble and were absorbed by the larger banks, who were more easily able to cut staff and improve profit margins. Den Danske Bank, the largest, was formed by a merger of Den Danske Bank, Copenhagen Handelsbank and Provinsbank. The main provincially based bank is Jyske Bank whose headquarters are in Silkeborg.

The Girobank, privatised in 1993, was formerly part of the Post Office and was widely used for transactions by government utilities, companies and individuals. It was not however allowed to lend money. Now that it is a limited company there are no such restrictions and its loyal customers provide a sound basis for its operations. At present it is the fifth largest Danish bank. Danish banks also provide insurance services, and some insurance companies provide banking services.

Personal Banking. Opening a bank account in Denmark is straightforward. If you are a cautious type you will probably choose one of the big five banks mentioned above, depending on your location. As tends to be the case with banks other than those in the UK, there will be charges for servicing your account even when it is in credit. Banking hours are normally 9.30am to 4pm on weekdays, except Thursdays when they are extended to 5.30pm.

Money Transfers. There are several possibilities for transferring money to and from Denmark. For transfers from the UK there is a minimum charge of around £15. The lowest fees are charged by the Co-op bank and the UK Girobank. Sending a cheque will lead to delays and will cost more than an electronic transfer.

Internal Payments System. Danish banks have a very efficient debit card system as they all share the same one, *Dankort,* which can be used in over 46,000 shops as an instant debit card and in all cash points. More than half of adult Danes use a Dankort; there is an annual charge of kr150 (approx. £12/US$17.50). There is also a Dankort/Visa for use in Denmark and abroad, but the most popular foreign credit card is Eurocard which has twice as many holders as Dankort/Visa.

TAX AND THE EXPATRIATE

As a result of the different tax regimes which exist in different countries there are major complications involved in a move overseas. This does not just apply to tax affairs in the host country; a move will conjure up many tax implications in one's home country also. Many globetrotters simply leave home without informing the tax authorities in their own country. While the UK tax authorities have always been quite indulgent, as long as you can show that you were away for a whole tax year, the Internal Revenue Service in the US is much stricter. If you have already arranged a job in advance in Denmark, then it would be advisable to obtain some information from the tax authorities in your home country before leaving, thus ensuring that no unnecessary tax is paid. If your tax affairs are complex, e.g. you own property or you have income in more than one country, then you will probably need to consult a tax adviser. These can be found in specialised magazines such as *FT-Expat* or *The Expatriate*.

The Question of Residence

Anyone who spends more than six months (183 days) per year in Denmark has to pay Danish tax on his or her worldwide income unless they are eligible for the Expatriate Tax Regime (see below). Taxable income includes income from work, letting and leasing, trade enterprises, returns on investment, annuities and speculative capital gains. Before moving to Denmark it is therefore important to consider where one's main residence will be for tax purposes. The important point to note is that one does not necessarily escape one country's income tax and become subject to another's just by moving there. It all depends on where the tax authorities consider one is resident for tax purposes, and also where one is ordinarily resident or domiciled – not necessarily the same thing. The terms resident, ordinarily resident and domiciled are not defined in the UK Tax Acts but are based on legal precedent.

Procedure for UK Residents

The situation is reasonably straightforward if you are moving permanently abroad. You should inform the UK Inspector of Taxes at the office you usually deal with of your departure and they will send you a P85 form to complete. The UK tax office will require certain proof that you are leaving the UK, and hence their jurisdiction, for good. Evidence of having sold a house in the UK and having rented or bought one in Denmark is usually sufficient. If you are leaving a UK company to take up employment with a Danish one then the P45 form given by your UK employer and evidence of employment in Denmark should be sufficient.

If you are eligible for a tax refund in respect of the period up to your departure you should complete an income tax return for income and gains from the previous 5 April to your departure date. It may be advisable to seek professional advice when completing the P85; this form is used to determine your residence status and hence your UK tax liability. You should not fill it in if you are only going abroad for a short period of time. Once the Inland Revenue are satisfied that you are no longer resident or domiciled in the UK, they will close your file and not expect any more UK income tax to be paid.

If you are moving abroad temporarily then other conditions apply. You are not liable for UK taxes if you work for a foreign employer on a full-time contract and remain abroad for a whole tax year (6 April to 5 April), as long as you spend less than 183 days in a year, or 91 days a year averaged out over a four-year period, in the UK. Several part-time jobs abroad may be considered as full-time employment. If you are considered a UK resident and have earned money working abroad then taxes paid abroad are not deductible. If you spend one part of a year working abroad and the rest in the UK you may still be considered non-resident for the part spent abroad, the so-called split tax year concession; this only applies to someone going abroad for a lengthy period of time.

Denmark has a double taxation agreement with the UK, which makes it possible to offset tax paid in one country against tax paid in another. While the rules are complex, essentially, as long as you work for a Danish employer and are paid in Denmark then you should not have to pay UK taxes, as long as you meet the residency conditions outlined above. For further information see the Inland Revenue publications IR20 *Residents and non-residents. Liability to tax in the United Kingdom* which can be found on the website www.inlandrevenue.gov.uk. Booklets IR138, IR139 and IR140 are also worth reading. Booklets can be obtained from your local tax office or from:

Non-Resident Claims, Fitz Roy House, PO Box 46, Nottingham NG2 1BD; ☎0115-974 1919; fax 0115-974 1919; www.inlandrevenue.gov.uk.

General Services Unit, St. John's House, Bootle, Merseyside L69 9BB; ☎0151-472 6214/6216; fax 0151-472 6067.

Procedure for US Citizens

The US Internal Revenue Service (IRS) expects US citizens and resident aliens living abroad to file tax returns every year. Such persons will continue to be liable for US taxes on worldwide income until they have become permanent residents of another country and severed their ties with the USA. If you earn less than a certain amount abroad in one tax year then you do not need to file a tax return. The amount in 2001 was $7,200 for a single person; other rates apply for pensioners, married persons, heads of household, etc.

Fortunately the USA has a double taxation agreement with Denmark so you should not have to pay taxes twice on the same income. In order to benefit from the double taxation agreement you need to fulfil one of two residence tests: either you have been a bona fide resident of another country for an entire tax year, which is the same as the calendar year in the case of the US, or you have been physically present in another country for 330 days during a period of 12 months which can begin at any time of the year. Once you qualify under the bona fide residence or physical presence tests then any further time you spend working abroad can also be used to diminish your tax liability.

Because Denmark does not have a binational social security or totalisation agreement with the USA, US citizens will have to pay social security contributions when working in Denmark, unless they are working for a foreign employer in the oil and gas sector (see below).

As regards foreign income, the main deduction for US citizens is the 'Foreign Earned Income Exclusion' by which you do not pay US taxes on the first $80,000 of money earned abroad (as of 2002; the amount of the exclusion has in recent times gone up by $2,000 every year). Investment income, capital gains, etc. are unearned income. If you earn in excess of the limit, taxes paid on income in Denmark can still be used to reduce your liability for US taxes, either in the form of an exclusion or a credit, depending on which is more advantageous. The same will apply to Danish taxes paid on US income.

The rules for US taxpayers abroad are explained very clearly in the IRS booklet: *Tax Guide for US Citizens and Resident Aliens Abroad,* known as Publication 54, which can be downloaded from the internet on www.irs.gov.

Personal Income Tax

It is well-known that taxes in Scandinavia are some of the world's highest, mainly in order to support the welfare largesse and superb infrastructure. Denmark has the highest direct taxation of all, as well as the highest indirect taxes. Direct taxes add up to 32% of GDP, indirect taxes to 16% and social security contributions a mere 1.7%. Virtually all public expenditure in Denmark is covered by the direct and indirect taxes so there are almost no other taxes for individuals to pay. The other burden of taxation falls on companies and organisations.

The annual personal tax-free allowance stood at kr33,400 (approx. £2,700/ US$3,900) in 2001. The bottom bracket tax rate is 5.5%. Middle bracket tax rate of 6% is payable on income up to kr177,900; the top rate of 15% on income above kr276,900. Municipal tax is levied at, on average, 32.5%. In addition there is the Labour Market Contribution (AM or unemployment insurance) at 8%, the special pension savings tax (SP) at 1%, and the small supplementary pension contribution (ATP), which does not exceed kr894 per annum. After these last three have been taken off, the rest of your monthly salary (minus your personal allowance) is subject to a 39% withholding tax; the final tax bill is adjusted later.

Tax Administration. In Denmark tax assessment for employees is almost completely automatic. The employers pass on employees' details direct to the tax authorities as do banks and insurance companies which gives details of salaries paid, interest received and payments to pension schemes; individuals pay provisional monthly tax calculated on an estimate of taxable income. In November the tax office issues a preliminary tax assessment with a tax card for the following year, which goes directly to your employer unless the authorities hear otherwise.

You will receive an income tax return form in March or April stating your income and deductions for the previous year. It is then up to you to correct any discrepancies; your tax return must be filed with the municipal tax authority not later than 1 May each year; failure to file in time carries a penalty. You then have until July 1 to pay any outstanding tax. If you pay later then interest is added on. Any overpayment of tax will be refunded in the year following the year of income. If you disagree with your tax assessment you should contact the local tax administration. If you are still not satisfied you can go to the local Tax Appeals Tribunal, or eventually to the National Tax Appeals Tribunal.

If you still receive payments in your country of origin you will need to fill in the form: *Selvangivelse for udenlandsk indkomst*; you will not be taxed on income received before you moved to Denmark. Further details can be found in the brochure: *When moving to Denmark* issued by the Ministry of Taxation.

Those in search of temporary work who get a job, however temporary, should try to rush off and get their own tax card (*skattekort*) from the Skatteforvaltning (Gyldenløvesgade 15, 1639 Copenhagen; ☎33 66 33 66; www.tax.dk *or* www.skm.dk) and give it to the employer themselves the same day. The reason for not delaying is that otherwise tax will be deducted at the emergency rate of 60% and you will not be able to claim it back until six months after the calendar year in which you worked. Fortunately, the authorities are extremely scrupulous about repaying any excess tax, even after you have long since left the country. The Skatteforvaltning opens from 10am to 2pm daily with an extra hour (4pm to 5pm) on Thursdays.

Other Taxes

From 1994 the highest rates of income tax were partly reduced, and higher taxes imposed on fringe benefits and capital gains, with increases in the taxes on energy, water and waste (the so-called 'green' taxes). All these are taxes paid by companies, rather than individuals. As in some other European countries the municipalities levy a church tax on members of the Danish Christian Church which amounts to between 0.5% and 1.7% of individual incomes, depending on the area. It is somewhat surprising that, although most Danes hardly set foot inside a church during their lives, 88% of them elect to pay the church tax. You have to formally opt out of the church in order not to pay it. Owners of real estate are subject to a local property tax calculated on the value of the land, at 1% or 3%.

Highly-Paid Foreign Researchers

From 1992 a scheme was introduced for researchers and key employees to work in Denmark for short periods of time. Highly-paid foreigners whose work is deemed to be important for the Danish economy may be subject to only 25% tax for a period of up to 36 months over 10 years. Their income should be over kr50,900 (approx. £4,100/US$5,950) per month after the social security contributions. The minimum level of income rule may be waived, depending on the persons' status. Such workers' qualifications have to be vetted by the authorities. See the leaflet '25% Tax Scheme' available from the Ministry of Taxation.

A Note for Non-Residents

If you are employed in the oil and gas industry by a non-Danish employer, your employer will only be liable to withhold tax at 30%. If you are considered non-resident and hired out to a Danish employer, the employer may withhold tax at 30%, along with the AM and SP contributions. You may also be considered resident in both Denmark and another country and benefit from a more favourable tax regime.

Indirect Taxes

In contrast to some other EU states Denmark relies more on revenues from direct rather than indirect taxes. However, as in most European countries the largest indirect tax is VAT which in Denmark is levied at a standard rate of 25% on most goods and services. The EU is aiming towards standardisation of VAT rates throughout the EU but this is some way from fruition. In the meantime, Denmark has no graded rate of VAT, but some services, notably banking, real estate and medical are exempted. Exports are zero-rated. The other major indirect tax is car tax.

Information on Tax

Once you have the Personal Code Number (see *Residence and Entry Regulations*) your tax will be automatically deducted from your pay by the employer. Any questions on your tax can be addressed to the employer or failing that the Ministry of

Taxation, Nicolai Eigtveds Gade 28, 1402 Copenhagen K (☎33 92 33 92; fax 33 14 91 05; e-mail skm@skm.dk; www.skm.dk *or* www.tax.dk).

SOCIAL SECURITY

Denmark is famed for its excellent social security system, something that has attracted some foreigners to going and live there. Social welfare comes under the Ministry of Social Affairs. The municipalities deliver social services and receive grants from central government to cover the costs that they are not able to meet from their own budgets. The largest item is old-age pensions (72% of the total budget). For information on social security provision see the website www.sm.dk.

THE HEALTH CARE SYSTEM

The health care system of Denmark is part of the overall state health and welfare policy whose high standards are characteristic of the Scandinavian countries. The policy assures the entitlement of all citizens to good housing, wholesome food, good working conditions, pollution control and an adequate social network of back-up organisations. The health sector is administered by the local authorities who operate virtually all health care facilities. Everyone in Denmark, regardless of income, social and employment status is entitled to almost all health care services free of charge. Health care provision is 85% in the public domain, and is financed almost entirely by taxation.

The main elements of the welfare system were instituted in the first half of the 20th century when the organisational framework was created at a national level to supervise the health conditions of the nation and to supervise the local health personnel. Another major reform came in the 1970s when local government entities were expanded and given more responsibilities, which led to a decentralisation of health care to a local level.

The counties, of which there are 14, along with the municipalities of Copenhagen and Frederiksberg, are responsible for running and planning the main health care services, i.e. hospitals and primary health. The municipalities (*amter*) which are the local authorities (275 in all) are responsible for running and planning most of the social welfare system and also for certain auxiliary medical services: home nurses, infant health visitors, school health and child dental services. Overall organisation of health care comes under the Ministry of Health.

General Practitioners and Specialists

As in the UK, often the first point of contact with the health service is one of Denmark's approximately 4,000 GPs. Anyone from the age of 16 is allowed to choose his or her GP. GPs are responsible for referring patients to specialists in primary health care or hospitals; also to social services, health visitors and home nurses. All such facilities are free of charge, except for night-time emergency calls, for which there is a charge of kr300 (approx. £24.00/US$35). As in the UK, in the state sector, patients can only be referred to a specialist by their GP. You are expected to see the GP with whom you are registered; if you choose to see another one you have to pay a fee. Your local municipal health department will advise you where to find your nearest GP: look for *Kommunes Social- og sundhedsforvaltning* in the phone book.

Most hospitals in Denmark are run as publicly owned bodies, and those who work in them are civil servants. The number of hospitals and hospital beds has fallen sharply in recent years. The emphasis is now on making hospital stays as short as possible and treating as many patients as possible as out-patients or in places other than hospitals. For an ambulance call the emergency number 112.

Useful Addresses

Rigshospitalet, Blegdamsvej 9, 2100 Copenhagen Ø; ☎33 45 33 45; www.rigshospitalet.dk.
Sundhedsministeriet (Ministry of Health), Slotsholmsgade 10-12, Copenhagen K; ☎33 92 33 60; e-mail sum@sum.dk; www.sum.dk.

Dispensing Chemists

All dispensing chemists (*apoteker*) in Denmark are authorised by the state, which decides their number and location. The National Health Insurance Scheme refunds some of the patients' prescription costs. The elderly, the chronically sick, and the infirm pay no charges for medicines. There is one 24-hour chemist in Copenhagen at Steno Apotek, Vesterbrogade 6.

Dentists

Dentists (*tandlæger*) are free to set up clinics where they wish; there are also municipal clinics. Adults have to pay about 70% of dental expenses. The rest may be reimbursed by private medical insurance. All children up to the age of 18 are entitled to free dental care at a municipal dental clinic. In an emergency call: Tandlægevagten, Oslo Plads 14, Copenhagen; ☎35 38 02 51.

The E111

The UK Department of Health advises that UK nationals do not require form E111 to obtain free, or mainly free, medical treatment in Denmark – presentation of a British passport is enough. You should apply for a refund of medical costs from the local municipality, with receipts, before you leave Denmark. The first kr500 (approx £40/US$58) of your treatment will not be refunded. Further information can be found in the Leaflet T6, *Health Advice to Travellers,* obtainable in post offices in the UK, or on the internet on www.doh.gov.uk/hat. If you are an EEA citizen living in the UK, but not a UK national, visiting Denmark then you do require the E111; the application form can be found in Leaflet T6.

Once in Denmark if you require minor treatment you can go to any doctor, dentist, hospital or any other part of the health care system, where you will be treated free of charge, as long as you can produce your British passport. For further information contact the local commune's social and health department: *Kommunes Social- og sundhedsforvaltning.*

US and other non-EEA citizens do not qualify for free medical treatment until they have been officially resident for six weeks. They will need private medical cover for the first part of their stay.

Private Medical Insurance

Those who are going to Denmark seeking work, or who spend a few weeks or months a year there, may require private medical insurance to cover the balance of the cost not covered by the E111 (see above). If you already hold private health insurance for the UK, you will find that most companies will switch this for European cover once you are in Denmark. With the increase of British and foreign insurance companies offering this kind of cover, it is worth shopping around as cover and costs vary.

One of the best known UK companies is Expacare (e-mail info@expacare.net or visit www.expacare.net), who are specialists in expatriate healthcare offering high quality health insurance cover for individuals and their families, including group cover for five or more employees. Cover is available for expatriates of all nationalities worldwide.

ExpaCare – high-quality health insurance cover, for individuals or families living abroard. To find out more...

For a copy of the **International Health Plan** brochure for individuals or groups (minimum of 5 employees) please email **info@expacare.net** or visit **www.expacareworld.net**

ExpaCare is a trading name of JLT Healthcare Limited. Regulated by the General Insurance Standards Council.

Other Benefits

Maternity Benefits, Denmark has the most generous maternity benefits in Europe. Employees qualify for benefit of up to kr2,758 (approx. £225/US$320) a week for up to 30 weeks, made up of four weeks before and 14 weeks after confinement, and concurrently, two weeks' paid paternity leave for the father; plus an extension of another 10 weeks for father or mother, and another 2 weeks for fathers only. To qualify one has to have worked at least 120 hours in the previous 13 weeks.

Child Benefit, There are equally generous allowances for children. The basic allowance for children is graduated from kr12,000 to kr8,600 annually depending on age. There are further allowances for children of single parents and pensioners. If you adopt a foreign child you can receive a one-time grant of kr34,000.

Most parents can find a place for their under-school age child in a nursery. About 90% of 3 to 5 year old children are in nurseries.

CRIME AND POLICE

The Police

As elsewhere in Scandinavia crime is not rampant on the well-lit streets. However it would be a mistake to assume that they are devoid of danger. Denmark has its share of anti-social and criminal elements, often linked with drugs and other addictions.

Should you need their assistance, the police are typically polite and helpful, and most will speak good English. The police are not used to dealing with civil disturbances, however, and many foreigners were astonished when they saw police firing on a crowd of rioters in Copenhagen at the time of the Maastricht referendum, wounding several in the process. The police service has a useful website, listing their various offices, and giving an annual report in English at: www.politi.dk.

The courts come under the Justice Ministry (www.jm.dk) and operate at three levels: the Lower Courts, of which there are 84, deal with the majority of cases; the High Courts of Justice, of which there are two, handle cases not dealt with by the Lower Courts; the Supreme Court of Judicature deals with appeals from the Lower Courts.

In addition there are three specialised courts: the Maritime and Commercial which handles trade and shipping disputes, the Rent Tribunal, and the Labour Tribunal.

LOCAL GOVERNMENT

In addition to the national parliamentary elections, local elections are held every four years. Local mayors and chairs for local committees are elected by the locally elected councillors from among themselves.

The municipalities are very important at local level. They collect both national and local taxes and are responsible for providing most of the social welfare budget of their area. In addition they run the local schools, libraries, rest homes and other public institutions. They are also responsible for various authorisations such as building permits.

Elections for Denmark's 16 county councils are held simultaneously with local government elections. A county council is mainly the local executive of the country's political administration and as such has limited powers.

In accordance with a 1994 EC directive, EU citizens living in another member state have the right to vote and stand in local elections, as do all foreign residents in Denmark.

SOCIAL LIFE

Most of us know little about how Danes tend to enjoy themselves. The Danes have their hedonistic side. The relationship between Denmark and Sweden is a bit like that between France and Germany. The Swedes come here in search of a good time. As with all the Scandinavians the Danes are more outgoing when the sun is shining, and in summertime they inhabit the outdoors as much as possible; campsites, beaches, cycling tours and yachting are all good ways to meet the Danes at their most enjoyable pastimes. In winter they become more hearth-oriented and practise the Danish art of *hygge*. This modern version of wassailing involves inviting some well-chosen friends to one's well-heated and insulated home to share a cosy and intimate evening with plenty of *skoaling* (toasting). The creation of a convivial atmosphere is probably the Danes' way of creating a defence against the isolation and suicidal tendencies to which Scandinavians enduring a long winter seem particularly prone. As a foreigner you may have to wait a bit longer to be invited to *hygge*. When you are, remember to take flowers for your hostess and not to drink from your glass or make a toast before your host does, and not to make jokes about their Royal Family.

An important rule to remember in Scandinavia is the so-called *Janteloven* or Law of Jante, the 'you are no better than we are' law, a quote from a well-known novel from the 1930s. Essentially nobody should consider themselves superior to anyone else; bosses and employees tend to be on a more equal footing and it is quite OK to speak your mind with your boss. The social system aims to iron out inequalities between people, by making it difficult to be very rich or very poor. Danes consider themselves to be very well off, and believe that people in other countries should follow their model. There is a great deal of concern for social injustice around the world in general; to some extent Danes tend to think that other countries are worse off than they really are.

While the Danes are generally well-disposed to other Nordics, their relationship with Sweden is much more complex. It would be presumptuous of foreigners to make jokes about Denmark or neighbouring Sweden, even if the Danes do it themselves. The Danes are very patriotic and proud of their country, and quite touchy about criticism.

THE DANES

As with the rest of Scandinavians there is a strong emphasis on toughness and independence which is bred into the Danes from the time they are born. Although Danes are generally tolerant and friendly, they do not have much time for idle chit-chat. They are generally less polite towards each other than they are towards foreigners. While they love a good argument with their friends they will be very cautious about expressing their opinions to a foreigner. They are not as suspicious of outsiders as the Norwegians, and more outgoing than the Swedes, but it still takes a long time to make close friends.

Some foreigners perceive Danes as arrogant or cold, because they are not easily drawn into conversations with strangers. North Americans will, in particular, find that their familiar style of relating to strangers does not go down all that well here. Because of their strongly socialistic mentality, Danes are generally more sympathetic towards Britain than towards the United States, but once one has gained their confidence the Danes are very amicable and make staunch friends.

Social Attitudes and Practices

One aspect of the Danes which people may find refreshing is their relaxed, no-nonsense way of dealing with most things including social and sexual issues and the openness about sexual matters generally. Danes are not at all easy to shock. Danish women are emancipated, straightforward and broad-minded. They have achieved an equality within their culture that few other European nations can boast. Such open-mindedness and independence, underpinned by a welfare state that ensures that all situations are supportable has led to an increase of partnerships that are not formalised by marriage. Denmark has the highest percentage of babies born outside wedlock of any EU nation, and one of the highest divorce rates – two out of every three marriages fail. However, owing to a policy of providing sex education in all schools, unwanted teenage pregnancies account for many fewer births than in other developed countries, like Britain and France.

On the whole, one should remember that while the Danes are very sophisticated and cultured people with a kind of French *art de vivre*, this is still basically a Germanic culture, with a multitude of written and unwritten rules which one should try to observe so as not to upset your fellow citizens. Not being punctual is considered extremely impolite on social occasions and bad practice in business. When using public transport or driving you should follow the rules as strictly as the locals. In social situations, Danes are quite compulsive in expressing gratitude and appreciation, so going round saying *tak* (thankyou) several times to anyone who does you a favour or a kindness is essential.

Entertainment and Culture

The nearest the Danes get to the festival of the midnight sun (which occurs further north in Scandinavia), is June 23rd (St Hans Eve) when huge bonfires are lit across the country and particular songs are sung.

The Danes are great readers (perhaps something to do with the long winters). Public libraries are well stocked and carry a large foreign language section (mainly English and some French). To join a library you will need a *sygesikringskort* (social security card). The Danes are also fervent patrons of their many annual arts festivals including the Roskilde Rock Festival end of June/beginning of July, the Copenhagen Jazz Festival and many more. Details can be obtained from the Danish Tourist Office in your own country. In Denmark itself look for flyers and free sheets advertising events or get the complimentary music monthly *Kappa*. In the arts generally, Denmark is well regarded: the Royal Danish Ballet, based in Copenhagen is internationally well thought of.

Sport

Football is regarded as the national sport of Denmark which takes great pride in having been the European football champions in 1992, although they have been slipping down the league ever since. The Danish fans are known as *roligans* (a pun on the word for quiet) which makes them somewhat different from their British counterparts.

In a country as flat as Denmark it is hardly surprising that cycling is very popular. Additionally, it is the main form of transport for many Danes, and cities and main roads are equipped with numerous cycle paths. Such is the consideration given to cyclists that they also have right of way over other traffic.

Sailing is another favourite Danish pastime, and with many coastal villages and havens with marinas it is no wonder that almost every locality has its own little regatta as well as other events. Windsurfing has also gained in popularity. Finding the wind is no problem, but you need to be well insulated.

CONVERSION CHART

LENGTH (NB 12inches 1 foot, 10 mm 1 cm, 100 cm 1 metre)

inches	1	2	3	4	5	6	9	12	
cm	2.5	5	7.5	10	12.5	15.2	23	30	

cm	1	2	3	5	10	20	25	50	75	100
inches	0.4	0.8	1.2	2	4	8	10	20	30	39

WEIGHT (NB 14lb = 1 stone, 2240 lb = 1 ton, 1,000 kg = 1 metric tonne)

lb	1	2	3	5	10	14	44	100	2246
kg	0.45	0.9	1.4	2.3	4.5	6.4	20	45	1016

kg	1	2	3	5	10	25	50	100	1000
lb	2.2	4.4	6.6	11	22	55	110	220	2204

DISTANCE

mile	1	5	10	20	30	40	50	75	100	150
km	1.6	8	16	32	48	64	80	120	161	241

km	1	5	10	20	30	40	50	100	150	200
mile	0.6	3.1	6.2	12	19	25	31	62	93	124

VOLUME

1 litre =	0.2 UK gallons	1 UK gallon = 4.5 litres
1 litre =	0.26 US gallons	1 US gallon = 3.8 litres

CLOTHES

UK	8	10	12	14	16	18	20
Europe	36	38	40	42	44	46	48
USA	6	8	10	12	14	18	

SHOES

UK	3	4	5	6	7	8	9	10	11
Europe	36	37	38	39	40	41/42	43	44	45
USA	2.5	3.3	4.5	5.5	6.5	7.5	8.5	9.5	10.5

SHOPPING

Normal shopping hours are from 8am or 9am to 5.30pm. Large supermarkets are often open later on most evenings but there is general late shopping on Fridays until 7pm or 8pm. Most shops are closed on Saturdays from 1pm until Monday morning with the exception of bakers which (sometimes) open on Sunday mornings. On the first Saturday of the month, shops are allowed to open from 9am to 5pm. There are also kiosks (døgnkiosker) which keep longer daily hours and are open daily. Supermarket chains include Brugsen, Irma and Netto. The last, Netto is a minimalist retailing concept which involves displaying goods in cardboard boxes on the floor, in a warehouse environment. This concept emerged from the recession of the early 1990s. More convivial perhaps are the fresh produce markets which most towns hold on Wednesdays and Saturdays.

You can buy groceries until midnight each day at the City Market, Central Station in Copenhagen, and at railway stations in Odense, Århus and Aalborg.

Part of the high cost of shopping in Denmark is due to the sales tax of 25% which is levied on most goods and is included in the price.

METRICATION

Denmark uses the metric system in all respects: the standards of measurement are recognisable to English speakers. Temperature is always measured in Celsius. In all cases measurements are quoted as a decimal and not a fraction. In the long run it is much easier to learn and think in metric rather than to always try to convert from metric to imperial. To facilitate this process a metric conversion table (including clothes and shoe size conversions is) given.

PUBLIC HOLIDAYS

Denmark does not have an excessive number of public holidays, but they are taken seriously with all shops etc. firmly closed on the appropriate day.

New Year's Day	1 January
Palm Sunday	
Maundy Thursday	
Good Friday	
Easter Sunday	
Easter Monday	
Store Bededag	4th Friday after Easter
Ascension Day	May
Constitution Day	5 June
Whit Sunday	June
Whit Monday	June
Christmas Eve	24 December
Christmas Day	25 December
Boxing Day	26 December

RETIREMENT

BACKGROUND INFORMATION

By all accounts the Germans are more likely to want to retire within Denmark (which has a common border with Germany), than Britons are. Many Germans enjoy regular holidays in Denmark and have built up the kind of relationship with areas of the country that the British have with certain parts of France. An additional attraction is the German-speaking population of southern Jutland. The Germans would not even find the Danish winters particularly severe. Britons on the other hand traditionally seek to retire to climes sunnier than their own where the property and the living expenses are generally cheaper than at home. Denmark does not fulfil any of these criteria and so would probably only be considered as a place to retire to by those who had a connection with Denmark built up over many years.

Theoretically, those of Danish retirement age (67 years) and older can be well off in Denmark with its generous welfare provisions. Health and hospital care is almost totally free and there is extensive provision for care in their own homes for the very elderly and infirm. Where special housing has to be built for the elderly it takes into account that each resident should have an independent apartment and facilities, in other words the institutional approach to care of the elderly has all but vanished except in the case of the very old, the very frail and the demented.

There is a basic universal pension of about kr4,400 (approx. £355/US$510) monthly for a single person based on the number of years worked, topped up with up to kr1,650 monthly under the ATP (Labour-market supplementary pension) scheme, and a further annual lump sum of up to kr2,500 from the Special Pension scheme. There is a further universal supplementary pension, to take care of those whose pension is insufficient to live on. Pensions can be supplemented by government grants for such things as rent, spectacles and television licence fees. In addition, to top up their government pension, many retirees have paid into pension funds or private pension plans. To qualify for Danish pension rights you will need to have lived in Denmark for at least 10 years between the age of 14 and 66, including the five years preceding retirement. If you reached the age of 60 after 1 July 1999 you can claim your pension from the time you turn 65.

Those who plan to have an active retirement in Denmark will have no difficulty finding things to do. Danes are born clubbers and form associations at the drop of a hat. There are many pensioners' societies and clubs for socialising and also courses, excursions and entertainment. There are cheap travel deals (usually at 50% reduction) for retired people on all public transport and internal air services.

There are also reductions for pensioners who want to take evening classes.

At day care centres and other centres for the old, there is an increasing emphasis on getting the old to take a greater part in the organisation of their daily lives by means of user councils which can influence the way local authorities plan the future in the field of management of the elderly so that they get the most out of their lives.

Once retired people finally become octogenarian (and many in Denmark do), Denmark's reputation for pioneering care for the over-80s enables them to stay in their own homes or alternatively in sheltered housing combined with activity centres. Those in their own homes are visited regularly by medical and home help staff as required – on an entirely free basis.

Nursing Homes. Where nursing home accommodation becomes unavoidable, residents have to pay rent amounting to a percentage of their pension and other income depending on the system of payment in force in their locality. Local councils have a choice of ways of charging the residents for stays in nursing homes. Under one scheme they can pay 15% of their income plus electricity and heating. Charges are also made for other benefits (meals, occupational therapy and so on) received in the nursing home but the benefits are normally optional.

Special Considerations

Until 1990 it was not possible for any foreigners other than those who had held residence permits for at least five years previously to buy property in Denmark. This regulation was changed to bring Denmark into line with other EU countries where free movement of all citizens, workers, pensioners and students from a another member state means they can buy property in Denmark without having to fulfil this qualification (which still applies to non-EU nationals). You do not require official authorisation to buy a home for your own use. On the other hand, you cannot buy a summer house in Denmark until you have been a resident for five years.

Retired people should note that they will need a residence permit in order to get a personal code number (CPR or *personnummer*) which is a prerequisite for using the national health service (see *Residence and Entry Regulations*).

UK State Pensions

Should anyone be in a position to move to Denmark to retire and wish to collect their British pension, there is no reason why they cannot have it paid to them in that country in local currency, as this is provided for under EU regulations. It will probably not work to their advantage, as the cost of living is much higher in Denmark than in Britain and Danish pensions take this into account and are more generous (see above). Additionally there are currency fluctuations to take into account as sterling could be devalued against the euro at some time in the future.

Both those who have yet to claim and those who are already claiming a state pension should contact the DWP Pensions and Overseas Benefits Directorate, Newcastle-upon-Tyne NE98 1BA (☎0191-218 7777; www.pensionguide.gov.uk) for details of payment arrangements for UK state pensions. For those who do not plan to spend periods longer than three months at any one time in Denmark, the easiest course of action is to leave the state pension to mount up in the UK and to cash it in on returning. In the case of a longer or permanent stay in Denmark the pension can still be paid to a UK bank account; alternatively you can have the pension paid to you in Denmark, usually on a monthly or quarterly basis by filling in form E121 issued by the DWP in Newcastle-upon-Tyne.

If someone has worked in one or more EU countries then they will receive pensions from each country but only in proportion to the number of years worked.

UK Personal Pension Plans

Rising costs of welfare provision everywhere are causing governments to reduce the levels of benefit on offer. The increasing cost of provision is coupled with a rapid increase in the numbers of elderly people, which is going to reach its peak in two or three decades, so it is no wonder that the personal pension plan business has taken off in the UK. However those with personal pension plans should contact the company or financial consultant concerned for details of how the money can be paid in Denmark. Usually the money will be forwarded in sterling, but some of the larger personal pension plan insurers can send foreign currency cheques, though an annual fee will be charged. You will need to ascertain the most financially advantageous way of receiving payment of the pension. If it cannot be paid in Denmark, you may need to maintain a UK bank account and stand the cost of currency exchange yourself.

Expatriates can invest in offshore pension plans run from offshore centres such as the Isle of Man and the Channel Islands. There would be no UK tax demands on the interest on such pensions, which would be paid in full, but they would almost certainly attract tax in the country where they were being paid. The status of tax havens is likely to change from 2003, with the partial abolition of banking secrecy in the EU.

Foreign & UK Wills

As a general rule Danish inheritance tax (*arveskat*) will be levied on your worldwide assets, if you were domiciled in Denmark at the time of your death. Since inheritance taxes are higher in Denmark than in the UK (and far more so than in the US) you need to make plans to protect your assets outside Denmark from the Danish tax inspectors. If you have substantial assets, then taking early professional advice will save your heirs a great deal of money. Danish regulations do not allow you to disinherit your family members in the way that you can in some countries. Unless you have started an offshore company, or put assets in the names of family members, then the Danish law will override the provisions of a foreign will.

The rate of inheritance tax depends on the relationship between the heir and the deceased. For parents and children, the rate is 15% of the estate exceeding kr205,000 (approx. £16,600/US$24,000). This is subject to annual revisions. For other beneficiaries, the rate is 25% up to kr205,000, and then 36.25% or the excess. No tax is levied on inheritance from a spouse. If you choose to make a gift to your relatives then gift tax (*gaveskat*) is levied at the same rate, except for a tax-exempt amount of kr45,600 every year.

SECTION II

WORKING IN DENMARK

EMPLOYMENT

PERMANENT WORK

TEMPORARY WORK

BUSINESS AND INDUSTRY REPORT

STARTING A BUSINESS

EMPLOYMENT

THE EMPLOYMENT SCENE IN DENMARK

Denmark became industrialised comparatively late by European standards, and industrial manufacturing reached its peak after the Second World War. Before that, the economy was largely based on agriculture. The number of independent farmers in Denmark is about 55,000, one of the highest percentages of the population of any EU state, but less than a quarter of the number at the end of World War II. However, Denmark's agricultural legacy can be seen in the high level of agricultural exports, though these days technological methods predominate. Processing is largely managed by farmer-owned co-operative societies, however, only one-seventh of them employ permanent help.

About 65% of production is livestock based. This was not always so; the Danes went over to livestock production only at the end of the 19th century because of a collapse in the price of wheat. Denmark is now one of the world's leading suppliers of bacon and processed meats. In fact, the pig population of Denmark is a staggering 12 million (more than twice the human one). The farmers' co-operatives have invested heavily in projects for additional meat processing, ready meals and so on in anticipation of expanded export markets. Horticulture is also important with flowers and potted plants for export being the mainstays.

The food and drinks industry is dominated by five giant companies: Carlsberg (whose British venture, Carlsberg Tetley has a large brewery in Northampton), Danisco, MD Foods, Danish Crown and Vestjydske Slagterier. Two of Denmark's largest companies, MD Foods (a dairy giant, now part of Arla) and Danish Crown (the largest abattoir and meat processing group) are co-operatives.

Danish food companies have been notably successful in recent years, thus ensuring a high international profile. One such company is Chr. Hansen Laboratorium which established its reputation as a producer of rennet (essential to cheese-making), but which has rapidly expanded into natural food additives, and allergy treatment and testing, so that it has become a major player on the Danish stock market. A Danisco subsidiary, Danish Sugar has taken over plants in Germany and Sweden and has become Europe's fourth largest producer of beet sugar.

Denmark made its industrial mark through the production of components, rather than glamorous completed products and nowadays produces a range of small, very sophisticated items dependent on a high level of technology. Such products as thermostats, refrigerator compressors, hi-tech pumps, cement-making machines and high tension cables together comprise 70 per cent of Denmark's exports. FLS Industries is the world's leading supplier of cement mills and related machinery and equipment. FLS also comprises road haulage (DanTransport) and an aircraft maintenance group. In telecommunications GN Great Northern and Telecom Danmark have between them completed the ground breaking project of linking Russia to Western Europe by an underwater fibre-optic cable, while the Danish mobile telephone company Cetelco (part of the German Preussag group) has pioneered a mobile telephone which reduces the risk from antennae radiation thought to be a cause of brain cancers amongst frequent users of mobile phones.

Danish pharmaceuticals have also made their international mark. The Danish company Novo Nordisk is one of the world's two leading producers of insulin for diabetes treatment and a world leader in industrial enzymes.

Denmark's biggest single export market is Germany, followed by Sweden and the UK. Denmark has also achieved the rare distinction of being the only country in the EU which has a trade surplus with Japan. Fresh pork is its most lucrative export to Japan.

Another Danish speciality is furniture design (particularly tables and chairs) and manufacture. Denmark has been making itself highly competitive in this area and is currently in the process of a major export drive which has produced optimistic forecasts in financial circles, about the growing importance of this industry to the Danish economy.

Traditional luxury Danish exports include Royal Copenhagen china and silverware which have a considerable worldwide reputation. Several manufacturers of tableware have been amalgamated into the Royal Scandinavian group: see www.royalscandinavia.com.

Like many of its European partners, Denmark has moved steadily in one generation from largely industry-based manual employment to a white-collar and services employment base. The service sector has developed immensely recently as shipping, aviation, transport, trade in goods and money and tourism all become much more important. About 35% of all those employed in Denmark are in the public sector which is an increase of over threefold since 1960. The service sector now accounts for 71% of GDP, followed by industry, with 25%, and lastly agriculture, with a mere 4%.

The trend away from manufacturing to services, coupled with the fact that there are no extremely low incomes in Denmark means that the need for militant trades unions to resolve disputes between employees and owners over wage increases has largely disappeared. An indication of this is that the post-industrial Danish employee now rates job interest and security as higher priorities than the size of their wage packet.

Since about 1987 most industrial expansion has taken place in new development areas rather than in the old industrial centres. One area that has experienced notable commercial growth is the Jutland peninsular which now provides just over half of all jobs in the manufacturing industry. Denmark has about 11,700 factories of which fewer than 100 have have more than 500 employees. About 43% of the work force are employed by companies with a workforce of under 100, 36.5% in companies with 100-499 employees and 21% in companies of more than 500 employees. There are over 7,000 enterprises with a total work force of about

393,000. Employment breaks down regionally as follows:

Copenhagen	25.7%
Copenhagen metropolitan area	25.7%
Jutland	55.5%
Zealand, Funen and Islands	18.8%

RESIDENCE AND WORK REGULATIONS

The way in which residence regulations for foreigners are generally linked to one's employment position in Denmark means that it is not easy to remain in the country indefinitely while looking for work. Nationals of all EU countries have the right to go to Denmark for up to three months to look for work. If they find employment during this period they must go to the nearest *Direktoratet for Udlændinge* (Foreigners Bureau), where they will be granted a residence permit. Normally you should apply to the Foreigners Bureau before your three months is up. There are certain conditions for getting a residence permit, even when you have been offered a job. Certain minimum conditions as regards working hours and salary are required; also you have to be in an unemployment fund. It is required that the salary should be enough to live on. A minimum after tax of kr60,000 (approx. £4,850/US$7,000) per annum is usually acceptable.

When applying to the Foreigners Bureau, you should take your passport or other travel documents, a confirmation from your employer that you have a job, including details of duration, salary and so on, and confirmation that you have joined an unemployment fund.

If you are not a national of another EU, EEA or Nordic country then you are not allowed to work during your stay in Denmark (this prohibition applies even to unpaid work), unless you have obtained a work permit from the Danish Embassy or Consulate before leaving your own country, or the country in which you have had legal residence for the previous six months. As employment prospects in Denmark are somewhat limited by high domestic unemployment, labour and residence permits may only be obtained in very specific instances where a foreigner, rather than a Dane, is needed to fill the vacancy, or where highly specialised skills are required.

UNEMPLOYMENT

It is perhaps no wonder that many Danes put job security at the top of their priorities. The government's tough economic policies of the 1980s and 90s aimed at bringing down inflation and the budget deficit, resulted in rationalisation right across the board. As domestic demand fell and then export demand as Europe generally went into recession, unemployment shot up to 12%. In 2000 it went as low as 4.6% but the trend is now upwards again. The real unemployment rate in Denmark is closer to 11% as revealed by the social security statistics. At least 20% of people of working age (16-66), an approximate total of 510,000 are living on social security incomes related to unemployment benefit. Of these about 270,000 are covered by an early retirement scheme, one of the government's measures designed to help younger people find work, and another 185,000 are on reduced hours. Another scheme is to pay those in full-time work 80% of their salary for a sabbatical year to be used for study and updating their skills. Some unemployed people are even paid to go abroad for educational travel.

The unemployment situation in Denmark is paradoxical to say the least. Denmark has one of the highest participation rates – that is, percentage of people of working age actually in the labour market – in the world. There is a shortage of workers in some areas; people who go on working after 60 are given special incentives, while some receive subsidies to work fewer hours. The main difficulties in getting more people off social security and into jobs are related to lack of appropriate training, and the fact that so many people have become used to living off the state. The main focus is now on trying to provide more job training and educational programmes so making the labour force rotating and flexible to the demands of the market.

DEMAND FOR FOREIGN STAFF

Even before the European recession of the early 90s Denmark was not the easiest of EU countries in which to find work as there is a high level of skills amongst the workforce and great effort is made to update skills to fulfil the latest demands of the workplace. Unemployment, especially amongst young people, is high, which diminishes the chances for foreigners even further. There are areas where knowledge of Danish is not immediately necessary. English-speakers who have successfully moved to Denmark include photographers, graphic designers, musicians, teachers in international schools or teachers of English, and others with strong entrepreneurial skills.

It should also be borne in mind that multinational companies with branches in Denmark will often use English as the corporate language; that is meetings and records are in English. This is in the company's interests, otherwise foreign staff would not be interested in joining them. Although the majority of Denmark's companies employ fewer than 50 staff, there are some multi-national groups such as Asea Brown Boveri (a Swiss-based engineering giant) which have subsidiaries in Denmark, and which will provide employment at the higher levels. The European Environmental Agency is also now located in Copenhagen and employs a large number of expatriates.

WORKING CONDITIONS

Any British person who has visited Copenhagen or elsewhere in Denmark is usually attracted by the laid-back lifestyle and the air of affluence. However, there is a world of difference between visiting a country and living and working there with all the frustrations of daily life, which Danes experience just as much as anyone else. Denmark attracts an increasing number of foreign workers who find it congenial not only from a work point of view but who also find the high Scandinavian ideals about the treatment of the individual are not practised better anywhere in Europe. Denmark is also at the forefront of expertise in certain high technology products including precision components machinery and larger products such as the electronically advanced sailing vessels of the shipping group J Lauritzen.

Unlike Britain, Denmark has no official minimum wage. Salaries are generally lower in Denmark than in Britain for most professions. People at the bottom of the scale do rather better. The lowest wage paid in Denmark is about £7 per hour. The high taxes finance a comprehensive welfare state and superb infrastructure and most Danes are able to enjoy an enviable lifestyle. Industrial relations are good and companies adopt a humanitarian attitude towards their employees as does the Danish state generally. However, firms do not hesitate to divest themselves of excess labour when required. Perhaps the knowlege that the welfare state and state retraining programmes are there to take care of the needs and prospects of the unemployed makes it easier for them. Working surroundings are generally well designed. While the Danes are punctual and polite, they are also very outspoken, and are not afraid to criticise their superiors, which may come as a surprise to some Anglo-Saxons.

COMPARABILITY OF QUALIFICATIONS

Since Denmark became part of the Common Market in 1973, there has been nothing to prevent any EU national with the right skills and talent from seeking work in Denmark. If you need to have your qualifications assessed to see how they compare with those in Denmark, the body responsible for issuing opinions on the comparability of qualifications is the Danish branch of NARIC. In the first instance you should approach your job centre in the UK, or in Denmark if you are already living there, who will then ask NARIC for their statement on your qualification. There are two EU directives on mutual recognition of education and training; the first (89/48/EEC), covers qualifications gained through a course of study in higher education, the second (92/51/EEC), concerns post-secondary courses of over a year, and workplace training. You can also approach NARIC directly, but there will be a charge for the service. The Danish ENIC will also give opinions on the comparability of qualifications gained in the United States, Canada, Australia, New Zealand and South Africa.

If you have experience but no training, it is still possible to obtain a Certificate of Experience from the Department of Trade and Industry; the charge in 2001 was £80. You should first make sure that your type of work experience is covered by an EC directive by asking the authorities in Denmark or the DTI, who will try to send you a copy of the relevant directive, together with an application form and any available literature. There is an enquiry line on 020-7215 4004 (fax 020-7215 4489) or you can write to: Certificates of Experience Unit, Department of Trade & Industry, Kingsgate House, 66-74 Victoria Street, London SW1E 6SW.

If your qualifications are vocational or in hotel and catering, the motor trade, travel and tourism or office work and you want to know how your qualifications stand up against the Danish equivalent, you can consult the Comparability Co-ordinator through your local job centre or direct: The Comparability Co-ordinator, Employment Dept. Qualifications and Standards Branch (QS1), Room E454, Moorfoot, Sheffield SP1 4PQ; ☎0114-259 4144.

Useful Addresses

UK NARIC, ECCTIS 2000 Ltd, Oriel House, Oriel Road, Cheltenham, Glos GL50 1XP; www.naric.org.uk.

CVUU Danish Centre for Assessment of Foreign Credentials, ENIC/NARIC, Danasvej 30, 1780 Copenhagen V; ☎33 26 84 90; fax 33 26 84 91; e-mail cvuu@su.dk; www.cvuu.dk.

SOURCES OF JOBS

NEWSPAPERS AND THE INTERNET

UK Newspapers and Directories. The combined effect of the single European market and the implementation of the European Commission's Professional Qualifications Directives (see above) has not led to a spate of trans-continental job recruitment but there is a steady crop of advertisements from other EU countries appearing in the appointments pages of newspapers such as *The Times, The Financial Times, The Guardian, The Sunday Times, International Herald Tribune,* and so on. A specialist fortnightly newspaper, *Overseas Jobs Express* available only on subscription (Overseas Jobs Express, 20 New Road, Brighton, East Sussex BN1 1UF; ☎01273-699611; www.overseasjobsexpress.com) carries occasional adverts for jobs in Denmark. OJE also carries articles on working abroad by a range of working travellers and a substantial jobs section.

The Wednesday and Sunday issues of *Berlingske Tidende* (www.berlingske.dk) have the biggest number of appointments and jobs while *Politiken* is also worth consulting (though of course they are in Danish). If you wish to place an advert for a job wanted in either paper you can do so from the UK: Crane Media Partners (20-28 Dalling Rd, London W6 0JB; ☎020-8237 8601) are agents for *Berlingske Tidende* and Powers Turner Group (100 Rochester Row, London SW1P 1JP; ☎020-7630 9966; www.publicitas.com) deal with *Politiken.* You can also contact the papers directly via their websites: www.berlingske.dk and www.politiken.dk.

The main newspaper for Jutland is *Morgenavisen Jyllands-Posten* (www.jp.dk) also represented by Powers Turner Group in the UK. In Copenhagen there are plenty of job adverts in the twice-weekly *Den Blå Avis* (www.dba.dk) and the Sunday paper Søndagsavisen (www.son.dk). You can place free adverts in these papers. Alternatively a range of casual jobs in Denmark is included in the annual directory *Summer Jobs Abroad* available from Vacation Work (see inside back cover).

The Internet

As everywhere in Scandinavia, the Internet has become an important part of the recruitment process. The first site to try is the Eures site: www.eures.dk, where one can access many agricultural jobs. The British Embassy site also has advice for jobseekers: www.britishembassy.dk, but the embassy itself does not help people to find jobs. The Copenhagen Jobcentre has a site: www.koebenhavn.af.dk; also www.jobcentret.dk. Other AF sites can be found just by substituting the name of the town for Koebenhavn, or try searching on Arbejdsformidling. Many sites have a *job* link. The following is only a small selection of other websites: www.jubii.dk; www.bf.dk/jobs; www.jobindex.dk; www.jobbanken.dk, www.monster.dk.

Professional and Trade Publications

Every trade and profession has its own journal or magazine in Denmark as well as the UK. An exhaustive list of trade magazines can be found in media directories, for example *Benn's Press Directory, Ulrich's Periodicals Directory* and *Writers' and Artists' Yearbook,* which are available in major UK reference libraries.

Danish Publications. Jobs on farms might be obtained by advertising in the farming magazine *Landsbladet* (Vester Farimagsgade 6, 1606 Copenhagen K; ☎33 38 22 22; fax 33 32 30 46; www.landsbladet.dk). A leading publishing house *Teknisk Forlag* (Naverland 35, 2600 Glostrup; e-mail info@techmedia.dk; www.tekniskforlag.com), produces many journals for technical industries including engineering electronics, chemistry and plastics.

PROFESSIONAL ASSOCIATIONS

UK professional associations are a useful contact point for their members with regard to practising elsewhere in the European Union. During the negotiations involved in finalising the directives concerning the mutual recognition of qualifications throughout the EU, many professional associations negotiated with their counterparts in other member states and can therefore be helpful in providing contacts. Details of all professional associations may be found in the directory *Trade Associations and Professional Bodies of the UK* available at most UK reference libraries. It is also worth trying to contact the Danish equivalent of UK professional associations: the UK body should be able to provide the address.

You could also try consulting your trade union for information; as they may have some links with a counterpart organisation in Denmark. The website of the Danish Federation of Trade Unions can give you further leads: www.lo.dk.

UK EMPLOYMENT SERVICE

The employment services of the 15 EU countries, including those of the UK and Denmark are linked together by a computer network known as EURES (European Employment Services), by which information on specialist vacancies notified to the employment service in one country can be made available to the employment services in the others. At any one time there are over 5,000 vacancies on the system, including jobs for graduates and professionals. In addition the EU has trained 500 Euro-advisers, including six at British universities.

The British branch of EURES is based at the Overseas Placing Unit (OPU) of the Employment Service in Sheffield (Rockingham House, 123 West Street, Sheffield S1 4ER; ☎0114-259 6051/2). Most UK Employment Service offices have computer access to the vacancies held at Sheffield. The kinds of vacancies range from agricultural workers, computer programmers, medical personnel, teachers and bilingual secretaries to florists, upholsterers, chefs and entertainers. Most employers are looking to fill posts as quickly as possible; Danish farmers particularly favour the use of the EURES system. You can see the vacancies on-line at: http://europa.eu.int/comm/employment or www.eures.dk.

The Employment Service produces the booklet, *Working in Denmark,* available from their offices nationwide or from the OPU (see above).

UK RECRUITMENT AGENCIES

There are some agencies in the UK which specialise in finding overseas jobs for clients. In general, these agencies deal with a specific sector such as electronics, computers, secretarial, medical, English teaching, etc. and can only place people with suitable qualifications. As a rule, agencies are retained and paid by employers to fill specific vacancies and do not search on behalf of prospective workers, but there are also firms which maintain databases of jobs and will try to match you with the ones you are qualified for.

The Recruitment and Employment Confederation (36-38 Mortimer Street, London W1N 7RB; ☎020-7462 3260; www.rec.uk.com) issues a list of employment agencies who are members. Human Resourcing Consultancies (Chancery House, 53-64 Chancery Lane, London WC2 A1QS; ☎020-7406 5154; www.careermanagement.co.uk) publishes a useful guide entitled *The Job Search: A Practical Guide* in two versions, for *Executive and Professional Staff,* and for *Supervisory and Support Staff,* which deal with everything from researching the job market, CV's and letters of application, to the all-important interview technique, as well as providing notes on self-employment and personal finance.

Useful Addresses

Bilingua Group, Suite 1, 49 Maddox St, London W1R 9LA; ☎020-7493 6446; fax 020-7493 0168; www.bilinguagroup.com. International language recruitment specialists; contract, permanent and temporary personnel

CLC Language Services, 73 New Bond

Street, London W1; ☎020-7499
3365. Offers opportunities for Europeans and North Americans (where
valid work permits apply) to work in
EU countries at all levels from junior
secretary to senior sales executive.
Sectors include: sales, marketing and
market research, banking, import-
export, translating, interpreting,
management consultancy, pharmaceutical, media sales and general
commerce for secretaries.
Drake International, 20 Regent St,
London SW1Y 4PH; ☎020-7484

0800; fax 020-7484 0808; e-mail
overseasrecruitment@drake.intl.c
om. Specialise in hospitality staff
amongst others.
Merrow Language Recruitment, 3rd floor,
23 Bentinck St, London W1U 2EZ;
☎020-7935 5050; fax 020-7935
5454; www.merrow.co.uk.
Miller Brand Recruitment, 16 Wigmore
St, London W1H 9DE; ☎020-
7290 0985; fax 020-7290 0981;
www.eurorecruit.com/miller. Middle
and senior management.

EXECUTIVE/SPECIALIST RECRUITMENT AGENCIES

The following recruitment/search
agencies specialise in technical,
professional and other senior executive
appointments in Denmark:
Beechwood Recruitment Ltd. 219 High
Street, London W3 9BY; ☎020-
8992 8647; fax 020-8992 5658. Keeps
a technical appointments register for
qualified engineers with experience.
Capacital Search & Selection, Østergade 24 A, 1100 Copenhagen,
☎33 33 07 70; fax 33 33 08 80;
e-mail   dialog@capacital.dk;
www.capacital.dk.
Egon Zehnder International Ltd, Devonshire House, Mayfair Place, London
W1X 5FH; ☎020-7493 3882; fax
0171-629 9552; www.ezi.net. Associate Office in Copenhagen: Egon
Zehnder International SA, ADR-
Hemmelig, 9999 Hemmelig; ☎33
11 13 53.
Harton Rosenkilde Executive Search,
Esplanade 34G, 1263 Copenhagen
K; ☎33 15 45 15; fax 33 15 30 40;
www.harton-rosenkilde.dk.
Horton International, Store Kongensgade
92, 1264 Copenhagen K; ☎33 12

01 33; e-mail copenhagen@horton-
intl.com; www.horton-intl.com.
Laigaard and Partners A/S, Store Kongensgade 40H, 1264 Copenhagen K;
☎33 91 18 00; fax 33 91 18 03.
Marlar Bennetts International, 4 Glen-
cairn, 70 Ridgway, Wimbledon,
London SW19; ☎020-8947 1056.
Associate office in Copenhagen:
Rix Management, 4 Springforbivej,
2930 Klampenborg; ☎39 96 06 60;
www.rixman.dk.
Odgers Ray & Berndtson, 11 Hanover
Square, London W1R 9HD; ☎020-
7529 1111; fax 020-7529 1000; e-mail
info@ray-berndtson.co.uk. Associate
office in Copenhagen: Ray & Berndtson International, Nyhavn 63C, 1051
Copenhagen K; ☎33 14 36 36; fax 33
32 43 32; www.rayberndtson.com.
P-E International plc, Boundary Way,
Hemel Hempstead, Herts HP2 7SR;
☎01442 202 490; fax 01442-219
886; www.p-einternational.com.
*PriceWaterhouseCoopers Search & Selec-
tion,* PB 2709, 2900 Hellerup;
www.pwcglobal.dk.

THE DANISH STATE EMPLOYMENT SERVICE

The Danish state employment service (*Arbejdsmarkedsstyrelsen*) has its headquarters at Blegdamsvej 56, 2100 Copenhagen (☎35 28 81 00; fax 35 36 24 11; e-mail ams@ams.dk; www.ams.dk) and runs a chain of local labour exchanges (*Arbejdsformidlingen*). The addresses of AFs can be found in the telephone directory. The main Jobcentre in Copenhagen is at: Kultorvet 17, Box 2235, 1019 Copenhagen K (☎33 55 17 14 *or* 33 55 10 20; www.koebenhavn.af.dk, www.jobcentret.dk). There is a special branch which deals just with students who visit in person, the *Studenterformidlingen*, Tøndergade 16, Vesterbro. The casual work centre is next door at no.14.

It is advisable not to rely entirely on the effectiveness of the AFs, as with the fairly high unemployment in Denmark they may not have that many jobs on their books. The first place to go if you are looking for a job on spec would be *Use It*, Rådhusstræde 13, Copenhagen, which has a good stock of newspapers and magazines; you will also meet other foreigners in your situation. The libraries have all the necessary publications, and, if you are lucky, you may be able to use their internet terminals.

PRIVATE AGENCIES

There are a number of chains of general employment agencies that may have jobs in offices, factories, hotels and so on to offer to personal callers. In Copenhagen, two of the largest are *Adecco* (Trommesalen 5; ☎33 26 03 70) and *Vikar Denmark* (Norre Voldgade 9; ☎33 13 05 11). The grandiose-sounding *Royal Service Agency* (28B Nørregade; ☎33 13 30 99) is a good source of casual jobs, supplying much of Copenhagen's hotel industry. Other agencies can be found under *vikarbureauer* in the telephone directory, or look on the website: www.jubii.dk under *rekrutteringsfirmaer*.

CHAMBERS OF COMMERCE

Chambers of Commerce exist to serve the interests of businesses trading in both Denmark and the UK; they do not operate as employment agencies. They may be able to offer background information which can be helpful in the job-hunting process. Denmark has 30 chambers of commerce, as well as about 200 local units. Local chambers of commerce can be a useful source of information on a word-of-mouth basis, though it should be stressed that they are only able to help on a goodwill basis, as helping job-seekers is not part of their remit.

Chambers of commerce can provide names and addresses of member companies; these may be listed on their websites. The member companies are medium-sized or large organisations which may well have current or prospective vacancies. The chamber of commerce in Copenhagen can supply the addresses of others throughout Denmark.

Useful Addresses

The addresses of the main chambers of commerce are:
Copenhagen – *Det Danske Handelskammer Børsen,* Børsgade 8B, 1215 Copenhagen; ☎33 95 05 00; fax 33 32 52 16.
Jutland – *Den Jydske Handelsstands Centralforening,* Ny Banegårdsgade 45, 8000 Århus C; ☎86 13 53 55.
Fyn – *Odense Handelsstandsforening,* Albani torv 4, postboks 308, 5100 Odense C; ☎66 14 47 14; www.ihk-odense-fyn.dk.

MULTINATIONALS

Danish Companies Operating in the UK. A number of Danish companies have entered the UK market in fields as diverse as brewing and banking. However check first that the company you target is a Danish one as many importers of Danish products are British companies.

British Companies Operating in Denmark. It is possible to enter a British company in the hope of a transfer to Denmark. If you have connections with Denmark then there is some likelihood this approach could work. Although UK companies have been slower to enter the Danish market than other more obvious ones, there are many more large British companies now actively involved in Denmark. The British Embassy in Copenhagen (36-40 Kastelsvej, 2100 Copenhagen Ø; ☎35 26 63 75; fax 35 43 14 00) can supply a list of the major companies operating there.

International Companies. There are an increasing number of multinational companies whose branches and subsidiaries are found all round the world and these can offer possible employment prospects. Many addresses of such companies can be obtained through the respective chambers of commerce as discussed earlier. The company name may be different in each country for instance the Danish-based MD Foods International has invested in dairies in the UK, so often a certain amount of detective work is necessary to discover the extent of a particular company's operation in the UK and Denmark and the consequent potential for later being posted elsewhere.

Useful Publications

Kompass Denmark, lists a lot of (but not all) Danish companies, with precise details of subsidiaries, turnover etc. This can be more conveniently consulted on a CD-Rom at Tradepartners UK, and other business information centres (see *Starting a Business* section). *Major Companies of Scandinavia* (publ. Graham & Whiteside), lists the main companies in alphabetical order. *Europe's 15,000 Largest Companies* lists firms in order of size. Dun & Bradstreet's *Who Owns Whom,* gives British and American companies with Danish subsidiaries.

METHODS OF APPLICATION

ON SPEC APPLICATIONS

With the spread of the internet, it is now feasible to send speculative applications to companies by e-mail. The Danes are generally quite meticulous about replying to enquiries, although you should try to direct your e-mail to the human resources department if at all possible.

Danes pride themselves on their knowledge of English. If for some reason you feel that it is necessary, then you can have your letter or CV professionally translated into Danish by an agency such as the Institute of Translation and Interpreting (Exchange House, 494 Midsummer Boulevard, Central Milton Keynes MK9 2EA; ☎01908-255905; e-mail info@iti.org.uk), who will charge from £60 for 1,000 words. It would be advisable to try to make some Danish friends and thus have it done for nothing. If you are interested in networking with Danes or people interested in Denmark, you can try logging on to the Nordic Forum – www.nordicfolks.com, which is particularly active in North America. There are also Danish clubs in the UK (see above). The site www.danelink.com is aimed at Danes living in the UK, but carries useful information for non-Danes.

PERSONAL VISITS

Anyone who is in Denmark looking for a job may want to make enquiries in person as to the availability of employment. This involves not only responding to jobs advertised, but also canvassing potential employers on the spot. Before making an approach to a potential employer decide how you can best sell your skills, talents or experience. For example those looking for casual work in the tourist industry will find the fact that they speak English may not impress the Danes that much. You will instead have to emphasise your experience and enthusiasm for the job.

If you are travelling it is useful to have a web e-mail address such as Hotmail or Yahoo so that the employer can get in touch with you easily, rather than giving a phone number in a hostel.

If you are invited for an interview, you may be pleasantly surprised to find that the average Danish employer takes a lot longer to come to a decision than one in the UK. Danes like to take a long time before taking decisions. Thus an employer will talk to you for an average of 45 minutes as opposed to 25 minutes in the UK. The Dane will have made up their mind after 25 minutes; in the UK they would have decided after 10 minutes.

FORM, CONTENT & STYLE OF WRITTEN APPLICATIONS

In the vast majority of cases, no matter how one finds out about a job, it will be necessary to write a letter of application. This applies at all levels, except for unskilled work or casual employment. Unless an advertisement clearly states that a personal or telephone application is required, a letter is the best choice. The letter may have to be written in Danish and it is quite in order to have a professional translation made. On the other hand it is not advisable to suggest that one's command of the language is substantially better than it is.

In many ways the process of doing business in Denmark is relaxed and informal. This does not however apply to job applications, and impressions gained from correspondence are very important. In particular, the letter should be hand written, and tailored to the company/type of job for which you are applying, and appear individually prepared. The letter should be formal and respectful in style, clearly stating your reasons for application and the relevance of your qualifications and experience to the employment available. Abbreviations should be avoided, as should jokes which may not be understood. For further guidance on writing business letters, consult *How to Address Overseas Business Letters* by Derek Allen (publ. Foulsham).

CURRICULUM VITAE

At the core of any application is the curriculum vitae (CV). The CV should be no more than one page if possible. Ideally the CV should be tailored to the job advertisement so that it precisely matches the requirements of the post. The more work you do on your CV the better. For this reason, many people entrust the preparation and presentation of their CV to a company that specialises in this kind of service. They can usually be found by looking in the Yellow Pages under Employment Agencies. The cost is usually about £30 for a one-page graduate CV. Alternatively, refer to the publication such as *How to Prepare your Curriculum Vitae* by A.L. Jackson.

Note that for a potential Danish employer the CV should be modified to remove any abbreviations and explain any qualifications, and so on, which could be unfamiliar to a foreign reader. A CV should be on A4 paper; it is acceptable to send it by e-mail (unlike the letter of application which should appear personalised). It is always best to provide a succinct CV that you may consider too short than one which the employer will think overlong. You can then add in your letter of application that if any further information is required you will be happy to supply it. The style of CV should be conservative, i.e. giving education and work experience in chronological order, starting with the most recent first. Trying for the hard sell is not likely to make a good impression; you will have to back up what you say in your CV at interview.

ASPECTS OF EMPLOYMENT

SALARIES

Danish salaries are generally lower than those in the US, UK, France and Germany, although somewhat higher than those in Sweden and Finland. There is also the burden of high personal taxes and the cost of living. Some highly-paid foreigners can benefit from the 25% Taxation Scheme, but you need to earn a salary of over kr52,000 (£4,200/US$6000)per month after pension and labour market contributions to benefit from this scheme (see *Daily Life* 'Taxation').

There is no statutory minimum wage in Denmark, instead the trades unions and employers' organisations agree on a minimum wage as part of the Common Consent (see below). This agreement sets the standard for the basic wage on the general labour market. For instance in 2001, the unions representing cleaners agreed a minimum rate with employers of kr99.56, or over £8 an hour. However, taking into consideration vacation, sickness and overtime allowances, it is estimated that the average minimum value in real terms is about twice as much. Table 2 lists average monthly salaries in 2002.

TABLE 2 AVERAGE MONTHLY SALARIES		
Managing director	kr93,600	£7,500/US$10,950
Sales director	k66,000	£5,350/US$7,700
Sales manager	kr43,200	£3,500/US$5,050
Technical engineer	kr33,600	£2,700/US$3,900
Systems analyst	kr43,8000	£3,500/US5,100
Senior programmer	kr33,600	£2,700/US$3,900
Customer services assistant	kr18,720	£1,500/US$2,200
Accounts clerk	kr20,400	£1,650/US$2,400

EMPLOYER AND EMPLOYEE ORGANISATIONS

There are two central organisations, the Danish Employers' Confederation (www.da.dk), and The Danish Confederation of Trade Unions (www.lo.dk) which govern industrial relations. There are other, smaller, employer and employee organisations, but the DA and LO are by far the largest.

Employer Organisations

The entire labour force of Denmark constitutes about 2.8 million. Approximately 45 employers' organisations, representing 29,300 employers, who between them employ about half a million people, belong to the DA.
Employee Organisations. There are about 90 Danish trade unions with 2.2

million members (roughly 80% of the workforce). This trade union membership level is one of the highest in Europe and gives the Danish trades unions a more significant role than in neighbouring countries. In some companies, you are obliged to join the trade union before you can start work. Members of trade unions have to pay into an unemployment fund, the *arbejdsløskasser.*

Instead of minimum wage legislation, there is a binding agreement known as the Common Consent between employers' organisations and unions. This sets the working hours and wages and is usually drawn up every two years. Normally a new agreement is concluded before the old one expires. If it is impossible to reach an agreement then the case will go to the Industrial Court or to an arbitrator agreed on by the two parties.

WORKING HOURS, OVERTIME AND HOLIDAYS

Scandinavians traditionally have the shortest working week and the worst absenteeism in Europe. In Denmark, the normal working hours are 37 per week. Employees are usually paid overtime but may also be given time off in lieu. The conditions vary depending on the company and are covered by the Common Consent agreement. Working conditions may also be negotiated between an individual and employer, as in the case of small companies. Executive positions are not covered by the overtime agreements.

Employees are entitled to five weeks paid holiday a year. Unlike wages, holiday pay is fixed by law. The employer pays a supplement of 12.5% of each employee's salary into a central vacation trust (*FerieGiro*). In April, the employee receives a money order from the *FerieGiro*, which can be cashed by the employee at any post office when it is accompanied by an endorsement from the employer saying when the holiday is to be taken.

Even if you have only worked for a few weeks you are still entitled to holiday pay in proportion to the period worked. In keeping with Denmark's reputation as the world's least corrupt country, foreigners who have worked in Denmark and then left will receive their holiday pay at the end of the tax year.

For longer-term employees the holiday period can be divided up over the course of the year but every employee has a right to 18 consecutive days of holiday during the main holiday period of 2 May to 30 September.

Any problems with holiday pay can be addressed to to *FerieGiro*: ATP-Huset, Kongens Vænge 8, 3400 Hillerød; ☎48 24 11 00; www.atp.dk.

WOMEN IN WORK

There are currently 82 women to every 100 men in the national workforce. This is not that high by Scandinavian standards, and may be partly explained by the fact that more and more women are choosing to take courses in higher education. Women have equal status with men in the work place and claim equal pay on principle. One of the factors in Scandinavia generally which has contributed to having such a large number of women in the workplace, is the availability of child care services outside the home. By 2002, 90% of pre-school (3-6 years) children were using kindergarten facilities.

Maternity Benefits and Parental Leave

All women are entitled to four weeks leave before a birth and up to 24 weeks post-natal leave. From the 14th week after the birth the mother can opt to transfer all or part of the remaining leave to the father. Otherwise all fathers are entitled to two weeks paternity leave starting from the day of confinement, and another two weeks at the end of the mother's leave.

While she is on maternity leave, a mother has a right to 50% of her salary during the first 14 weeks. Most employers will pay the full salary for the 14 weeks, and some even for the whole period of leave. The employer is reimbursed by the state from the third week, at the 50% rate. After 14 weeks the state pays social welfare of about kr3,200 (approx. £260/$375) per week.

SOCIAL SECURITY AND UNEMPLOYMENT BENEFIT

CLAIMING UK UNEMPLOYMENT BENEFIT IN DENMARK

If you are thinking of going to Denmark to look for work, it is worth knowing that you can continue to receive UK unemployment benefit at UK rates for three months in Denmark. This is only applicable if you have already been unemployed for a month in the UK. It is essential to apply as soon as you can, as entitlement to transfer benefit expires after three months. You will need to have paid full Class 1 contributions during the two tax years previous to the one you are claiming in. You should contact your usual benefit office who will in turn contact the International Services branch of the Inland Revenue (see above for address). They will issue a form E303, the document which is needed to claim benefit in another EU country. In order to receive the medical care you are entitled to under Danish regulations for unemployed people you should also ask for the form E119 at the same time. For general information about benefits and social security in EU countries, ask for forms SA29, either from your Jobcentre or from the Pensions and Overseas Benefits Directorate, Department for Work and Pensions, Tyneview Park, Whitley Rd, Benton, Newcastle-upon-Tyne NE98 1BA; www.dwp.gov.uk.

SOCIAL SECURITY IN DENMARK

Denmark has a highly developed system of social security which has come under criticism from opponents of its policy of paying young people more money than they would receive if they were a trainee with an employer. About 20% of people of working age (i.e. 16-66 years old) are living on social security. About 130,000 received unemployment benefit in 2002 and a further 85,000 were on 'reactivation' schemes, namely workfare. The total number receiving some kind of social security benefit or pension comes to 2.2 million. Social security is enormously expensive for Denmark and is funded by high personal taxation (see Chapter Four, *Daily Life, Taxation*). Until the 1960s unemployment benefits totalled a mere 40% of earnings. They now go up to a maximum of 90% of the earnings of a skilled worker (about kr143,000 – approx. £11,500/US$16,750 per annum) which is available more or less indefinitely.

Unemployment insurance (*A-kasserne*) in Denmark is administered by the trade unions. You have to have paid into a trade union fund for at least one year and have worked at least six months during that year, before you can claim social security. In order to be able to pay into a fund, you have to prove you have worked at least five weeks full-time (or are about to). If you only work part-time then you pay less into the fund and claim correspondingly less unemployment benefit should you need to. If you do not pay into a trade union fund, then you pay into a fund of your choice depending on your particular profession; all the funds are listed on the employment ministry's website: www.arbejdsministeriet.dk.

DANISH PENSIONS

The Danish pension system is more generous than that of the UK. The basic pension amounts to kr6,250 (approx. £500/US$730) per month for a single person, without taking into account private pension schemes.

The normal age for a retirement pension is 67 but you can be entitled to an early pension under certain specified circumstances. The minimum period of residence before a pension can be claimed at all is three years. In order to receive a full old-age pension 40 years of residence is required between the ages of 15 and 67. If the period of residence is shorter, the pension is calculated in fortieths of a full pension, proportional to the number of years of actual residency. Applicants for an early pension must have lived in Denmark for at least four-fifths of the period between the age of 15 and the age at which the pension is awarded. Where the period of residence is shorter, the amount of the pension is calculated in proportion to the actual number of years of residence.

Recently introduced is a new pension scheme whereby people from the age of 60 can reduce their working hours and receive compensation from the state. Or they can take early retirement at that age, as long as they have paid into an approved pension fund for 20 out of the previous 25 years.

Those between 50 and 67 in permanent need of care are in addition entitled to early retirement pensions when health and/or special circumstances justify it. Depending on the degree of disability, they qualify for normal, medium or maximum early retirement pensions (altogether 265,000 people in 2000).

Foreigners can claim a Danish pension provided they have lived in Denmark for at least ten years between the ages of 15 and 67 with five of these years immediately prior to the application for a pension. Special allowance is made for refugees accepted by Denmark who may now claim the years of residence in their own country as residence in Denmark for the purpose of calculating their pension.

UNEMPLOYMENT BENEFITS & SICKNESS PAY

Just under three-quarters of the national labour force (over 2 million employees) pay into an unemployment fund. Should they become unemployed, the fund will pay out a proportion of unemployment benefits. The main cost of unemployment benefit is however borne by the government. Membership fees of an unemployment fund vary among the different trades and the average is about kr6,000 (approx. £480/US$700) per annum.

Unemployed people who are members of an unemployment fund receive benefits which amount to about kr2,900 weekly up to a maximum of 90% of their former salary. If the individual is not a member of an unemployment fund then social welfare provides all benefits due.

Unemployment benefit is only paid out if you have worked for 52 weeks in the previous three years. It will not be paid if you left your job voluntarily, or were dismissed for misconduct, or if you refuse an offer of alternative employment.

Sickness Pay

An employee is entitled to sick pay if they have been working for a minimum of 13 weeks, and if they have worked for at least 120 hours in the 13 weeks before becoming ill. Often under employer/employee agreements employees are entitled to receive full pay during the first 120 days of illness. If you are paid by the hour however, you can claim only a maximum of 90% of your salary up to a ceiling of about kr2,900 (approx £235/US$340) per week.

If you are ill for more than three days and up to five days, your employer can ask you to sign a declaration stating that you are ill. For illness that lasts longer than five days your employer has the right to a medical certificate (for which the employer pays) from a doctor stating the nature and expected duration of your malady.

PERMANENT WORK

COMPUTERS/INFORMATION TECHNOLOGY

Those who work in computing and can speak another European language are almost always able to find jobs in the European Union. British computer science graduates are highly thought of and many get jobs by approaching recruitment agencies that specialise in computer personnel.

Useful Addresses & Publications

Computer Contractor/Computing, two magazines published by VNU Business Publications. Both carry masses of advertising by computer contractors wanting to hire personnel for Britain and abroad.

Dux International, 15 Princeton Mews, 167-9 London Rd, Kingston-on-Thames, Surrey KT2 6PT; ☎020-8547 0100; fax 020-8547 0400; www.duxrecruitment.com. Specialises in computer vacancies in Europe.

Elan IT Resource, Bregnerødvej 132B, 3460 Birkerød; ☎45 90 28 00; fax 45 90 28 01; www.elanit.dk.

OCC Computer Personnel, 108 Welsh Row, Nantwich, Cheshire CW5 5EY; ☎01270-627206; www.occ-computing.co.uk.

Track International, PO Box 1, Perranporth TR6 0YG; e-mail track@trackint.com. IT professionals in Europe.

Capacital Search and Selection, Østergade 24A, 1100 Copenhagen K, ☎33 33 07 70; fax 33 33 08 80; e-mail: dialog@capacital.dk; www.capacital.dk.

TEACHERS

There are a number of international schools in Denmark who recruit teachers from abroad. A list is given in the Daily Life chapter, under 'International Education'. Agencies which can give you information about working in Danish schools are:

Council of British Independent Schools in the European Community (COBISEC): Lucy's, Lucy's Hill, Hythe, Kent CT21 5ES; tel/fax 01303 260857; e-mail cobisec@cs.com; www.cobisec.org.

European Council of International Schools: 21 Lavant Street, Petersfield, Hants GU32 3EL; ☎01730-268244; fax 01730-267914; e-mail ecis@ecis.org; www.ecis.org.

ECIS North America: 105 Tuxford Terrace, Basking Ridge, New Jersey 07920, USA; ☎908-903-0552; fax 908-580-9381; e-mail malyecisna@aol.com; www.ecis.org.

World-wide Education Service Ltd, Canada House, 272 Field End Road, Eastcote, Middlesex HA4 9NA; ☎020-8582 0317; fax 020-8429 4838;e-mailwes@wesworldwide.com; www.wesworldwide.com.

MEDICAL STAFF

Qualified medical staff who are interested in working in Danish hospitals can try consulting the weekly journal of the Danish Medical Association which can be obtained directly from the DMA (Trondhjemsgade 9, 2100 Copenhagen O) in which hospital staff vacancies are advertised. A complete list of hospitals and other medical institutions can be obtained from the same source for kr300, as well as a useful booklet Information for Doctors Migrating to Denmark.

In order to obtain authorisation to practise as a doctor in Denmark, the National Board of Health (Holbergsgade 6, 1057 Copenhagen K; ☎33 92 33 60; fax 33 93 15 63; e-mail sum@sum.dk; www.sum.dk) has to be contacted after an offer of a job is received, but before it is taken up. Generally, the DMA emphasise the difficulty of finding a post in Denmark as there is likely to be a surplus of doctors for some years to come. The DMA may be able to advise which specialties are in demand.

The regulations governing applications from foreign doctors to work in Denmark are given in the leaflet *Guidelines for the Registration of Doctors of Medicine with a Degree from Abroad*, available from the Danish National Board of Health (*Sundhedsstyrelsen*) at the above address.

TEACHING ENGLISH

As already mentioned, there is less demand for English teachers in Scandinavia than elsewhere in Europe because of native proficiency. Contracts are therefore more often than not part-time and tend to be focused on English for Business. Danish language schools are also very much geared to preparing candidates for the Cambridge English Examinations. The FOF organisation, which has 10 branches, is the best source of work. An advantage of working in Denmark is that wages are controlled by law. For teaching the starting rate is about kr150 per lesson (approx. £12/US$18); once you are established you can earn up to kr275 a lesson.

Useful Addresses

Cambridge Institute Foundation, Vimmelskaftet 48, 1161 Copenhagen K; ☎33 13 33 02. Contracts generally last from October to May and are renewable.

FOF (Folkeligt Oplysnings Forbund), Frederiksborggade 20, 1., 1360 Copenhagen K; ☎33 11 19 80; fax 33 32 70 47.

FOF, Lyngby-Taarbæk, Hovedgade 15D, 2800 Lyngby; ☎45 96 01 00; fax 45 87 28 46.

Frit Oplysningsforbund, Frederiksborggade 21, 1360 Copenhagen K; ☎33 93 00 96; fax 33 33 00 96.

THE EUROPEAN ENVIRONMENT AGENCY

In February 1994 the European Commission announced that a number of new European Institutions would be located in various major European cities with briefs as diverse as harmonising trade marks, design and models in the internal European market, and a monitoring centre for drugs and drug addiction. The institution allocated to Copenhagen was the European Environment Agency (not to be confused with the European Economic Area whose acronym it shares). The EEA moved to Copenhagen (6 Kongens Nytorv, 1050 Copenhagen; www.eea.eu.int), from Belgium in autumn 1994, and has a permanent staff of about 50, recruited through, amongst other publications, the *Official Journal of the European Communities,* which can be consulted at any of the regional offices of the European Commission. Competition for the main posts is extremely tough: hundreds of applications are received for every post. Clerical staff are recruited locally in Denmark, while scientific positions are advertised internationally as they fall vacant. The Agency is entirely independent of the European Commission and functions as an environmental liaison office for all the EU countries.

TEMPORARY WORK

This section deals with seasonal jobs, for instance in agriculture, childcare and tourism as well as a variety of possibilities through agencies. Temping is something which many people might have to do before they find a long-term post. Teaching English as a foreign language is dealt with above.

AGRICULTURE

Agriculture is an important part of the Danish economy. Denmark produces about three times the agricultural produce, and consumables from food technology subsidiaries, that it needs for home consumption. At least 70% of Danish agriculture produce is exported and about 60% of its food products. Its world share of the bacon market is 33%, 22% for fresh pork, and 14% for combined dairy products. The food industry provides 30% of Denmark's industrial turnover. More interestingly, it has a 32% share of the grass and clover seed market. Although the industry is dominated by farmer-owned co-operatives, often with a short-term profit motivation, there are still a reasonable number of fruit picking jobs, especially on the island of Funen. The most prevalent crops are tomatoes (grown all summer), strawberries (picked in June and July), cherries (picked in July and August) and apples (picked in September and October). It may be necessary to travel quite widely in Denmark to find work, as there is no concentration of fruit farms in one area; some of the larger farms are to be found around Århus and east and west of Odense. It is recommended to have a tent and a bicycle to get around. The work is paid at quite reasonable piece rates at about kr6 (approx. 50p/US$0.70)per kilo, but starting dates and working hours are unpredictable.

Surprisingly, it may also be possible to find a job on a farm by advertising in the farming magazine *Landsbladet* (Vester Farimagsgade 6, 1606 Copenhagen K). The best results have come from those who have mentioned previous farming experience (which might include working on a kibbutz/moshav) in their advert. It is also important to provide a contact telephone number. A typical monthly wage after tax and including bed and board might be £500.

Organic farms are another possibility and you could start by contacting the Danish version of WWOOF, the worldwide organic farm organisation which is VHH (c/o Inga Nielson, Åsenvej 35, 9881 Bindslev, Denmark; e-mail info@wwoof.dk; www.wwoof.dk). You will need to send £5/US$10/kr50/€10 for a list of about 25-30 organic farms in Denmark, which you then contact individually. Organic farms in Denmark are usually run by alternative communities, of which there are many, with the result that they may not be very compatible with the market economy. Though you may be fed and housed, learn valuable agricultural techniques and be otherwise well looked after, you should not expect any remuneration.

The Agricultural Council or *Landsbrugrådet* (3 Axeltorv, 1609 Copenhagen V; ☎33 14 56 72; fax 33 14 95 74), is the umbrella organisation for all major farmers' organisations in Denmark.

Useful Addresses

The International Farm Experience Programme. National Agricultural Centre, Stoneleigh Park, Warwickshire CV6 2LG; ☎01203-696578. Arranges placements on Danish farms for British subjects with at least two years practical experience of farming/horticulture.

Exchanges from the USA and Canada to Denmark can be arranged by:
The International Agricultural Exchange Association (Servicing Office) 1000 1st Avenue South, Great Falls, Montana 59401 United States of America.
IAEA Servicing Office, No. 206, 1505-17 Ave. S.W. Calgary, Alberta T2T OE2 Canada.

For fruit-picking the simplest approach is to contact the Jobcentret which specialises in placing foreigners in this kind of work: Vestsjælland Employment Office. They will approach farmers on your behalf. They claim to have up to 4,000 jobs available at the height of the season. Also look at www.eures.dk/seasonalwork.htm. Some fruit farms

even have websites, which shows how keen they are to find workers at the moment:
Alstrup Frugtplantage, Alstrupvej 1, Alstrup 8305 Samso; ☎86 59 31 38; fax 86 59 31 38; e-mail elicc@samso.com; www.alstrupfrugt.subnet.dk. Strawberry picking can be between May and July but usually from beginning of June. Free campsite but no accommodation provided.
Birkholm Frugt & Bær, V/Bjarne Knutsen, Hornelandevej 2 D, 5600 Faaborg; ☎62 60 22 62; e-mail birkholm@strawberrypicking.dk; www.strawberrypicking.dk. Strawberry picking. Campsite and washing and cooking facilities provided.
Earth Work Ltd, 8 Beauchamp Meadow, Redruth, Cornwall TR15 2DG; ☎01209 219934. Agency looking for workers on an island in Denmark.
Vestsjælland Employment Office, Smedelundsgade 16, 4300 Holbæk; ☎59 48 12 00; fax 40 31 74 32; e-mail euresjue@postb.tele.dk; www.eures.dk.

AU PAIR AND NANNYING

Going as an au pair to Scandinavia, might seem like taking the proverbial coals to Newcastle, since au pairs from Scandinavia have become something of a cliché. Despite its potential drawbacks (awful parents, abominable children and sexploitation) being an au pair/nanny/mother's help in Denmark, is well regulated. It is also probably the best way to learn the language inexpensively, though not necessarily by chatting with the family who will probably speak English, but by attending subsidised or free classes locally.

There has been a big increase in the numbers of au pairs going to Denmark from North America, hence the Immigration Service has added a section for au pairs to its website: 'Guide concerning the Au-Pair System'; see www.udlst.dk. Non-EU au pairs do not require a work permit, but they must show that they are suitably qualified to benefit from a stay in Denmark. For further details see: Susan Griffith, *Au Pair and Nanny's Guide to Working Abroad* (Vacation Work; www.vacationwork.co.uk).

UK au pair agencies may in the future not be able to arrange placements abroad, hence it is advisable to contact an au pair organisations in Denmark. These agencies are involved both in sending young Danes abroad as au pairs, and with incoming au pairs. Pocket money starts at about kr3,500 (approx. £280/US$400) per month.

Useful Addresses

Au Pair International, Sixtusvej 15, st. tv., 2300 Copenhagen S; ☎32 84 10 02; fax 32 84 31 02; e-mail: info@aupairsinternational.dk; www.aupairsinternational. dk.

Exis-Europair, Postboks 291, 6400 Sonderbeg; ☎74 42 97 49; fax 74 42 97 47.

Scandinavian Au-Pair Center, Saturnusgatan 240, 260 35 Ödåkra, Sweden; ☎+46 42 20 44 02; fax +46 42 32 82 39; mobile +46 706 94 37 24; e-mail: scandinavian@aupair.se; www.aupair.se.

TOURISM

Although Denmark's summers tend to be brief, much like Scottish ones, they can be very fine. In any case, the country has a lot to offer besides a healthy climate as the rapid expansion of the tourist industry shows.

Four per cent of the total number of jobs (roughly 120,000) in Denmark are in the tourist industry and the number is set to increase. Many of the new jobs are likely to be in new tourism organisations. The Danish government also plans to target marketing at southern and central Europe, so anyone with a proficiency in languages from these areas might be able to get a job in this sector.

Menial temporary jobs in hotels in main tourist cities are reasonably easy to find, though you will probably have to do a lot of leg work going round in person to ask for work in hotels and restaurants. It may pay off to start with the biggest establishments as vacancies obviously occur on a large scale. This has happened in the past at the Copenhagen Sheraton where you are likely to get the unskilled jobs like chamber staff and kitchen porter.

Another common source of jobs are the foreign fast-food restaurants such as Burger King and McDonalds, whose turnover of staff is almost as fast as their food. Their wages are comparatively low but still a useful standby.

For those who prefer not to be cooped up indoors, the British company Eurocamp runs a campsite in Denmark for which it needs campsite couriers, children' couriers and administrative couriers. Further details from Eurocamp: Overseas Recruitment Department (Ref. SJ/02), ☎01606-787522.

VOLUNTARY WORK

There is a variety of possibilities for volunteer work in Denmark. If you are applying from the UK, you can apply through various umbrella workcamp organisations such as the Christian Movement for Peace, Quaker Work Camps, or the United Nations Association.

If you are already in Denmark you can contact Mellemfolkeligt Samvirke, Borgergade 14, 1300 Copenhagen K; ☎77 31 00 00; fax 77 31 01 01; e-mail ms@ms-dan.dk; www.ms.dk. This is one of the few ways you can get a job in the Danish territories of Greenland and the Faroe Islands as well as in Denmark. MS organises from 20 to 30 workcamps which usually last two or three weeks. The camps mainly involve construction work, either renovatory or from scratch, of communal buildings or facilities, located in small communities, for whom such buildings are an important part of daily social interaction. Volunteers pay their own travel costs but everything else is provided.

Another Danish-based organisation is the Swallows of Denmark (the Danish Branch of Emmaus International) which raises funds for projects in India. They organise fortnight-long work camps in Denmark which involve collecting saleable goods.

Useful Addresses

Youth Action for Peace, Methold House, North Street, Worthing BN11 1DU.
Swallows of Denmark, Ulandsforeningen Svalerne, Osterbrogade 49, 2100 Copenhagen O; ☎35 26 17 47; fax 31 38 17 46.
United Nations Association (UNA) Wales, International Youth Service, Temple of Peace, Cathays Park, Cardiff CF1 3AP.

TRAINING AND WORK EXPERIENCE SCHEMES

One of the problems for those leaving school or university is their lack of a proven track record in the job market. The European Commission has come up with various schemes for young people to go on work exchanges in Europe, mainly SOCRATES. In the UK SOCRATES exchanges are arranged by the Central Bureau.

ICYE organises stays for those aged 16-30 in over 25 countries worldwide, including Denmark. The normal stay is one year and comprises college work combined with social work. There is a charge of about €3,000 for your stay.

Useful Addresses

Central Bureau for Educational Visits and Exchanges, British Council, 10 Spring Gardens, London SW1A 2BN. ☎020-7389 4157; fax 020 7389 4426; e-mail socr ates@britishcouncil.org; www.centralbureau.org.uk/socrates. Arranges many types of European exchanges for a range of ages and qualifications.

ICYE (International Christian Youth Exchange), Dansk ICYE, Skolebakken 5, 8000 Århus C; ☎86 18 07 15; fax 86 18 07 61; www.icye.org/denmark.

DIRECTORY OF MAJOR EMPLOYERS IN DENMARK

The following are some of Denmark's top companies in terms of turnover and number of employees.

Company	Employees	Type of Company
A.P. Møller Group	30,000	Shipping, etc.
Carlsberg	23,460	Brewing
Danfoss	6,012	Thermostats
Danisco	3,556	Food, beverages
Danish Crown	19,500	Meat products
Dansk Shell	650	Oil
Danske Bank	19,600	Banking
Det Danske Trelastkompagni	3,478	Timber
DSA	4,910	Supermarkets
DSB	10,922	Railways
East Asiatic Company	6,000	Foodstuffs, beverages
FLS Industries	18,000	Cement-making equipment
IBM Danmark	4,479	Documentation
ISS	253,000	Office maintenance, industrial cleaning services
J Lauritzen Holding	15,000	Shipping, shipyards
Lego AS	5,583	Toys
Lego System	3,912	
MD Foods	6,832	Dairy products
Monberg & Thorsen Holding	2,759	Construction
Norsk Hydro Danmark	3,135	Oil refining
Novo Nordisk	8,146	Pharmaceuticals
Post Danmark	25,472	Postal service
SAS	23,607	Air transport
Skandinavisk Tobakskompagni	4,900	Tobacco & furniture
Sophus Berendsen	2,975	Pesticides
Superfos	3,008	Conglomerate
Tele Danmark	15,000	Telecommunications
Vestjydske Slagterie	4,391	Meat products

BRITISH & MULTINATIONAL COMPANIES WITH BRANCHES, AFFILIATES OR SUBSIDIARIES IN DENMARK

Amersham Pharmacia Biotech Slotsmarken 14, 2970 Hørsholm. (Biotechnology).

Astra Zeneca A/S Roskildevej 22, 2620 Albertslund. (Pharmaceuticals).

Atlas Copco A/C Postbox 1349, 2600 Glostrup. (Compressors).

Baxenden Scandinavia A/S Fulbyvej 4, Pederborg 4180 Soro. (Chemicals and pharmaceuticals).

Black & Decker A/S Hegrevang 268, 3450 Allerød. (Machine Tools).

Boeg-Thomsen A/S Nybyvej 11, 4390 Vipperod. (Foodstuffs and beverages).

Canon Denmark A/S Vasekær 12, 2730 Herlev. (Office equipment).

Castrol A/S Esplanaden 7, 1263 Copenhagen K. (Petrochemicals).

Colgate-Palmolive A/S Smedeland 9, 2600 Glostrup. (Healthcare).

Compaq Computer A/S/ Kongevejen 2, 3460 Birkerød. (Computers).

Corus Denmark Hans Edvard Teglers vej 7, 2920 Charlottenlunnd. (Metal products).

A/S Dansk Shell Kampmannsgade 2, 1604 Copenhagen. (Petrochemicals).

DEB Swarfega Denmark Teglværksvej 6, 5620 Glamsbjerg. (Chemicals and pharmaceuticals).

Dell Computer Amager Strandvej 60, 2300 Copenhagen S. (Computers).

DOW Agrosciences A/S Sorgenfrivej 15, 2800 Kgs Lyngby. (Chemicals).

Euro-matic A/S Baldersbuen 8, 2640 Hedehusene. (Plastics).

Fisons A/S Kongevejen 100, 2840 Holte. (Chemicals and pharmaceuticals)

Goodyear Dunlop Tires Denmark A/S Fabriksparken 1, 2600 Glostrup. (Rubber goods).

Hewlett Packard Kongevejen 25, 3460 Birkerød. (Computers).

Hoechst Marion Roussel A/S/ Slotsmarken 14, 2970 Hørsholm. (Pharmaceuticals).

Hoover A/S Frydenborgvej 27K, 3400 Hillerød. (Electrical and electronic equipment).

Invensys APV Products Platinvej 8, 600 Kolding. (Heat exchangers).

Johnson Matthey A/S Frederikssundsvej 247 D, Copenhagen. (Metal products).

Minolta Denmark A/S/ Valhøys Allé 160, 2610 Rødovre. (Office equipment).

Nokia Denmark A/S/ Frederikskaj 5, 1790 Copenhagen V. (Mobile phones).

Oracle Denmark ApS Lautrupbjerg 2, 2750 Ballerup. (Software).

P&O Ferrymasters A/S Kristiansgade 8, 2100 Copenhagen Ø. (Freight storage and transport).

Pfizer ApS Lautrupvang 8, 2750 Ballerup. (Pharmaceuticals).

PricewaterhouseCoopers Toldbuen 1, 4700 Næstved. (Accounting and auditing).

Procter & Gamble A/S Køgevej 50, 2 tv, 2630 Taastrup. (Healthcare products).

Reckitt Benckiser Scandinavia A/S Vadstrupvej 22, 2880 Bagsværd. (Foodstuffs and beverages).

Rockwool International Hovedgaden 584, 2640 Hedehusene. (Isolating materials).

Siemens A/S Borupvang 3, 2750 Ballerup. (Computers).

Smithkline Beecham A/S Lautruphøj 1-3, 2750 Ballerup. (Chemicals and pharmaceuticals).

Xerox A/S Borupvang 5, 2750 Ballerup. (Office equipment).

Birkerød. (Computers).

STARTING A BUSINESS

The majority of foreigners residing in Denmark are there for work or career reasons. However, there is another option available in the Single European Market which is to set up or buy a business in another EU country.

Starting a business abroad need not necessarily be reserved for established business people or multinational companies. In addition to the regular large-scale opportunities, recent administrative simplifications within the EU have made a point of providing encouragement to small- and medium-sized enterprises (SMEs) and individual entrepreneurs to set up businesses in other EU nations. Such businesses can take almost any form: running small shops, art courses, letting agencies, providing bed and breakfasts or running a job agency are just some of the commercial enterprises started by foreigners in other EU countries. The main limitation in Denmark that one has to bear in mind is that many Danes prefer to do things for themselves, so trying to set yourself up as a plumber or painter and decorator would not be likely to work. There is more scope in creative types of work, such as photography or graphic design if you feel that you can compete with the high standard of the locals.

Inevitably the cultural differences between Denmark and the UK, and the difficulties of the language, will make this a challenging undertaking. It is likely that anyone who sets up business in Denmark will already have some connections there. In Denmark, unlike France, Spain and Portugal, you cannot expect some types of business to thrive on the custom of fellow expatriates, or holidaymakers of your own nationality visiting the country. In addition, the extra difficulties caused by a lack of familiarity with foreign procedures could prove a serious drawback. Denmark is a very bureaucratic country, but you can at least expect to have procedures explained to you in English. In the beginning it could be wise to seek out a Danish business partner or company with compatible interests with which you can have a joint venture until you have found your feet.

Denmark has recently become alert to the potential of the newly opened-up markets of Eastern Europe and the Baltic Republics, which it is strategically positioned to exploit once economic conditions improve there. Foreign investors may also like to consider ways of cashing in on these markets. Furthermore, Denmark has already begun talks with Germany and Sweden on the possibility of building a fixed link between Lolland (the island artificially linked to southern Zealand) and Germany across the Fermarn straits. This would reduce distribution time not just to Germany but to the new markets of eastern Europe.

THE BUSINESS CLIMATE

There are estimated to be about 2,000 foreign-owned businesses operating in Denmark. While some of these are high profile companies with international interests (e.g. Lego, Carlsberg, East Asiatic Company, Sophus Berendsen), large multinationals do not predominate here. The majority of enterprises (about 75%) have fewer than 50 employees, and are family-owned. Although small companies have some advantages, notably in lead-in times (i.e. the speed with which they can produce new products), they are at a disadvantage in a pan-European field when competing with big companies in research and export drives. The government has therefore encouraged companies to merge or to network with other SMEs to produce a greater momentum in these areas. The state has also invested heavily in efficient distribution systems, reducing the time from the order to the receipt of goods by the customer to one of the shortest in Europe.

The small population of Denmark means that it has strict limitations as a market. Most Danish companies are therefore expanding through exports. For anyone who is competent and experienced in international marketing there are opportunities, as this is one of the few areas where the Danes are short on expertise, although they are more likely to turn to their neighbours and commercial collaborators, the Swedes, before they head-hunt non-Scandinavians.

Hitherto, an important trading union for the Scandinavians has been the Nordic Union. Since 1954 citizens of Nordic states have had a common labour and trade market. There is also a Nordic investment bank and shared commercial and environmental protection laws. In addition the Nordic countries have harmonised their technology in practical ways so that it is, for instance, possible to use the same mobile telephone in Copenhagen or Helsinki. Although the NU has worked beneficially for past decades in the areas of agriculture, industrial policy and natural resources, Denmark along with Finland and Sweden looks more and more to the European Union for export markets.

FINANCIAL CONSIDERATIONS

Loans

Businesses can use the banking services of both commercial and savings banks while mortgage credit institutions can give loans for commercial agricultural properties, companies and ships as well as residential dwellings. The choice of the type of loan will depend on tax considerations and the assessment of individual business income. One mortgage credit institution, Industriens Realkreditfond, specialises in mortgages for businesses. About half of all mortgage credit in Denmark is loaned to commercial enterprises. Further information on mortgage credit institutions can be found in the chapter *Setting up Home*.

The institution Finance for Danish Industries (FIH – Finansieringsinstituttet for Industri og Håndværk A/S, will provide medium and long-term financing for various business requirements including machinery and building acquisitions, marketing and for mergers and takeovers. Generally serial loans are granted and the first repayment is deferred until the third year and entire repayment lasts over a period of four to 20 years.

Useful Addresses

Finance for Danish Industries, FIH – Finansieringsinstituttet for Industri og Håndværk A/S, LaCoursVej 7, 2000 Frederiksberg; ☎38 16 68 00; fax 38 16 68 01; e-mail info@fih.dk; www.fih.dk.
Industrial Mortgage Fund (Industriens Realkreditfond): Bredgade 40, 1260 Copenhagen K; ☎33 42 10 00.
Information Office for Foreign Investments in Denmark (Informationskontoret for udenlandske investeringer i Danmark), Søndergade 2, 8600 Silkeborg; ☎86 82 56 55; www.investindk.com.

IDEAS & PROCEDURES FOR SETTING UP BUSINESS IN DENMARK

Help and Information

In order to help foreigners who want to invest in Denmark, the Ministry of Foreign Affairs has set up an Investment Secretariat. This bureau offers a range of services which include establishing contact with the various authorities, other organisations and commercial companies. It also, helps to arrange fact-finding visits; provides information on investment conditions and help with feasibility studies and market research. The Secretariat will also undertake to find a Danish business partner for foreigners wishing to form a commercial liaison. Even once the desired contacts have been made, assistance is sustained during the setting up of business and afterwards.

Danish embassies and consulates general can also assist in providing information for proposed business set-up and investment in Denmark as can chambers of commerce and special agencies in Denmark.

Useful Addresses

Agency for Investment and Development of Trade and Industry in Greater Copenhagen, via Copenhagen Science Park, Symbion A/S, Fruebjergvej 3, 2100 Copenhagen; ☎39 17 99 99. The agency offers specific business service programmes to foreign companies considering the Copenhagen area as a possible location.
Danish Chamber of Commerce (Handelskammeret), Børsen, 1217 Copenhagen K; ☎33 91 23 23; fax 33 32 52 16; www.handelskammeret.dk.
American Chamber of Commerce, Christians Brygge 28, 1559 Copenhagen V; ☎33 932 932; fax 33 13 05 17; www.amcham.dk.
The Danish Federation of Small Industries, Lille SCT Hans Gade 20, 8800 Viborg; ☎86 62 77 11; fax 86 61 49 21; www.hvri.dk.
Ministry of Foreign Affairs (Udenrigsministeriet), Asiatisk Plads 2, 1448 Copenhagen K; ☎33 92 00 00; e-mail

info@investindk.com; www.um.dk.
National Bureau of Statistics, 11 Sejrøgade,
2100 Copenhagen Ø; ☎39 17 39 10;
fax 31 18 48 01; www.dst.dk.
Royal Danish Embassy, 55 Sloane Street,
London SW1X 9SR; ☎071-333

0200; www.denmarkemb.org.
Royal Danish Embassy, 3200 Whitehaven Street, NW Washington
DC 20008-3683; ☎202-797-5300;
www.denmarkemb.org.

Registration of Foreign Enterprises

Citizens from the EU are free to set up a business in Denmark on the same terms
as Danish citizens. For other details of residence regulations in Denmark for EU
citizens, see *Residence and Entry* chapter. All new foreign commercial enterprises
have to be registered with the Danish Trade and Companies Agency, Erhvervs &
Selskabsstyrelsen (Kampmannsgade 1, 1780 Copenhagen V; ☎33 30 77 00; fax
33 30 77 99; e-mail eogs@eogs.dk; www.eogs.dk), and must be managed by one
or more persons whose residence is in the European Union.

Normally, if a non-EU citizen wishes to establish a business in Denmark it can
only be done if Danes have a reciprocal right with the country concerned. Non EU-
nationals have to obtain authorisation from the Ministry of Justice/*Justitsministeriet*
(Slotholmsgade 10, 1216 Copenhagen K; ☎33 92 33 40; www.jm.dk) if they
wish to purchase commercial (or residential) property. It is usually easier for non
EU-nationals to obtain permission to buy industrial property than residential
property.

Government Investment Incentives for Foreigners

Denmark operates several business subsidy programmes none of which is
particularly substantial except for shipping and agriculture which are earmarked
for preferential treatment. Incentives generally take the form of financial support
such as loans or guarantees which may or may not have to be paid back either
in part, or in full. Other incentives include free export assistance and other
information and advice. Anyone interested in investing in Denmark should contact
the Ministry of Trade and Industry, Investment Secretariat (10-12 Slotsholmsgade,
1216 Copenhagen K; ☎33 92 33 50; fax 33 12 37 78; www.em.dk), for further
information. Table 3 lists areas in which assistance is given.

TABLE 3   AREAS FOR WHICH INCENTIVES CAN BE PROVIDED:

○ Product development and enhanced production methods – state
   grants and subsidised loans.
○ Expansion of small companies including refurbishing/constructing
   premises and upgrading equipment – interest-subsidised loans.
○ For small companies' export, environmental and energy projects
   – interest subsidised loans.
○ Shipping: for building of new ships of minimum gross 100 tons and
   rebuilding same in a Danish shipyard – interest-subsidised loans.
○ Energy: for installation of renewable energy sources (solar, wind,

compost heating) and cost efficient energy projects – subsidies.
○ Environmental technology – subsidies for investment in reducing pollution.
○ Hiring & Training Staff: subsidies for the hiring of long-term unemployed if this causes an increase in overall staffing; retraining subsidies and subsidies for staff participating in research and development outside Denmark.
○ Export: assistance to enable enterprises to carry out research to find new export markets and to prepare sales material. A definite export project qualifies for a guarantee against losses on foreign debts and security for export loans.
○ Consultation: export assistance and counselling on production methods is available free or at a low cost. Also counselling on product development, market information and management.
○ Regional Development: the Danish state subsidises development in high unemployment areas. Subsidies or subsidised loans are granted to companies prepared to establish or relocate in such areas where they provide jobs and raise income levels.
○ Agriculture: The European Commission guarantees mininum prices and guarantees export subsidies for farmers. In addition, there is a range of support schemes aimed at the agricultural sector including subsidies for consultants who provide an advice service to farmers and temporary assistance in case of illness.
○ Information Technology: subsidies for research and development are available where they are deemed valuable to Danish business conditions.

Useful Addresses

Invest in Denmark, Danish Trade Council, Ministry of Foreign Affairs, 2 Asiatisk Plads, 1448 Copenhagen K; 33 92 11 16; fax 32 54 05 33; e-mail info@investindk.com; www.investindk.com.
Regional Investment:
Horsens Business and Innovation Centre, Tobaksgaarden, 10 Allégade, 8700 Horsens; ☎75 61 18 88; fax 75 61 31 99; erhverv@horsenskom.dk; www.horsens-erhverv.dk.
Randers Trade Office (& Business Centre),

Erhvervenes Hus, 12 Tørvebryggen, 8900 Randers; ☎86 40 10 66; fax 86 40 60 04. Has an excellent database on companies in the region.
Trade Office for Silkeborg, Viborgvej 24, 8600 Silkeborg; ☎86 81 54 67. Very active trade office for Silkeborg and the region keen to help companies wishing to set up a new enterprise.
Viborg Industrial Development Council, Gammel Vagt, Postbox 4, 2 Ll Sct. Hans Gade, 8800 Viborg; ☎86 62 67 77; fax 86 61 35 50.

BUSINESS STRUCTURES

Limited Liability Companies

Denmark has two types of limited company: private and public, and the legislation to which they are subject differs for each of the two types.

Public Limited Company (Aktieselskab A/S). The minimum capital required for the formation of a public company is kr500,000 (approx. £40,000/US$58,500 The main difference between a private and a public company is in the minimum capital required for formation. Also if the capital is reduced to less than 50% of the registered capital by losses, the board of directors (*Bestyrelse*) is required to call a general meeting of shareholders to consider remedial measures.

A public limited company should be incorporated by at least three founders. It is not essential that the founders subscribe capital and the company may be owned by an individual shareholder. At least two of the founders must be residents of any EU nation (exceptions can be made by special agreement with the Minister of Industry). The founders have to sign a formation agreement. The company must have articles of association which must include the name and objectives of the company, the resident address of the company, the amount of share capital, the number of board members and the accounting year, which need not follow the calendar year.

All companies have to apply for registration with the Danish Commerce and Companies Agency within six months of the formation agreement being signed. Companies may however, begin carrying out business as soon as the formation agreement is signed. However rights against third parties are not possible until registration has taken place. Until the company is registered, the General Management, the Board of Directors and the founders are personally liable.

All public limited companies must have a minimum of three directors on the board. The board is elected by the annual general shareholders' meeting. The board of directors elects at least one general manager (*direktør*). The general manager can be elected to the board but not as its chairperson.

Private Limited Company (Anpartsselskab ApS). For an ApS, a minimum capital of kr125,000 is required. If the company sustains losses of more than 40% of the registered capital, it must be recapitalised or dissolved.

Generally the formalities for the formation and increases in capital are less restrictive for private than for public companies. A private company is required to have a board of directors, unless it is a small private company, in which case the articles of association may allow that a board is not created. This exemption will not apply if staffing reaches a level where there is a statutory obligation to have employee representation on the board. This type of entity is designed to facilitate the establishment of small companies with limited liability, for example strictly family held businesses.

The presentation and audit of annual accounts is the same for both private and public companies. There is an additional requirement for a private company to make its annual accounts public through the Trade and Companies Agency (www.eogs.dk).

If a private company is reorganised into a public one, a special valuation report must be prepared and endorsed by external valuers, regardless of the capital status of the company.

Partnerships

A partnership is not governed by a rigorous framework of regulations and composition and methods of operation are flexible. There are two main types and partners can be individuals or limited liability companies:

A general partnership (Interessentskab I/S). This can be formed by two or more persons that operate a business as co-owners for profit. Many professions form partnerships. Although partnerships are free to operate in a manner of their choosing, the method of operation must be set down in a formal set of agreements.

Tax is levied on the share of the profits taken by each member of a partnership. If they wish, partners can elect to be taxed in accordance with the Business Tax Act which enables them to be taxed in part, similarly to an enterprise operating as a single company.

Limited Partnership (Kommanditselskab K/S). A limited partnership is useful where some partners wish to invest in a company but do not want liability. A limited partnership is taxed similarly to a full partnership. A limited partnership may comprise two or more individuals or companies of which at least one (the general partner) must be fully liable for all the liabilities of the partnership. Other members are liable only to the extent of the financial stake they have in the company.

Limited partnerships are often used by high tax individuals to raise funds for the acquisition of depreciable assets such as machinery and buildings. The general partner in such instances would be a financial company. The assets would then be leased commercially. Leasing is generally cheaper than interest expenses owing to capital allowances. By claiming these allowances, taxes payable are postponed until the assets are disposed of.

Joint Ventures

A joint venture is defined as 'any combination of two or more enterprises associated for the purpose of pursuing a business objective'. Legally two unrelated, incorporated or unincorporated businesses conducting business as a non-corporate joint venture are treated as a partnership, albeit one with limited scope and duration. For tax purposes they are also treated as a partnership.

Sole Proprietorships

Sole proprietors have a special place in Danish economic history as many Danish firms began as single person enterprises including some international Danish companies. The sole proprietorship (*enkeltmandsfirma*) is suitable for those engaged in trading, farming and in the provision of professional services. There is no specific legislation for this type of enterprise. Registration at the registry of trade is optional and free of charge.

For tax purposes sole proprietors are taxed on business and any other additional income. The Business Tax Act (1987) allows the proprietor to choose to be taxed in the same way as a limited company.

Trusts and Foundations

Trusts are not recognised in Denmark. However both commercial and non-commercial foundations can be established. In order to qualify as a foundation there are certain criteria which must be met:

- The capital must be separated from the founder's capital so that it cannot be re-acquired by the founder, founder's spouse or their offspring under 18 years.
- A board of directors must be appointed and include at least one independent member.
- The foundation must have one or more clearly defined objectives.
- The foundation must be a separate legal entity responsible for its actions and able to assume rights.

Foundations exist in various types in Denmark. The two main distinctions are between commercial and non-commercial foundations. The former must be registered with the Trade and Companies Agency while non-commercial ones do not have to register. Both types are liable for tax.

Branches of Foreign Companies

A foreign company wishing to establish a branch in Denmark has to register with the Danish Trade and Companies Agency who require specific information regarding the identity and particulars of the parent company. The parent company's annual accounts and annual reports must be filed with the DTCA. A branch has also to file a tax return, which must include details of taxable income and capital and debts.

For tax purposes branches of foreign companies are handled like incorporated companies. The branch and the parent company form an entity. The branch cannot deduct interest on loans granted by the parent company or deduct royalties that are paid to the parent company for the use of rights. Such transactions are deemed capital transfers and do not confer any fiscal benefits.

RUNNING A BUSINESS

Employing & Dismissing Staff

Denmark's social security system is almost entirely funded through the tax system. Pension schemes require compulsory employee contributions. The *Arbejdsmarkedets Tillægspension* (ATP) or Supplementary Pension Scheme is run by employers jointly with the labour organisations. The employee pays one-third and the employer two-thirds of the contributions to ATP. Workers also pay 1% of their income into the Special Pensions (SP) scheme; employers are not liable. Self-employed workers have to contribute to the SP scheme, and the AM (labour market contribution).

There is also an education and training scheme for young workers and the unemployed, *Arbejdsmarkedsuddanelsesfonden* (AUD) which is run by the Ministry of Labour and to which employers contribute.

Foreign workers from EU and Nordic countries may be exempted from pension contributions under EU regulation 1408/71, or if they are from a country that has a totalisation agreement with Denmark; note that the USA does not have such an agreement.

Dismissing Staff. The notice period of termination of employment is fixed by the Employees Act which stipulates the following notice periods:

Length of Employment	Period of Notice Required
O up to five months	one month
O up to 2 years & 5 months	three months
O up to 5 years & 8 months	four months
O up to 8 years & 7 months	five months
O thereafter	six months

For employees who have been employed for 12, 15 or 18 or more consecutive years there is a supplementary compensation of one, two or three months salary respectively.

The employment terms for hourly paid employees are governed by collective agreements. There is no legal minimum notice period. An example of an agreement with skilled industrial workers could be:

Period of Employment	Period of Notice Required
O less than nine months	nil
O more than nine months	21 days
O more than three years	49 days
O more than six years	70 days

For employees over 50 years of age whose employment period exceeds 9/20 years, the notice period would be 90 days/120 days.

TAXATION

The Danish tax system depends more on direct taxes (income tax and corporate tax) than on indirect taxes. In many EU countries the reverse is the case. Whereas individual income tax in Denmark is levied by both central and local governments, corporation tax is levied only by the central government. Personal taxation in Denmark is notoriously high; the corporation tax, which is the principal tax on businesses has been lowered to 30%.

Tax is paid on a current year basis in two tranches on 20 March and 20 November. Final settlement is in November. The main indirect taxes are VAT at a uniform rate of 25% on most goods and services, and various excise duties of which car tax is one of the most excessive. Most banking, real estate and medical services are exempt from VAT and exports are zero rated. The threshold for compulsory VAT registration is a turnover of kr20,000 (approx. £1,600/US2,340) per annum. For further information see the publications listed below.

Excise duties are levied on tobacco and spirits, wine, beer, motor vehicles, most energy sources and petroleum.

Useful Addresses

American Chamber of Commerce, Christians Brygge 28, 1559 Copenhagen V; ☎33 932 932; fax 33 13 05 17; www.amcham.dk.

British Embassy Commercial Department, Kastelsvej 36, 2100 Copenhagen Ø; ☎26 46 00; www.britishembassy.dk. Produces a detailed report *Financial Services in Denmark* covering banking, mortgage credit, insurance and pension funds. Also provides much other useful information for British businesses setting up in Denmark, from business practices and etiquette to a list of Danish lawyers with expertise in drawing up agency/distributer agreements.

Danish Chamber of Commerce, Main office: Børsen 1217 Copenhagen K; ☎33 95 05 00; fax 33 32 52 16. Branches and sub-branches all over Denmark. The Danish Chamber of Commerce is the principal organisation for international trade and industry and the service sector. For many foreigners it is the first point of contact for starting a business in Denmark.

Den Danske Bank, International Trade Promotion, 2-12 Holmens Kanal, 1092 Copenhagen K; ☎33 44 00 00; fax 39 18 58 73; www.danskebank.dk. Produces leaflets, *Setting Up in Denmark,* and *Taxation of Business Operations in Denmark;* offers a range of banking services to companies in Scandinavia and worldwide, including helping establish business contacts and in the acquisition of Danish companies by foreign ones.

Ernst & Young, National Office, Tagensvej 86, 2200 Copenhagen N, Denmark; ☎35 82 48 48; fax 35 82 48 00; www.ey.dk.

Industri-og Handelsstyrelsen/National Agency of Industry and Trade, Regional Development, Tagensvej 137, 2200 Copenhagen N.

KPMG C Jesperson, Borups Allé 177, PO Box 250 Frederiksberg; ☎38 18 30 00; fax 38 18 30 45. KPMG is one of the world's largest accountancy firms and has branches throughout Denmark. Publishes a free guide, *Investment in Denmark.*

Mortensen & Beierholm, Vester Søgade 10,1, 1601 Copenhagen V; ☎33 12 68 11; fax 33 32 37 73. Part of the worldwide organisation of accounting firms known as HLB International. Has eight other branches in Denmark especially experienced in co-ordinating activities between different countries.

PriceWaterhouse Coopers, Strandvejen 44, 2900 Hellerup; ☎39 43 39 45; fax 39 45 39 87.

Trade Partners UK Information Centre, 66-74 Victoria Street, London SW1E 6SW; 020-7215 5444/5; fax 020-7215 4231; www.tradepartners.gov.uk. See Denmark country profile on website.

Useful Publications

Business Denmark: journal of the American Chamber of Commerce in Copenhagen (see above).

Doing Business in Denmark, published by PriceWaterhouseCoopers in 1999; download from website www.pwc.dk.

Kraks Business Directory, available on the internet: www.krak.dk.

Finland

SECTION I

LIVING IN FINLAND

GENERAL INTRODUCTION

RESIDENCE AND ENTRY REGULATIONS

SETTING UP HOME

DAILY LIFE

RETIREMENT

GENERAL INTRODUCTION

DESTINATION FINLAND

To many, Finland, or Suomi as it is known in Finnish, evokes images of polar bears and snowy landscapes. While there is quite a lot of snow in winter (although not as much as there used to be), there are no polar bears. Elk and reindeer are very typical of this country, which sees itself as a bridge between East and West, but very keen to be considered a full member of Europe. The name 'land of 10,000 lakes' is more than accurate. Depending on how you define a lake, Finland is said to have 188,000 of them. Finland is also official home to Santa Claus and the Moomintrolls. Finnish design flair has had a universal impact. Nokia controls some 35% of the global mobile phone market. The Marimekko company played a large part in promoting bold, colourful designs for the masses during the 50s and 60s.

The institution of the sauna exemplifies Finland more than anything else: there is one sauna for every three residents. As they say: first build the sauna and then the house. Here the Finns discard their clothes and their reserve. The sauna is much more than a place to sweat out grime; in the past it was used for caring for the sick, for childbirth, and even for smoking meat. The other great institution is the summer house next to a lake, where the people go to commune with nature in the summer. The Finns are intensely attached to their country and proud of their independence, which only came about in 1917. Their culture is founded on democracy and equality. There is probably no other country in the western world where men and women are on such an equal footing. The Finns are a peace-loving people, something which was commented on as long ago as the first century AD by the Roman historian Tacitus, in the oldest known description of the Finnish people. The Finns' resolve and solidarity were tested to the utmost during World War II when the country narrowly escaped reconquest by the Russians.

Like Sweden, Finland joined the European Union in January 1995 following a referendum in which 57% of voters (the turnout was about 75%) voted for membership. The small Finnish farmers mostly abstained in this vote, in the knowledge that they faced oblivion when their country was opened to agricultural imports from the European Union. However, the instability of the former Soviet Union (with which Finland shares a long border), convinced the majority of the people to vote for EU membership, thus ensuring Finnish independence for a long time to come.

Additionally Finland had to repair the damage wrought on the economy by the worst recession for 60 years, which began in 1990 and was exacerbated by the loss of about 60% of their regular export market as a result of the disintegration of the Russian empire, with which trade was mostly on a barter basis. Concern about the former Soviet Union and its ageing nuclear reactors are two things that greatly trouble the Finns. Fortunately, entry into the EU has revitalised the economy; Finland was also in the first wave of EU members to adopt the euro in 2002. The capital, Helsinki, at last free from Russian influence, has blossomed and is fast becoming a cosmopolitan and trendy place for foreigners and expatriates. Quality of life is very high in Finland, and many immigrants from more southerly countries in Europe swear that they will never leave. Apart from the tangible advantages of excellent public transport, a virtual absence of atmospheric pollutants and low crime levels, Finland offers something of even greater value, namely, a culture that has not been spoilt by modern amenities and lifestyles. There is a genuineness and straightforwardness about the people which are quite rare in the modern world, something that draws from ancient traditions that seem to have been lost elsewhere.

It would be naïve to say that there is no downside to living in Finland, and that can be summed up in one word: the climate. Whereas a Brit or an American can look forward to the first signs of spring in March, even in Helsinki one will have to wait another two months for signs of new life. Finns have traditionally been great travellers, and they have emigrated in large numbers to North America, driven by poverty rather than a desire to leave their country behind. These days Finland offers far more opportunities to the young and ambitious, and they are more likely to spend a few years abroad and then return home. Nonetheless, Finland is facing a looming crisis in recruiting enough highly qualified workers: the baby-boom generation born just after the war is reaching retirement age and will have to be supported. In the first place, Finland has opened its doors to Russians and Estonians who have at least one Finnish grandparent, as a way of finding skilled workers who can adapt to the climate, and cope with the language.

Finland has the smallest number of resident foreigners of any European country (under 2% of the population, or 95,000 people), but the number is increasing quite rapidly. About 2,300 of the foreign residents are British, and the number increases by about 100 every year; there is about the same number of US citizens, most of them with family ties to Finland. Other groups include Somalis, Turks, Iraqis, Iranians, Vietnamese and other refugees, who have considerable difficulty in adapting to such an alien environment. For northern Europeans, Finland is an increasingly attractive place to live, and there is a considerable willingness on the part of the Finnish authorities to make integration into their country as smooth as possible.

PROS AND CONS OF MOVING TO FINLAND

Those seeking employment in Finland will find an affluent country, which has recovered with amazing speed from the devastating recession of the early 90s, which saw unemployment reach 20% in 1993 (compared with a low of 3% in 1990). In 2001 unemployment was down to a seasonally-adjusted total of 10%; the figure is much higher in winter than in the rest of the year. The Finnish economy is, however, heavily dependent on just one company, Nokia, and the benefits of the high-tech boom are by no means evenly spread over the whole country; but given the Finns' remarkable track record in dealing with national crises, the odds are that this is a country with an exceptionally bright future.

Pros
- Helsinki is one of the world's least polluted capitals.
- Extremely efficient transport systems.
- Ideal for sailing, skiing and fishing, depending on the season.
- Very low national crime rate, even in Helsinki.
- Most Finns speak some English; many fluently.
- High standard of living.
- Locals are generally friendly and helpful.

Cons
- Unemployment is higher than in UK and USA.
- Helsinki has a noticeable problem with drunkenness, especially at night.
- Seasonal depression is acute in the long winters.
- Winters are so cold that the sea around Helsinki freezes (but you can skate on it).
- Alcohol is expensive, more than double UK prices.
- Not all locals are easy to get to know.
- Finnish is one of Europe's most difficult languages.

POLITICAL AND ECONOMIC STRUCTURE

The key to understanding the contemporary politics and economy of Finland lies partly in knowing something of its national history. The first settlers were nomadic tribes from the Urals and Volga region, the Finno-Ugrians. From the Viking era political control rested with Swedish-speaking settlers who were encouraged to colonise the area, partly to ward off the danger of encroachment by Russia. The Swedish Empire eventually collapsed and Finland became an autonomous Russian province in 1809. Swedish remained the official language until the 1870s even though only one-seventh of the population spoke it. Finnish identity was redefined in the 19th century with the publication of the *Kalevala,* a collection of Finnish legends, by Elias Lönnrot. The nationalist movements which developed from the 1860s ensured the status of the Finnish language was enhanced to the point that it became the main language at the turn of the century.

Finland's status as an autonomous Grand Duchy with its own constitutional laws lasted until 1899 when Russia decided to 'Russify' Finland by making Russian the official language of the top administrative cadres and by banning indigenous newspapers. Thus began a period of Russian oppression, which became more severe from 1908 when Russia started to govern Finland directly from Moscow.

The downfall of the Tsarist regime in Russia, signalled by the October Revolution, relieved the Finns of Russian domination, and separatists seized the chance to declare Finland independent on 6 October 1917. While agreeing to Finnish independence the Russians also supplied Bolshevik-inspired radicals in Finland with weapons, leading to a long and bitter civil war between the nationalists and the radical revolutionary party. The government forces prevailed and early in 1919 Finland finally became a republic. Finland was a founder member of the Nordic Council in 1925, an organisation that has become more and more important since the 60s.

The struggle between extreme left- and right-wingers continued into the 1930s. Finland moved closer to Nazi Germany, to counter the threat on its eastern borders from the Russians. In November 1939 the Soviet Union moved in (with the secret approval of the Germans), but, to everyone's surprise, the Finns managed to throw them back. The Russians soon mounted a better-organised campaign, and Finland had no option but to ally itself with Germany to regain its lost territories, without doing anything to bring about a Germany victory over the Soviet Union. Consequently, Finland lost more territory with the settlement after the end of the war and had to pay war reparations to the Allies. Note that the Finns generally do not refer to the Second World War (as far as Finland is concerned), but to the Winter War (1939-1940) and the Continuation War (1941-1944).

With their economy in ruins and their people starving, the Finns were forced to sign a treaty of mutual co-operation with the Soviet Union in 1948. In spite of Finland's supposed neutrality the Russians now dictated Finnish politics, using embargoes and military pressure to ensure their neighbours' compliance, a situation that only ended with the end of the Cold War in 1990. The threat to the country's independence has now passed with Finland's entry into the European Union.

Government

The Finnish constitution, enacted in 1919, remained much the same until the Constitution Act was passed in 2000. Two hundred members of the uni-cameral parliament (the *Eduskunta*) are elected every four years (next elections 2003). The country is divided into 14 electoral districts from which representatives are elected by proportional representation. In addition there is a representative from the self-governing province of Åland Islands.

The head of state is the President of the Republic (currently Tarja Halonen, the first female President, expected to serve until 2006), elected by direct popular vote every six years. Before 1988 the President was selected by an electoral college of 301 who were themselves chosen by proportional representation. There are two ballot papers for presidential elections, one for the presidential candidates and the other for the electoral college. If there is no outright winner for President then he or she will be selected by the electoral college.

The President used to have wide-ranging powers, which have been curtailed by the Constitution Act of 2000. Supreme power is vested in the people represented by Parliament. Parliament selects the Prime Minister (currently Paavo Lipponen), who in turn selects a government team, which is confirmed by the President. The President's role is as a figurehead; he or she still has influence on foreign policy and security matters, but the EU has more and more say in foreign policy matters.

Political Parties

Historically, post-war Finnish political parties represented two main areas of interest: urban and rural. This distinction has become less obvious since the Agrarian Union party changed its name in 1965 to the Centre Party (KP) which is basically liberal and currently the party with the most representatives in Parliament. There are two other main parties: the Finnish Social Democrat Party (SDP) which represents the moderate left, and the National Coalition Party (Kokoomus/KOK) which is the conservative party.

Other parties in declining order of importance in Parliament are:

Left-Wing Alliance: communist and socialist.

Swedish People's Party (RKP): Represents the Swedish-speaking minority.

Greens: Elected to Parliament for the first time in 1983.

Finnish Christian League (SKL): Gained first parliamentary seat in 1970, then resigned in June 1994 over Finland's application for EU membership.

The Economy

Finland only had an embryonic industrial base in the early part of the 1950s. Agriculture and forestry were the main occupations of a large part of the working population and forestry products were the main exports. Finland still relies on forestry exports to a large degree, and they make up some 40% of export volumes and about half of all revenues. In the 50s individual incomes were very modest. A rapid period of growth at 5% per annum from the 50s to the 70s led to a great expansion of the cities (over half of the housing in Finland was built in 20 years from the mid-60s). This meant that in two decades Finland reached a very high standard of living, became specialised in new industries and experienced considerable urbanisation. From the 1950s exports had been led by metal and engineering industries, which did much to promote the growth of the economy. Later, imports of crude oil from the Soviet Union under a bilateral trade agreement also helped the expanding economy.

From the 1980s Finland's economy joined the worldwide boom but became over-heated due to excessive borrowing to fund corporate investment. It is estimated that Finnish banks had to write off a total of £2.2 billion in unrecoverable debts by 1993. Fortunately, the Finnish economy has prospered since entry into the European Union, with an average annual growth rate of 4.6% between 1995 and 2001. The public debt is still relatively high by Finnish standards at 50% of GDP in 2001 (€73 billion – approx. £45/US$63 billion), although considerably lower than the EU average of 73%.

With the entry into the Single Market the economy has had to open up. It was only in 1993 that foreign companies were allowed to own Finnish ones, an innovation that led to a share-buying boom from abroad. Foreign companies have been slow to widen their operations in Finland, and most interest has come from Scandinavia. As a consequence of Finland's small domestic market and rather specialised economy, outward investment has outstripped inward investment by about 50%. After a downturn at the end of 2001, business confidence is on an upward trend again, however, much depends on the economic outlook for Finland's two main export markets, the United States and Germany.

Since the break-up of the Soviet Union, Finland has tried to promote itself as the business centre of the 'New Northern Europe'. Since the former Soviet economies have performed very poorly in the last decade, with the exception of the Baltic States of Estonia, Latvia and Lithuania, it remains to be seen what advantages Finland can gain from the new political set-up in its region. On the downside, cheap imports of wood products from Russia have become a serious threat to Finland and Sweden's dominant position in this area.

The economy base is a mixture of private and state ownership. State industries are still considered, to some extent, to be the bedrock of the economy. Valtionrautatiet (the national railways), Finnair, the national carrier, and the Finland Post Corporation are 100% owned by the state. The state still held over half the shares in Kemira (chemicals) and Sonera (formerly Finland Telecom) at the end of 2000, and large stakes in a number of leading and diversified enterprises. Some firms have been wholly privatised, such as Neste (chemicals) and Tampella (metals). The state's monopoly on alcohol sales will end in 2002 in accordance with EU regulations.

GEOGRAPHICAL INFORMATION

Area and Main Physical Features

Suomi Finland, the Republic of Finland, is one of the Nordic countries located in the far north-east of Europe; only Iceland lies further north. Strictly speaking it is neither geographically nor culturally part of Scandinavia, but for the sake of convenience most people assume that it is. One third of its area of 338,000 square kms/130,000 square miles lies within the Arctic Circle. In total area, Finland is the fifth largest European country in Europe after Germany, France, Spain and Sweden. In the north of the country is Lapland, a part of a huge wilderness that cuts a swathe also across Norway and Sweden, and which has its own regional culture and traditions.

Finland is a long, thin country (maximum length 1,160km/720 miles; maximum width 543km/337 miles), and therefore, not surprisingly, there is a considerable difference in the landscape from north to south. The south is characterised by gently rolling landscapes which become hillier and more forested as you go north. About 60% of Finland is tree-covered, which makes it the most densely forested country in Europe. Physically, much of the country is lowland, which falls gradually to the south and south-east. The only mountainous region is the north-west tip of Enontekiö towards Norway, where there are peaks of 1,000m/3,280 feet. The highest point is Halti, at 1,328m/4,356 feet.

Like Canada, Finland is a land of lakes. There are about 188,000 in total representing 10% of the surface area of Finland. Statistically, this works out at 37 metres/121 feet of lakeside for every inhabitant. The largest, Lake Saimaa (4,400 square kms/2,734 square miles) is also Europe's fourth largest expanse of water. However, the lakes tend to shallowness with an average depth of 7m/22 feet and the deepest at 95m/305 feet.

Neighbouring Countries and Coasts

Finland has a frontier of 2,570kms/1,596 miles, of which 1,269kms/788 miles is with Russia, 716kms/444 miles with Norway and 586kms/364 miles with Sweden.

To the south and west Finland is bounded by the Baltic Sea and the Gulfs of Finland and Bothnia. The shallow Baltic is the largest area of brackish water in the world. The coastline is approximately 1,100kms/683 miles. Finnish islands are as profuse as its lakes: about 30,000 of them lie scattered mainly off the south and south-west coasts. The autonomous region of the Åland Islands is among those to the south-west.

Regional Divisions and Main Towns

Finland is divided into 12 provinces (*lääni*): Uusimaa, Hame, Turku-Pori, Kymi, Mikkeli, Keski Suomi, Kuopio, Vaasa, Pohjois-Karjala, Oulu, Lappi and Åland. The general administration in each province is carried out by a provincial board headed by a governor appointed by the President. Under the provincial board come the local authorities with *nimismies* (sheriffs), of which there are 224. In the ancient historical boroughs, a magistrate may be appointed instead of a sheriff. Both functionaries represent the highest legal authority in their province.

Helsinki (Helsingfors in Swedish), the nation's capital since 1812, is the largest city with a population of 556,000. The populations and the Finnish/Swedish names of the other largest towns are:

Espoo/Esbo	214,000
Tampere/Tammerfors	200,000
Turku/Åbo	175,000
Vantaa/Vanda	170,000
Oulu/Uleåborg	110,000
Lahti/Lahtis	97,000
Kuopio	86,000
Pori/Björne	83,000

Population

The original inhabitants were a combination of settlers (Lapps) who arrived after the last Ice Age and tribes who arrived most probably from the Urals and the Volga via the East Baltic region at the beginning of the Christian era. In the 1750s, the population for the whole Finnish land was under half a million (the population of Helsinki today). By 1870 it had reached 1,769,000 and in the next 45 years it doubled. It was not until after World War II that it reached 4 million after which the birth rate declined. The current population of 5 million was reached in 1992, making Finland one of the most sparsely populated nations in Europe. Only Iceland and Norway have fewer inhabitants. There are minority groups: the Lapps/Sami of whom there are about 4,400, the majority of whom live in the Lapp/Sami districts of Enontekiö,

Inari, Utsjoki and Sodankylä and the gypsies of whom there are about 5,500, who live mostly in the south. The population of the Åland Islands is Swedish-speaking as they were part of that country in former times.

In the Helsinki metropolitan area, which includes the towns of Espoo, Vantaa and Kauniainen, now has 1 million inhabitants making it easily the most densely populated area of Finland. Over half of the country's total population live in the three southwest provinces comprising 15% of Finland.

It has been forecast that the population of Finland will actually decline. This is in part due to the low birth rate (ironically Finnish males have the highest sperm count in the world), and partly due to emigration. A total of about 250,000 Finns are estimated to have left the country for Sweden, while 280,000 have gone to the US, about 20,000 to Canada, and 10,000 to Australia during this century.

Climate

The Finnish climate is classified as temperate, but winters are extremely cold. Seasonal temperatures are influenced by the internal waters of Finland and the surrounding oceans: for instance the west winds blow from the Atlantic after warming up over the Gulf Stream.

There are two main climatic zones in Finland: the Arctic north and the temperate south. In summer temperatures in the north are about 3°C lower than in the south. The average maximum for July is about 20°C, although temperatures can go as high as 30°C. Winter lasts from November to mid-March and is very cold with average minimum temperatures in Helsinki of -20°C the coldest months being January and February. The north is much colder; snow cover lasts from mid-October to mid-May, and, in the extreme north, the sun does not rise for nearly six months. In contrast there can be as many as 70 nightless days in the brief Arctic summer. The warm summers invariably cause a plague of mosquitoes and gnats, worst in the north and lakelands where liberal use of insect-repellent is essential.

The parts of the country which are consistently the warmest are the southwest and the Åland Islands.

REGIONS' REPORT

Information Facilities

Although Finland does not suffer the annual tourist invasion of other, more sun-baked European destinations, tourism nevertheless provides an important source of revenue, and tourists are well-catered for with nationally-run offices and organisations. The most important is the Finnish Tourist Association, which publishes the official guides. All large tourist centres have a tourist office and most districts have a tourist manager responsible for developing and co-ordinating tourism in their area. Addresses of some of the main tourist offices are given below.

THE SOUTHWEST INCLUDING HELSINKI

Helsinki (*Helsingfors* in Swedish) was founded in 1550 by the Swedish King Gustav Vasa; Finland's new Russian masters made Helsinki the capital in place of Turku in 1812. Set on a peninsula, it has a convenient grid layout; the centre has changed little since the 1890s. Helsinki and the southwest are the cultural and industrial heartland of Finland, but every Finn will tell you that Helsinki is not at all typical of Finland. Fortunately, in spite of its size, the city has still kept some of its village atmosphere. The current influx of Russians and other foreigners is giving the city the same cosmopolitan atmosphere that it had in earlier times. Among the southwest's cultural attractions are the former capital Turku as well as Porvoo and Pori. The latter holds an annual international jazz festival.

The Coast, Archipelago & the Åland Islands

The mass of islands off the southwest are known as the Turku archipelago and are now a maritime national park. This region is popular with tourists, and many Finns have holiday cottages there. It is especially favourable for sailing; tides are minimal and the water of the Baltic is less salty than many seas as little salt water percolates through the straits of Denmark. In fact the Baltic is mainly topped up by the rainfall and rivers of Finland. As you might expect, the warmest part of the country has no shortage of popular resorts including Ekenäs, Hanko, Hyvinkää, Hämeenlinna, Kotka, Kouvola, Kuusankoski, Naantali and Lohja.

The Åland Islands (6,500 of them), are set in the Gulf of Bothnia between Sweden and Finland. For historical reasons they are Swedish-speaking, although an autonomous region connected to Finland. They have cultural ties with both Sweden and Finland. The only town of any size is Mariehamn. The main industry of these islands used to be shipping and fishing but these days tourism is becoming more and more important. 'Rod-and-line safaris' are big business in these parts.

Main Tourist Offices

Finnish Tourist Board, 30-35 Pall Mall, London SW1; ☎020-7839 4048; e-mail mek.lon@mek.fi; www.finland-tourism.com/uk, www.mek.fi.

Finnish Tourist Board, 655 Third Ave, New York, NY 10017; ☎212 885 9700; fax 212 885 9739; www.finland-tourism.com.

Finnish Tourist Board, Eteläesplanadi 4, 00200 Helsinki; ☎09 4176 9300; fax 09 4176 9301; www.mek.fi.

Helsinki City Tourist Office, Pohjoisesplanadi 19, 00200 Helsinki; ☎09 169 3757; fax 09 169 3839; www.hel.fi.

Åland Tourist Office, Storagatan 8, 22100 Mariehamn; ☎018 240 00; fax 018 242 65; www.goaland.net.

Pori Tourist Office, Raatihuone, Hallituskatu 9A, 28100 Pori; ☎02 6211 273; fax 02 6211 275; www.pori.fi.

Turku Touring, Aurakatu 4, 20100 Turku; ☎02 262 7444; fax 02 262 7674; www.turku.fi.

THE FINNISH LAKELAND

The part of Finland known as the Lakeland or Saimaa Lakeland, after its largest lake, is where the majority of Finland's 188,000 lakes are situated. This veritable maze of waterways lends itself to exploration, with its links formed by rivers, straits and canals. There are many lake steamers offering varied itineraries, and because the lakes are shallow they are not too cold for swimming. The mosquito is the biggest threat to enjoyment of this beautiful region.

The biggest tourist centre and Finland's second city is Tampere on the western edge of the Lakelands, which extend as far north as Iisalmi, and east as far as the frontier with Russia. The western edge of Lakelands also includes Hämeenlinna (the birthplace of Sibelius) and Lahti, a winter sports centre, while Jyväskyla, which lies further north is renowned for its modern architecture. The eastern region of the Lakelands contains the vast Saimaa lake and a profusion of interconnected lakes with no fewer than 33,000 islets within them. It is possible to follow a network of waterways between the major towns such as Savonlinna, Mikkeli and Kuopio.

Main Tourist Offices

Häeenlinna Tourist Office, Raatihuoneenkatu 11, 13101 Hämenlinna; ☎03 621 3374; fax 03 621 2764; www.hameenlinna.fi.

Kuopio Info, Haapaniemenkatu 17, 70110 Kuopio; ☎017 182 584; fax 017 261 3538; www.kuopioinfo.fi.

Mikkeli Tourist Service, Hallituskatu 3a, 50100 Mikkeli; ☎015 151 490; fax 015 151 625.

Savonlinna Tourist Service, Puistokatu 1, 57100 Savonlinna; ☎015 517 510; fax 015 517 5123.

Kaupungin Matkailutoimisto, Verkatehtaankatu 2, 33101 Tampere; ☎03 3146 6800; fax 03 3146 6463; www.tampere.fi.

BOTHNIA

The west coast area lies on the gulf of the same name, across which lies Sweden. This is the main agricultural region whose coast has long, sandy beaches. The islands between Vaasa and Kokkola have old fishing villages; many coastal houses are of the traditional wooden type. Vaasa, and the coastal area around it, has a large concentration of Swedish speakers. Further north is the university town of Oulu which is a centre of the computer industry. The inland town of Seinäjoki has municipal buildings designed by the internationally renowned architect Alvar Aalto. Other main towns on the coast are Jakobstad and Raahe. There are ferry connections with Sweden from Vaasa and Kokkola.

Main Tourist Offices

Kaupungin matkailutoimisto, Mannerheiminaukio, 67100 Kokkola; ☎06 831 1902; fax 06 831 0306; www.kokkola.fi.

Oulu Tourist Services, Torikatu 10, 90100 Oulu; ☎08 5584 1320; fax 08 5584 1711; www.oulutourism.fi.

Vaasan matkailutoimisto, Kaupungintalo, PL 3, 65101 Vaasa; ☎06 325 1145; fax 06 325 3620; www.vaasa.fi.

EASTERN FINLAND

The eastern part of Finland lies between the lakelands and Lapland and and has characteristics of both at its southern and northern limits. It is a sparsely populated area of thick forests and clear lakes. The southern part, roughly the Joensuu-Ilomantsi district, is known as the cradle of Karelian and Orthodox culture whose influence was at its strongest at the turn of the century, especially on literature. The best internationally known Finnish literary work, the *Kalevala,* a collection of epic folk poetry published in 1835 by Elias Lönnrot, was written after his travels, mainly in Karelia, to search for and record folklore. These traditions underpin rural values which are at the heart of most Finns' culture.

The region is also popular with Finns for spectacular hiking, shooting the rapids and winter sports. North from Kainuu and Kuusamo the character of the landscape becomes more like Lapland.

Main Tourist Office
Karelia Expert, Koskikatu 5, 80100 Joensuu; ☎013 267 5223; fax 013 123 933; www.jns.fi.

LAPLAND

There are no towns of any size in Lapland and it would be extremely difficult to live and work there, unless you were skilled with reindeer. However, the inspiring if desolate landscapes are attractive as a place to get away from the world, especially hiking trips where you are still likely to see the Sami, itinerant reindeer herders whose way of life has changed little with modern times. The region is characterised by rivers, swamps and some forested valleys. In the northernmost regions there is only tundra and scrubland. The four main towns of the region are Rovaniemi, Kemijärvi, Tornio and Kemi. There are reckoned to be 200,000 people inhabiting this vast region of 100,000 square miles, which works out at two inhabitants per square mile. About 4,000 of these are Lapps; there are about 600 Skolt Lapps who belong to the Orthodox Church. From September to January there are round-ups of the estimated half a million reindeer, and reindeer-driving competitions attract participants from all over the region.

Lapland is the official home of Santa Claus, known as *Joulupukki* in Finnish. Rather bizarrely, *Joulupukki* actually means 'evil Christmas stud goat' in Finnish; Santa somehow got mixed up with a goat spirit that demanded presents at Christmas. Santa inhabits a log cabin in Santa Claus Village near Rovaniemi, and is on duty all the year round to meet tourists. Here he has to answer more than 1 million letters a year, with the help of his secretaries; he expects payment up front for letters. He is on the internet at www.santaclausoffice.fi.

Main Tourist Offices
Kemi Tourist Info, Kauppakatu 29, 94100 Kemi; ☎016 259 690; fax 016 259 465; www.kemi.fi.
Rovaniemen matkailutoimisto, Koskikatu 1, 96200 Rovaniemi; ☎016 346 270; fax 016 342 4650; www.rovaniemi.fi.

GETTING TO FINLAND

Air

Flying is the quickest and cheapest way to get to Finland from the UK and the USA. The flight time from London Stansted is only 2 hours 50 minutes; coming back takes half an hour longer. The cheapest single fares from London are with Buzz Airlines, with offers starting from £45.00 (excluding tax). For return flights there are offers as low as £99.00 on www.ebookers.com with Finnair, British Airways and SAS, with flights from London Heathrow, Gatwick and from Manchester. The Finn-Guild in London offers special deals to its members for a similar price. From North America, only Finnair offer direct flights to Helsinki from New York; there are also direct flights three times a week from Toronto in the summer. Otherwise you will have to change in Stockholm or elsewhere. Prices for return flights vary between $450 return low season to $900 high season. It may be cheaper to fly to London first. If you fly Finnair or SAS it is possible to add on very cheap flights within Finland to your return ticket. In the case of SAS these are with their partner Air Bothnia.

Useful Addresses

Buzz Airlines, www.buzzaway.com.
Finnair, 14 Clifford St, London W1S 4BX; ☎0870-241 4411; fax-020 7629 7289; www.finnair.co.uk.
Finnair, 228 East 45th Street, New York, NY 10017; ☎212-499-9000; fax 212-499-9059; www.finnair.com.
Finn-Guild, 33 Albion St, London SE16 7GJ; ☎020-7237 4589; fax 020-7231 4261; e-mail guild-travel@finn-guild.org; www.finn-guild.org.

Sea and Rail

There are no direct rail links to the rest of Europe, nor are there any direct ferries from the UK. There are several ferry connections a week from Germany to Helsinki and nearby Hanko, leaving from Rostock, Travemünde and Lübeck; the journey takes from 21 to 36 hours. There are also daily ferries from Stockholm to Helsinki (14 hours) and from Umeå to Vaasa further north. One may also take the ferry to Turku (or Åbo) from Stockholm, and then the train to Helsinki, or stop off in the Åland islands on the way.

RESIDENCE AND ENTRY REGULATIONS

CURRENT POSITION

Finland is comparatively speaking one of the newest members of the European Union, having joined on January 1st 1995. Finnish entry and residence regulations were changed as early as January 1994 when the European Economic Area (EEA) agreement came into effect. Under these regulations nationals of other EU countries do not need work permits. Furthermore, residence permits will automatically be given for stays of longer than three months, provided that you can support yourself and you have no criminal record in Finland. Nationals of other Nordic countries (Sweden, Denmark, Norway and Iceland) are entitled to be treated exactly the same as Finnish citizens for however long they wish to remain in Finland.

Finland signed up to the Schengen agreement on 25 March 2001. The main implication for travellers is that border controls are in theory abolished for anyone entering from another Schengen country (in 2002 this included 13 EU countries, as well as Norway and Iceland, but excluded the UK and the Irish Republic).

Family members of EU or EEA citizens who are not themselves EU or EEA citizens will still have to comply with the visa requirements for non-EU/EEA nationals and will have no right of residence on their own account, but only if joining the EU/EEA national.

PASSPORTS AND IDENTITY CARDS

EU and EEA citizens arriving in Finland need a valid passport or approved identity card. Finland recognises identity cards issued by the following nations: Austria, Belgium, France, Germany, Italy, Liechtenstein, Luxembourg, the Netherlands and San Marino. As with all EU countries, Finland still has the right to refuse entry to or deport EU citizens who are deemed likely to become a public charge or engage in illegal or immoral activities (e.g. sex-workers). Note that if you arrive in Finland in a car on a ferry you may be breathalised.

ENTRY FOR EU NATIONALS

Nationals of the UK and other EU countries can travel to Finland to look for work and then take up permanent residence; they do not have to seek prior permission or obtain an entry visa. In other words, there is no difference at this stage whether someone is entering Finland as a tourist or a potential resident. Registration with the police or any other authority on arrival is not necessary. It may be necessary, however, to obtain a Personal Identification Number in order to open a bank account and have access to various services.

Those who have a job to go to in Finland, or who intend to look for one on arrival, must apply for a residence permit within three months of entering Finland. In practice, it is advisable to go to the Aliens Permit police office if you have any intention of working, even if it is only for a short time. Note that you always go to the Aliens Police first, even if your dossier is actually dealt with by the Immigration Office.

RESIDENCE PERMIT

Residence permits are granted by the local police authorities in the place of residence and are valid for up to five years if employment lasts longer than one year. After five years, renewal or permanent residence can be applied for. The renewal of a residence permit may be restricted if the applicant has been unemployed for more than one year before the first permit expired.

If the period of work is for less than one year then a residence permit will be granted for the period of employment only. Work can be started before the permit has been obtained. Although work permits are no longer required by EU citizens wishing to work in Finland they still need to obtain an employer's certificate before applying for the residence permit.

After receiving the residence permit you have to go on the population register (see below).

ENTRY FOR NON-EU NATIONALS

Non-EU nationals need to apply for a Schengen visa from their nearest Finnish embassy or consulate; US, Canadian, Australian and New Zealand citizens will normally be given a three-month visa when they land in a Schengen country, assuming that they have funds to support themselves. If you arrive in Finland from another Schengen country then it is possible that your passport will not be checked at all. Visa and passport information can be found on the Finnish Foreign Ministry website: www.finland.formin.fi/english. The Interior Ministry also has some general information on its website: www.intermin.fi/eng/schengen.

Non-EU nationals who wish to stay in Finland for more than three months have to apply for a residence permit before they leave their country of origin. If you arrive on a Schengen visa and plan to stay for longer than one month you will need to submit an official notification of new residence within three days of arrival to the Immigration Office. In Helsinki this is located at Siltasaarenkatu 12A (☎09 476 5500). In most cases, your hotel will already have notified the authorities of your arrival. If you have not been registered at a hotel, then there are special forms for this available from caretakers of apartment blocks, or from a post office or registration office (*maistraatti*).

Non-EU nationals planning to work or undertake some kind of training scheme will also need a work permit. This condition is relaxed for foreign employees staying in Finland for less than six months, whose work is deemed to be essential to the economy; this mainly applies to IT and telecoms specialists. The authorities are very strict about non-EU nationals starting work before they have all the necessary papers. If coming as a trainee on a recognised practical programme then a trainee work permit (valid for one to 18 months) should be applied for.

Students

Students who have arrived on a visa and who successfully pass an entry examination, are given a residence permit for one academic year at a time by the local police authorities. They must be able to satisfy the authorities that they have funds or scholarships that will cover study and living expenses and are expected to deposit funds of €5,000 (approx. £3,000/US$4,350) in a Finnish bank. A similar deposit is expected at the beginning of each academic year. Sponsored/exchange students must show proof of acceptance. A student also has the right to work while studying and no permit is required.

Trainee Work Permit.

Trainee Work Permits are granted to those coming to Finland to carry out practical training in their own professional or academic field. The main body authorised to issue trainee permits is the Centre for International Mobility (CIMO). Candidates must submit a written statement of employment from the prospective employer and a certificate signed and authorised by CIMO to the Finnish Embassy or Legation in their home country which will stamp the trainee work permit (Status B5) into the applicant's passport. After this, a residence permit will automatically be granted for the same period as the work placement.

ENTERING FINLAND TO START A BUSINESS

EU nationals who wish to carry out entrepreneurial activities or be self-employed in Finland must have a certificate of registration of a business or trade, or other suitable evidence of the type of business being carried out before applying for a residence permit.

REGISTRATION

Anyone, regardless of nationality, who is going to stay in Finland for more than one year has to fill in the 'Registration Information on a Foreigner' form at their local Register Office (*maistraatti*) in order to be included on the population register. This formality requires presentation of your passport and a valid residence permit. On this basis you will receive a Personal Identification Number (PIN) which allows you to apply for a sickness insurance card, or *KELA kortti*. Note that you can apply for the PIN as soon as you arrive, if you think that you will require it, for example, to install a telephone. Anyone who moves house within Finland has to submit a Notice of Moving to their Population Register Office.

NATIONALITY & CITIZENSHIP ONCE IN FINLAND

On expiry of the five-year residence permit, an employee may apply for a further five-year renewal, or a permanent residence permit. An employee also becomes eligible to apply for Finnish citizenship after five years. Men between 18 and 60 are liable for call-up to the armed forces, or may be expected to take part in military exercises after having completed their military service, but only Finnish citizens can serve in the armed forces.

Useful Addresses

Embassy of Finland, 38 Chesham Place, London SW1X 8HW; ☎020-7838 6200; fax 020-7235 3680; www.finemb.org.uk.

Embassy of Finland, 3301 Massachusetts Ave NW, Washington, DC 20008; ☎202-298 5800; fax 202-298 6030; www.finland.org.

British Embassy, Itäinen Puistotie 17, 00140 Helsinki; ☎09 2286 5100; fax 09 2286 5262; www.ukembassy.fi.

US Embassy, Itäinen Puistotie 14B, 00140 Helsinki; ☎09 171 931; www.usembassy.fi

Ministry for Foreign Affairs, Passport and Visa Unit, POB 176, 00161 Helsinki; ☎09 134 151; fax 09 1341 5684; e-mail oik-33@formin.fi; www.formin.finland.fi/english.

Ministry of the Interior, Kirkkokatu 12, Helsinki; ☎09 1601 1;

www.intermin.fi. Any questions about residence permits can be addressed to the customer service.

Aliens Permit Police Office, Punanotkonkatu 2, Helsinki; ☎09 1891.

Directorate of Immigration, Siltasaarenkatu 12A, 00530 Helsinki; ☎09 476 5500; e-mail ulkomaalaisvirasto@uvi.fi. Information in English can be found on the Directorate of Immigration's website: www.uvi.fi/englanti.

Ministry of Labour, Fabianinkatu 32, 00100 Helsinki; ☎09 18561; fax 09 1856 9181; www.mol.fi. Contact for any questions concerning work permits.

Population Register Office, Albertinkatu 25, Helsinki; ☎6954 4312.

Ombudsman for Foreigners, Mikonkatu 4, Helsinki; ☎18 561.

SETTING UP HOME

Foreigners living and working in Finland tend to be concentrated in the Helsinki metropolitan area where over a million inhabitants are based. The urban areas commenced their sprawl during the mass exodus from the countryside to the towns during the 50s and 60s. There was already a housing shortage following the destruction brought about by World War II. According to the government, there is now adequate housing for all. For foreigners the situation is not so simple, but everything depends on where you want to live, of course.

HOW DO THE FINNS LIVE?

Most of the housing stock dates from after 1970, and is therefore in good condition. About 90% of dwellings have all the modern amenities; some 10% of units have no bath or shower, but there are public saunas to take their place. Double doors and double-, or even triple-glazing are standard in modern dwellings. The traditional type of wooden house also survives, especially in the countryside; when equipped with a tiled ceiling-high stove, indoor temperatures can be overwhelming. It is said that Finns are still distrustful of city life; their ideal is 'a lakeshore cottage in the middle of a town'. There are about 450,000 summer cottages; most Finns aspire to own one.

Roughly two-thirds of dwellings are owner-occupied, although the term 'owner-occupied' does not necessarily mean the same as in other countries. Rented accommodation accounts for some 30% of units. About 0.8% are Right of Occupancy dwellings, a form of tenancy falling between rental and ownership; other forms of tenure account for the rest. In the past there were restrictions on foreigners buying property in Finland, but these have now been abolished.

Foreigners, especially those from North America, may find Finnish dwellings have very small bedrooms, even if the living rooms are of a good size. The necessity of having a sauna in one's house or apartment cuts down on the amount of floor space.

THE HOUSING FUND OF THE REPUBLIC OF FINLAND

Finland has had an organised housing strategy since the 1950s, and has used original and ingenious methods of financing construction which the rest of the world could learn a lot from. Housing policy comes under the Ministry of the Environment through the HFRF ('Housing Fund of the Republic Finland') or ARA in Finnish, which deals with all aspects of housing except for the payment of housing allowances. ARA has two main functions: the financing of housing and quality control of all types of housing.

The ARA's budget is strictly separated from the state budget; although grants may be made by the state to the ARA when the need arises. The role of the state in building has increased enormously recently; some 75% of dwellings have been built with some form of state subsidy in the last few years. The ARA grants state ARAVA loans for building and renovation of housing intended for rental or right-of-occupancy, to municipalities, housing corporations, associations and foundations. Commercial loans are supported through interest-subsidy schemes targeted at housing companies. Direct government loans for construction have virtually ceased. Part of the interest on housing loans to individuals is tax-deductible. Most loans are taken out with commercial banks; there are few mortgage institutions as such.

In order to cut down on the public debt, the ARA securitises loans through a special-purpose company known as Fennica, using the backing of its high-quality loan portfolio to raise funds on the commercial market. This was the first public securitisation sponsored by an agency of a European central government. Further details on how housing is financed in Finland can be found on the ARA website: www.vyh.fi/ara.

RENTING

Forms of ownership and tenancy in Finland are somewhat different from those in other countries. About 54% of houses are detached or semi-detached; 43% of dwelling units are in blocks of flats. Many blocks of flats are owned by housing companies; members hold a share in the company which entitles them to the right of possession – that is, the physical control and occupancy – of an apartment. Shares can be bought and sold, or used as security for a loan, but the building and land remain the property of the housing company. In return for managing and maintaining the building the housing company collects a maintenance charge. There is a board with a manager and auditor. Residents have the right to be informed about the running of the building they live in. Tenants who fail to pay maintenance charges can be evicted for a maximum of three years while the arrears are recouped.

In order to apply for a state-subsidised (ARAVA) rental dwelling, you should first go to the municipal housing office to find out if your income is low enough to qualify. Your application will have to be accompanied by a tax certificate, an income certificate and an extract from the population register. You will then be placed on a waiting list. Further information on rental can be found in a booklet *Key Information for Tenants* published by the Central Central Union of Tenants (see www.vuokralaistenkeskusliitto.fi for an order form, or call 09 477 1301).

In the free-market sector, rent regulation was abolished in 1995. Rental values vary widely over the country. In central Helsinki the average rent is about €16 (approx. £10/US$14) per square metre per month. Government-subsidised rentals average €6.50 nationally; in the non-subsidised sector the average is €7.50. An average dwelling has 77 square metres of floor area. Rental contracts can be for any length of time; typically they are for three years or more. The lessor has the right to increase the rent annually in line with the inflation index, or lessor and tenant can negotiate a new rent. If no agreement is reached, then the tenant can leave after six months during which the rent remains unaltered. Foreigners often find themselves renting a house or flat from a Finn who has gone abroad; the contract may be for one year, with an option for another two years, or vice versa. Properties are advertised in newspapers such as *Helsingin Sanomat* and also on the internet through the DIME website: www.dime.net owned by Alma Media; 65% of estate agents advertise properties on this website.

As stated in *Key Information for Tenants*, it is important to find out whether the person who is renting you the property is the legal owner, and whether they have permission to sublet their property. The lessor can ask for a deposit of up to three months' rent; in most cases the deposit is two months' rent. The period of notice – in the case of a non-fixed term lease – from the lessor's side is three months if the lease is shorter than one year, or six months where it is over one year. From the tenant's side it is always one month. Notice of termination should be done by registered letter.

The lessor has an obligation to keep the dwelling in a habitable condition; the tenant is not liable for ordinary wear and tear. It is advisable to have a written agreement on the responsibilities of the two parties for the upkeep of a property to avoid disputes. Where disputes arise, one may have recourse to one of the housing courts that operate in the main Finnish cities. These have one representative from the Central Union of Tenants, and one from the Finnish Real Estate Federation, as well as a professional judge.

If you come to Finland to work for a local company your accommodation may be arranged for you. If you come looking for a job or are on a low income, the situation can be difficult. In Helsinki there is a 10-year waiting list for public housing, and Helsinki natives are at the top of the list. If at all possible, you should try to get yourself declared homeless. There is intense competition for private rented accommodation; if you are unable to speak Finnish you will be at a disadvantage. Following changes to the law in 2001, many rental agencies now claim to only rent to companies, or to customers who register with them. The rental agency can charge the owner of a property a fee of 1.22 times one month's rent, but it is now becoming more common for the prospective tenant to be charged.

Right of Occupancy Apartments.

A recent innovation which is in between renting and buying is the so-called 'Right of Occupancy' apartment whereby the occupier pays up to 15% of the value of the property plus monthly rent. This gives a high degree of security of tenure without the full expense of purchase. ROO housing is intended for those aged 18 or over, who are unable to afford other housing. Fewer than 1% of dwellings fall into this category.

BUYING

Prices of dwellings vary greatly over the country. As a rough guideline, a property in the Helsinki region will cost about twice as much as one in the rest of the country. In 2001, a flat in an older block of flats in the Helsinki area cost on average €2,100 per square metre (approx. £1,300 or US$1,800). There are few flats available smaller than 50 square metres. In the suburbs, such as Vantaa, a traditional four-bedroom wooden house may fetch €300,000 (approx. £186,000/US$260,000). The prices in the rest of the country are half as much, but there is wide variation between the affluent centres of high-tech industry and the more impoverished centre and north. Loans are generally taken out through commercial banks; some foreign banks in Finland will also grant loans.

Useful Addresses

Estate Agents in Finland:
Helsingin Liiketeollinen Kiinteistönvälitys Oy, Mikonkatu 13G 186, 00100 Helsinki; ☎09 684 0680; fax 09 6840 6840.
Huoneistomarkkinointi Oy, Mannerheimintie 4, 00100 Helsinki; ☎09 680 851; fax 09 646 852.
Suomen SKV-Yrityspalvelu Oy, Sinimäentie 10C, 02630 Espoo; ☎09 8269 1230; fax 09 8269 1250 (commercial property).
Suomen Kiinteistöliitto ry (The Finnish Real Estate Federation), Annankatu 24, 00100 Helsinki; ☎09 166 761; www.skvl.fi.

Housing Organisations:
Association of Tenants and Home Owners in Finland, Käenkuja 3-5 N, 00500 Helsinki; ☎09 716 800.
Finnish House Owners' Association, Kulosaaren Puistotie 42, 00570 Helsinki; ☎09 684 9055.
Housing Reform Society, c/o VVO, PO Box 40, 00301 Helsinki; 09 43 6311.

Finance

In Finland the majority of loans for property purchase are organised through banks (about 70%) and the rest through a variety of institutions including savings and co-operative banks, insurance companies and central and local government.

Useful Addresses

Aktia Bank, ☎010 247 5000; www.aktia.fi.
Merita Bank, ☎09 165 431745; www.merita.fi.
Merita Bank plc, 19 Thomas More St, London E1W 1YF; ☎020 7265 3333.

Merita Bank, 437 Madison Ave, New York NY 10027; ☎212 318 9300.
Sampo Bank, ☎0200 2580; www.sampo.fi.
Suomen Hypoteekkiyhdistys (Mortgage Organisation), PL509, 00101 Helsinki; ☎09 228
   361; fax 09 647 443; www.hypoteekkiyhdistys.fi.

UTILITIES

Finland is a world leader in CHP (combined heat and power generation). Industries and electricity utilities jointly own co-generation plants where excess energy, such as coolant from power stations, is channelled into the municipal district heating network. The by-products of wood-processing are particularly useful for this. The Ministry of the Environment website has a great deal of information on energy efficiency in buildings. Gas is hardly used at all for domestic purposes; the gas supplied by Russia goes to industry. Finland also has four nuclear power stations; the waste is likely to be buried deep underground in Finland itself.

For information on electricity and heating contact *Helsingin Energia* on their free helpline for household customers: 09 0800 1 400 010 or see their website. The website www.motiva.fi also has information on energy efficiency.

Useful Addresses

Fortum Power and Heat, POB 40, 00048 FORTUM; ☎010 4511; fax 09 6185 8200;
   www.fortum.com.
Helsingin Energia, Kampinkuja 2, 00090 Helen, Helsinki; ☎09 6171; fax 09 617
   2360; e-mail helsinki.energy@helsinginenergia.fi; www.helsinginenergia.fi.
Ministry of the Environment, POB 380, 00131 Helsinki; ☎09 19 911; fax 09 1991
   9545; www.vyh.fi/eng.
Motiva Center for Energy Efficiency, PO Box 462, 02151 Espoo; ☎09 456 6090; fax
   09 456 7008; www.motiva.fi.

RELOCATORS

The task of relocators is to help employees of foreign companies to settle in quickly when posted abroad. Their services are not cheap, but they save employers a lot of money by ensuring that transfers are done as smoothly as possible. Services range from helping with immigration formalities, finding accommodation to looking at schools, to being on the end of a phone for 24 hours a day in case of emergencies.

Useful Address

Transite, Kasarmikatu 14 b 19; 00130 Helsinki; ☎09 260 9203; fax 09 260 9201;
   e-mail info@transite.fi; www.transite.fi.

REMOVALS

Personal Effects

EU citizens may import personal effects free of customs duties. In accordance with EU regulations, certain goods which could be a threat to public security or to animal or plant health are prohibited. Persons coming from outside the EU may import personal property which has been in use at their normal place of residence for at least six months prior to leaving. Such goods can be imported over a 12 month period, or in advance of arrival, with the permission of the customs authorities (see the website www.tulli.fi for details).

IMPORTING A CAR

Anyone who is taking up residency in Finland may import one motor vehicle, duty free, for private use, provided that he or she has owned it outside Finland, and been resident outside Finland for at least one year prior to importation. After the vehicle has been imported it may not be sold, hired out, or lent to anyone other than a family member (which includes couples living together but not married), until two years from the date of clearance have expired. In the event that the vehicle is damaged beyond repair before the two years are up, you may hand it over to your insurance company or sell it to a scrap dealer without paying duties and taxes provided that you have been granted tax relief.

All cars imported into Finland whether from an EU or non-EU country are liable for Car Tax. A car is considered as part of removal goods if it has been in use for at least six months prior to arrival in Finland. As an example, a 12-month-old car valued new at US$35,000 could attract tax of US$1,450. The precise details of Car Tax can be seen on the website www.tulli.fi. Car Tax will be dealt with when you register your car at the local Vehicle Administration Centre, which must be done within 30 days of arrival. Your car cannot be registered until it has been inspected and you have obtained motor insurance.

Insurance

Third party motor insurance is compulsory in Finland. Claims are dealt with by the *Liikennevakuutuskeskus* (Finnish Motor Insurers' Centre), Bulevardi 28, 00120 Helsinki; ☎09 680 401; fax 09 6804 0391; www.vakes.fi/lvk.

Useful Addresses

Tullihallitus (National Board of Customs), P.O. Box 512, 00101 Helsinki; ☎09 614 3800; fax 09 614 3813; www.tulli.fi.
Vehicle Administration Centre, Fabianinkatu 32, 00530 Helsinki; ☎0100 7800; fax 09 6185 3600; www.ake.fi.

IMPORTING PETS

Cats and dogs may be imported from the UK or Ireland without an import permit or health certificate if they travel directly to Finland or through any of the following countries: Sweden, Norway, Iceland or Ireland. Airlines and shipping companies will give the necessary information about the transportation of animals. If the animal is travelling overland through any country not mentioned above, then a rabies vaccination certificate is required.

Cats and dogs from the USA or Canada will require a health certificate and rabies vaccination. See the Finnish Ministry of Agriculture website: www.mmm.fi/eeo. The UK Department for the Environment, Food and Rural Affairs (DEFRA) gives information about re-importing pets into the UK. Call 0870-241 1710 or e-mail pets.helpline@defra.gsi.gov.uk.

DAILY LIFE

THE FINNISH LANGUAGE

In Finland there is not a great incentive to learn Finnish as most Finns speak a little English and many can converse fluently in it. However, in order to integrate yourself to a greater degree, you should aspire to learn some Finnish, not least because you will have greater access to Finnish culture. Unfortunately, Finnish is not for the faint-hearted as it is a difficult language to learn. Finnish is part of the Finno-Ugrian group of languages, which includes Estonian, Lappish and, more distantly, Hungarian. One of the main characteristics of these languages is the number of cases (15 in Finnish) appearing as suffixes. Cases broadly equate with prepositions in other languages. However these are not the only Finnish suffixes. There is a whole range of them, which alter the sound of the stem word in various ways. Articles do not exist and there is no grammatical distinction of gender; e.g. the same word *hän* is used for he and she.

As regards pronunciation, Finnish is reliable in that every letter is always pronounced the same. It is important to observe the stress on the first syllable of each word.

Words can be strung together to form a complete word of unwieldy length which at first can be rather intimidating. After you have acquired a basic vocabulary you can usually recognise the constituent bits of long words. Finnish has a claim to fame in that it has the longest palindrome (a word that spells the same forwards and backwards) found in any language, *saippuakauppias,* meaning soap salesman. Words likely to prove more useful in daily life are loanwords from languages that may be more familiar: *pankki* (bank), *sekki* (cheque) are fairly obvious, and *kauppa* (shop) is derived from the German *kaufen* (to buy).

As Swedish is Finland's second official language and spoken by 5.7% of Finns, place-names generally appear in both languages. Most Swedish-speakers are concentrated in the west and south-west and in the Åland islands. The use of Swedish is declining, and it is being replaced by English as Finland's second language. Sami and gypsies living in Finland have their own languages.

Learning Finnish

As you would expect, evening classes in Finnish are not commonplace in the UK. The best source of information is probably the University College London's School of Slavonic and East European Studies (Registry, Senate House, Malet Street, London WC1E 7HU; ☎020-7862 8517; www.ssees.ac.uk), which can provide a list of Finnish courses in the United Kingdom and in Finland. The Finnish UKAN organisation has information on courses in Finnish in other countries. The Finn-Guild promotes the study of Finnish in the UK at schools and also runs occasional one- or two-day courses for adults. Facilities for studying Finnish in the USA are shown on the University of Minnesota website: http://carla.acad.umn.edu/lctl/access.html.

Some Finnish universities run evening classes at reasonable prices. The courses at Helsinki University are very popular; the beginners' courses fill up quickly so book early. Linguarama may be able to arrange instruction in Finnish in the UK; they also run a language school in Helsinki. There is a self-study language course published by Routledge with two cassettes: *Colloquial Finnish* by Daniel Abondolo, available in some libraries.

There are some resources for Finnish on the internet. The site www.uta.fi gives a basic grammar of Finnish. There is a limited 1,800 word on-line dictionary at www.dictionaries.travlang.com; there are more complete dictionaries on www.yourdictionary.com. The Academic Bookstore in Helsinki lists every Finnish course in existence on its website: www.akateeminen.com; another list can be seen on the Finnish Embassy website in Washington DC: www.finland.org.

Useful Addresses

Finn-Guild, 33 Albion St, London SE16 7JG; ☎020-7237 7736; fax 020-7231 4261; www.finn-guild.org. As well as providing information about courses, scholarships and examinations, the Finn-Guild sells Finnish language courses on CD, and publishes the quarterly, bilingual newsletter *Horisontti*, through which one can make contact with Finnish speakers.

Finnish Institute, 35-36 Eagle Street, London WC1R 4AJ; ☎020-7404 3309; fax 020-7404 8893; info@finnish-institute.org.uk; www.finnish-institute.org.uk. The Finnish Institute in London is a cultural development agency that promotes Finnish excellence in the arts and sciences. Its mission covers the United Kingdom and Ireland.

Open weekdays Monday to Friday 10.00am-4.00pm.

UKAN *(Council for Finnish Studies at Universities Abroad)*, CIMO, POB 343, 00531 Helsinki; ukan@cimo.fi. Promotes the teaching of Finnish abroad.

University of Helsinki Language Centre, POB 33, 00141 Helsinki; ☎09 1912 3234; fax 09 191 22753; www.helsinki.fi/kksc/language.services.

Audio-Forum, 4 Foscote Mews, London W9 2HH; ☎020-7266 2202; www.ndirect.co.uk. Publishes Finnish language course. USA: Audio-Forum, c/o Jeffrey Norton Publishers, 96 Broad St, Guildford, CT 06437, USA; ☎203-453 9794; e-mail info@audioforum.com; www.audioforum.com.

SCHOOLS AND EDUCATION

Pre-School

As more than three-quarters of mothers in Finland go to work, childcare for the under-sevens is a priority. This area is under the control of the Ministry for Social Affairs and Health who are responsible for providing municipal day-care centres or registered child-minders. The state is legally obliged to provide day-care for children under school age. If a nursery place is not available the state provides financial compensation. Foreigners only qualify for the compensation if they can prove that they are going to stay in Finland for more than two years, as this is a 'residence-based' benefit. Since 2001 all six-year-old children are entitled to pre-school education.

Junior and Secondary Schooling

Schooling is compulsory for nine years from ages 7 to 16. The 10th year is optional. The educational system was reformed in the early 1970s when the basis of a comprehensive system aimed at reducing social and regional inequalities was laid down. Before the 1970s secondary schools were mostly fee-paying and private; now most are run by the municipalities. The range of compulsory subjects at junior level (forms 1-6), is an ambitious mixture of the practical, the mind-stretching and the creative: mathematics, religious knowledge, environmental studies, Finnish or Swedish (depending on mother tongue), foreign languages (English), history, social studies, civics, biology, geography, physical education, music, arts and handicrafts.

At senior level (forms 7-9) the same subjects are taught with the exception of environmental studies. Compulsory subjects at senior level include chemistry and physics, home economics and the second official language. At the senior level optional subjects are available including economics, other foreign languages, agriculture and computer studies.

Forms 10-12 (ages 17-19 years) are known as senior secondary school of which there are two types in Finland: the three-year *lukio* which roughly corresponds to a UK sixth form or a French baccalaureate class, i.e. the academic line, and the more practical vocational schools. Students study Finnish, Swedish, 1-3 foreign languages, maths, physics, chemistry, geography, biology, psychology, religious knowledge, art or music and hygiene. Some of these are compulsory subjects, others optional. Special *lukios* exist for fostering talent in music, art and physical education. At the end of a full 12-year education, students will have studied English for 10 years, Swedish for three, and possibly another language. Some Finnish-speaking parents send their children to Swedish-medium schools, since these are reckoned to offer a better education, and their offspring will become fluent in Swedish.

After three years the students sit a very competitive national matriculation exam, either in spring or autumn, to qualify for university entrance. There are usually some 30,000 qualified candidates for 18,000 university places, some of which are reserved. This results in a surplus of able candidates who have failed to get into university, who then have to reconsider their options. Many take a vocational education or go to work.

The organisation of general education is the responsibility of the municipality. Teaching, materials and school meals are all free. Children who live more than 5km from the school are provided with free transport. The state subsidises local authorities' education budgets by as much as is necessary to maintain them to the required standard. There is no limit to the state subsidy, which can be 100%.

Current Trends in School Education. In the sparsely populated areas of Finland schools can be very small with only two or three teachers teaching classes in which the age difference can be as much as four years. There have been moves in recent years to reduce class sizes generally and also to decentralise decision-making. Teachers and school boards have increasing freedom to run their local schools.

Higher Education

Finland's first university was the Royal Academy of Turku which was founded in 1640 at a time when Finland was part of Sweden. In 1828 the RA was transferred to the new capital Helsinki. Before Finnish independence in 1917, two other institutes of higher education were in existence and two additional universities were created immediately afterwards. Today there are 16 universities and four academies of art with a total student enrolment of 80,000, of whom about 2,000 are international students from about 40 countries. Helsinki is the largest university (26,000 students), followed by Turku and Tampere (10,000 students each). The technology university in Espoo (near Helsinki) has 9,000, Oulu has 8,000 and Jyväskylä 7,000 students.

Vocational Institutions and Polytechnics

Vocational training leads to a vocational degree. The basic training takes 2-3 years; in the near future all basic training will last 3 years. This will include on-the-job training of 6 months. Students who have successfully completed a vocational degree may then go on to a polytechnic or university.

Recently many vocational institutes have merged to form polytechnics and the process of consolidation is still going on. At the last count there were some 32 polytechnics. Polytechnics offer courses with a vocational emphasis lasting 3½ to 4½ years. Studies at vocational institutions and polytechnics are basically free. Adults may also pursue vocational training at these institutions. Further information can be found on the National Board of Education website: www.oph.fi; see also www.minedu.fi and www.hut.fi.

Student Grants and Loans. Students can apply for non-returnable state grants, or state-guaranteed low interest bank loans. Other state contributions to the cost of studying include subsidised hostels, health care and meals.

Useful Addresses

SAKKI, (Finnish Federation of Vocational Trainees), Siltasaarenkatu 3A, 00530 Helsinki; ☎ 09 772 1480; www.sak.fi.
National Union of Finnish Students (SYL), Kalevankatu 3 A 46, 00100 Helsinki; ☎ 09

680 3110; http://mail.syl.helsinki.fi.

Scholarships, Grants & Exchange Programmes

There are various international, European and Finnish organisations which can offer the above to students from abroad. CIMO publishes several brochures on studying in Finland, including: *An Overview of Higher Education in Finland, Higher Education in Finland, Polytechnics in Finland*, and several more. See their website for the full list.

Useful Addresses

Centre for International Mobility (CIMO), PO Box 343, Hakaniemenkatu 2, 00531 Helsinki; ☎09 7747 7033; e-mail cimoinfo@cimo.fi; www.cimo.fi.
The Academy of Finland, Hämeentie 158, 00550 Helsinki, ☎09 774 881; www.aka.fi.
Ministry of Education, Meritullinkatu 10, 00170 Helsinki; ☎09 134 1711; www.minedu.fi.
National Board of Education, Hakaniemenkatu 2, 00530 Helsinki; ☎09 774 775; fax 09 7747 7865; www.oph.fi/english.

Degrees

Until 1994, all Bachelor's or Master's degrees required about 5-7 years of study. However, in 1994 three-year bachelor degrees in humanities and science subjects were introduced. Government policy is to provide appropriately trained graduate researchers for the workplace particularly in science and technology subjects. This has been achieved by increasing the number of students in the sciences at the expense of the arts and social sciences.

Adult and Continuing Education

A parallel system of informal education exists alongside the full-time degree or diploma oriented education system. Originally conceived as a way of providing a general education and stimulating leisure time, adult education has steadily become more directed towards vocational training. Vocational education may involve training to upgrade skills, or training for a new vocation. Various organisations and associations run courses which are partly state-subsidised. For instance, the national network of workers' institutes nowadays has more than 600,000 students. They offer mainly evening classes in the traditional general and leisure subjects; also classes covering the senior secondary school syllabus (but usually without final certification), as well as vocational training. See websites www.ktol.fi and www.vsy.fi/faea/index.html for information on workers' institutes and adult education.

The folk high schools (*kansanopistot*) and academies are mainly residential; they have about 7,000 students a year and offer a similar mix of courses and vocational training. See the website: www.kansanopistot.fi.

Most universities have summer schools open to all. Only part of the tuition is at university level, the rest supplements vocational or upper secondary education.

International Schools

There are international, English, German, French, Russian and Jewish schools in Helsinki. Lessons are given partly in Finnish and partly in the language of the school. These schools are private, and charge fees for tuition.

Useful Addresses

Deutsche Schule, Malminkatu 14, 00100 Helsinki; ☎09 694 4464; fax 09 694 6927; www.dsh.edu.hel.fi.

The English Kindergarten, Y.E.S., Leinikkitie 20, Vantaa; 09 873 1078; fax 09 873 4698.

English School, Mäntytie 14, 00270 Helsinki; ☎477 1123; fax 09 477 1980; www.eschool.edu.hel.fi.

Helsingin ranskalais-suomalainen koulu (French-Finnish School of Helsinki), Raumantie 4, 00350 Helsinki; ☎09 561 551; fax 09 5615 5207; www.hrsk.edu.fi.

The International School of Helsinki, Selkämerenkatu 11, 00180 Helsinki; ☎09 686 6160; fax 09 685 6699; www.ish.edu.hel.fi.

MEDIA & COMMUNICATIONS

Newspapers

The Finnish press made its debut with the publication of a newspaper in Turku in 1771. A few magazines also appeared about the same time. The first regular newspaper was not published until 1809 when Finland was an autonomous Russian Grand Duchy. In the 1820s more newspapers appeared, but in Swedish. They include the oldest newspaper still being published today *Abå Underrättelser,* founded in 1824. The oldest Finnish-language journal is *Uusi Suomi* founded in 1847.

Today there are about 55 daily newspapers in Finnish and Swedish, with a combined circulation of 3.2 million, or 660 copies per 1,000 inhabitants. UNESCO statistics show Finns to be the world's third largest consumers of newsprint. There are about 10 leading newspapers, none of which is truly a national newspaper except perhaps *Helsingin Sanomat.* The daily *Uusi Suomi* has a page summarising the news in English. The main papers are: *Helsingin Sanomat, Ilta-Sanomat, Aamulehti, Turun Sanomat, Iltalehti* and *Kauppalehti.* The press receives state subsidies most of which go to the politically-affiliated papers.

Overseas newspapers, including US and British ones, can be bought at the *Academic Bookstore* in Helsinki (Pohjoisesplanadi 39).

Magazines

It is not possible to state the exact number of magazines in Finland because of the tradition of leafletting and private publishing that goes on there. The Post Office has over 1,000 publications on its delivery list. Many magazines are reviews and trade and professional journals. The leading magazines are a mixture of general interest, women's and cultural and political reviews.

Television & Radio

The Finnish Broadcasting Company (*Oy Yleisradio Ab*) known as YLE was established in 1926; it had a virtual monopoly on broadcasting until the 1950s. YLE's radio output consists of the usual array of programmes plus one unique claim to fame: *Nuntii Latini* (News in Latin) launched in 1989, a five-minute summary of worldwide events broadcast every Friday on international shortwave. Details of broadcasting times and wavelengths for radio programmes broadcast internationally can be obtained from YLE Radio Finland (Box 78, 00024 Yleisradio, Finland; www.yle.fi). You can listen to both recorded and live programmes in English via www.yle.fi/rfinland/english. Radio Finland broadcasts Finnish language lessons on Fridays and Saturdays.

In 1956 *Helsinki Tesvisio* and *Tampere Tamvisio* were granted broadcasting licences for television programmes. In 1957, a third company MTV (now renamed MTV3 to avoid confusion with Music TV) came into being and linked up with YLE which subsequently took over the Tesvisio and Tamvisio which became TV2. Although YLE and MTV3 work together they are entirely separate organisations. A third channel, TV3 started transmitting in 1986 and is a joint venture between YLE, MTV3 and Oy Nokia Ab. English Sky Channel and French ECS channel are available via satellite and cable. Since 1988, Swedish programmes have been available on TV4 which is aimed at Swedish subscribers in Finland and can only be received in the coastal zone where most of them live. Many English-language channels and the French TV5 are relayed by satellite and can be received by those with the appropriate equipment. The cable company HTV has over 100,000 subscribers in the Helsinki area. Almost half the programmes shown on the three main Finnish channels are home-grown. The most popular of these are Finnish films and serials.

Post and Telephone

Post. Postal services are highly efficient; letters posted before 5pm are guaranteed to get to anywhere except the most remote locations in Finland the next day. Stamps can be bought at newsstands, bus and railway stations, and post offices. As with other Scandinavian countries, it is necessary to specify when sending items abroad whether you want them to go 'A Prioritaire' (first class) or B economy class; there is a small difference in the price. It is necessary to put a sticker on Prioritaire items. The central post office in Helsinki, next to the main railway station, is open 9-6 Monday to Friday.

Telephone. There is a bewildering variety of different telecoms operators; the Finnet association includes 49 private operators. The telecoms market was deregulated early on, thus there is intense competition for customers and a host of special offers. The Helsinki area supposedly has the highest number of telephones per head of population in the world. The first place to try would be the local Sonera shop. The partly-privatised Sonera was formerly the state-owned Telecom Finland. Their website – www.sonera.net – explains all their tariffs in English. For private subscribers in Helsinki one company to contact is Elisa

Communications (once known as the Helsinki Telephone Company): ☎0800 9 5001; e-mail kotiasiakkaat@elisa.fi; www.elisa.com. The basic installation charge for a landline or 'analogical' phone, is €125 (approx. £77/US$108); there is a monthly rental fee of €12.5. Other well-known companies are Telia and Radiolinja.

The Helsinki telephone directory has a page of instructions in English. The area code for Helsinki metropolitan area is 09. Codes for other areas all start with 0. For direct dial international calls 00 is the international access code, followed by the country code, the area code and the subscriber's number. To call Finland from overseas dial the international access code then 358. There are cheaper access codes for phoning abroad, such as 990 and 999.

Most public telephones operate with phonecards. Colourfully designed phonecards (*tele puhelukortti*) of €5, €10 and €20 values, are sold by Sonera shops, R-Kiosk newsstands, post offices and other outlets such as bus stations in the vicinity of public telephones. Even a local call will cost a minimum of 50 cents.

The Finnish yellow pages are available on-line on: www.keltaisetsivut.fi, with some English explanations. The business pages – www.yritystele.fi – may be more useful for looking up businesses if one knows the Finnish word for the type of business one is looking for. One can also search for subscribers using their phone number.

CARS AND MOTORING

Foreigners may drive in Finland using their national driving licence for 12 months. After this time they have another six months in which to apply for a Finnish licence but may not drive their car. One can apply for a Finnish licence six months after arrival. Driving on your national licence after the 12 month period is illegal and your car could be impounded. The initial point of contact for the exchange of licences is the local police station. The same rules apply to North American citizens. Licences from some countries (notably China) are not recognised in Finland, and holders have to take the Finnish driving test.

Finland has an excellent road network of over 45,000km and congestion problems are almost unknown. There are no toll roads. Snow is a problem away from the main population centres, especially when it melts. The Road Administration (*Finnra*) has masterminded a road weather service supplying road users with weather forecasts complete with radar and satellite images, as well as webcams with pictures of roads: see www.tiehallinto.fi/eindex.htm. Elk and reindeer sometimes wander on to the highways and the former can cause considerable damage if collided with. Any collision, including those with elk and reindeer, should be reported to the police. Speed limits are 80kph except where indicated otherwise, and 100kph on motorways. In the summer the speed limit goes up to 120kph. Speed limits can be changed according to conditions using electronic signboards.

- ○ **Accidents and Breakdowns.** The countrywide number for all emergencies is 112.
- ○ **Parking.** In Helsinki and major towns parking is controlled by meters from 8am to 5pm Monday to Saturday. Sundays are free. The

maximum parking time varies between two and four hours. There are various ingenious new ways to pay for parking time, including using your mobile phone, or with a scratchcard from a R-Kiosk. *Pysäköiminen kielletty* means no parking. There is a parking information centre: e-mail palvelu@kv.hel.fi.

O **Petrol.** Petrol stations are open generally 7am to 9pm, six days a week. They generally also open on Sundays in holiday areas during summer only.

O **Regulations.** As with other Scandinavian countries, motorists and motorcyclists are required to drive with headlights any time of day or night outside built-up areas and regardless of weather conditions. Special winter tyres are compulsory from November to March.

TABLE 4	ROAD DIRECTIONS
aja hitaasti	slow
kelirikko	frost damage
keskusta	town centre
irtokiviä	loose stones
liukasta	slippery surface
lossi	ferry
räjäytystyö sulje radiolähetin	danger, explosives, switch off your radio
tietyö	road works

Useful Addresses

Touring Club, Autoliitto, Hämeentie 105A, 00550 Helsinki; ☎0200 8080 *or* 09 7258 4400.

Finnish Motor Insurers Bureau, Bulevardi 28, 00120 Helsinki; ☎09 680 401; www.vakes.fi/lvk.

Vehicle Administration Centre, Fabianinkatu 32, PL 120, 00530 Helsinki; ☎0100 7800; www.ake.fi.

TRANSPORT

Air. Internal flights are operated by Finnair, whose head office is at Asema-aukio 3, Helsinki (☎818 77 50; www.finnair.fi). There are more than 20 domestic airports and the flights are among the cheapest in Europe. There are discounts on certain routes at weekends. For the over-65s and young people aged 12-23 there is a 50% discount (with some restrictions). Buses to Helsinki-Vantaa airport from the city take about 40 minutes. For airport and flight information dial 02 00 46 36.

Rail. Finland has 6,000 kms (3,700 miles) of rail network. The railways are run by Finnish state railways (*Valtionrautatiet*; information 09 707 5700). There is an online English timetable at www.vr.fi. Seat reservations are required for Express

(EP) trains and InterCity (IC) trains. There are reductions for groups of three or more and for children under 12 years.

Bus. There is a network of long-distance buses, 300 of which depart from Helsinki daily with connections to all parts of the country. The majority are run by the ExpressBus company (www.expressbus.com). Bus fares are sometimes cheaper than second class rail fares. Rural areas are often served by post buses. Fares and timetables can be consulted on-line at www.matkahuolto.fi. *Matkahuolto* is the organisation that co-ordinates bus travel and runs the bus stations. There is a national timetable enquiry line on 0200 0400; calls cost €1 per minute. Each city also has its own number for enquiries, e.g. Helsinki 0200 4010; Tampere 0200 4031; Turku 0200 4021.

Useful Addresses

Oy Matkahuolto Ab, Simonkatu 3, 00100 Helsinki (☎0200 4000 for enquiries); www.matkahuolto.fi.
Helsinki Coach Station, Simonkatu 3; ☎0200 4090.

Boat. Apart from the ferry traffic criss-crossing between Finland and Sweden and further afield, there is an abundance of steamers and motor boats on the lakelands of Finland. One of the most popular, and cheapest ferry routes (if you can stand the drunken Finnish company) is between Helsinki and Tallinn, the Estonian capital. Finns use these trips to indulge in alcohol both internally and to bring back duty frees; the ferries, operated by several companies, are almost literally awash with the stuff. The trip can cost as little as €15 (approx. £9/US$13). Tallinn is a starting point for the rail journey (1,300 miles) to St Petersburg. There are direct trains from Helsinki to St Petersburg every day.

Within Finnish waters, main routes include those between Hämeenlinna and Tampere, Tampere and Virrat and various routes on the Saimaa Lake. The lakes of Päijänne and Inari also have regular services as does Lake Pielinen. Car ferries and overnight lake steamers with cabins also exist. Most lake services are aimed at holidaymakers and so they go at a leisurely pace and are not particularly economical.

City Transport. In the larger towns and cities urban transport is excellent and integrated. In Helsinki, for instance, tickets for the bus, tram, suburban rail lines and ferries to the Suomenlinna Islands are all linked in a common fare system. Multi-trip tickets (10 rides) can be bought in advance and work out slightly cheaper. Single tickets are cheaper if you buy them at a R-Kiosk or station. There are various cheap deals including renewable 30-day season tickets, for which a photo is required.

After midnight you may have to resort to taxis (*taksi*). Fares are generally more expensive in towns than in the country. The basic fare is about €4 (approx. £2.50/US$3.50) and extra kms are €2. Higher charges are made in the evenings (6pm-10pm; Saturdays from 2pm) and the highest charges are from 10pm to 6am.

BANKS AND FINANCE

The Bank of Finland (founded 1811; www.bof.fi) is the central bank that regulates bank rates and currency. Its activities are supervised by parliament. The Finnish currency before the euro was the *markka*. It was devalued in 1993, reducing its value by over a third, which made Finland much better value for foreigners at least for a while. After a major banking crisis in 1993, many banks merged. The main operators are Merita (part of the Swedish Nordea group), Sampo (formerly Leonia), Aktia and Okopankki, and some 20 savings banks.

Banking Services. There are no restrictions on foreigners opening bank accounts in Finland; banks generally prefer clients to have a Finnish Personal Identification Number; a valid passport may also be acceptable. Newly arrived immigrants can ask the Population Register office to send a provisional number to the bank by post. Customers are obliged by law to account for the nature and number of transactions. Assets can be moved freely in and out of Finland, but banks retain the right to ask about the origin of one's assets. Bank cards that accompany a current account can be used in almost all the many automatic cash machines (*pikapankki*) countrywide. Money can be withdrawn using foreign cashpoint and credit cards where you see the orange Otto sign. There is also no charge for paying bills via a cash machine. If you pay these by bank transfer the charge is €1-2. When arranging a transfer you must produce proof of identity.

Internet banking is becoming more and more popular. It is possible to make payments for expensive items by transferring funds yourself to the payee's bank account via the internet; you will then receive a proof of payment from the bank.

Banking hours are generally Monday-Friday from 9am or 9.15am to 4pm or 4.15pm. There are some regional variations.

Money. Finland's national currency is now the euro made up of 100 cents. Coins come in denominations of 5, 10, 20, 50 cents, and €1 and €2: notes come in €5/10/20/50/100/200/500. Finland was the first country in Euroland to abandon using 1 and 2 cent euro coins, thus proving beyond any doubt that this is one of the most expensive countries in Europe. The euro was worth about 62p sterling, or 87 US cents in 2002.

TAXATION

In common with other Scandinavians, Finns have long been subject to swingeing personal taxation. In 2001 Finland had the third highest tax burden in the EU, after Sweden and Denmark. In 1993 there was a major reform of the tax system starting with the lowering of personal and corporate tax rates. In 1994 full value-added tax (*aruonlivävero*) was introduced to broaden the tax base. Value added tax now raises virtually as much as state income tax. The main personal taxes are national income tax (*valtionvero*), municipal income tax (*kunnallisvero*) and net wealth tax (*varallisuusvero*). Other taxes include inheritance and gift tax, withholding tax and stamp duty. The main indirect tax is VAT, generally charged at 22%. Food, tobacco, alcohol and water are taxed at 17%; books, medicine, transportation, accommodation services, and entrance to sporting and entertainment events are charged at 8%. A number of items are zero-rated, including cemetery services and the sale of wild berries and mushrooms by the person who picked them.

Income Tax For the tax year 2001 personal income tax was lowered, supposedly as a response to tax cuts in Germany, Finland's main trading partner. The personal allowance is now €11,100 (approx. £6,900/US$9,600). The lowest rate of income tax is 14% on income between €11,100 and €14,300. There are further rates of 18%, 24%, 30%, and 37% which starts on income over €54,660. Note that even if you pay little state income tax, you are still liable for municipal income tax, which in Helsinki stands at 16.5%, and social security taxes. If your total tax bill exceeds 70% of your income then the excess has to be refunded.

The tax office in Helsinki has a foreign adviser who speaks English, and some free handouts (not necessarily up-to-date) on the taxation of foreigners. The office is at Haapaniemenkatu 7 (☎ 09 731 120). As it is located next to a motorway it is best approached along Vetehisenkuja and Näkinsilta. The Finnish tax system is explained in the book *Taxation in Finland 2001,* published by the government publishers Edita Oy, and available from the Edita bookshop at Annankatu 44. It is updated every two years.

Taxation for Foreigners and Trainees. There are some allowances made for foreigners working as trainees on an approved scheme organised by CIMO (see *Education* above) and for full-time students under the age of 25 at a foreign college; if they work for less than six months, they are entitled to a deduction of €510 a month from their taxable income. The tax office or CIMO will give further information on the precise conditions.

If you are going to work in Finland for less than six months your employer will collect 35% 'tax-at-source' (*lähdevero*), sometimes called 'withholding tax', unless they are instructed otherwise by the tax office, and you will not have to fill in a tax return; in this situation you cannot claim any tax deductions. If you are deemed to be a 'foreign expert' you may pay tax at 35% for up to two years, provided your income is at least €5,800 (approx. £3,600/US$5,050) per month for the whole period of employment. This last condition is waived for teachers in higher education and those who do scientific research 'for the public good'. Teachers from the UK may be eligible for complete tax exemption, if they can show they are paying tax in the UK.

Tax Administration. Taxation for individuals relates to the calendar year. Tax returns must be filed by 31 January of the following year. If the individual has a professional income the deadline for filing is extended to 1 March. If the individual has a business income and their financial period ends between 1 January and 1 October or 2 October and 31 December then the filing dates are 1 January and 1 April respectively. For details of tax on businesses see *Starting a Business.*

The Ministry of Finance bases the final assessment for tax on the returns which are normally dealt with by October of the year following the tax year. Taxpayers receive a final tax bill. If the tax paid exceeds the final assessment the difference is refunded in December. If the individual needs to pay more tax then it normally has to be paid in three tranches in December and the following two months.

HEALTH CARE

Finland has a hybrid system of health care, with public and private sectors. The public part is financed by the government and the municipalities. The private sector is also open to all citizens and is partly subsidised but is much more expensive than the public sector. If you go to a private doctor you may claim some of the costs back from the state. The advantage of the private sector is that you can go to a specialist without waiting. While the standard of health care is high, there is a looming shortage of health care staff, which will have to be filled by foreign workers. In 2001 the doctors went on strike for six months, seeking to make good cuts in pay that were imposed during the recession of the mid-1990s.

Health Care Centres.

Public health care centres (*terveyskeskus*) provide local medical services including ante-natal and post-natal clinical services and pre-school health care. All newborn citizens in Finland are issued with a healthcard which is kept up-to-date throughout their school years. Apart from centres offering valuable services including those for expectant mothers, and mothers and infants, there are private centres (*lääkäriasema*) where authorised doctors practise medicine in parallel with their hospital duties.

Health centres are also responsible for providing the local ambulance service. Call 112 in a medical emergency. There is one 24-hour pharmacy in Helsinki, the University Pharmacy, at Mannerheimintie 96, ☎020 320 200 or 09 4178 0300. For emergency dental treatment call 09 736 166 up to 9pm. There is also a nursing advice helpline on 09 10023.

Health centre fees vary in different localities. The charge may be €20 (approx. £12/US$17) for the first visit, or €10 for the first three visits in a given year. Further appointments are free of charge.

Students. Students in higher education have their own health care scheme which does not exclude them from using the public and private systems. The Finnish Student Health Service FSHS (*Ylioppilaiden terveydenhoitosäätiö – YTHS*), has a student health care centre in every university town open to all student union members. Most basic services are free but for specialist ones, e.g. psychologist, there is a small fee.

Hospitals

Finland has 21 hospital districts; the municipal governments within each district are responsible of the upkeep of their central (i.e. general) hospital(s). The state pays a contribution to the costs depending on the means of the district. To supplement the main hospitals there are smaller local hospitals which are required to provide treatment in three specialist fields. Supplementary hospitals are maintained by the local authorities and are established on a voluntary basis.

Private hospitals are rare in Finland, where the local communities have become the traditional providers of healthcare. In an emergency one may go directly to the outpatients' department of a general hospital. Otherwise call 112 for an ambulance. There is a call-out fee. The main hospital for emergencies in Helsinki is: Maria Hospital, Lapinlahdenkatu 16, Building 15C; ☎09 3106 3231.

SOCIAL SECURITY

Finland's social security system is excellent, especially pre-natal, post-natal and childhood services, but it has not reached the same level of munificence as that of its Scandinavian neighbours. The system is financed from taxes and contributions from insured people and employers; it consumes about 18.5% of the budget. Social security encompasses five areas of requirement: health insurance and maternity, pensions, unemployment security, workers' compensation and occupational disease insurance, and subsistence benefits. Detailed information in English about the social security system can be found on the website: www.kela.fi.

Health Insurance

All Finnish workers contribute to the health insurance scheme administered by the National Pensions Institution which is open to all residents of Finland. Health Insurance contributions entitle you to medical examination, laboratory and x-ray facilities and subsidised physiotherapy. As in most countries there is a charge for prescriptions, except in the case of the chronically sick. Your employer pays a contribution of 1.6% of your salary for state health insurance; the employee pays 1.5%. In the private sector, most insurance companies deal with health insurance as well.

Treatment as an out-patient is chargeable; you will not have to pay more than €590 (approx. £260/US$513) over a 12-month period. There is a charge of €21 per day as an in-patient, which covers all services. The cost of private medical attention is also partly subsidised but is much more expensive to the patient. Only part of doctors' fees and examination costs will be refunded; other procedures have to be paid for in full.

The dental treatment scheme provides free dental treatment up to the age of 17. After this, there are reductions in the cost of some dental treatments if you are a member of the state health insurance scheme.

In order to make use of Finland's health insurance scheme, the resident has to obtain a sickness insurance card from the local social insurance office (*kansaneläkelaitos*) known as KELA for short.

Since the UK and Finland have a reciprocal health-care agreement UK nationals do not require the E111 form. You only need to show your passport to obtain treatment. There are fixed non-refundable charges for treatment in hospital. Part of the cost of medicines will be refunded. US citizens need to take out private health insurance.

Private health insurance is advisable to meet the cost of any health treatment that may be required. Expacare (e-mail info@expacare.net or visit www.expacare.net) are specialists in expatriate healthcare offering high quality health insurance cover for individuals and their families, including group cover for five or more employees; cover is available for expatriates of all nationalities worldwide.

Benefits

Unemployment Benefit. Most workers belong to voluntary unemployment benefit schemes run by the trades unions. Eligibility for unemployment benefit is restricted to those who have been subscribing to a fund for a minimum of 10 months before becoming unemployed. There is an upper limit on annual benefits payable and also for those paid within a three-year period. The employer and the state fund the major part of the unemployment benefit while the employee contribution is much less.

Anyone not covered by an unemployment fund will have their unemployment benefit paid by the state, for up to 500 days, on condition that they are able and willing to work. The benefit is aimed at covering only the basic needs; housing allowance is a separate benefit paid by the municipality. If your entitlement to benefit runs out you then fall back on the 'labour market subsidy'; in practice no one is left destitute. In the case of immigrants this is called the 'integration allowance'.

Child Benefit. The parents of all children under 17 are entitled to family allowances. Children under three years command an increased benefit. Municipalities run day-care centres for pre-school aged children of working parents. Such parents receive a monthly allowance. Despite the obligation imposed on municipal authorities by the government to provide day care facilities for all pre-school children this has so far not been achieved and there is considerable variation among the municipalities.

SOCIAL LIFE

As with other Nordics, Finns have a reputation for reticence and a disinclination to make small talk. Bertolt Brecht unkindly stated that the Finns were the only people who could be silent in two languages. Often this is ascribed to the Finns' modesty about speaking a foreign language in case they make mistakes. There are reckoned to be some regional character differences: for instance the inhabitants of Karelia and Savo are considered jollier and keener on socialising than those from Håme and the southwest. Life in Finland tends to operate at a relaxed pace and Finns place a lot of emphasis on comfort. This was not always the case: their not-too-distant forebears rated determination and fortitude against adversity (summed up by the word *sisu*) as the most important characteristic of the Finns. Sisu is also the name of a brand of foul-tasting liquorice sweets. As they say, when a Finn decides to do something they will try to see it through to the end.

The Finns are great coffee drinkers and virtually any event that can be, is celebrated with a gathering for cakes and coffee. Outdoor barbecues (*grilli*) are also very popular. Another good way to socialise with Finns is to take up a sport. Sports are probably the Finns' most common pastime whether it is ski-ing or ice hockey, swimming, walking, cycling or jogging and so on. In recent times, Finland has had the highest rate of male heart attacks in the European Union; male life expectancy is only 73 years. The situation is changing since many are now adopting healthier eating habits, partly thanks to propaganda aimed at wives and partners by the government.

Finns also have the Scandinavian bent towards melancholia, particularly in winter when many of them are inclined to drink to excess. However, younger Finns are tending more to treat drinking as a pleasure rather than as an alcoholic marathon. Drinking and dancing the tango or foxtrot or *humppa* are traditional Finnish methods of warding off winter blues. In summer, Finns are generally more optimistic and expansive and most take a month's holiday in the country. For this reason it is difficult to do any kind of business in July. Many have summer cottages near the lakes, others take their camping gear and move round the country. Such times are good opportunities to meet Finns in their natural surroundings. Increasingly, though, Finns are taking holidays in the southern European countries.

It is probably a cliché, though one reiterated by the Finns themselves, that they are at their most relaxed in that great Finnish invention, the sauna (pronounced 'sow-una'). Along with the clothes goes the reserve it seems. The sauna was not always a place for washing and cleansing by steam, but a kind of community medical centre where children were born and the sick cared for. The best kind of sauna is a wood-fired one. Ideally the sauna should be near a lake for the essential cold plunge afterwards. In the countryside virtually every property has an adjoining sauna and the whole family go together. Sooner or later, the foreign resident will be invited to sweat out grime and cares and thrash him or herself (or someone else) with a bunch of fragrant birch twigs (*vihta*).

Manners and Customs. When dealing with Finns remember that they like to be addressed, at least initially, by their professional titles such as Director, Doctor, Professor etc. The Finns (women included) shake hands very firmly on meeting. They often look you straight in the eye when talking to you, something one quickly becomes used to. Honesty and reliability are national characteristics. While the Finns' conversation tends to be matter-of-fact, they are not as taciturn as they are made out to be, and they can become quite talkative after a drink or two.

The Finns are very pleased to talk about their country, since they have only recently emerged from the shadow of Russian domination to become full members of Europe, but the acid test for acceptance into Finnish society is being able to speak the Finnish language. There is prejudice against immigrants, and anti-immigrant violence, the worst of which has been in the town of Joensuu near the Russian border. White persons will not encounter much discrimination, but one should do everything to learn Finnish as quickly as possible if one is going to settle here.

Food and Drink

Finnish dietary staples are filling and insulating ones. A typical Finnish breakfast consists of porridge, dark Finnish rye bread, eggs, ham and so on. Lunch is regarded as the main meal of the day; expect heavy soups and stews, and lots of fish dishes in typical restaurants; imported burger houses and pizzerias have also made their mark, and there are more and more Russian restaurants. Typical ingredients of home cooking are meat or fish, potatoes, vegetables and dairy produce. In addition there is a host of regional dishes. In the north, reindeer meat is a speciality; reindeer-tongue sausages are a delicacy. Sometimes meat and fish are mixed as in *Vorschmack* (peppered beef and herring), or the Finnish version of *en croute, Kalakukko* (fish baked in black bread), which is from eastern Finland.

Seasonal fruits like wild strawberries, blueberries and the slightly later lingonberries and cranberries are delicacies; the rarer cloudberries and arctic brambleberries are used to flavour vodkas.

The traditional liquid accompaniment to a meal is most likely to be milk or sourmilk (even for adults), though beer is also very popular.

Alcohol. It is a myth that all Finns are alcoholics, though they do tend to overimbibe at weekends. Average yearly consumption is only 0.01% higher than in the UK. Beer is served in *tuoppi* glasses which are 30% bigger than a pint. Homegrown spirits include Finlandia and Koskenkorva vodkas. Until 2001 the alcohol trade was controlled by the state-owned monopoly Alko. From 2002, in line with EU regulations, alcohol can be imported or produced or sold by anyone with a licence. What the consequences of this liberalisation might be no one can tell at the moment.

CRIME AND POLICE

For those concerned about prodigious crime rates in their home countries, Finland can be a pleasant surprise. Rates of crime are still comparatively low, although increasing in the big cities. A brochure aimed at foreign students and trainees does give a brief caution about not wandering around Helsinki railway station at night. This is however countered with the reassuring, *You do not need to panic about your handbag or wallet.*

The police are more guardians of the peace than trouble-shooters and the only dealings most foreigners are likely to have with them are for mundane administrative matters such as renewing residence permits. The majority of incidents dealt with by the police are domestic disputes, public drunkenness or traffic accidents. One of the busiest times of the week for the mobile police in Helsinki is Friday night. The clear-up rate for crimes has gone down gradually over the years; about 45% of crimes of solved, but 82% of violent crimes are cleared up. According to police statistics, the average foreigner is almost four times more likely to commit a crime than a Finnish national. The emergency number for the police is 112.

METRICATION

For information on the metric system including a conversion chart see under *Metrication* at the end of the *Daily Life* chapter in the section on Denmark.

PUBLIC HOLIDAYS

1 January	New Year's Day
6 January	Epiphany
March/April	Good Friday
March/April	Easter
March/April	Easter Monday
1 May	May Day
May	Ascension Day
May	Whitsun/Pentecost
June	Midsummer Eve and Day
1 November	All Saints Day
6 December	Independence/National Day
25 December	Christmas Eve, Christmas Day
26 December	Boxing Day

RETIREMENT

Finland is not a country that most people would consider retiring to unless they had some prior connections there. These days it is increasingly likely that Finns will emulate other northern Europeans, by retiring to Mediterranean countries where they can enjoy sunshine all year round. The only advantages of retiring in Finland would be the high level of general amenities, the relatively low pollution and the good welfare provisions for the elderly provided by the state. Probably the main disadvantage from the point of view of retirees is the long winter and the cold. Peter Ackroyd, the travel writer, describes it as 'an elemental cold, a cold which invades the body and leaves it stunned'.

Municipalities are responsible for the care of the aged at local level. Many different services are provided at a nominal cost and they include daily help with domestic chores including cooking, cleaning and shopping. There are community centres for the elderly which function as information bases as well as centres for social activities. Some centres are attached to homes for the elderly. The emphasis in housing for the elderly is to create an environment where they can be as independent as possible. Many are housed in service flats and houses where home helps and home nursing services provide the essential back up. Other services provided by the state include bathing, pedicure, hairdressing and a clothes service.

Residence and Entry

It is possible to enter Finland as a retiree with funds to support yourself. You are required to register with the police and obtain a residence permit within three months; this will be granted to EU and EEA citizens, dependent on their financial status.

For further details, see chapter on *Residence and Entry Regulations*.

The Right to Remain

Once you have entered Finland and registered you have the right to remain indefinitely on a renewable residence permit. After a permanent stay of two years it is possible to apply for a permanent residence permit. After five years you become eligible to apply for citizenship.

Finnish Pensions

The pensionable age is 65 for both men and women. It is possible to go into early retirement, or unemployment retirement (for the long-term unemployed), from the age of 60. There is also a 'part-time' pension from the age of 56, although this scheme is still subject to review.

National Pension. According to the Social Insurance Institution (KELA), Finnish citizens living in Finland are entitled to a national pension if they have lived in Finland for a total of at least three years after reaching the age of 16. Employees from EU member countries and their family members are treated the same for national pension purposes. Citizens of other countries are entitled to a Finnish national pension if they have lived in Finland for an uninterrupted period of five years after the age of 16. To receive the full national pension one needs to have lived in Finland for 40 years between the ages of 16 and 64.

Everyone employed in Finland has to make contributions to the national pension scheme administered by KELA, which employers also contribute to. The maximum amount of the national pension in 2001 stood at €460 (approx. £285/US$400) for single persons per month, and €400 for married persons. The amount of the national pension is influenced by the pensioner's other income, such as earnings-related pensions. For instance, a person whose monthly earnings-related pension exceeds about €870 for married persons and about €960 for single persons will not receive any national pension. In 2001 the average pension was about €950 monthly.

Earnings Related Pensions. The system of earnings-related pensions was introduced in stages in 1963 which will continue taking effect until 2002. Earnings-related pensions are proportional to total earnings and length of service and accumulates at the rate of 1.5% of pay annually. A person who has worked for the full 40 years will receive the full 60% pension subject to certain limits. Pensions are in fact considered taxable income. Only those receiving the minimum flat-rate and earnings-related pension are entitled to tax exemption on their pensions.

There are certain fields of employment which have their own separate pension arrangements and systems, notably employees in the public sector, the church and maritime jobs.

Earnings-related pensions are managed by private insurance companies and pension funds and foundations, and are co-ordinated by the Central Pension Security Institute (*Eläketurvakeskus*), Opastinsilta 7, 00520 Helsinki; ☎09 774 77 033; www.etk.fi.

Part-time Pensions. This is a scheme that comes under the earnings related pensions. A worker may, from the age of 56, cut their working hours to 16-28 hours a week; the earnings from the part-time job should amount to 35-70% of the previous established earnings from the full-time job. The pension amounts to half of the difference in earnings between the full-time and the part-time job. So the person gets the salary from the part-time work and the pension.

Places of Worship

Finns are almost all Lutherans (at least those who go to church). On Sunday mornings there is an Anglican service at the Mikael Agricola Church, Tehtaankatu 23, Helsinki (☎09 490 424). There are also services in Turku and Tampere; call 09 680 1515 or 09 490 424 for more information.

Clubs and Societies

The best way to have an interesting social life is to find other foreigners via clubs and societies. Your embassy can give you names and addresses of contacts. The following are some expatriate organisations that can help put you in touch with other foreign residents:

Finnish-British Society, Puistokatu 1b A, 00140 Helsinki; ☎09 687 7020; fax 09 687 7021; e-mail finnbrit@finnbrit.fi; www.finnbrit.fi.

League of Finnish-American Societies, Mechelininkatu 10A/2, 00100 Helsinki; 09 41 333 700; www.sayli.fi.

Finnish Cricket Association, e-mail andy.armitage@kolumbus.fi; ☎0400 298 266.

SECTION II

WORKING IN FINLAND

EMPLOYMENT

PERMANENT WORK

TEMPORARY WORK

BUSINESS AND INDUSTRY REPORT

STARTING A BUSINESS

EMPLOYMENT

THE EMPLOYMENT SCENE

As with most Western economies, Finland was hit by a steep recession starting in 1989. This setback followed a period of unprecedented expansion in the 1980s when the economy was growing at 10% a year for several years and unemployment was at an all-time low of 3%. In Finland's case, the recession was exacerbated and prolonged by the loss of one of its main export markets with the collapse of the Soviet Union. Finland recovered quickly thanks to its immense paper and forestry industries, and its accession to full EU membership, as well as to the government's prescience in vigorously promoting communications and other high-tech industries. Now unemployment has come down to 10% (April 2002) job prospects appear more positive, but Finland still remains vulnerable to any global economic downturn.

Since Finland is a member of the EU, one would expect foreign workers to move there in greater numbers. Finland has an increasingly large foreign population (although still very small compared with other EU countries), mostly Russians, Swedes and refugees from the Third World. The Finns are some of the best, if not the best, linguists in the world, whilst speaking one of Europe's most difficult languages. There is an immense language barrier for foreign workers to overcome and not that many are prepared to commit themselves to living in a country with such a harsh climate. Should the Russian and Baltic economies develop, then there would certainly be many more international companies who would set up in Finland. Going to Finland on a traineeship is quite feasible; CIMO and other organisations listed below will be able to help.

If you go to Finland to look for temporary work, you are likely to find it more difficult than in other countries. There are far more temporary work agencies in other Scandinavian countries than in Finland. Casual work is also considerably harder to find than in countries with larger populations.

One factor which may aid the foreign jobseeker is the generous benefit system in Finland which discourages the locals from taking the most menial kinds of work. A modest number of unskilled jobs are available for foreigners in hotels (ask the tourist office for a list), and to a lesser extent on farms. The government lays on a large array of courses for the new and long-term unemployed to update their skills. A high level of training is very much the norm in Finland as is job mobility. Finns tend to move from job to job gaining experience, rather than spend years with the same company. Many emigrate permanently in order to escape high taxation and the climate. It has recently become more common for Finns to return home after a few years of working abroad, but with an economic downturn they are more likely to stay away.

An inherent disadvantage in the permanent job scene is that there is not the diversity of fields that you might expect to find in other industrially developed countries. Finland concentrated for many years on its two main industries, forestry and heavy engineering; the creation of new areas of expertise came later than in many other European countries. Engineers, which Finland churns out of its universities in thousands, are overly abundant for the jobs available, so prospects are not good for foreign engineers unless their technical skills are outstanding. Tourism, ICT, language services and international marketing are some of the areas where foreigners with the appropriate qualifications and experience have reasonable prospects for finding work.

In spite of relatively high unemployment, Finland will soon face a labour shortage, because those who were born in the baby boom years just after the war are reaching retirement age. Menial jobs will be increasingly filled by Russian and other immigrants. Jobseekers from the European Union should see their chances improve as well, now that employers are becoming more open-minded about employing foreigners.

SOURCES OF JOBS

Newspapers

British and International. If you are looking for work before you go and you have experience and qualifications for teaching English, then you may find suitable adverts in the *Times Educational Supplement* (published Fridays), the education pages of the Tuesday edition of the *Guardian* and the professional paper the *EFL Gazette* (see under English Teaching) all of which have carried adverts from Finnish English-language schools in the past.

Finnish Newspapers. Advertising in some Finnish newspapers has produced results in many cases. One of the best newspapers for this is *Helsingin Sanomat,* a daily newspaper with the widest area of readership in Finland, which is published every day including Sundays. *Helsingin Sanomat* is represented in the UK by Crane Media Partners (20-28 Dalling Rd, London W6 0JB; ☎020-8237 8601).

Some regional newspapers:
Aamulehti PL 327, 33101 Tampere; ☎931-666 111; fax 666 259; www.aamulehti.fi.
Demari, PL338, Helsinki 00531; ☎09 701 041; fax 09 761 0567; www.demari.fi.

Ilta-Sanomat, PL41, Helsinki 00089 SANOMAT; ☎09 1221; fax 09 1223 419; www.iltasanomat.fi.
Kaleva, Lekatie 1, Oulu; ☎08 5377 111; fax 08 5377 195; www.kaleva.fi.
Kauppalehti, PL 380, 00101 Helsinki; ☎09 50 781; fax 09 507 7644; www.kauppalehti.fi. Financial and business.
Turun Sanomat, Kauppiaskatu 5, 20100 Turku; ☎02 269 3311; fax 02 269 3274; e-mail info@ts-group.fi.
Helsingin Sanomat, Töölönlahdenkatu 2, POB 56, 00089 SANOMAT; ☎09 1221; fax 09 122 3259; international@sanoma.fi; www.helsinki-hs.net/news.asp.

The Internet

As elsewhere in Scandinavia, the internet is used a great deal by jobseekers and employers. Most job vacancies are posted in Finnish and sites tend to be entirely in Finnish, constituting an almost impenetrable barrier. However, it may be feasible to post one's CV on a website with the help of a Finnish speaker. A simpler procedure would be to look for the UK website of a Finnish company, such as Nokia. Finnish employers are generally good about answering e-mails; but as everywhere else it is usually necessary to combine an e-mail with a fax or letter or phone call.

Internet access is free in libraries in Finland, and some libraries are open on Sundays. The best place in central Helsinki is at the Lasipalatsi or Glass Palace, Mannerheimintie 22-24; the terminals were bought with a grant from Bill Gates. The Helsinki employment office recommends the following sites: www.mol.fi (Ministry of Labour); www.minedu.fi/rekrytointi/avoim.html; www.jobline.fi; www.uratie.fi; www.rekry.com; www.kyky.net.

The UK Employment Service

Any office of the UK National Employment Service can be used to access the Overseas Placing Unit (OPU) in Sheffield which handles the processing of vacancies within the EU. The Employment Service also produces a booklet – *Working in Finland* – with some basic information on immigration, the health care system and advice on how to best find work. Although vacancies in Finland are likely to be few, it costs nothing to register and so is worth trying.

Comparability of Qualifications. If you are not sure how your professional qualifications compare with those in Finland, you can consult the National Academic Recognition Information Centre (NARIC) office at the Ministry of Education. Your job centre in the UK or Finland will approach the NARIC office on your behalf. If you want to study in Finland you should approach the educational institution directly. The Ministry of Education points out that in many cases it is difficult to compare foreign qualifications with those gained in Finland.

Euro-Advisors. In order to provide help to those seeking work abroad, there are a number of Euro-advisors based at the OPU in Sheffield and several UK jobcentres. The EURES system can be consulted online at Jobcentres. Not many jobs are listed for Finland as a rule. In the summer of 2001 there were a handful of jobs for au pairs, nursery assistants and health care workers, as well as vacancies for five welders and 50 forest wardens (summer only). The latter would probably be expected to speak Finnish since the advert was entirely in Finnish. See the site: http://europa.eu.int/jobs/eures.

Claiming UK Unemployment Benefit While Looking for Work Abroad. Provided that you are receiving contributions-based benefit and have been registered unemployed for a minimum of four weeks you can arrange to have your benefit paid abroad for up to three months. You have to be registered at the Finnish employment office (*työvoimatoimisto*) as looking for work before you can make your claim at the KELA office. For further details ask at your local benefit office.

Useful Addresses

Comparability Coordinator, Employment Dept., Qualifications and Standards Branch (QSI), Room E454, Moorfoot, Sheffield SP1 4PQ; ☎0114 2594144.
Overseas Placings Unit, Employment Service (0PS 5), c/o Moorfoot, Sheffield SP1 4PQ.
UK NARIC, ECCTIS Ltd, Oriel House, Oriel Road, Cheltenham, Glos GL50 1XP; ☎01242-260010; fax 01242-258611; www.naric.org.uk.
NARIC, Ministry of Education, PB 29, 00023 Valtioneuvosto; ☎09 134 1711; www.minedu.fi.

UK Recruitment Agencies

There are some agencies in the UK which specialise in finding overseas jobs for clients or which recruit for corporate clients. Generally speaking such agencies deal with a specific sector, for instance, electronics, secretarial, accountancy and so on, and will only consider job applicants with the appropriate qualifications. The Recruitment and Employment Confederation (36-38 Mortimer Street, London W1N 7RB; ☎020-7462 3260; www.rec.uk.com) issues a list of employment agencies who are members, some of them have connections with Finland

Useful Addresses

Berndtson International, 6 Westminster Palace Gardens, Artillery Row, London SW1P IRL; ☎020-7222 5555; www.rayberndtson.com. One of the few recruiters that encourages speculative application and keeps its own register. Office in Helsinki: Ray & Berndtson Oy, Bulevardi 5A; ☎09 607 300.
Egon Zehnder International Ltd. Devonshire House, Mayfair Place, London W1X 5FH; ☎020-7493 3882; fax 020-7629 9552; www.ezi.net. Accepts speculative applications. Helsinki office: Erottajankatu 19B,

5th Floor, 00130 Helsinki; ☎09 684 00 30; fax 09 684 00 333; e-mail ezihelsinki@ezi.net.
Heidrick & Struggles, 3 Burlington Gardens, London W15 3EP; ☎020-7075 4000. In Helsinki: Heidrick & Struggles, Erottajankatu 9A, 00130 Helsinki; ☎09 251 1250; e-mail he@h-s.com.
Korn/Ferry International, Pohjoisesplanadi 37A VII krs, Helsinki; 09 612 2560; fax 09 612 25656.
Marlar International Finland, e-mail cv@marlar.dk; www.marlar.dk/fin/marlar.htm.

Mec-Rastor Pricewaterhouse Coopers Oy, Kimmeltie 1, Espoo; ☎09 469 71. *Transearch International UK,* Watson House, 54 Baker St, London W1U 7BU; 020-7009 5800. Helsinki office: Transearch Finland Oy, Fredrikinkatu 48A.7, Krs 00100 Helsinki; ☎09 694 2866; fax 09 694 2810.

Finnish State Employment Offices

The Finnish state employment offices are known as *työvoimatoimistot* of which there is one in every town and several in Helsinki. The *Helsingin Työvoimatoimisto* (Employment Office of Helsinki) can be reached on ☎09 7021; the office in the wealthy suburb of Espoo is on 09 805 7755 or 09 455 4022. Employment offices are generally open from 9am to 4pm; some from 8am to 3pm. At the time of going to press virtually all employment offices in Finland were state ones though there are plans to establish private services which might lead to more job openings or even create business opportunities for foreign businesses willing to open branches in Finland. For further information on regional employment services in Finland, contact the Ministry of Labour, POB 34, 00023 GOVERNMENT, Finland; ☎09-18 561; fax 09-1856 9181; e-mail tyovoimatoimisto@mol.fi; www.mol.fi.

TYPES OF WORK

Executive Recruitment

The best possibilities are in marketing, finance, accountancy, general management, linguistic services, training, and development of new technology. By joining the EU Finland has ended an era of isolation from mainstream European trade and is in need of individuals who can provide skills which will aid communication and liaison with other European countries. For some executive jobs, a knowlege of Finnish would not be essential initially. In multinational companies, the corporate language is often English, thus removing the main barrier to foreign applicants.

Teaching

Teachers should consider applying directly to schools in Finland where some programmes are taught in English. These include the English School and the International School in Helsinki, both of which have kindergartens attached. See the list under *Daily Life.* In addition, certain mainstream Finnish state comprehensive and upper secondary schools and vocational institutes have been teaching some subjects in a variety of languages including English since 1991. In 2001 there were comprehensive school classes in English at Helsinki, Espoo, Tampere, Turku, Oulu, Jyväskylä, Kirkkonummi Kuopio, Lappeenranta, Lahti, Taruma, Rovaniemi and Vaasa state schools. The Espoo-Vantaa Technical College and Vaasa Technical College also teach some programmes in English. The Ministry of Education will give you further information; see under 'Education' in the *Daily Life* chapter.

SHORT-TERM WORK

Au Pair Work and Family Stays

This is an option for both young men and women. EU citizens do not need a work permit. There are few, if any, agencies outside Finland that can help you find an au pair placement. In Finland you can try Allianssi and CIMO. A proven method of obtaining au pair work is by advertising in a Finnish newspaper (see above). You can do this in English, or find someone to translate your advert into Finnish or Swedish. *Helsingin Sanomat* (the Helsinki daily paper) advertises a few domestic situations most days. One former au pair also recommends putting up flyers in places where they are likely to catch the eye of busy parents, such as at playgroups in affluent city suburbs. You should stress the fact that you are an English-speaker as most Finnish parents are keen to have their offspring proficient in English. Pocket money generally works out at €350-€500 monthly. The Finnish Youth Cooperation Alliance, Allianssi, is a non-profit youth exchange organisation which deals with small numbers of placements with Finnish families for six to 12 months. The pocket money is €350 (approx. £210/US$300) a month for about 30 hours work a week.

Part of Finland's international trainee exchange organisation, CIMO, organises a Family Programme whereby you can stay with a Finnish family for one to three months in summer or up to 12 months beginning any time of year. Participants are expected to help families with their English as well as housework, gardening and looking after children. There are also openings for those with farming experience. The Family Programme is open to 18 to 23-year-olds who can speak English, German or French

Useful Addresses

Allianssi, Olympiastadion, Eteläkaarre 00250 Helsinki; ☎09 348 24305; fax 09 491 290; e-mail info@alli.fi; www.alli.fi/indexeng.html. Finds placements for foreign au pairs in Finland.

CIMO, The Centre for International Mobility, POB 343, 00531 Helsinki, ☎09 774 77033; fax 09 774 77064; e-mail cimoinfo@cimo.fi; www.cimo.fi.

Teaching English

Swedish is Finland's second official language, but English has already displaced it as most people's second language. Despite the prevalence of English teaching in the national school curriculum, there is still an increasing requirement for special English language tuition in a variety of establishments, including private kindergartens, vocational colleges, business schools, folk schools and universities. There are over 30 private English language schools in Helsinki alone, and over 160 in the country as a whole.

It can also be profitable to advertise yourself as a freelance teacher of English. The going rate for private lessons starts at €20 (about £12/US$17 per hour).

Useful Organisations

British Council, Hakaniemenkatu 2, 00530 Helsinki; ☎070-18731; fax 018725. Can provide a list of private schools in Helsinki only. The British council runs its own schools and offers one- or two-year contracts. Perks include a tax-free salary and help with airfares and relocation costs. Anyone applying for work with the BC should normally have the RSA/Cambridge/Trinity Diploma. Preference is given to expatriates already on the spot such as spouses of those with jobs in Finland.

Federation of Finnish-British Societies, Puistokatu 1b A, 00140 Helsinki; www.finn-brit.fi. There are at least a dozen Finn-Brit Societies around Finland which employ teaching staff. The largest one in Helsinki (see above address) takes on a number of experienced teachers and less experienced graduates as teaching staff. The other Societies around Finland also employ teachers though to a lesser extent than the main branch in Helsinki. Contracts are generally for nine months and airfares are paid for. Applications should arrive by the end of February and interviews (in London) take place in April. Accommodation can also be arranged.

Berlitz Language Services, Mikonkatu 9, 00100 Helsinki; ☎09 668 9460; fax 09 668 94646; www.berlitz.com.

Linguarama Suomi Oy, Annankatu 26, 00100 Helsinki; ☎09 680 3230; fax 09 603118; UK office: Oceanic House, 85 High Street, Alton, Hants GU34 1LG. Linguarama offers language training for business. Offers graduates with a TEFL certificate and six months basic experience a short training course that qualifies them to teach in Linguarama's own centres in Helsinki and Lahti.

Richard Lewis Communications, Länsituulentie 10, 02100 Espoo; ☎09 4157 4700 is a British-based organisation that specialises in providing language training for business people and professionals. Their UK address is Riversdown House, Warnford, Hampshire SO32 3LH; ☎01962-771111; info@rlcglobal.com; www.crossculture.com.

Trainee Schemes

CIMO (Finnish Trainee Placement Programme). It is possible to arrange a trainee post in Finland through CIMO, Finland's International Trainee Exchange Programme (POB 343, 00531 Helsinki; www.cimo.fi) through which the Finnish Ministry of Education actively encourages trainees to come to Finland for short-term paid work. Trainees from abroad receive a statutory minimum trainee wage (slight less for agriculture than for other types of work).

There is a wide range of work categories covered by this programme which includes all of those types mentioned below. In order to qualify for the CIMO programme, you must be at least a year into undergraduate studies, preferably with an additional year of related experience, and be aged 18 to 30.

CIMO Contact Organisations Abroad. You can either contact CIMO direct or apply through an organisation in your own country. Some of the main contacts are listed below:

Canada: Canadian Federation of Student Services, SWAP, 243 College Street, 5th

Floor, Toronto, Ontario M5T 2Y1. Also: Youth and Personalities Exchange, International Higher Education, External Affairs and International Trade, Canada, 125 Sussex Drive, Ottawa, Ontario K1A OG2.

UK: Central Bureau for International Education and Training: 10 Spring Gardens, London SW1A 2BN; ☎020-7389 4004; fax 389 4426; www.britishcouncil.org/cbiet.

United States of America: Association for International Practical Training, 10 Corporate Center, Suite 250, 10400 Little Patuxent Parkway, Columbia, Maryland 21044-3519; ☎410-997-2200; fax 410-992-3924; e-mail aipt@aipt.org. (Hotel/Culinary applicants).

United States of America: The American-Scandinavian Foundation, Scandinavia House, 58 Park Avenue, New York, NY 10016; ☎212-879-9779; e-mail info@amscan.org; www.amscan.org. (Technology, horticulture and forestry students).

United States of America: Interexchange, 161 Sixth Ave, New York, NY 10013; ☎212-924-0446; fax 212-924 0575; www.interexchange.org.

United States of America: Future Farmers of America, National FFA Center, 5632 Mt Vernon, Memorial Highway, Alexandria, Virginia 23309-3600; www.ffa.org. (Farming students).

IAESTE. The International Association for the Exchange of Students for Technical Experience, based in the UK at the Central Bureau for International Education and Training in London (see above address), is a worldwide organisation. This is one of the best-known organisations for trainees looking for posts in industry. Those in Finland can range from working on the factory floor to helping with research and development. Students should apply for work in an area related to their studies. Some IAESTE contact addresses are:

Canada: IAESTE Canada, POB 1473 Kingston, Ontario K7L 5C7, Canada; ☎613-533 2030; fax 613-533-6869; e-mail Canada@iaeste.org.

United States of America IAESTE US, c/o The Association for International Practical Training, 10400 Little Patuxent Parkway, Suite 250, Columbia, Maryland 21044-3510; ☎410-997-3068; fax 410-997-5186; e-mail USA@iaeste.org.

Other Types of Jobs Available

EU nationals in particular should note that they can access the following jobs in Finland, such as those below, by contacting organisations in their own countries, Finnish employers direct or by applying on the spot in Finland.

Agriculture, Forestry, Horticulture. These programmes can involve arduous, physical, hands-on experience but may also involve working in a specialist institute, for instance in an enviromental protection department of a large company. Farming proper in Finland requires an appreciation of the problems of agriculture in a cold climate. While other European farms are spring planting, Finnish ones may be under a metre of snow. You need two years practical experience to get on the International Farm Experience programme which. Farming jobs for three to 12 months can also be arranged through the International Farm Experience programme in the UK (YFC Centre, National Agricultural Centre, Stoneleigh Park, Kenilworth, Warwickshire CV8 2LG; ☎01203-696584; fax 01203-696559).

It is also possible to get casual work in horticultural nurseries by contacting them direct or visiting in person. There are quite a few in the Helsinki area.

Hotels, Catering and Tourism. It is possible to get a hotel job by writing directly to some of Finland's hundreds of hotels, especially those in tourist resorts like Hämeenlinna. A list of hotels can be obtained through the Finnish tourist office in your own country. The only hotel it would not be advisable to apply to is the Arctic Hall Hotel at Jukkasjärvi which is a giant igloo built in December; in March it melts. Smart international hotel chains like Intercontinental of which there is one in Helsinki, may prefer to take trainees through CIMO as they will consider them more motivated. Those studying tourism or related subjects can work in travel agencies and Finnish offical tourist offices. Trainee chefs, waiters, bar and housekeeping staff are also eligible to go through CIMO.

One hotel that advertises for kitchen and waiting staff in Britain, is the *Hotel Ruotsinsalmi* (Kirkkokatu 14, Kotka 10). A charge of £45 per month for board and lodging is deducted if needed. The only snag is that a knowledge of Swedish is required and if possible Finnish as well.

Social & Voluntary Work. There is plenty of scope for voluntary work in Finland. There are traineeships in old people's homes, in youth work and on summer camps with young Finns or a more international participation. As well as applying through CIMO there are some international voluntary work camp organisations in Finland:

Allianssi, Olympiastadion, Eteläkaarre, 00250 Helsinki; ☎09 348 24305; fax 09 491 290; e-mail info@alli.fi; www.alli.fi/indexeng.html. Arranges international workcamps in Finland.

KVT, Raulhanasema, Veturitori, 00520 Helsinki, runs summer work camps. In the UK you should apply through International Voluntary Service (IVS, Old Hall, East Bergholt, Colchester, Essex C07 6TQ; www.sciint.org). US residents see www.sci-ivs.org.

Valamo Monastery 79850 Uusi-Valamo, nowadays only takes volunteers with special skills, such as icon-painting, translating and editing texts into English, acting as guides for English-speaking visitors (in summer), etc. A full day's work is expected in return for keep.

ASPECTS OF EMPLOYMENT

Salaries

It may come as a surprise that Scandinavian salaries are some way behind Germany and the UK and that Finns are generally paid less than other Scandinavians. North American salaries are much higher. Typical salaries are €100,000 (about £62,000/US87,000 per annum) for a managing director, €52,000 for a sales manager, €22,000 for a customer services assistant. There is a statutory minimum rate of pay for men and women in manufacturing of about €10 (approx. £6,29/US$8.70) per hour. There is a minimum statutory wage for industrial trainees which varies between €700 and €1,000 per month, depending on the category of work. The cost of living is higher than in the UK and far higher than in the USA.

Salaries are negotiated by collective bargaining agreements between the trade unions and the employers' federations. The salaries of managerial and professional staff are usually negotiated directly by the employee and employer and often individual contracts drawn up. Tables 5 and 6 list monthly earnings from 2002 in the public and private sectors.

TABLE 5   PRIVATE SECTOR MONTHLY EARNINGS

Bank manager	€4,700	£2,900/US$4,000
Computer programmer	€2,500	£1,550/US$2,200
Clerical Worker	€1,600	£990/US$1,400
Industrial worker (paper and pulp)	€2,400	£1,480/US$2,080
Production manager	€4,000	£2,480/US$3,480
Sales manager	€5,000	£3,100/US$4,400
Shop Assistant (foods)	€1,400	£870/US$1,200
Waiter	€1,500	£930/US$1,300

TABLE 6   PUBLIC SECTOR MONTHLY EARNINGS

Bus/tram driver	€2,100	£1,300/US$1,800
Senior teacher (secondary school)	€3,000	£1,860/US$2,600
Cleaner	€1,500	£930/US$1,300
Cook	€1,650	£1,000/US$1,430
Electrician	€2,200	£1,350/US$1,900
Engineer	€3,100	£1,920/US$2,700
Assistant Librarian	€1,900	£1,150/US$1,650
Nurse	€2,100	£1,300/US$1,830
Physician	€4,650	£2,880/US$4,040
Social Worker	€1,900	£1,180/US$1,650

Fringe Benefits and Perks

Apart from bonuses paid to executive staff, the only perk widespread in Finland is a payment of an additional 50% of the regular salary during the employee's holiday time. Some employers also provide, or subsidise, meals and transport, and even housing.

Working Hours, Overtime and Holidays

The law governing working hours states that a regular working week consists of 40 hours a week, eight hours a day. As in other northern European countries lunch breaks are not usually longer than one hour. The normal working day begins at 8.30am and ends at 5pm, but with flexible working hours many jobs can be arranged around other commitments. The recession has caused Finnish employers to be more adaptable; schemes for job sharing and allowing employees sabbaticals to enrol on a study year or further their skills with additional training have been introduced.

The normal annual holiday allowance in addition to public holidays, is five weeks, one week of which must be taken during winter. Most try to take their holidays in July.

Overtime is normally restricted to a maximum of 200 hours per year on weekdays and 120 hours for weekends. Legislation also governs the payment for overtime: for the first two hours on weekdays and Saturdays the rate is a minumum of time and a half. The rate for more than two hours on a weekday and Sunday work is at least double. The Labour Council may allow up to a 50% increase in overtime subject to special terms of negotiation.

Trade Unions

Finland has a high level of union membership in the main industries. This ranges from about 65% in the services sector to nearly 95% in the metal and paper industries. It is not compulsory to belong to a union but the unions are important in the area of collective bargaining and the major ones set the pattern for wage increases nationally. During the recession wage hikes were almost non-existent; since 1996 they have been averaging over 3% per annum, higher than the rate of inflation.

Employment Contracts

As in other countries a written contract of employment is not essential. If there is no written contract the national labour laws govern the terms of dismissal. Employers may therefore consider a written contract desirable, depending on the type of employment. Some employers insist on a trial period of about three to four months before offering a more permanent contract.

Termination of Contract. Theoretically employers and employees have equal rights to terminate employment contracts. However, in practice is is more difficult for an employer to terminate a contract than an employee. As an employee you cannot be dismissed except in exceptional circumstances such as *force majeure* or serious misconduct. Employees cannot be dismissed for illness, pregnancy, religious, political or other beliefs, or trade union activity. If there is a reduction in the volume of work the employer has to try to find other work for employees.

Dismissal periods are laid down in collective bargaining agreements or specific employment contracts. If there is no contract then the dismissal time may be based on the length of service, but must be a minimum of two months.

If an employee wishes to terminate a contract a minimum of one month's notice must be given. For fuller details of the terms of dismissal see 'Employing Staff' in the chapter *Starting a Business*.

Maternity Benefits, Parental Leave & Employment Rights

Parents are entitled to maternity, paternity or parents' leave from work when their child is born. Allowances are paid at the rate of 80% of pay. The mother also gets a maternity benefit in cash, or in the form of a maternity pack of baby items which is valued at twice the amount of the cash benefit. Table 7 contains a summary of the benefits.

TABLE 7   SUMMARY OF MATERNITY/PATERNITY BENEFITS

- O   Maternity benefit.
- O   Child allowance (paid from 0-17 years).
- O   Maternity, paternity and parents' allowance (0-9 months).
- O   Child home care allowance (1-3 years).
- O   Child day care (1-5 years) and day care for school children (6-10 years).
- O   Leave of absence to look after children at home 1-3 years.
- O   Partial leave of absence (shorter working hours) 1-4 years.

Child Care. There is a choice of possibilities from the above. Children under three can have a place in a communal day centre or the parents can have an allowance for the child to be cared for at home after the end of their maternity/paternity allowance. In some cases the parents' choice may be dictated by the circumstances in their area where there is a shortage of municipal, pre-school day care places. Parents of children who are sick can apply for compensation for loss of earnings if they stay at home to look after them.

Women at Work

Europe seems to lag behind Scandinavia when it comes to equal opportunities for women at work. However by the high standards of Scandinavia opportunities in Finland are not considered the best – Sweden generally comes out top in this respect. Nonetheless, career opportunities for women are improving helped by a significant female presence (38%) in the Finnish parliament and a few top industrial jobs. It is tempting to attribute this partly to the high rate of heart attacks amongst Finnish males, which makes women seem a better bet when it comes to coping with stressful jobs, and even creates opportunities (such as those in politics), for them. While Finnish society tends towards accepting women as equal at work, there is still some way to go. For example, in 2002 the average monthly earnings for regular work for men was €2,500 (approx. £1,550/US$2,175) and for women €2,100. A number of high-profile jobs are held by, or have recently been held by women in Finland. At the time of writing, the President, the Speaker of Parliament and the Mayor of Helsinki were all women; a woman was also recently Governor of the Bank of Finland.

The work force is made up of 48% women and 52% men, more or less the same ratio as in other Scandinavia. Having a family is compatible with developing career prospects where desired, thanks to generous maternity and paternity leave, child allowances and state and commercial child day care provisions. About 70% of 3-6 year-olds are in day care, less than in Sweden, Norway and Denmark; 25% of 0-2 year-olds are in day care.

Income Security

Most income security comes from employee and employer contributions to statutory insurance which covers sickness, accident, pension and unemployment insurance. As in most European countries, most of the burden of contributions is borne by the employer. The types of income security available are:

Sickness Insurance. Patients and those convalescing from illness or injury are entitled to a daily allowance calculated at 80% of average earnings.

Industrial Accidents. Employees' contributions cover accidents at work, occupational diseases and accidents while commuting to or from work. Intangibles may also be taken into account. Compensation at the rate of 80% of earnings is paid, as well as the cost of treatment, rehabilitation and so on. In the event of a fatal accident survivors' pensions where appropriate as well as funeral expenses are paid.

Unemployment Security. Employees who are members of a trade union are paid from union funds, a daily allowance that is usually 60% of normal income up to a period of two years. After that the unemployed person receives a flat-rate unemployment allowance from the state as do employees who are not affiliated to a trade union.

An income allowance is paid to those whose income is not sufficient to cover daily outgoings. The amount is tailored to need and is paid by the local authorities.

Long-term unemployed people over 60 can claim an unemployment pension (see *Retirement* chapter).

BUSINESS AND INDUSTRY REPORT

Finland's industry is said to have three 'legs': the forest sector, metals and engineering, and high tech. Although industrialisation began around 1860, heavy engineering only took off after World War II, when Finland was forced to find goods to export to pay off its war reparations. The country has long been one of the world's major exporters of paper, along with packaging, pulp and chemicals associated with paper-making. The formerly state-owned Valmet company is a world leader in the area of paper-making plant. The Finns have also been acquiring paper producers in the USA and elsewhere. The forestry products sector is also a major player, although recently under pressure because of cheap Russian exports.

In metals and engineering, Outokumpu Oy pioneered the flash smelting of copper, one of Finland's most significant inventions. Ship-building is also still thriving. The well-known Fiskars company, makers of scissors, has been in existence since it was started by Belgian immigrants in the 17th century. Kone is one of the world's leading manufacturers of elevators. The third pillar of Finland's industry, high-tech, has developed rapidly in recent years thanks to the foresight of the government and a certain degree of luck; a particular feature in this field is the close co-operation of the state, industry and research institutes.

The eventual aim is to make Finland into an information- or knowledge-based society. Virtually every Finn has a mobile phone and the Nokia company is the world leader in mobile phone technology; 90% of its operations are outside Finland. While Finns joke that a company that manufactures everything from rubber boots to mobile phones cannot be any good, they take enormous pride in Nokia's success.

The Finnish government identified lack of investment in training as a major weakness in their economic strategy during the recession of the early nineties; consequently investment in training has increased on average by 5% every year since 1995, with the result that according to some surveys, Finland now has the world's best-trained workforce. Finland also leads the world in the development of electronic commerce; it rates as third in terms of ownership of computers, and third in competitiveness after the USA and Singapore.

The Finns are particularly proud of their record of innovation and patents. The first talking pictures or movies were developed by one of the country's greatest inventors, Eric Tigerstedt, at the beginning of the last century. Some products have now become household names, although few consumers would associate them with Finland. One example is Benecol, makers of cholesterol-reducing margarine and other foods. Another is the Linux freeware operating system. Finnish researchers are playing a leading role in the development of many innovative products, including neural networks, low-temperature physics, biotechnology and genetics, to mention but a few.

Most industry is in the highly developed southwest of the country, while the paper industries are in the south-east next to the lakes and rivers that supply the huge amounts of water needed. Agriculture has gone through a transformation following the country's accession to the EU. For several years investment plummeted but this trend has now been entirely reversed. Most small farms were forced out of business; along with the rationalisation into larger units has come an ongoing fall in the price of farming products.

The gap between the prosperous south and the under-developed north is understandably marked. The TE-Keskus (formerly the Finnish regional development fund) finances or subsidises industries which provide substitutes for imports, as well as others such as fishing, tourism and fur-farming in the north.

DIRECTORY OF MAJOR EMPLOYERS

The Finnish Trade Centre website lists the country's top companies: www.talouselama.fi. The following is a selection of some of the top companies in Finland in terms of employees and turnover:

Nokia, P.O.B. 226, 00045 Nokia Group; ☎09 18071; fax 09 652 409; www.nokia.com. Telecommunica- tions, paper, rubber tyres, electronics. Over 60,000 employees. *Neste,* PL 20, 02151 Espoo;

☎010 45 15; fax 010 452 50 15; www.nestechemicals.com. Mainly oil, also chemicals and plastics. Over 32,000 employees.

Metso Corporation, P.O.B. 1220, Helsinki 00101; ☎020 484 100; fax 020 484 101; www.metso.com. Mainly wood and machinery, but very diversified. Over 32,000 employees.

Kone Corporation, P.O.B. 8, Munkkiniemen puistotie 25, 00331 Helsinki; ☎020 4751; www.kone.com. Metals, lifts and metal instruments. Over 23,000 employees.

UPM-Kymmene Oy; POB 1079, Mikonkatu 15A, 00101 Helsinki; ☎0204 1511. Chemicals, plastics, forestry, metals. About 17,000 employees.

Outokumpu Oy, P.O.B. 140, 02201 Espoo; ☎09 4211; fax 09 421 3888; www.outokumpu.com. Metals. Over 17,000 employees.

Fortum Corporation, Keilaniementie 1, Espoo; ☎010 4511; fax 010 45 24920; www.fortum.com. Refining, distribution and marketing of energy, engineering. Over 16,000 employees.

Metsä-Serla Oyj, Revontulentie 6, 02100 Espoo; ☎010 4611; fax 010 469 4355; www.metsaserla.com. Mainly forestry. Over 15,000 employees.

Metra Oy Ab. P.O.B. 230, John Stenberginranta 2; 00101 Helsinki. Paper, machinery. Over 15,000 employees.

Stora-Enso Oy, P.O.B. 309, Kanavaranta 1, 00101 Helsinki; ☎020 4613; fax 020 462 1471. Forestry, chemicals, plastics. Over 14,000 employees.

Valmet Corporation, PL 587, 40101 Jyväskylä; ☎020 48 21 50; fax 020 48 21 51; www.valmet.com. Metals. About 11,000 employees.

Kesko Oyj, Satamakatu 3, 00161 Helsinki; ☎010 53 11; fax 09 17 43 98; www.kesko.fi. Wholesale and retail trade. Over 11,000 employees.

Sonera Corporation, P.O.B. 154, 00051 SONERA; ☎020 401; fax 020 40 60025. Over 10,000 employees.

Kemira Oy, P.O.B. 330, Porkkalankatu 3, 00101 Helsinki; ☎09 10 86 11; fax 09 10 862 1119; www.kemira.com. Chemicals. Over 10,000 employees.

A. Ahlström Oy, PL 329, 00101 Helsinki; ☎09 50 39 11; fax 09 503 97 09; www.ahlstrom.com. Paper, packaging, pumps. Over 10,000 employees.

Huhtamäki Van Leer Oyj, Länsituulentie 7, 02100 Espoo; ☎09 68 68 81; fax 09 66 06 22. Foods, food processing. About 10,000 employees.

Rautaruukki Oy, PL 93, 92101 Raahe; ☎09 41 77 11; fax 09 41 77 62 88. Metals. Over 9,000 employees.

International and British Companies in Finland

A list can be supplied by the British Embassy in Helsinki; ☎09 2286 5100.

Software

Hewlett Packard Oy, PL 68, 02201 Espoo; ☎09 887 21; fax 09 887 22 77.

ICL Invia Oyj, PL 458, 00101 Helsinki; ☎09 5671.

Microsoft, Jaakonkatu 2, 01200 Vantaa; ☎09 52 55 01; fax 09 878 8778; www.microsoft.fi.

Novell Finland Oy, Lars Sonckin Kaari 14, 02600 Espoo; ☎09 502 951.

Oracle Finland Oy, PL 47, 02201 Espoo; ☎09 8046 61; fax 09 8046 62 00; www.oracle.fi.

SAP Finland Oy, Valkjärventie2, 02130 Espoo; 09 2536 4400.

Siemens Oy, PL 60, 02601 Espoo; ☎010 511 5151.

Sybase Finland Oy, Martinkyläntie 43, 01720 Vantaa; ☎09 7250 2214.

Viatek Ltd, PL 4, 02101 Espoo; ☎09 43011.

STARTING A BUSINESS

BUSINESS BACKGROUND

Finland was slower than other Scandinavian countries to develop industrially and the process only really began after World War II. There ensued several decades when the forestry and metal industries were the backbone of the economy. Over the last 20 years Finland has grown into a world leader in telecommunications (Nokia controls 35% of the world market in mobile phones). Also very developed are the freight transport and consumer durables industries. Companies such as Oy Sisu-Auto Ab which makes trucks and port tractors, and the Metso Corporation which manufactures paper for magazines and newspapers worldwide, are multi-nationals. The Metra company is a world leader in diesel engines. Chemicals and pharmaceuticals are industries that have been added in recent years, as have oil refining and fertiliser production. Finland continues to be second only to Canada in the production of pulp and paper.

There is a worldwide market for Finnish-designed functional objects such as scissors, cutlery and furniture, and decorative ones such as glass, not to mention textiles. Leading companies include Marimekko textiles, Iittala glass and Arabia ceramics.

For many years Finland maintained restrictions on foreign companies part-owning or buying up Finnish ones. In 1989 the government took the first positive steps towards dismantling the legal restrictions on foreign investment in Finnish companies. These were finally lifted on 1 January 1993 in preparation for Finland's entry into the European Union.

The status of foreign-owned businesses in Finland is the same as that of home-grown ones. The government offers subsidies for starting up businesses in development areas. Freight subsidies and special financing deals are also available. Subsidies are available on a countrywide basis for various purposes including: research and development, export promotion, and machinery and equipment purchases.

As Finland has only recently opened up fully to foreign investment, there are considerable commercial possibilities awaiting companies and individuals. These include access to the emerging economies of the Baltic Republics and Russia with which Finland has long-established links. St Petersburg and Estonia are the most lucrative potential markets. There is now more tourist interest in these areas and a need for services for travellers.

With one of the highest jobless rates in the European Union (10%), there is no shortage of labour available in Finland. Far from resigning itself to permanent high unemployment, Finland is currently making huge investments in training schemes for its human resources aimed at producing individuals whose skills are tailored to the requirements of industry, particularly in the area of new technology. Finland's advanced technology industries include dental, medical and automotive equipment. Finland also has the largest technical research facility in Scandinavia, VTT (see *Useful Addresses* below), whose main laboratories are within the Helsinki University campus.

The Finnish economy has made an impressive recovery from the depression of the first half of the nineties. Finland is now a full member of the European Union and part of Euroland. Finnish interest rates are determined by the European Central Bank, and are therefore quite low at the moment. The government is also committed to cutting taxes in line with German and EU policies, a move that is seen as essential to maintain the competitiveness of Finnish industry.

PROCEDURES INVOLVED IN BUYING OR START-ING A NEW BUSINESS

The Ministry of Trade and Industry in Finland provides help and advice on setting up a business in Finland. There is also the Invest in Finland Bureau, set up in 1992 to promote inward investment and to push Finland as a major gateway to the Baltic and Eastern European markets.

Investment Incentives

Foreign companies are eligible for government incentives on the same basis as Finnish companies. There are special incentives for so-called development regions or 'structural adjustment areas' which include most of northern and central Finland. Investments likely to attract government support include manufacturing, tourism and business services.

Start-up loans for businesses are now handled by the TE-Keskus or TE-Centralen on behalf of the Ministry of Trade and Industry (MTI):

Business Subsidies. Granted by the Ministry of Trade and Industry and its regional offices. Business subsidies take the form of regional investment aid, aid for small businesses or development subsidies for SMEs (small and medium-sized companies). The level of subsidy varies from 20 to 40% depending on the category of the region where the investment is taking place.

Subsidies for SMEs. There is a special investment and start-up package for small companies with no more than 50 employees and an annual turnover not exceeding €5 million (approx. £3/US$4.3 million). For SMEs with no more than 250 employees and a turnover not exceeding €20 million there is a development subsidy for improving competitiveness in the international marketplace.

Other Incentives. Tax reliefs are provided by the local tax authorities in development regions. These include a refund of the stamp duty (usually at 4 to 6%) on the purchase of industrial real estate for starting or expanding business operations.

Transportation subsidies are provided by the Ministry of Trade and Industry for firms in development regions. The Ministry also provides grants for the promotion of exports, covering up to 50% of the cost of market research, brochures and sales costs during the start-up period, and it will give grants for attending trade fares abroad.

Useful Addresses

Trade Partners UK Library, Kingsgate House, 66-74 Victoria Street, London SW1E 6SW; ☎020-7215 5444/5; fax 020-7215 4231; www.tradepartners. gov.uk.

Finnish Foreign Trade Association, POB 908, 00101 Helsinki; ☎09 46 951; www.finlandtrade.com.

Finnish Science Park Association, Tykiskönkatu 4D, 20520 Turku; www.tekel.fi.

Invest in Finland Bureau, Aleksanterinkatu 17, POB 800, 00101 Helsinki; ☎09 6969 125; fax 09 6969 2530; www.investinfinland.fi.

Ministry of Trade & Industry, Commission for Foreign Investment, Aleksanterinkatu 4, 00101 Helsinki; ☎09 160 3672; www.vn.fi.

TE-Keskus (Employment and Economic Development Centre), Maistraatinportti 2, 00241 Helsinki; ☎09 2534 2111; fax 09 2534 2000; www.te-keskus.fi. Provides funds for start-up and development, investment in fixed assets and operating capital. Grants soft-, long- and short-term loans and guarantees.

Small and Medium Enterprises Foundation, Unioninkatu 14, 00130 Helsinki; ☎09 7511 7511; fax 09 7511 7500; www.pkt.fi.

Technology Development Centre of Finland (TEKES) POB 69, 00101 Helsinki; ☎010 521 51; fax 09 694 9196; www.tekes.fi. Provides grants and loans as high as 50% for research and technical development. Also credits for as much as 75% of salaries, raw materials, machinery, subcontracting, travel and patents.

VTT Technical Research Centre of Finland, P.O.B. 1000, 02044 VTT; ☎09 4561; fax 09 456 7000. Deals with among other things technological and related economic research and development and international cooperation.

Grants Controlled by the European Commission

There are hundreds of business grant regimes which are overseen by the European Commission. A useful comprehensive listing is contained in *The European Grants Directory.* Private and public sector grants, grants for voluntary organisations and individuals are all available. The directory is published annually by European Consultancy Services (01482-651695) and costs £15 including postage.

BUSINESS STRUCTURES AND REGISTRATION

There are several business forms which are recognised in Finland:

Limited Company.

*O*sakeyhtiö, or *oy*: an *oy* is the type of business entity most found in Finland. It is the only corporate form in which capital is divided into shares and liability is assumed by the company itself. The Limited Companies Act (*Osakeyhtiölaki*) of 29 September 1978 has been overhauled to allow both private and public limited companies. The main difference between public and private companies is the amount of share capital needed: €8,000 (approx. £4,950/US$6,950) for a private company; €80,000 for a public company.

Under the new law, a limited company will be considered a private limited liability company unless the shareholders elect to adopt the public limited company form. If there is a change to a public form, the articles of the company will have to be amended and the company must have evidence of a share capital of not less than €80,000. The company will be deemed to have become a public company only after its articles of association have been recorded in the trade register.

Partnerships.

Partnerships are the most usual form adopted by small entities, and there are two main kinds: the general (denoted by *ay*) and limited (called *ky*). In a general partnership, the partners are jointly and severally liable for the obligations of the partnership. In a limited partnership, at least one of the partners has unlimited liability.

There is the minimum of formalities for creating this type of business. The parties involved enter into a partnership agreement and register it with the Trade Registry and the tax authorities.

There are no minimum capital requirements for partnerships and the partners may be individuals or companies.

Joint Venture.

Joint ventures, otherwise known as 'silent partnerships', come about when one partner (a company or an individual) runs the partnership's business affairs on behalf of the other partners. Limited companies with shares owned by the partners also adopt the joint venture system.

Sole Proprietor Status

The most appropriate form for individual entrepreneurs is usually sole proprietorship (*yksityisen elinkeinonharjoittajan perusilmoitus*) which must be registered with the trade registry (cost €60; (£37/US$52). A sole proprietor has unlimited personal liability for company debts. For accountancy purposes, sole proprietorships are treated the same as partnerships.

Branches of Foreign Companies

An application to start a branch of a foreign company must be submitted to the local administration office in Finland. The application should comprise a copy of the trade registry document from the company's own country and an officially certified Finnish translation. Also a document confirming the decision by the board of directors to establish a branch in Finland, with a Finnish translation. The documents will be forwarded to the trade registry. The application to the trade registry must be signed by the person who is going to be in charge of the branch in Finland. He or she must be resident in Finland.

Accounting requirements are the same as for domestic corporations, but there is no requirement for an external audit. If the branch's turnover exceeds €1.6 million, the branch has to file financial statements with the trade registry within six months of the end of the tax year.

Registering a New Company

There are certain formalities involved in establishing a new company in Finland. These are normally handled by lawyers, accountants or commercial banks providing a complete formation package. A draft of the articles of incorporation of the company has to be submitted to the trade registry which must be notified about the proposed registration of a new company. The registration must be submitted within six months of establishing a corporation, otherwise its incorporation will be deemed to have lapsed. The registrar is responsible for gazetting the formation of a new company in the *Virallinen Lehti* (Official Gazette). In Helsinki the trade registry is at Arkadiankatu 6A (☎09 6939 500; www.prh.fi). The office at Albertinkatu 25, in the same building as the *Maistraatti* or city hall, only registers housing associations. Companies owned by citizens of countries outside the European Economic Area should approach the Ministry of Trade and Industry first.

The forms that you need to submit can be seen on the trade registry website: www.prh.fi/lomake.htm. The Business Information System website, www.ytj.fi,also carries a lot of useful pages. When your business is registered you will receive a number (*Y-Tunnus*) and your details will be put on the trade registry's electronic information network. Anyone can have free access to information on businesses at the trade registry.

The company officially becomes an entity at the first share issue. It usually takes about three months to complete all the formalities needed to form a corporation.

Cost of Starting a New Company

Apart from the minimum share capital needed to start a public or private company (see above), there are normally advisor's fees which are generally low (about €1,000-€2,000; £620-£1,240/US$870-US$1,740) as are registration fees. At present the fee for registration is €250. An amendment notice costs the same. It is also possible to obtain 'off the shelf' companies for less.

IDEAS FOR NEW BUSINESSES

Most countries are keen to encourage inward investment and Finland is no exception. Business people will find that there are many incentives for business start-ups or for investing in Finnish businesses. Finland is also very keen to promote Finnish products abroad, so any foreigner with languages and proven international marketing skills would have an excellent chance of talking themselves into a job. The types of business which could be started in Finland with a reasonable prospect of doing well would be private employment agencies (as yet virtually unknown there), software, graphic design, copy-writing, and language schools.

RUNNING A BUSINESS

Employing Staff

Contracts. Managerial and professional staff are normally provided with individual contracts whereas other types of staff are protected by a barrage of regulations enshrined in the Employment Contract Law and the Work Safety Law. Wage rates and conditions are to a large extent governed by collective bargaining agreements.

Trade Unions. Trade Unions are particularly strong in the metal and paper industries where 95% of employees are signed-up members. They are less strong in the services sector where membership is about 60%. Trade unions are important in the collective bargaining process.

Wages and Salaries. Minimum wages are usually fixed by agreement between management and unions. The average worker's hourly wage is about €13 (approx. £8/US$ 11) for men and €11 for women.

Social Security Contributions. Other expenses which are largely paid by the employer are the compulsory social security contributions for pensions, sickness and disability, occupational accident and unemployment insurance. The employer pays about 75% of the total. Contributions do not normally have to be paid for foreign employees staying in Finland for less than one year.

Termination of Employment. In theory employers and employees have equal rights to terminate employment contracts. However, termination by the employer is hedged about with restrictions. For instance employees may only be dismissed for exceptional reasons. Employees may not be sacked for illness or pregnancy, or for taking part in a strike or other union activity. If there is a temporary reduction in the volume of work, the employer is bound to try to find other work for the employee.

Periods of notice required for both parties are usually defined by collective bargaining agreements. If this is not the case the length of time varies according to length of employment. The minimum is two months' notice from the employer's side and one month from the employee's.

If the employee is deemed to have been unlawfully dismissed the employer has to pay a financial penalty equivalent to three to 20 months' wages.

Taxation

The principal taxes affecting businesses in Finland are corporation tax and VAT, though they are also liable for capital gains tax and stamp duties in certain circumstances. In a sole proprietorship, personal income tax is payable. Among innovations designed to bring Finland into line with other EU countries, the corporation tax basic rate has been lowered to 29%. The tax year for companies depends on the financial period of the company concerned. If the company's financial period ends between 1 January and 1 October, the tax return must be filed by 1 January of the following year. Alternatively companies whose financial period ends between 2 October and 31 December must file tax returns by 1 April of the following year.

For limited companies, partnerships and the self-employed, the tax is usually paid in 11 advance instalments based on an estimate made by the local tax office. Late payment incurs a penalty of 1% per month.

Final assessments of tax returns are usually completed by October of the year following the tax year. If the tax office calculates that an overpayment has been made, the difference is refunded, usually by December. If the reverse is the case and the tax office has underestimated your liability, then any additional tax due has to be paid in December. If the amount is considerable, it may be paid over three consecutive months.

Tax Audits. The tax authorities have the right to inspect the books of any company. Large companies are subject to regular audits, about every five years, but there are not enough resources to give small companies the same treatment.

Tax on Partnerships. For tax purposes a partnership's income is calculated in the same way as a company's taxable income and then allocated among the partners. An individual's share of the partnership income is divided into capital income and earned income. Capital income is usually calculated at 15% of the partnership's net assets. The remainder is regarded as earned income. The division of income is not applicable to corporate partners.

VAT. VAT is levied at 22% on most goods and services sold by businesses.

Capital Gains Tax. CGT is tougher on companies than on individuals. Where companies have assets such as real estate or shares which are not reported to the tax authorities as business assets, they may not claim indexation in calculating the gain as an individual would be allowed to do. Their calculations must be based on the purchase price, whereas an individual can usually deduct 30% or sometimes 50% of the sales price before calculating the gain.

Stamp Duty. Businesses are liable for stamp duties: at 1.6% on transfers of shares. However, stamp duties are not levied on transactions on the stock exchange or so-called OTC (over-the-counter) dealings. Loans from banks or other financial institutions are liable for a 1.5% stamp duty on the amount borrowed and if the loan is raised abroad then there is a 0.5% loan tax. Other stamp duties for which businesses may be liable include a 4-6% rate on transfers of real estate.

Accountancy and Auditing Requirements

Finland passed a new Accounting Act in December 1992 to comply with the EU's company law directives. A company must present financial statements annually within three months of the end of the accounting year and these must be presented for adoption to a general shareholders' meeting to be held no later than six months after the end of the accounting year. Within two months of the financial statements being adopted, companies should file a certified copy of their statutory accounts with the Trade Registry, including consolidated accounts with an auditor's report. All of these are then made available for public inspection.

Limited liability companies must appoint at least one independent auditor who must be Finnish, or a permanent resident of Finland. If there is more than one auditor, only one need be Finnish. If the company is a large one then one of the auditors must be authorised or working for a company authorised by the Central Chamber of Commerce. A large company for this purpose is defined as one which:

- Is listed on the stock exchange.
- Whose share capital and restricted reserves exceed €350,000 (approx. 217,000/US$304,000).
- Whose average number of employees exceeds 500 during the previous two accountancy years.
- If the company fulfils only number two above, it is sufficient for the auditor to be authorised at local level by the chamber of commerce.

Useful Addresses

Central Chamber of Commerce of Finland, Aleksanterinkatu 17, 00100 Helsinki; ☎09 6969 69.

Euro Info Centre, Helsinki Chamber of Commerce, Kalevankatu 12, 00100 Helsinki; ☎09 228 606; www.euro neuvontakeskus.com.

Oy Ernst & Young Ab, National Office, Kaivokatu 8, 00100 Helsinki; ☎09 172771; fax 09 622 1223. Main Finnish branch of chartered accountants Ernst & Young providing full business service including public accounting, tax and management consulting.

Finnish Association for Accounting Firms, Salomonkatu 17A, 00100 Helsinki; ☎09 694 4077; fax 09 694 9596.

Finnish Employers' Confederation (STK). Eteläranta 10, 00130 Helsinki; ☎09 17281; www.stk.fi.

Finnish Institute of Authorised Public Accountants, Fredrikinkatu 61A, 39, 00100 Helsinki; ☎09 694 2255; fax 09 693 1567.

National Board of Patents and Registration (Trade Register), Arkadiankatu 6A, P.O. Box 1140, 00101 Helsinki; ☎09 6939 500; fax 09 6939 5328; www.prh.fi.

Useful Publications

There is a considerable amount of information available both on the internet and in published form on starting a business. The Chamber of Commerce, Ministry of Trade and Industry and other bodies will be pleased to help entrepreneurs. The official bookshop, Edita, at Annankatu 44, has a large stock of useful books, mostly in Finnish. English publications include:

Establishing a Business in Finland, Edita Oy.

Taxation in Finland, Edita Oy. Published every two years.

An Enterprise of Your Own?, Ministry of Labour. Small leaflet available at jobcentres; also on the website www.vn.fi in PDF format.

Starting Your Own Small Business in Finland, Reindeer Books, Karina.

Finnish SME Sector in the EU, Ministry of Trade and Industry.
European Labour Law, by Roger Blanpain. Frequently updated.

Patents, Trademarks & Copyrights

Laws on the above are in line with other EU countries. Asserting a right over a patent, design or trademark normally entails registering with the National Board of Patents and Registration.

Patents. The application for a patent must be in Finnish and submitted by a resident of Finland, or a company registered in the EEA. The patent takes effect from the date of the register of the application and is in force for 20 years. The issuing process may take up to five years for a foreign patent.

Trademarks. The registration of a trademark is similar to a patent except that it is in force for ten years and can be renewed for further 10-year periods. The fee is €170 (€185 for renewal). The definition of a trademark is:

- A device.
- One or more letters, words or numbers.
- A distinctive arrangement of goods or packaging.

Once a trademark has been registered, the owner has the exclusive right to use it as a distinguishing symbol for their goods or packaging. It is possible to still have the sole right to a trademark even without registering, if it has an established reputation and has become generally associated by the business community or customers in Finland with a particular owner's goods.

Copyright. The copyright act is for creative, literary or artistic work. The categories included are: written or spoken fictional or descriptive renderings and may be musical, dramatic or cinematographic, fine art, architectural, artistic handicraft or industrial art or design. The copyright entitles the owner to the exclusive right to control the work by producing copies and making the work available to others. Since 1991 computer programmes have come under the copyright act as they are considered literary works.

Miscellaneous Intellectual Property. Designs can be registered for five years and renewed twice for a total of 15 years. Methods and chemical products cannot however be protected. Utility models are technical solutions which are not sufficiently unique to warrant a patent but which involve progressive inventive processes. These are protected for four years and are renewable for another four years.

When naming your company or product or setting up a foreign company in Finland you should check that the words in the title or product name do not mean anything laughable or worse in Finnish. Conversely some words are acceptable in Finnish that are not in English. You cannot however call your company Bonk Business Inc. as this firm already exists in Helsinki. Bonk means a mechanical noise in Finnish.

Norway

SECTION I

LIVING IN NORWAY

GENERAL INTRODUCTION

RESIDENCE AND ENTRY REGULATIONS

SETTING UP HOME

DAILY LIFE

RETIREMENT

GENERAL INTRODUCTION

DESTINATION NORWAY

Set on the edge of the North Sea and the Arctic Ocean, Norway often seems to be more of a European outpost than a fully paid-up European country. This is hardly surprising – geographically Norway is separated from mainland Europe by a narrow strip of water, it lies in northerly latitudes, and its most southerly point barely reaches as far as the far north of Scotland. Politically and economically too, Norway has retained a certain independence from Europe; this was particularly apparent in the November 1994 referendum when a narrow majority opted to stay out of the European Union despite the fact that Norway had joined the European Economic Area in January of the same year.

Reasons for voting against joining the European Union tended to have a more idealistic basis than an economic one, although, as things have turned out, the decision was the right one. Norway sees itself as a unique country which does not want to be told what to do by the bureaucrats of Brussels. Centuries of domination by Denmark and later Sweden, and the German occupation, have left them wary of outside interference; there is a strong sense of wanting to preserve national identity and culture. Much of the opposition came from Norway's traditional farming and fishing communities who were anxious to protect their livelihoods. Most of the support for membership of the EU came from big business, the media and the political parties. As the country is rich in oil and gas resources, Norway is in a position to stay self-sufficient for the time being and is doing much better outside the EU than its neighbour Sweden.

However, it would be a mistake to see Norway as an isolationist country that is constantly casting suspicious glances over its shoulder. Norway pursues an idealistic foreign policy, and is at the forefront of peace-making initiatives around the world. There has long been a genuine desire to promote social equality, although recent political developments have shown a movement away from the socialist agenda of the past. The small population of 4.5 million enjoys a disproportionate amount of national wealth thanks to discoveries of oil and gas in the 1960s. Norway is over 1,000 miles/1,600 km long and its national identity has been strongly influenced by its geography, as small farming communities have developed in isolation from each other. Norway was already a wealthy country before the discovery of oil; the challenge it faces is how to spend its unexpected wealth wisely before the oil and gas run out.

Norway and the Norwegian way of life remain largely unknown to most outsiders. Not that many people can identify the dramatist Ibsen, the composer Grieg, or the painter Munch with Norway. The explorers Amundsen and Heyerdahl are more readily identified as Norwegian. Once a year Norway is in the international spotlight when the Nobel Peace Prize ceremony is held in Oslo, although Nobel himself was Swedish, and the prizes are awarded by the Swedish Academy of Sciences. Anyone who goes to Norway will be impressed by the beauty of the natural landscape; few would disagree that Norway has the best scenery in Europe.

Norway is inevitably having to accept the presence of more and more immigrants, rather than just tourists, which in itself is a challenge to a country that has in the past seen mass emigration because of economic hardship. The idea of Norway as a country where people want to go to start a new life takes some getting used to.

PROS AND CONS OF MOVING TO NORWAY

Historically the Norwegians have earned a reputation for being less than welcoming to foreign workers; a general ban on immigration was imposed in 1975. Until Norway's membership of the European Economic Area (EEA) from 1994 gaining a work or residence permit in Norway was very difficult (although exceptions were made for specialist skilled workers for the oil and gas industry) and this situation still holds for non-EEA nationals.

Yet Norwegians are far from being insular and narrow-minded towards foreigners *per se*. Few European nations are as generous, welcoming and friendly although the Norwegians are usually rather less effusive when showing it than their southern European counterparts. Reasons for keeping a fairly closed door policy lie with history and economics rather than mere insularity. Until the second half of the present century life in Norway was a hard battle to gain a subsistence level of existence from poor unyielding soil, and a valley in Norway could rarely support more than one or two farming families. Like their Viking ancestors, many Norwegians turned west in search of opportunity and wealth, and the 19th century saw a mass emigration of over 750,000 Norwegians to America (a third of the population). In present-day Norway there is a strong environmental awareness and concern about overcrowding and encroachment on the country's beautiful green spaces.

One of the main drawbacks which immediately strikes foreigners who take up work in Norway is the hefty cost of living. There are many reasons for this – heavy farming subsidies, high taxes and the cost of imports being a few. Whilst wages are generally correspondingly good, opportunities for saving in Norway are diminished by high costs – food and drink in particular are very expensive. Set against this is a country with excellent social and welfare services, a very low crime rate and some of the most stunning scenery in Europe. English is widely and excellently spoken throughout Norway and amongst all sectors of the population with the possible exception of the elderly. However, not being able to speak Norwegian could adversely affect your job prospects, and your social acceptance. While the rules of the European Economic Area grant the right to all member nationals to look for work in all member countries, this does not affect the individual employer's right to hire or not to hire.

PROS AND CONS OF MOVING TO NORWAY

Pros:
- Strong economy
- Excellent social security system
- High standard of living
- English widely spoken
- Friendly, helpful people
- Glorious scenery
- Open access to the job market for EEA nationals

Cons:
- Very high cost of living
- Not as geared to employing and housing foreigners as the rest of Europe
- Authorities not all that helpful to casual job seekers
- Very long distances to travel between places
- Long, dark, cold winters
- High taxes

Norway is considerably less geared towards employing foreigners than mainstream Europe and finding work and accommodation can be more of a struggle than in other parts of Europe. There are opportunities, however, and the North Sea oil fields off Norway's western coast have provided wealth and work opportunities for the British, Americans and French in particular. The Norwegians claim to have a special affection for the British although they are less than happy about pollution, specifically the acid rain, which blows over from Britain. This is quite a sore point – in 1987 when the then British Prime Minister Margaret Thatcher visited Oslo the police had to mobilise the riot squad for the first time ever because of protests against acid rain.

Norwegians are great lovers of folklore and nature and the population has a lot of it to enjoy. Of all the Scandinavian countries, Norway has the most glorious scenery which is ever changing and always superb. Sports and the Great Outdoors are very important in Norway and this holds true all year round. Set against the natural beauty is the fact that the country is in a northerly position which inevitably means dark, snowy winters.

POLITICAL AND ECONOMIC STRUCTURE

Until the discovery of North Sea oil in the 1960s both weather and terrain had a powerful influence on Norway's development as a nation. As an outpost on the northern end of the North Sea, Norway has played a relatively low-key role in international affairs and only truly emerged onto the European scene in the second half of this century.

Recorded history of Norway begins only in about 800 AD; the ancestors of the Norwegians were Germanic tribes who probably entered Scandinavia from the north. Until about 500 BC most Norwegians were migratory hunters, but a deteriorating climate led to the development of settled communal farming. From this, small communities emerged which were democratic in nature, and by the eighth century, Norway comprised a number of small independent kingdoms which were isolated from each other by the mountainous terrain. The attractions of doing business abroad, as well as a shortage of farmland in Norway itself, led the Norwegian Vikings to pillage their way across Britain and Ireland in the eighth century and move further west into Iceland. Their ocean-going longships, which were equally suited to sailing up river estuaries (the word Viking means 'people who sail up creeks'), enabled them to strike at lightning speed against the sedentary communities of Western Europe. Iceland, the Faroe Islands and Greenland were largely settled by Norwegians exiles. Around 1000 AD Leif Eriksson set up a colony in North America named Vinland; although the location is not entirely certain it may have been in Newfoundland. The Viking era was more or less over by 1066 when Harald Hardråda made an unsuccessful attempt to conquer England, just before William the Conqueror's successful invasion.

Christianity was brought to Norway in the 12th century although the earlier paganism lingered on until after the Reformation. The Hanseatic League was formed during the Middle Ages and in Norway operated principally from the harbour of the then capital, Bergen. The League was a chain of European and Baltic cities with shared trading agreements – an early forerunner of the European Community. Squabbles over succession to the Norwegian throne were a constant feature of medieval Norway; the arrival of the Black Death in 1349 devastated Norwegian farming communities and decimated the nobility. A period of comparative stability came to Norway and to all of Scandinavia when Norway, Sweden and Denmark were united in 1397 by Margrethe widow of King Håkon of Denmark, who persuaded Norway and Sweden to hand over their crowns to her five-year-old nephew Erik.

The union was beset by difficulties and Norway came increasingly under Danish influence and in 1536 was relegated to a humble Danish province. The union with Denmark survived until 1814 when, following the defeat of Denmark in the Napoleonic Wars, Norway was united with Sweden. Initially this was an uneasy alliance, with Norway subservient to Sweden. The 19th century saw a period of domestic reform and economic growth in Norway, the country prospered and by the late 19th century it had the third largest merchant navy. Overpopulation in rural areas lead to widespread emigration to America.

The tide of nationalism of the late 19th century washed over Norway and in 1905 a plebiscite voted overwhelmingly for dissolution of the union. Norway was declared an independent monarchy and a Danish prince elected to the throne as King Håkon VII.

Although Norway remained neutral in World War I and at first profited greatly, things went downhill after sanctions on trade with Germany were imposed by the USA, and half the merchant shipping fleet was sunk by U-boats. The end of the war saw a huge rise in state expenditure, runaway inflation and industrial unrest. As the economy declined the Norwegian Labour Party became the dominant force in politics from 1927 and has remained a powerful force to the present.

Norway wanted to remain neutral throughout World War II but the Nazi invasion, aided and abetted by the treachery of Defence Minister Vidkun Quisling, brought Norway under German occupation. King Håkon abdicated and fled to Britain where he worked with the Norwegian exile movement. With the surrender of Germany in May 1945, he returned with his son Crown Prince Olav to a tumultuous reception which sealed the popularity of the monarchy in Norway.

At the end of the war the retreating Nazis razed many towns and villages in northern Norway. A programme of rebuilding began, industry was expanded and modernised and the standard of living rose faster than in most other European countries. The discovery of oil and gas in the North Sea in 1969 led Norway into a period of unprecedented prosperity and the Socialist government introduced a comprehensive social welfare programme, while ensuring that the wealth from the oil fields would be invested wisely for the country's long-term future. Post-war Norwegian socialism has been generally middle-of-the-road, aiming to create social equality and opportunities for everyone.

Economy

Norway operates as a free-market economy. Over 95% of industrial companies have less than 100 employees but these account for half of the industrial labour force and for more than half of production. Foreign companies account for about 10% of production. Only a few larger industries are state-owned but they account for nearly half of the GDP. The largest company in Norway, Statoil, is partly privatised and Norsk Hydro is 51% state-owned. Agriculture is strongly subsidised, fishing to a lesser extent and the state actively participates in the oil industry. Norway is particularly rich in natural resources, of which the most important are oil, gas, hydroelectric power, metal ores, forestry and fish. Hydroelectric power from Norway's numerous natural water sources forms the basis of much of the electricity which powers Norwegian industry.

Only about 3% of Norway's elongated landmass is cultivated. Most farms are small family affairs with less than 1% having more than 125 acres. Norway has about 65,000 self-employed farmers. The main agricultural product is livestock. The country has over three million chickens, just over a million sheep and nearly a million cattle. The majority of agricultural land (56%) is used for mowing and pasture lands; the principal crops are grain, peas, oil seed, potatoes and root crops. The most fertile food growing area is in the south. Despite the inauspicious climate and poor growing conditions, Norway is self-sufficient in livestock products and produces an impressive 59% of its own food. This is done mainly by huge subsidies: 10% of the national budget goes on farming subsidies and much of this is spent on small farms which are not economically viable.

About one-third of Norway consists of forests which provide the basis for the wood-processing industry. Wood is a small but important export commodity; about 22.9% of the land area in use is productive forest. Half of Norwegian farms depend on forestry as a second source of income. The paper and pulp industry, of which the forests form the basis, has been a growth export area for Norway.

Fishing plays a similar role for farmers as forestry. Only half of Norway's fishermen claim fishing as their sole occupation and many farmers fish as a seasonal occupation. With an extensive coastline and multiple varieties, fish is a staple fare with cod the most prolific catch. Only about one-third of the haul is for human consumption with the rest being processed as fish meal and oil. Fish and fish related products account for over 14% of traditional commodity exports per year.

The shipping industry has traditionally played an important part in the Norwegian economy. After considerable setbacks, bankruptcies and closures in the late 1980s the shipping market has taken an upward turn and Norway now has one of the world's largest merchant fleets. Norwegian shipping giants Kvaerner have become the world's third largest ship owners.

The Norwegian economy experienced huge growth following the discovery of the Ekofisk oil and gas fields in 1969. North Sea oil brought considerable wealth to Norway's 4.5 million population. In the 1970s oil and gas became the most important exports and by the 1980s rivalled the total value of traditional commercial exports. Money from the oil and gas fields was injected into Norway's declining industries, into the welfare, education and the transport systems, leading to a consequent increase in the standard of living. Like Britain, Norway was hit hard by the decline in oil prices in 1986 and experienced 6% unemployment and many bankruptcies. One of the problems facing the Norwegian economy is the need to promote and develop the traditional commodity exports and knowledge-based industries to prevent overdependence on the oil reserves. The government has responded by instituting a queue system for oil and gas developments. 64,000 Norwegians work in the oil sector.

An offshoot of the oil and gas industries has been the growth of the engineering industry. About one-third of manufacturing consists of the production of equipment for the petroleum industry. Electrical equipment, electronics and telecommunications also play a significant part in the Norwegian economy.

Norway spends more money per capita on foreign aid than any other country, through its aid organisation, NORAD. Unemployment in Norway is currently about 3.5% (not including people on job creation schemes), relatively low for a Scandinavian country, but there is a shortage of specialised workers. The oil industry, in particular, could not function without foreign expertise. Inflation is tending to rise towards 3% (2002); interest rates are high at 7%.

Government

Norway has a constitutional monarchy and a multiparty political system. The parliament or Storting has 165 members who sit in two chambers – the Odelsting and the Lagting. Members are democratically elected every four years and the Prime Minister and State Council are nominally selected by the monarch with the approval of the Storting.

The monarch's role is as symbolic head of state and the current king, Harald V has reigned since 1991. The role is an exclusively male affair as the constitution allows succession only through the male line. Generally the Norwegian monarchy is low-key with pomp and ceremony being kept to a minimum. There was something of a crisis in 2000 when Crown Prince Håkon announced his intention to marry an unmarried mother, Mette-Marit Tjessem-Høiby. The marriage went ahead in August 2001, and most Norwegians are now quite happy with Mette-Marit as their future queen.

The Norwegian constitution was drafted in 1814 when Norway and Denmark dissolved a 434-year-old union. Eclectic in nature, the constitution draws on

British political traditions, the US constitution and notions of Liberty, Equality, Fraternity, embodied in the French Revolution. Amendments can be made to the constitution by a two-thirds majority in the Storting.

Candidates for the *Storting* are nominated from each of Norway's 19 counties or *fylker* and the number of candidates representing each *fylke* depends on the size of its population. From before World War II to the mid-1960s Norwegian politics has been dominated by the *Norske Arbeiderpartiet* (DNA) or Labour Party. This was followed by a series of coalition governments in which no single party held a majority. Gro Harlem Brundtland, Norway's first woman prime minister, headed governments in 1981, 1986-1989 and 1990-1996. She was followed by a Labour-only government under Thorbjørn Jagland.

A centre-right coalition came into power under Kjell Magne Bondevik from October 1997 to March 2000. Bondevik's first government fell after a vote of no confidence, and was followed by 20 months of Labour government under Jens Stoltenberg. Bondevik returned to power after fresh elections in October 2001, with a coalition made up of the Christian Democrat Party, the Conservative Party, and the Liberal Party. The opposition is made up of the Labour Party, the Centre Party, the Socialist Left, the Progress Party, and the Red Electoral Alliance.

Norway is a member of NATO, the Council of Europe and the European Economic Area. In a 1972 referendum Norway voted against joining the European Community, opposition coming largely from among farmers and fishermen who feared the loss of subsidies, but there was also opposition from young urban professionals who saw joining as a threat to national identity. The result was a vote of 52.5% against joining. The country reconsidered membership in the autumn of 1994. The referendum then produced an almost identical narrow majority against joining (52.2%). Even the fact that the Swedes had decided to join the EU had no impact on the attitude of the Norwegians towards membership.

Euroscepticism and a traditional independence, as well as a sense of security from the reserves of the North Sea oil and gas were the main reasons behind Norway's opting out. Some industrialists have expressed concern about the future implications for Norway's activities in the commercial world. In addition to this Norway will have limited bargaining power in seeking concessions from the European Union and there are fears that the country may suffer from isolation over international issues of trade and the environment.

Although Norway does not seem likely to join the EU in the foreseeable future, she has been part of the European Economic Area since 1994, thus giving other EEA nationals a number of rights in the Norway, in particular the right to work, and some social security rights.

GEOGRAPHICAL INFORMATION

Area

Norway occupies a total area of 150,000 sq miles/386,958 sq km including Svalbard (Spitsbergen), the remote northern islands which lie 400 miles (640 km) north of the mainland. Norway is approximately the size of the United Kingdom or California and comprises an elongated, thin landmass which bears some resemblance to a tadpole with the broader southern end as the head. At over 1,000 miles/1,600 km long, the country would reach Rome if it was pivoted on Oslo and is so long that the weather maps on the nation's TV screens divide the country into two. In places however, it is less than five miles wide. Western Norway has a jagged, fjord-indented coastline which measures 4,300 miles/2,650 km (excluding the fjords) and is studded with about 50,000 tiny islands. The country stretches from latitude 57° 57'N at Kristiansand to 71° 11'N at the North Cape and about half of the country lies above the Arctic Circle.

Norway is a neighbour of Sweden (they share a 1,000 mile/1,619 km border) and Finland and Russia in the north. The former Soviet Union shares Svalbard with Norway in a fairly easy relationship.

About two-thirds of Norway's terrain is mountainous – the average elevation is 1,600 feet compared with an average of 1,000 feet for Europe as a whole. Traditionally this has made transport and communication difficult and accounts for the fact that even today many farms are isolated in valleys. The Hardanger plateau in Southern Norway is Europe's largest mountain plateau covering 4,600 square miles/11,900 square km. Large areas of Norway are covered in forest but the soil is poor agricultural land.

Population

Norway is the fifth largest country in Europe but has the second lowest population density after Iceland. With just over 4.5 million inhabitants Norway has approximately 34 inhabitants per square mile/13 per square km. Over 500,000 people live in Oslo; half the country's population lives in the Oslo region. Other main cities' estimated populations are: Bergen 218,000, Trondheim 140,000 and Stavanger 101,000. The majority of the population lives in the south; the far north is very thinly populated. Low birth rates have reduced population growth; an increasing proportion of the population are elderly because of high longevity. There is a surplus of about 20,000 of immigration over emigration.

The north is home to 90% of the 20,000 Sami population of Norway. The Sami form an ethnic minority whose culture and language have much in common with that of the Sami of Northern Sweden and Finland. There are very few truly nomadic reindeer herders left amongst the Sami and only about 2,000 of them live on the Finnmark Plateau. Despite this they have clung fiercely to their own identity and in 1989 were granted their own parliament the *Sameting.*

Norway has historically operated a fairly open-door policy towards refugees and visitors to Norway are often surprised that this land of mainly blond, blue-eyed people has a surprisingly multi-cultural mix of races and religions. Although it has had a particularly good record on granting refuge to refugees, Norway currently operates a very strict immigration policy. Racism is a problem that is taken very seriously by the government, and discussed quite openly; unfortunately, a certain degree of suspicion of outsiders is a trait of the Norwegian character that cannot easily be changed. The population is rising steadily; there is a net surplus of immigration over emigration of 20,000 per year.

Climate

As you would expect, Norway is not the best place to go for a sun tan; nonetheless, it would be wrong to lump the whole of Norway together as a cold northern country. Its length means that there is considerable variation in climate. Norway is warmer than its northern position should warrant owing to the benevolent effect of the Gulf Stream, which means that the fjords do not, as a rule, freeze over even in the far north. The west coast experiences an average annual temperature of 7°C/45°F and the Lofoten Islands which fall inside the Arctic Circle experience well above average winter temperatures for the latitude because of warm southerly air currents.

The west coast of Norway experiences frequent gales and weather changes because of North Atlantic cyclones. It has fairly cool summers, mild winters and up to 80 inches/2030 mm of rain. Eastern Norway is more sheltered because of the mountains; summers are relatively warm whilst winters are cold. Average rainfall for the east is less than 30 inches a year. In the far north, winters are long, snowy, cold and dark, and summers are brief, bright and surprisingly warm. Temperatures are generally mild in Norway thanks to the Gulf Stream but it can be dark and bleak in winter. Tables 8 and 9 list average monthly temperatures and rainfall.

TABLE 8   AVERAGE TEMPERATURES (DEGREES CENTIGRADE)

Month	Oslo	Bergen	Trondheim	Tromsø
January	−4.7	1.5	−3.1	−3.5
February	−4.0	1.3	−2.6	−4.0
March	−0.5	3.1	−0.4	−2.7
April	4.8	5.8	3.5	0.3
May	10.7	10.2	8.2	4.1
June	14.7	12.6	11.6	8.8
July	17.3	15.0	14.7	12.4
August	15.9	14.7	13.6	11.0
September	11.3	12.0	9.8	7.2
October	5.9	8.3	5.4	3.0
November	1.1	5.5	1.8	−0.1
December	−2.0	3.3	−0.7	−1.9

TABLE 9   AVERAGE RAINFALL IN MM

Month	Oslo	Bergen	Trondheim	Tromsø
January	49	193	57	96
June	71	135	68	59
Courtesy of Statistics Norway, the Royal Ministry of Foreign Affairs.				

For more immediate information about the weather in Norway contact the Norwegian Weather Bureau, (*Det Norske Meteorologisk Instituttet*), Klima-avdelingen, Niels Henriks Abels Vei 40, 0371 Oslo; ☎22 96 30 00; www.dnmi.no.

There is usually plenty of snow throughout the country in winter and skiing is as much a means of local transport as it is a sport. It is sometimes claimed that the Norwegians are born wearing skis and the oldest pair of skis found in Norway dates back 2,600 years. Generally road transport is good even in winter – centuries of bad weather have taught the Norwegians a thing or two about keeping the roads open; but inevitably some of the minor roads may be closed.

Midnight Sun and Northern Lights

With so much of the country within the Arctic Circle, northern Norway experiences a considerable amount of midnight sun. From 13 May to 29 July the midnight sun is visible from the North Cape (Nordkapp). The further south you go, the less one can experience it. Generally summers in Norway have very long hours of daylight and in winter correspondingly long hours of night. Adjusting to these extremes takes time and even Norwegians experience difficulty sleeping in the long summer nights. Long hours of darkness in winter can lead to seasonal affective depression although reflections from the snow can make things lighter than they normally would be.

The northern lights (or aurora borealis), can be seen in the north in winter. Viewing is often better just below the Arctic Circle than above it. The lights appear as shimmering colours in a clear night sky. The usual colour is green but they can be red and yellow too.

REGIONAL GUIDE

Norway is a large country with a small population. The mountainous terrain which divides region from region may account for the fact that neighbours in the next valley may speak a different dialect and may be regarded as slightly foreign. In the past, rural families tended to be isolated and self-sufficient, cut off in a valley whose soil was not good enough to support more than one or two farms. Today Norwegians still appreciate having plenty of space; towns tend to be small and spread out. In the north the Sami people do not acknowledge national boundaries and move freely between Norway, Sweden, Finland and Russia.

Most English-speaking foreigners are to be found in the south, in Oslo, Stavanger and Bergen.

Information facilities. Whilst you may find the authorities and other organisations rather monosyllabic with individual enquirers, there is a great deal of information on the internet in English, which compensates for the cautiousness about saying too much. The government site http://odin.dep.no/engelsk will give you all the necessary links to the ministries and even to the websites of members of the royal family. Most tourist offices have their own websites, except for those in the far north; they usually provide free maps and brochures. Libraries in Norway generally have free internet access. Norway has few tourist offices abroad; where there is no tourist office, you can contact the nearest Norwegian embassy.

Useful Addresses

Norwegian Tourist Board, 5 Regent Street, London SW1; ☎020-7838 6255; e-mail infouk@ntr.no; www.visitnorway.com.
Scandinavian Tourist Board, 655 3rd Ave, New York, NY 10017; ☎212-885-9700; www.visitnorway.com.

The country can be divided into the following regions:

The Østland (Eastern Norway)

Østland contains more than half of Norway's population most of whom live in the capital city of Oslo (pop. 510,000). Oslo itself is vast, comprising 454 square kilometres of which only a small proportion is city, the rest being taken up with areas of forest, beach and water. Oslo is not only an attractive city, with superb public transport and amenities, it also boasts several world-class museums, including the Viking Ships Museum and the Edvard Munch Museum (Munch is mostly known for his expressionist masterpiece, The Scream). As well as the tourist office there is a Youth Information Service, Use It (see below).

Oslo is bounded on the east by Oslomarka – an area of seven adjoining forests which is larger than Greater London. The land extending south-eastwards towards the Swedish border is relatively fertile lowland which is intensively cultivated for cereal grains. Forests in this area form a significant proportion of farm acreage and the region has just over half of Norway's total forest resources and fully cultivated land. The southern coastline of the Østland which faces across to Denmark is densely populated with small towns and coastal villages, the most significant of which is the city of Kristiansand on the southern tip of Norway.

Norway's most popular ski resort, Lillehammer, is located about 113m/180km north of Oslo. It became famous as the site of the 1994 Winter Olympics, although it is in fact a year-round tourist resort.

Useful Addresses

Norges Informasjonssenter, Brynjulf Bulls plass 1, 0250 Oslo; ☎22 83 00 50; e-mail touristinfo@oslopro.no; www.oslopro.no, www.visitoslo.no.
Use It, Møllergata 2, 0179 Oslo; 22 41 51 32; fax 22 42 63 71; e-mail useit@unginfo.oslo.no; www.unginfo.oslo.no.
Kristiansand Tourist Office, Vestre Strandgate 32, Kristiansand; ☎38 12 13 14; e-mail soerreis@online.no; www.visitsorlandet.com.
Turistkontor Lillehammer, Elvegata 19, 2609 Lillehammer; 61 25 02 99; fax 61 26 96 55; www.lillehammerturist.no.

Vestland (Western Norway) and the Fjord Country

The narrow coastal zone of southwestern Norway is characterised by a jagged coastline of fjords cutting into the mountainous region of the main land. It contains Norway's two major cities of Stavanger and Bergen. The Jæren Plain south of Stavanger is exceptionally fertile because of mild winters and long growing seasons. Stavanger itself is a major industrial centre built on a fjord.

Once predominantly known for its fish canning industry, Stavanger became wealthy on the oil riches of the North Sea and was in danger of becoming the Dallas of Norway, but has remained an attractive well-preserved city thanks to money being invested in restoration as well as in local industry and social services. Stavanger marks the beginning of the Fjord Country which stretches north to the great Hardanger Fjord, encompassing Bergen, the Fjord capital, past the Sognfjord and Nordfjord to the less well-known Geirangerfjord.

Bergen, about 100 miles north of Stavanger is the former capital of Norway and is a beautiful city built on seven hills around a harbour. Once a major trading centre for northern Europe, Bergen operated as a hub of the German Hanseatic League. Today it is the most cosmopolitan town of Norway although many Norwegians feel that the Bergenese suffer from an inflated sense of their own importance and have never quite resigned themselves to the fact that Bergen is no longer the capital. Further north from Bergen is the Sunnmore District with Ålesund at its centre and a major engineering area. Many large smelting plants are built on the Vestland fjords, taking advantage of the hydroelectric resources of the area. This is also the centre for Norway's furniture industry.

Useful Addresses

Bergen, Slottsgaten 1, PO Box 4055 Dreggen, 5835 Bergen; ☎55 55 20 00; fax 55 55 20 11; e-mail mail@visitBergen.com; www.visitBergen.com.

Turistinformasjonen Stavanger, Rosenkildetorget 1, Pb.11 Sentrum, 4001 Stavanger; ☎51 85 92 00; fax 51 85 92 02; e-mail info@visitStavanger.com; www.visitStavanger.com.

Trondelag, Nordland and Troms

Standing just above the western fjords, Trondelag and Nordland are two long thin counties. Trondelag in the south represents the last contact with the gentler forested regions of the south and leads into Nordland where the Arctic Circle and the wilderness begin. The major town of Trondelag is Trondheim in the south, an attractive medieval town, which is Norway's third city and former home to the early Norse parliament. The major attraction today is the Nidaros Domkirke, a medieval cathedral and Scandinavia's largest surviving medieval building. South east of Trondheim is the marvellously preserved 18th century mining town of Røros. Northern Trondelag is scenic but thinly populated and leads into Nordland.

At Mo-i-Rana, just before the Arctic Circle, is an enormous steel plant built just after the war to revive the local economy. From here towns are few and far between and the railway runs out at Bodø. To the northwest are the Lofoten Islands – a string of mountainous islands which are famous for their bird life. Adjacent to the Lofoten Islands on the mainland is Narvik, an important iron-ore town with an impressive, if not particularly attractive, industrial complex. During the war Narvik was heavily bombed by the Germans and many British soldiers lost their lives here. From Narvik the population becomes even more sparse and the only major town is Tromsø in the county of Troms.

Tromsø has been saddled with the absurd nickname of 'Paris of the North', possibly because it houses the world's most northerly university and cathedral.

In fact it is a large fishing town with four filleting factories, but also several museums. From Tromsø it is possible to fly to Svalbard.

Useful Addresses

Turistinformasjon Tromsø, Storgata 61/63, Tromsø; ☎77 61 00 00; fax 77 61 00 01; www.destinasjontromso.no.
Turistinformasjon Trondheim, Munkegata 19, 7013 Trondheim; ☎73 80 76 62; fax 73 80 76 70; www.visittrondheim.com.
Nordland Tourist Office, Postboks 434, Storgata 4a, 8001 Bodø; ☎75 54 52 00; fax 75 54 52 10; e-mail nordland@nordlandreiseliv.no; www.visitnordland.no.

The Far North

Finnmark is Norway's most northerly county and its most extensive. Although it covers 15% of the entire country it is inhabited by just under 2% of the population. Despite being on the same latitude as Alaska, Finnmark is easily accessible by car, public transport and domestic planes. Many of the towns, villages and farms of the region were destroyed by the Germans at the end of World War II, but they were rapidly rebuilt and consequently are architecturally uninspiring. The biggest town is Alta with a population of 14,000, but the main attraction of Finnmark is the landmark of North Cape.

Just South of Alta is Kautokeino, home to the largest Sami community in the country. The Sami have in the past been known as 'Lapps', but this term is not used any longer. The Sami are different ethnically from the other Scandinavians and have more in common with the Siberians. For a long time they were discriminated against by the Norwegians and Swedes, who tried to suppress their language; recently they have been a greater degree of autonomy, and have their own parliament, the Sameting, in Karasjok. The administrative capital is Vadsø.

Between mid-May and the end of July, Finnmark experiences up to 24 hours of daylight; between the end of November to the end of January it is in almost constant darkness. The landscape is a vast, sparsely populated wilderness of mountain ranges, fells and wild windswept coastline.

UsefulAddresses

Alta Turistinformasjon, Sorenskriverveien 13, Postboks 80, 9500 Alta; ☎78 44 00 20; e-mail post@visitnorthcape.com; www.visitnorthcape.com, www.Finnmarksnett.no.
Samelandssenteret Tourist Office, Karasjok; ☎78 46 69 00; www.Finnmarksnett.no.

Svalbard

Svalbard, or Spitsbergen as it is known outside Norway, consists of two main islands and many smaller islands 400 miles/640 km north of the mainland. It is just 600 miles/960km south of the North Pole and is surrounded by pack ice throughout the winter. The islands are rich in coal and have been mined since about 1900. Sovereignty over Svalbard was granted to Norway after World War I but Norway currently shares the islands with Russia. Svalbard is also home to the polar bear.

Info-Svalbard, Postbox 323, 9171 Longyearbyen, Svalbard; ☎79 02 55 50; fax 79 02
55 51; e-mail info@svalbard.net; www.svalbard.net.

GETTING THERE

Air

Unless you have the time to take a ferry, flying is the most convenient way of
getting to Norway from the UK and US. Only SAS (Scandinavian Airlines
Systems) has direct flights from North America to Oslo. Ryanair offers by far
the cheapest flights to Norway, but the airport they fly to is 65 miles south of
Oslo; seats can be booked online from any country in the world. Because of the
importance of the oil industry, there are daily flights to Stavanger and Bergen
from the UK. There are flights to Kristiansand via Copenhagen on SAS and
British Airways. Note that routes may change.

Braathens, Newcastle International Airport, Woolsington, Newcastle-upon-Tyne
NE13 8BZ; ☎0191-214 0991; www.braathens.no. London/Newcastle to Oslo/
Bergen/Stavanger/Trondheim.
British Airways, ☎0845-77 333 77 *or* 0845-606 0747; www.british-airways.com.
London/Manchester to Oslo.
British Midland Airways, ☎0870-607 0555; www.flybmi.com. London to Oslo.
Coast Air, Postboks 126, 4262 Avaldsnes, Haugesund Airport, Norway; ☎0345-
222111 (UK); www.coastair.no. Aberdeen to Haugesund/Bergen; Newcastle to
Oslo.
KLM uk, Endeavour House, Stansted Airport, Stansted, Essex CM24 1RS;
☎08705-074 074; www.klmuk.com; London to Oslo/Bergen; Aberdeen to
Stavanger/Bergen.
Ryanair, ☎08701-569 569; www.ryanair.com. London to Oslo Torp.
SAS, 52-53 Conduit Street, London W1; ☎0845-607 2772; www.scandinavian.net.
London to Oslo/Stavanger; Aberdeen to Stavanger; Manchester to Oslo.
SAS (USA), ☎800-221-2350; www.scandinavian.net. New York to Oslo.

Ferry Services

Ferries run from Newcastle to Norway all the year round. There is also a service
from Lerwick in the Shetland Islands to Bergen run by Smyril Line, once a week
from mid-May to mid-September.
DFDS Seaways, Scandinavia House, Parkeston Quay, Harwich, Essex CO12 4QG;
☎08705-333 000; www.dfdsseaways.co.uk. Newcastle to Kristiansand.
Fjord Line, Norway House, Royal Quays, North Shields, Tyne & Wear NE29 6EG;
☎0191-296 1313; e-mail fjordline.uk@fjordline.com; www.fjordline.com.
Newcastle to Stavanger/Haugesund/Bergen.
Smyril Line, fax +298 315707; www.smyril-line.fo.

RESIDENCE AND ENTRY REGULATIONS

THE CURRENT POSITION

Since joining the European Economic Area, Norway has been bound by the agreement of 1 January 1994 which states that all nationals of the European Union (EU) and the European Free Trade Area (EFTA) states have the right to live and work in any of the member countries. Citizens of member countries (Austria, Belgium, Denmark, Finland, Germany, Greece, Iceland, Ireland, Italy, Luxembourg, the Netherlands, Norway, Portugal, Spain, Sweden and the United Kingdom) are allowed to enter Norway with the intention of looking for work and do not need to secure a work permit before entering the country.

In 1975 Norway imposed a ban on immigration for economic reasons. Until its membership of the EEA, Norway operated extremely tight controls on foreigners wanting to work and live in Norway, but this has to some extent had to change as Norway comes to terms with the EEA agreement. There are currently more than 300,000 foreigners living and working in Norway. The majority are Europeans (about 100,000) and most of these are from other parts of Scandinavia. In principle, members of EEA states now have the same rights as Norwegian nationals as regards employment, wages and working conditions, although there are still unofficial barriers. Exceptions to this rule apply to certain public sector jobs such as police work.

REQUIREMENTS FOR BRITISH CITIZENS

British citizens can enter Norway and stay for up to three months, but if you are going with the intention of looking for work or to take up permanent residence you need to register with the police. Visas are not required for British citizens entering Norway.

ENTERING TO WORK – EEA MEMBERS

Any EEA national can stay in Norway for up to three months to look for work but must be able to fully support themselves financially during this time. Given the high cost of living in Norway this is not something to enter into lightly.

If you do not find work within the three month period but would like to extend your stay in Norway you should report to the local police before the three months expire. The authorities allow EEA citizens to remain for up to six months to look for work; this period may be extended if you can show that you have a realistic chance of finding a job soon. You may be expected to provide proof that you can continue to support yourself; the Norwegian authorities reserve the right to ask you to leave the country if you do not satisfy this condition. The authorities are not allowed to discriminate against non-Norwegian speakers.

If you take up short-term work and your total stay in Norway does not exceed three months you will not need to apply for a residence permit, nor do you have to report to the police.

Residence Permit

Whilst work permits are no longer required for EEA nationals who live and work in Norway, residence permits are required for stays of more than three months. You can start work in Norway before you have obtained a formal residence permit. A residence permit is usually valid for up to five years but may be extended if the grounds on which it was granted still apply, or can be shortened if you are not intending to stay for the whole period. For students a residence permit is usually granted for one year at a time and is renewable.

When you find work you must apply for a residence permit. To do this go to the nearest police station and present your passport, two photographs, and a document of Confirmation of Employment (*ansettelsesbevis*) which your employer should provide or which you can get from the police station. You will be given an application form with instructions specifying the required documents. When your application has been processed you will be notified of the outcome by the police. If you apply through an embassy the procedure is the same but your application will be dealt with by the Directorate of Immigration (*Utlendingsdirektoratet*).

If you have a firm offer of employment which extends beyond three months before you arrive in Norway you can apply for a residence permit when you arrive. Again, you will need to go to your nearest local police station and present your passport, two photos and confirmation of employment.

You can also apply for a residence permit prior to departure for Norway – application forms can be obtained from embassies. If you already have a residence permit before arriving in Norway you should report to the local police within seven days of arriving. Family members of EEA nationals working in Norway are entitled to residence permits even if they themselves are not EEA nationals.

Commuting

If you work in Norway but are permanently domiciled in another EEA country and return to your country of origin once a week you will not be required to have a residence permit. You will, however, have to report to the local police within a week of the day your work in Norway started. If you spend a number of weeks working in Norway followed by a number of weeks in your home country you will still need a residence permit.

Residence in Norway

Any EEA national can live in Norway provided they can support themselves, regardless of whether they work or not. This also applies to students and retired people. You must apply for a residence permit (see above) within three months of your arrival and you must provide additional proof that you are able to support yourself financially and that you have sufficient health insurance. You can also apply for a residence permit via your nearest embassy. All foreigners who apply for a residence permit are subject to a test for tuberculosis.

Entering To Start A Business

EEA Citizens have the right to establish or purchase businesses in Norway; professionals such as doctors, architects etc, have the right to set up practice (for validation of professional qualifications see *Employment* chapter). In most cases a government permit is required and the enterprise should be registered with the Register of Business Enterprises (*Foretaksregisteret*). For further details see the chapter *Starting a Business*.

Self-Employment

EEA nationals have the right to acquire or establish a business in Norway on a self-employed basis but must comply with the usual regulations for setting up a business. See *Starting a Business*.

Providing a Service

It is not necessary to start a business in Norway if you are intending to offer professional services such as those of a lawyer or architect, but you must be prepared to submit details of the type of service you are offering, the length of time you are offering it for, and provide proof that you will be receiving sufficient payment to support yourself whilst in Norway.

Unemployment Benefit

If you have been registered as unemployed in the UK for at least four weeks before coming to Norway, and have been drawing contributions-based income support, you will be entitled to have your benefit paid to you in Norway. It should be borne in mind however that the cost of living is very high and you may not be able to live on the benefit level paid in the UK.

ENTRY FOR NON-EEA NATIONALS

Norway joined the Schengen agreement in March 2001, along with the rest of the Nordic countries. A Schengen visa entitles you to remain in the Schengen area for 90 days out of six months. Your passport will be checked at the point of entry into the Schengen area; you may not be checked at all at the border when entering Norway. If you look particularly poverty-stricken you may be subjected to questioning. Controls are more stringent coming from Finland than from other neighbouring countries. US, Canadian, Australian and New Zealand nationals do not require a visa to enter Norway for up to three months, only a valid passport.

Those seeking work in Norway from countries other than those of the European Economic Area still have to face Norway's stringent laws on working and living in Norway. Normally you will need to have a firm offer of a job and a work permit, as well as your residence permit, before coming to Norway; it is forbidden to come with the intention of looking for work. The time required to process an application (usually done through the embassy) is about three months. Usually the work permit will limit you to working for a specific person or company, for a specific length of time and at a specific place. The employer must arrange or provide suitable accommodation and the employee must be physically fit, and literate in their own native language. There is a compulsory test for tuberculosis.

In the case of specialist skilled workers, particularly in the technical field, it may be possible to apply for a work permit when already in Norway; you should consult your prospective employer and nearest embassy.

Foreign nationals who are required to have a visa to enter Norway and who are granted a residence permit have the right to leave and return to Norway within the time for which the permit is valid. If there is doubt about your eligibility for a residence permit you case will be dealt with by the Directorate of Immigration (*Utlendingsdirektoratet*), not the police.

If a residence permit is not granted, applicants may appeal in writing to the local police or the Foreign Ministry. The appeal will be forwarded to the Ministry of Justice via the Directorate of Immigration.

PART-TIME WORK

Usually to be classed as employed you will need to work at least half of a full-time position. If you work part-time you must be able to prove that you are earning enough to support yourself in Norway.

NORDIC NATIONALS

Under the terms laid down by the Nordic Council, founded in 1952, all citizens of Nordic countries (Norway, Sweden, Denmark, Finland, the Faroes, Iceland and Greenland) are granted the freedom to travel without passports and work without work permits in other Nordic countries.

Useful Addresses

Norwegian Embassy, 25 Belgrave Square, London SW1X 8QD; ☎020-7591 5500; fax 020-245 6993; e-mail emb.london@mfa.no; www.norway.org.uk.

Norwegian Embassy, 2720 34th St. NW, 20008 Washington DC; 202-333-6000; fax 202-337-0870; www.norway.org/embassy.

Norwegian Consulate, 825 3rd Ave 38th Floor, New York, NY 10022-784; ☎212-421-7333; fax 212-754-0583; e-mail cg.network@mfa.no; www.norway.org.

British Embassy, Thomas Heftyesgate 8, 0244 Oslo; 23 13 27 00; fax 23 13 27 41; e-mail britemb@online.no; www.britain.no.

United States Embassy, Drammensveien 18, 0244 Oslo; ☎22 44 85 50; e-mail oslo@usa.no; www.usa.no.

Utlendingsdirektoratet (Directorate of Immigration), Postboks 8180 Dep., 0032 Oslo; ☎23 35 15 00; fax 23 35 15 01; e-mail udi@udi.no; www.udi.no.

Foretaksregisteret (The Register of Business Enterprises), 8901 Brønnøysund; ☎75 00 75 00; e-mail firmapost@brreg.no; www.brreg.no.

Ministry of Petroleum and Energy, Postboks 8148 Dep., 0333 Oslo; ☎22 24 90 90; e-mail postmottak@oed.dep.no; www.oed.dep.no.

SETTING UP HOME

Moving to Norway is not as common an occurrence as it is to other parts of Europe; information is not as easy to come by as in some countries, although the internet has improved matters. Norway is quite a diverse country. In general one can say that life in Oslo and in the rest of the country are very different. The far north is also a special case.

HOW DO THE NORWEGIANS LIVE?

Norwegians enjoy a high quality of life, and one of the highest per capita incomes in the world, thanks largely to the oil and gas reserves off the west coast. Even small farms which would normally be struggling to survive make a decent living because of state subsidies. Society is largely consumerist with most households possessing the latest state of the art technology. Satellite and cable TV and the video have transformed viewing habits even in remote areas. Many Norwegians own two homes, one of which is the holiday hut or *hytte*, often larger than the actual permanent home, and used as a retreat where the Norwegians can get back to nature. The largest concentration of the population, 50%, live in and around Oslo, whilst the rest are divided over a wide area. The most thinly populated area is Finnmark in the North with 1.8% of the population.

While there are inevitably a number of cramped apartment blocks in Oslo, housing is spacious by European standards. The majority of Norwegians own their own homes and the average number of persons per household is 2.3. Norway has a near 50% divorce rate and there is a striking number of single home-occupiers. First-time young Norwegian buyers receive heavily subsidised home loans and it is not unusual for Norwegians to build their own houses.

ACCOMMODATION

Many of the more casual, seasonal or voluntary jobs will come with accommodation provided – this is the norm in farm work, hotel work and au pair work. Workers recruited by recruitment agencies for engineering and technical work will usually have access to a Norwegian representative at the place of work who will put them in touch with landlords. In sectors where a large number of foreign workers are employed, simply asking colleagues and friends will usually produce something. Some recruitment agencies may expect you to stay in a hotel for an initial one or two nights until accommodation is arranged and you may be expected to pay for this yourself. There are hostels and the seamen's mission if you are stuck.

Renting

The explosion in property prices of recent years has created something of a crisis in the housing market. These days municipal rented housing only represents 5% of all housing. Social housing is reserved for the needy, or people with 'social' or health problems. The government embarked on an ambitious programme in 1998 to build 50,000 non-commercial rental dwellings in the following 10 years. Rents will be regulated and kept low. At the moment about 20,000 units are built each year in total. For more information see the Norwegian Tenants Association website: www.lbf.no.

Newly arrived foreigners will generally find themselves looking for rented accommodation on the open market. Property (*eiendom*) in Norway is usually rented for one or two years and is often fully furnished. Rent is usually paid one month in advance, with a two-month deposit. Most estate agents in Norway rent as well as sell property. If you are moving into rented accommodation make sure there is a written contract signed by both parties.

Because of the shortage of rented accommodation in Oslo, agencies have sprung up who will charge you for arranging accommodation. You can look at the website www.finn.no for advertisements. The Use It website: www.unginfo.oslo.no/bolig/meglere.php lists rental agencies. There is very little available in central Oslo under NOK7,000 per month (approx. £550 or $790). For this you will get a two-room flat in an apartment block. Prices are somewhat cheaper in Bergen; in the oil town of Stavanger rents are far more reasonable.

You may be able to sub-let a property for a few months, or even find a room in someone else's house for a modest price. In the case of a *framleie* or sub-let in a housing co-operative property it is necessary to find out if the owner has permission to sub-let. Prospective tenants are asked to come at the same time for a *visning* or viewing. *Use It* suggests taking some references or other evidence of good standing to give yourself a better chance. You can expect to be asked for a deposit equivalent to two months rent.

TABLE 10	USEFUL TERMS
areal	surface area
bad	bath
bolig	house
delvis møblert	partly furnished
dep./depositum	deposit
etasje	storey
hyggelig	cosy
kjeller	basement
kjøkken	kitchen
kvm	square metres
leilighet	apartment

lys	bright
møbl./møblert	furnished
rom or *hybel*	room
soverom	bedroom
umøbl./umøblert	unfurnished

Buying Property

Foreigners wanting to buy property in Norway must apply for a concession. The exception to this is that foreign citizens who are permanently domiciled in Norway can buy property concession-free. The intention to remain for more than a year is regarded as permanent domicile. The purchase of property entails a registration fee of 2.5% of the property price and an official stamp duty payment. Norwegian mortgages are arranged in similar ways to British mortgages; you will need to apply through the Norwegian banks.

Houses for sale are advertised extensively in the national and local press. The website www.finn.no is the most convenient place to find ads. Look under *til salgs* (for sale). A flat is indicated by the word *leilighet* and a family house by *enebolig*. A *tomannsbolig* is a semi-detached house. There are some terraced houses or *rekkehuser*. Housing is hard to find, particularly in Oslo and Bergen, but estate agents will usually succeed in finding you at least a rented home within 30 days.

Prices have shot up recently; there was a 166% rise between 1993 and 2001; but prices were only 81% higher in 2001 than in 1987, a peak year. Apartment prices have gone up much more than houses. A 5- or 6-room apartment in a good location can be worth more than a detached house. Prices in Oslo are far higher than the rest of the country; a small apartment can cost NOK1 million. Other expensive areas are Asker, Bærum and the Akershus county around Oslo. Table 11 lists property prices in NOK: as a basis for comparison, NOK10,000 is worth approx. £790/US$1,130 and NOK15,000 is worth approx. £1,185/US$1,695.

TABLE 11	PROPERTY PRICES PER SQUARE METRE FLOOR AREA		
	80m² flat	115m² rowhouse	150m² detached house
Oslo	NOK21,900	NOK17,200	NOK18,800
Bergen	NOK17,100	NOK11,600	NOK12,400
Kristiansand	NOK16,400	NOK10,500	NOK11,100
Stavanger	NOK16,500	NOK11,600	NOK12,400
Trondheim	NOK17,500	NOK12,800	NOK12,600

January 2002: Figures courtesy of NEF, EFF, Finn.no, and ECON.

Norwegian property is not usually advertised in foreign newspapers. You can view properties on the internet; the best site is www.finn.no. This will tell you exactly how much your mortgage will cost you per month, and the amount of deposit (*kontantinskudd*) you will have to put down. This is generally 20% of the total price.

Forms of Ownership

In common with other Scandinavian countries there is more than one kind of ownership.

- *aksje:* literally a 'shareholding' in a housing co-operative. You pay monthly service charges, and a monthly contribution *(fellesgjeld)* towards the co-operative's mortgage, as well as a down-payment.
- *andel:* a share in a communally-owned house or apartment block. Otherwise similar to an *aksje*.
- *annet:* 'other', ownership form not specified.
- *eier/selveier:* freehold, i.e. full ownership.
- *obligasjonsleilighet:* contract leasehold apartment; tenants hold bonds in an apartment block.

A general source of information is the Norwegian Homeowners Association, or Huseiernes Landsforbund, Fred Olsensgate 5, 0152 Oslo; ☎22 47 75 00; e-mail post@huseierhl.no; www.huseierhl.no.

Mortgages

Mortgages operate in much the same way as in the UK, except that one deals with banks rather than specialised building societies. The main disadvantage of Norwegian mortgages is that you generally have to pay a 20% deposit. Interest rates are higher than in the rest of Europe as well; repayment rates were between 7.45% and 8.25% in 2002. There are special deals for first-time buyers between 18 and 34 whereby the bank will lend a sum equivalent to the full *lånetakst* or loan value, as long as this does not exceed 90% of the market value *(verditakst)* of the property. The loan value is generally calculated at between 80 and 85% of the full value, and is given in advertisements.

There is a choice between variable interest rate *(flytende rente)* and a fixed rate *(fast rente)*. One can also have both, a *fleksibel rente*. Failure to make payments on time results in a 15% penalty being added on to the payment.

Estate Agents

You will need to deal with a Norwegian estate agent when buying property; fortunately they generally speak some English. For details of estate agents contact the *Norwegian Association of Real Estate Agents (NEF)* (Inkognitogaten 12, 0258 Oslo; ☎22 44 79 53, fax 22 55 31 06; www.nef.no), or look in the Yellow Pages – www.gulesider.no – under *eiendommegler.* The Association has ten local associations covering the whole country and a total of 450 members. Choosing to use the services of a member of the association has several benefits. Members must pass an exam in Norway and are bound by ethical and professional codes.

The Association provides a leaflet *Information to Consumers* in English on its website. According to the official act relating to estate agency practice only authorised estate agents or advocates can deal in the selling of property and estate agents are bound to safeguard the interests of both the buyer and the seller by providing advice and information that is of importance to the implementation of the transaction. When buying a flat the prospective purchaser should be provided with written information about the rules, regulations, budgets, accounts etc, of the relevant housing company. Estate agents who fail to carry out the assignment in accordance with the law will be liable for any costs incurred by the buyer as a result.

Housing Co-operatives

There are over 100 *boligbyggelag* or housing co-ops in Norway. They own some 260,000 dwellings; the biggest one is OBOS in Oslo; see www.obos.no. A housing co-operative has the form of a private commercial company; members buy shares in the company, which entitles them to buy a house or apartment. Shares (*andeler*) can be traded on the open market; you can see the word *andel* in many house adverts. Buying a share in a co-op is possible for a foreigner who intends to stay in Norway permanently. The Norwegian Federation of Co-operative Housing Associations gives out information in English on its website: http://boligsamvirket.no.

A housing co-operative has a board of management. Meetings are held where tenants can air any grievances, and badly behaved tenants brought to account.

Legal Advice

You should certainly seek legal advice before embarking on a property purchase abroad. The British embassy website provides a list of English-speaking law firms; see www.britain.no.

UTILITIES

Norwegian homes have all the usual modern conveniences – and often a sauna too. As well as having some of the world's biggest oil and gas reserves, Norway has always had relatively cheap electricity from the thousands of waterfalls and watercourses in its mountainous terrain. Hydro-thermal energy accounts for nearly 60% of domestic energy consumption compared with 35% for oil and gas. Coolant from power stations is also used for central heating – so-called 'district heating'.

All Norwegian homes are well insulated against the elements; another common source of heating in Norway is the traditional log fire. The Norwegians recognise that chopping wood is an effective way of staying warm. The electricity supply in Norway is 220 volts and 50 hertz (cycle); American equipment with a 50/60 cycle label can be used in Norway with a transformer. Plugging equipment designed to run on 110 volts directly into the power supply here will most likely cause terminal damage. UK equipment will work fine with a simple adapter plug. There are many local energy suppliers; they can be easily found by looking under *energi* in the Gule Sider (Yellow Pages).

Useful Addresses

Oslo Energi, Customer information: ☎800 80 100; e-mail kundeservice@oslo-energi.no; www.oslo-energi.no for electricity. Call 22 92 50 00 for information on gas.

Viken Energinett AS, Sommerrogata 1, Oslo; ☎22 43 50 00; e-mail firmapost@viken.no; www.viken.no.

Recycling

The Norwegians are immensely concerned about the environment. Different kinds of rubbish can be sorted into different bags. Paper is generally collected once or twice a month. You will be expected to use the plastic bags supplied by the municipality. There are collection centres for bottles and tins. For information look under *renholdsverket* or *renovasjon* in the Yellow Pages.

Telephones

If you want a new telephone line installed or transferred to your name, this must be done by the partly state-owned Telenor. A new connection costs NOK760 (approx. £60/US$85) The monthly rental, or Abonnement, is NOK150. If you make very few calls, you can take out a cheaper Miniabonnement, for NOK117 a month. Ex-directory numbers are charged for. An ISDN line can be installed for NOK1,100; it is cheaper if you can install it yourself. There are other operators of fixed-line services, namely ElTele and GlobalOne. The main mobile companies are Telenor Mobile and Netcom. Telenor's customer service number is 05000; for mobiles 09000. For prices of services you can call the free number 800 31 031; or look at the website www.telenor.no.

REMOVALS

Moving anywhere holds inherent trauma but this is particularly the case when moving overseas. It is inevitably an expensive process and you should carefully consider what is essential and what is not. Household items in Norway are far more expensive than at home. The British Association of Removers (BAR) can provide a leaflet with hints for anyone planning to move overseas, and a list of removers. Send an SAE to the address below:

Useful Addresses

BAR, 3 Churchill Court, 58 Station Road, North Harrow, Middlesex HA2 7SA; ☎020-8861 3331; fax 020-8861 3332; e-mail info@bar.co.uk; www.barmovers.com.

Household Goods Forwarders Association of America, www.hhgfaa.org.

Overseas Moving Network International (OMNI), www.omnimoving.com.

Allied Pickfords, Heritage House, 345 Southbury Road, Enfield, Middlesex EN1 1UP; ☎0800-289 229; www.allied-pickfords.co.uk (UK) www.alliedintl.com (USA).

Crown Relocations, 5252 Argosy Drive, Huntington Beach, CA 92469, USA; ☎714-898-0961; e-mail general.ususa@crownpacific.com.

IMPORTING CARS

Regulations regarding importation of cars depend on your length of stay and whether you intend to take up permanent residence in Norway. If you have lived outside Norway for five years prior to entry, and owned your car for at least a year, you can generally import it tax-free. Otherwise the import duty and value added tax may actually exceed the value of the car itself. The Norwegian Directorate of Customs and Excise provide the English language leaflet RG-1098 which gives details about the importation and use of foreign-registered cars to Norway. The actual form that has to be filled out is known as RG-131. The regulations can be seen on the website: www.toll.no. For further information on car taxes, see the section 'Cars and Motoring' in the following chapter.

IMPORTING PETS

Norway is considered to be rabies-free. Cats and dogs can only be brought into Norway at manned border crossings. The animal must be accompanied by a Veterinary Certificate approved by the Norwegian Animal Health Authority (see below). The Veterinary Certificate consists of part I, the Health Certificate, and part II, the Vaccination Certificate. Both parts must be signed by an authorised veterinarian, within 10 days before leaving. The animal has to go to a vet for further treatment within a week of arrival. Note that certain breeds of dogs cannot be imported into Norway, e.g. pit bull terriers.

Different conditions apply to animals from rabies-infected non-EEA countries, which includes the USA except for Hawaii. As well as having the necessary Veterinary Certificate, the animal has to go into quarantine for four months; the only quarantine facility in Norway is about 70km from Oslo.

The Norwegian Animal Health Authority will supply further details of import requirements on request. If you are planning to return with your animal to the UK, you need to contact DEFRA at least nine months before you take your animal abroad (see below).

Useful Addresses

UK Department of the Environment, Food and Rural Affairs, ☎0870-241 1710; www.defra.gov.uk.

Independent Pet and Animal Transportation Association International Inc, www.ipata.com.

Statens Dyrehelsetilsyn (Norwegian Animal Health Authority), Postboks 8147 Dep., 0033 Oslo; ☎23 21 65 00; fax 23 21 65 01; e-mail post@dyrehelsetilsynet; www.dyrehelsetilsynet.no.

Dyrebeskyttelsen, Norwegian Society for the Protection of Animals, Karl Johans gate 6, 0154 Oslo; ☎22 20 23 00; fax 23 13 92 51; e-mail post@dyrebeskyttels en.no; www.dyrebeskyttelsen.no.

DAILY LIFE

Moving to Norway involves getting to grips with the day-to-day realities that influence life for the Norwegians. Whilst you will find most Norwegians helpful above and beyond the call of duty when asked, you will still have to deal with the frustrations as well as the excitement of coping with a new way of life. What follows is a run-down of some of the basic facets of daily life.

THE LANGUAGE

Most Norwegians have an impressive capacity for learning foreign languages. As a tiny nation of only 4.5 million they accept that if they want to be heard in the world they have to speak a language it understands and in practice this is English. English is mandatory in schools but many Norwegians will study French and German too. English is widely spoken in business, service industries, and by everyone from the king to the cashiers. The pervasiveness of the British and American media means that most Norwegians will hear English every day of their lives and many are keen to practise what they have learned on a native speaker.

Norwegian is a Germanic language, historically related to English. English absorbed a lot of Old Norse words during the period of the Viking invasions, although this is not perhaps all that obvious these days. The mountainous character of the landscape and lack of contact between communities has generated the many present-day dialects. Some dialects on the west coast still bear a strong resemblance to Icelandic, the most archaic of all the Scandinavian languages. Until about 1850 the official language was *Riksmål* – a written language which was heavily influenced by Danish resulting from the 434-year union of the two nations. After 1850 *Landsmål* or Country Language was created mainly out of rural dialects. After many disputes, a compromise was made by which both languages received equal status under the new names of *Bokmål* or Book Language for written Norwegian and *Nynorsk* or New Norwegian, for spoken language. In the spirit of national feeling of the 19th century it was decided to lessen Danish influence on the Norwegian language by three principal means: Danish words were exchanged for corresponding Norwegian dialect words; Danish soft consonants were replaced by Norwegian hard ones; and Norwegian syntax replaced Danish syntax.

The differences between *Bokmål* and *Nynorsk* are not very significant and *Bokmål* is usually the taught language – about 83% of school children use *Bokmål* as the main language in schools. Most newspapers and three-quarters of the programmes of the Norwegian Broadcasting Corporation are standardized in

Bokmål and 90% of all business publications are written in *Bokmål*. *Nynorsk* is heavily influenced by the Old Norse of the Vikings and is based on rural culture; it has suffered from 20th century urbanisation but about 15% of the country's fiction writers still use it. They are principally to be found in the west of Norway.

Norwegian uses the same writing system as English, but adds on three letters at the end of the alphabet: æ, ø and å. These are always placed last in telephone books and alphabetical listings.

The Sami or Laplanders in the north have retained their own language and in recent times have had active encouragement from the Norwegian government. The Sami language is used and taught in Sami primary schools, and the Universities of Oslo and Tromsø make provision for courses to be taught in the Sami language. There is a Sami teacher-training college at Alta.

Language Study

Books and cassettes on the Norwegian language are widely available and you may be able to borrow some from your local library. Norwegian is occasionally available through evening classes at local colleges of further education. Norwegian language courses can be arranged through the Berlitz School and Linguarama. A cheaper way to learn would be to find a Norwegian speaker in your area, through a local Scandinavian society.

Facilities for studying Norwegian in the USA are listed on the University of Minnesota website: http://carla.acad.umn.edu/lctl/access.html, under 'Less Commonly Taught Languages'. If you want to learn Norwegian whilst in Norway you can contact the local adult education organisation *Friundervisningen*, who will provide details of courses for foreigners. There are free Norwegian dictionaries on-line at: www.yourdictionary.com.

Useful Addresses

The Berlitz School of Languages, 9-13 Grosvenor Street, London W1A 3BZ; ☎020-7915 0909; www.berlitz.com.

Linguarama, Oceanic House, 89 High Street, Alton, Hants GU34 1LG; ☎01420-80899; www.linguarama.com.

Friundervisningen i Oslo, Torggata 7, 0105, Oslo; ☎815 00 380; fax 22 47 60 01; e-mail info@fu.oslo.no; www.fu.oslo.no.

EDUCATION

Schools

Ten years of basic education are compulsory for all of Norway's school children from the age of 6 to 16. Children attend a primary school from 6 to 13, and lower secondary school for the next three. After completing primary and lower secondary schools, students can attend the 3-year upper secondary schools for ages 16-19 and are then eligible to take examinations leading to university entrance. Compulsory subjects include Norwegian, English, maths, religion, music, physical education and science. In higher grades, students have the option of taking further arts and languages courses and vocational courses such as office skills and seamanship. Most Norwegian schools are free. In more remote rural areas classes are so small that different age groups may be taught in the same class at the lower levels.

Higher Education

The country currently has four universities: Oslo (founded in 1811), Bergen (1946), Trondheim (1968) and the world's most northerly university at Tromsø (1968). There are also specialised university institutions, such as the Agricultural University of Norway (Noragric) at Ås and the Norwegian School of Economics and Business Administration in Bergen. The higher education system was reformed in 2001, with the degree structure being brought into line with other European countries; there are now 3-year Bachelor degrees, 2-year Masters, and PhDs. Student grants and loans have been increased, and more colleges are being offered the opportunity to convert into universities.

Just over half of school students going on to further education attend vocational colleges and several thousand go to Folk High Schools. These are boarding colleges which offer 17-year-olds from rural backgrounds a one-year training course. All students are eligible for a government loan. For further information see the website: http://odin.dep.no/ufd/engelsk. About 9,000 foreign nationals study in Norway with the support of the State Educational Loan Fund. Adults have a right to attend any level of education, including primary. Every year 24,000 adults attend upper secondary courses.

Adult Education

Continuing education is hugely popular in Norway, which may be partly explained by the long months of darkness in the winter, and the desire to keep in touch with the outside world. Distance learning is also very popular. About 1 million adults attend adult education classes, which are organised by several bodies, including the municipalities and counties. Most of the Folk High Schools are boarding schools run by two organisations: the Folkhøgskoler, and the Christian Kristeligt Folkehøgskoler.

Useful Addresses

Christian Folk High Schools, Grensen 9a, 0154 Oslo; ☎22 39 64 50; fax 22 39 64 51; e-mail ikf@ikf.no; www.folkehogskole.no.

Folkehøgskoler, Karl Johansgaten 12, 0154 Oslo; ☎23 35 53 70; fax 23 35 53 80; e-mail if@folkehogskole.no; www.folkehogskole.no.

Folkeuniversitetet, Torggata 7, 0105, Oslo; ☎815 00 380 or 22 47 60 00; fax 22 47 60 01; e-mail info@fu.oslo.no; www.fu.oslo.no.

Norwegian Association for Distance Education, NADE/NFF, Gjerdrums vei 12, 0484 Oslo; ☎22 02 81 60; fax 22 02 81 61; www.nade-nff.no.

Utdannings- og Forskningsdepartmentet, Ministry of Education and Research, http://odin.dep.no/ufd.

VOX Voksenopplæringsinstituttet, Lørenveien 11, 0585 Oslo; vox@vox.no; www.vox.no.

International Education

Norway has a surprising number of international schools and classes most of which offer a choice of British style education and the International Baccalaureate (an international curriculum and university entrance examination). The cosmopolitanism of education is a legacy of the offshore oil industry which has led to increasing numbers of foreigners (principally English, American and French) taking up work and residency in Norway following the oil discoveries. The majority of schools are, understandably, on the west coast and both Stavanger and Bergen have English, French and American schools. Foreign children who have lived in Norway for more than three months must attend school.

The language of instruction is English in all the schools given below; all the schools are co-educational.

Sources of Information

European Council of International Schools, 21 Lavant Street, Petersfield, Hants GU32 3EL; ☎01730-268244; fax 01730-267914; e-mail ecis@ecis.org; www.ecis.org.

ECIS North America, 105 Tuxford Terrace, Basking Ridge, New Jersey 07920, USA; ☎908-903 0552; fax 908-580 9381; e-mail malyecisna@aol.com; www.ecis.org.

International Schools

Oslo International School, Gamle Ringeriksvei 53, 1340 Bekkestua; ☎67 53 23 03; fax 67 59 10 15; e-mail oslo.is@online.no; www.osলointernationalschool.no. Ages 3-18. IPC curriculum in primary school; otherwise IGCSE and IB.

The British International School of Oslo, Skovveien 9, 0258 Oslo; ☎22 44 49 16. 3-18. Offers UK and International Baccalaureate.

The International School of Bergen, Vilhelm Bjerknesvei 15, 5081 Bergen; ☎55 30 63 30; fax 55 30 63 31; e-mail murison@isb.gs.hl.no; www.isb.gs.hl.no. 3-16. Offers an international education.

Skagerak International School, PO Box 1545, 3206 Sandefjord; ☎33 48 43 70; fax 33 46 93 63; e-mail office@skagerak.org;

www.skagerak.org. 4-19. Offers the International Baccalaureate PYP, MYP and Diploma Programme.

The International School of Stavanger, Treskeveien 3, 4042 Hafrsfjord, Stavanger; ☎51 55 43 00; fax 51 55 43 01. 3-18. Offers US, UK and international education.

Stavanger British School, Gauselbakken 107, 4032 Gausel, Stavanger; ☎51 57 55 99; e-mail principal@stavanger-british-school.no; www.stavanger-british-school.no. 3-13. Offers UK and Common Entrance examinations.

Birralee International School, Bispegate 9C, 7012 Trondheim; ☎73 87 02 60; fax 73 87 02 65; e-mail birralee@online.no; http://birralee.wave.no. 4-13. Offers a modified UK curriculum.

MEDIA AND COMMUNICATIONS

Newspapers and Magazines

About 84% of the adult population read a daily newspaper – a slightly higher percentage than those watching TV. The Norwegians are avid news followers and over 150 national and regional papers are produced daily in Norway. The daily newspaper circulation is 2,900,000. Many papers are kept going by government subsidies, state advertising and loans; many smaller papers are the mouthpieces of political parties. The bigger city-based papers are more independent – the daily independent *Verdens Gang* claims the highest figure circulation with over 366,000 on weekdays. It is followed by the liberal paper *Dagbladet* with a weekday circulation of 221,000. The main business newspaper is *Dagens Næringsliv*.

A wide variety of popular, special interest and professional journals are published in Norway. Most large Narvesen kiosks sell English-language newspapers and the main public library (Deichmanske Bibliotek, Henrik Ibsens gate 1, Oslo) has a selection of international papers and periodicals in its reading room. The following are the websites of the main newspapers in Norway:

Aftenposten: www.aftenposten.no.
Bergens Tidende: www.bergens-tidende.no.
Dagbladet: www.dagbladet.no.
Dagens Næringsliv: www.dn.no.
Stavanger Aftenbladet: www.aftenbladet.no.
Verdens Gang: www.vg.no.

Books

In Oslo English language books can be bought from: *Erik Qvist* (Drammensveien 16, Oslo; ☎22 54 26 00) and *Tanum Karl Johan* (Karl Johansgate 43, Oslo; ☎22 41 11 00; www.tanum.com).

Television and Radio

The television network has expanded over the past few years. As well as the state channels NRK1 and NRK2, there is TV2, which shows adverts, and the American-owned satellite TV Norge. Norway also receives TV3, a channel which is common to Denmark, Sweden and Norway. Norway imports a significant amount of English and American TV, so even if you are several hundred miles inside the Arctic Circle you may still find your favourite programme showing on television. Satellite and cable TV are available in parts of Norway. The main cable channels are Telenor Avidi and UPC. To watch TV you need to have a TV licence; see the NRK website: www.nrk.no/info.

In summer English is broadcast on the radio on 106.8 FM. You can tune in to the English language NATO station all year round on 105.5 FM.

Post

The main post office is at Dronningensgate 15, Oslo and is open Monday to Friday 8am-8pm and Saturday 9am-3pm. The general opening times of other post offices are 8am-5.30 pm Monday to Friday and 9am-1pm on Saturdays. Stamps are also available from kiosks and stationers. Yellow post boxes are for local post; red post boxes for long distance and international. There are two rates for foreign mail: A-Prioritaire and B-Economique. You should ask for the right sticker. The Norwegian Post Office's website has some useful information: www.posten.no.

Telephones

The cheapest calling times in Norway are outside business hours: 5pm to 8am. Weekends are cheaper than weekdays. At the present time a local call costs a minimum of 2 NOK. Telephone cards can be bought at Telehuser (Telenor shops) and Narvesen and Mix kiosks.

A useful feature of the Norwegian telephone directory is a page of English instructions listed in the index. As well as the White Pages and Yellow Pages, there are also the Pink Pages which list all the business in area alphabetically. There is also a one-volume version that covers the whole of Norway. While the Yellow Pages are available online at: www.gulesider.no, you can only log on to the White Pages (www.telefonkatalogen.no) if you are on the population register. If you are looking for a business number, the site www.bizkit.no is very useful.

Calls from outside and inside a region normally have eight digits. Norway uses the international access code of 00. To call Norway dial: 00 47 followed by an eight digit number. To call the UK from Norway dial 00 44 followed by the area code and number. From Norway for the United States and Canada dial 00 1. For operator-assisted calls dial 117 for national calls and 115 for international calls. Most operators speak English. For numbers in for Norway and the rest of Scandinavia call 180 and for other international telephone numbers call 181

The area code for Oslo is 22. For emergency services dial: Police 112; Fire 110; Ambulance 113. All these are free of charge. For local emergency numbers outside Oslo dial the operator on 180.

CARS AND MOTORING

Roads

The principal road in Norway is the E6 Arctic Highway which runs from the southern tip on the Norway/Sweden border, north through Oslo and up through the northern towns of Trondheim, Mo-i-Rana, Narvik, Alta and up to Kirkenes on the Russian border. The E6 has branches off to most main towns north of Oslo including Ålesund, Kristiansund, Tromsø and Hammerfest. In the more populous south there is a reasonably good network of major and minor roads; the principal towns at the southern end of Norway are served by the E18. The further north you go the fewer the roads, reflecting both the increasingly wild terrain and the small population. There are only two main routes from Norway into Sweden in the north: the E75 at Trondheim and Route 70 just after Narvik. Given the harsh climate, major roads are well maintained in Norway, and of the 50,000 miles of road in Norway about two-thirds are hard-surfaced. Mountain roads may be closed up to seven months of the year.

The further north you go the less traffic there is and it is possible to drive for many miles on empty roads. Away from the major routes, roads often run through tunnels. There are many sharp twists and turns through the mountains and there may only be guard rails as a safety precaution. Roads along the west coast frequently run into ferry stops for which a charge is levied. Tolls on roads vary from NOK5 to NOK145 (approx £11.50/US$16.38). Norwegian roads are well signposted with information, directions and distances. Some roads in mountainous areas can be closed for the whole or part of winter. Petrol stations are frequent and those marked *Kort* operate for 24 hours. At 24-hour stations there is a slot to insert a credit or debit card directly into the pump. Diesel and unleaded petrol are widely available.

Driving Regulations

Driving is on the right; the important rule when driving in Norway is always to yield to a vehicle approaching from the right. Owners of right-hand drive cars should have their headlights adjusted so as not to dazzle oncoming drivers. Dipped headlights must be used at all times and seat belts are mandatory in both the front and back of cars.

During winter the use of studded tyres is compulsory. They can be rented (at a hefty price) if necessary. Studs can only be used on winter tyres with a tread of 3mm. Drivers of heavy goods vehicles have to use snow-chains. Many drivers carry snow-chains as a precautionary measure. Snow chains and studded tyres may only be used between November 1 and Easter Sunday, unless the weather requires them.

Seatbelts must be worn, front and back. You are required to carry a red warning triangle with you in case of breakdowns.

Speed limits are 50kph (30mph) in built up towns and cities and 30kph (18mph) in residential areas. On major motorways the maximum speed limit is 90 kph (55mph) and on other highways 80kph (50mph). Speed limits are very strongly enforced and most roads are monitored. Along main roads there are periodic warning signs of *Automatisk Trafikkontroll* (Automatic Traffic Monitoring).

Regulations concerning drink driving in Norway are strictly enforced. The allowable alcohol limit is a blood alcohol percentage of 0.05% or 0.5 promille, which means that you cannot drink any alcohol if you are going to drive. On Friday and Saturday night routine road checks are common and if you are stopped you may have to take a breathalyser test. If the result is positive you will be required to give a blood sample. Punishment is severe; you could lose your licence on the spot and foreigners are no exception to this. Fines of over NOK10,000 (approx. £790/US$1,130) are levied; more serious cases lead to automatic imprisonment. In practice most Norwegians don't drink and drive at all.

Breakdowns and Accidents

Norway has one of Europe's lowest rates of traffic accidents. In an average year about 300 people are killed, and 11,000 are injured in accidents. In such a mountainous country there are many roads that could be classed as hazardous; on the other hand the lack of traffic in most parts of the country makes driving relatively safe.

Two motoring organisations in Norway, the *KNA* and the *NAF*, can advise you on all aspects of motoring and breakdowns in Norway (see below). If you are a member of the UK motoring organisations, RAC or AA, you can get help through the NAF. Otherwise if you need breakdown assistance you have a choice between *Viking Redningtjeneste* and *Falken Redningskorps* (see below). In the case of a minor accident it is not usually necessary to call the police, but you are legally obliged to exchange names and addresses with the other driver involved. For a real emergency call the police (112) or ambulance (113)

Useful Addresses

Kongelig Norsk Automobilklub (KNA, Royal Norwegian Automobile Club), Parkveien 68, Oslo 2; ☎800 80 555; www.kna.no. Breakdown service: ☎800 31 660.
Norges Automobil Forbund (NAF, Norwegian Automobile Association), Storgate 2, Oslo 1; ☎22 34 14 00; fax 22 33 13 72; www.naf.no. Breakdown service: ☎810 00 505.
Falken Redningskorps, 815 68 888 (free) or 024 68; www.falken.no.
Viking Redningstjeneste, ☎800 32 900 (free) or 22 08 60 20; www.vikingredning.no.

Driving Licences

You can continue to drive in Norway for one year on an EEA licence or other recognised licence. Some licences from less developed countries may not be accepted. Once you have become a permanent resident, in effect after six months, you can exchange your licence for a Norwegian licence, as long as you are over 19, at a *trafikkstasjon*. If you want to have your licence returned in the future then you should inform the authorities, otherwise it may no longer be available.

Car Tax and Insurance

Car owners are liable for an annual road tax, the *årsavgift*, payable to the customs and excise. In 2002 this cost NOK2,310 (approx. £182/US$ 260) for private cars. The tax runs for a calendar year, and must be paid by the end of March. Once you have paid the tax you will receive a coloured sticker (*oblat*) to display in your windscreen. If the police notice that your sticker is out of date they will remove your licence plates without warning.

Third party insurance is compulsory, as is some level of personal injury insurance. Your licence plates will be confiscated if you are found to be without insurance.

Exporting a Vehicle from the UK

If you plan to take your car out of the UK for more than 12 months, you must notify its export to the Driver and Vehicle Licence Agency in Swansea; they will send you a certificate V561 for registering abroad. If you are going abroad for less than a year, you need to take the registration documents with you, or apply for a temporary certificate of registration from the DVLA. See the leaflet V526, *Taking your vehicle out of the country,* or the website www.dvla.co.uk for further information.

Useful Addresses

Automobile Association (AA), Overseas Department, PO Box 2AA, Newcastle-upon-Tyne, NE99 2AA; ☎0870 606 1615; www.theaa.com.
RAC Motoring Services, Travel Services, PO Box 1500, Bristol BS99 1LH; ☎0800-550055; www.rac.co.uk.
DVLA (Driver and Vehicle Licensing Agency), Exports Section, Swansea SA 99 1BL; ☎01792-783100; www.dvla.co.uk.

TRANSPORT

Air

There are regular daily flights to Norway from most major airports in Europe. Norway has international airports at Oslo Fornebu, Oslo Torp, Oslo Gardermoen, Bergen, Stavanger, Kristiansand, Trondheim and Haugesund. The main airport is now at Gardermoen 30 miles/50 km from Oslo. The main airline is the Scandinavian SAS run jointly by Norway, Denmark and Sweden. The other well-known Norwegian airline Braathens was taken over by SAS at the end of 2001 when it became insolvent.

Large, thinly populated distances make domestic flights a convenient form of travel in Norway, particularly in the north. Journeys which can take several days by road can be completed in hours by plane. The main domestic air companies in Norway are SAS, Braathens and Widerøe. Braathens SAFE (standing surprisingly for the South American and Far Eastern routes of the parent shipping company) operates 240 internal departures daily and serves domestic airports throughout the country, including Svalbard; routes are likely to be cut following the takeover by SAS at the end of 2001.

Useful Addresses

SAS, Ruseløkkveien 6, Oslo 3; ☎810 03 300; www.scandinavian.net.
Braathens SAFE AS, Ruseløkkveien 26, Oslo 2; ☎67 58 60 00; e-mail booking@braathens.no; www.braathens.no.
Widerøe Flyveselskap AS, Mustadsveien 1, Oslo 2; ☎810 01 200; www.wideroe.no.

Trains

The Norwegian State Railway System (NSB) operates five main lines from Oslo S (Central) Station and 2,600 miles of railway track. The northern line runs up the country, through Trondheim and reaches its most northern point at Fauske with a short western run to Bodø. There is also a train from Kiruna in Sweden to Narvik, further north. There are two southern lines: one covers the south coast to Stavanger and the other runs through Gothenburg and is the main connecting route with continental Europe. The western line takes a particularly scenic route from Oslo to Bergen. The eastern line runs through Kongsvinger to Stockholm in Sweden. From Trondheim you can take a ticket to Hell (literally) and carry on eastwards into central Sweden. You can also take a train south from Narvik on Sweden's Ofot line which takes you to Sweden's northeast coastline.

Norwegian trains are punctual, clean, comfortable and costly. Most offer special compartments for the disabled and for families with young children. You can buy first or second class tickets and sleeping compartments consist of one, two and three bunk cabins. On long journeys seat and sleeper reservations are compulsory. Tickets can be booked in the UK through Deutsche Bahn (German Railways).

Although Norwegian State Railways do not claim leaves on the line as an excuse for lateness they do occasionally have problems with wild elk wandering onto the line – over 500 elk are killed by trains each year and with each elk weighing an average of 120 stones they can cause substantial delays.

Useful Addresses

NSB, Jernbanetorget 1, Oslo; ☎22 36 37 80; www.nsb.no.
German Railways, ☎08702-43 53 63; e-mail sales@deutsche-bahn.co.uk.

Buses, Trams and the Underground

Nearly every sizeable settlement in Norway is served by buses; where a rail route runs out a bus route begins. This is particularly important in northern Norway where the railway ends at Fauske. Several bus routes are operated by the Norwegian State Railway. The buses travel as far north as North Cape and up to Kirkenes on the Russian border. The NOR-WAY Bussekspress company runs long-distance buses, including one from Oslo to Hammerfest, via Sweden and Finland. Call the free number 815 44 444 or see the website www.nor-way.no.

Oslo has a comprehensive tram and bus service which is efficient and clean. You can find details at every stop and information on public transport is also available from Oslo S Station. There is a skeleton night service. Oslo is also served by an underground – the *T-bane*. Its eight lines cover Oslo and go out to quite distant suburbs. The station entrances are marked by a T. For details contact the tourist information in Oslo S station.

Boat

Sailings from the UK to Norway are covered in *Getting There* at the end of the previous chapter. There are several ferry routes from Denmark to Norway, so it is possible to take the boat from Harwich to Esbjerg in Denmark, and then go on to Norway. Color Line runs a direct service from Kiel in northern Germany to Oslo, and services to Hirtshals and Fredrikshavn in northern Denmark.

In Norway the proximity of the sea and the coastline eaten into by fjords means that ferries form a significant part of the transport system. Ferries often provide short cuts and help avoid many extra road miles. In busy areas near Oslo ferries are also widely used by commuters in particular on the Oslofjord where the Horten-Moss ferry carries regular commuters between Vestfold and Østfold. Norway's most famous boat trip is the Coastal Express or *Hurtigrute*, which takes six days to travel from Bergen to Kirkenes and takes in 34 stops en route. Although the *Hurtigrute* is very expensive and tends to be a tourist's pleasure trip in summer, it sails throughout the year and is used by local people as a ferry service. It is ironic that *Hurtigrute* literally means 'Fast Route'.

Useful Addresses

Color Line, ☎810 00 811; www.colorline.com. Oslo to Kiel/Hirtshals; Kristiansand to Hirtshals; Larvik to Fredrikshavn; Sandefjord to Strömstad (Sweden).

DFDS Seaways, www.scansea.com. Oslo to Helsingborg/Copenhagen; Kristiansand to Gothenburg (Sweden).

Hurtigruten, ☎76 96 76 96; www.hurtigruten.no. Coastal route.

Stena Line, ☎23 17 90 00; www.stenaline.com. Oslo to Fredrikshavn.

BANKS AND FINANCE

The central bank of Norway – Norges Bank was founded in 1816. Today it primarily serves as the government's executive agency for credit and foreign exchange policy. Commercial banks (*forretningsbanker*) are set up as limited companies and were originally directed by the government to deal with national and corporate matters whilst the savings banks (*sparebanker*) were to deal with local matters. In practice there is not a great deal of difference between the two; whilst commercial banks offer long-term loans they can also do short-term loans such as overdrafts. Most savings banks are local banks. Originally they acted as a banking facility for the municipality and for arranging individual mortgages but today they offer the same services as commercial banks. Foreign banks were allowed to establish branches in Norway for the first time in 1984.

Bank opening times are Monday to Friday only between 8.15am-3.30 pm (Thursdays until 5pm) and they are closed on Saturdays. Credit and debit cards (*kredittkort* and *bankkort*) are used in the same way as in the UK. There are card readers in shops for the debit card. Another card is the *handlekort* or charge card which can be used at the outlets of one particular chain of businesses, such as petrol stations. You are sent a monthly bill. Bills can be paid with cheques, or with *avtalegiros,* a pre-filled-in cheque which you only have to sign and take to a bank.

Currency

The Norwegian currency is the Krone (literally translated means Crown). The plural is Kroner. It is usually written NOKalthough this rarely appears on price tags and Kr is used. One Krone contains 100 øre; there is still a fifty øre coin, although it is used less and less. Kroner come in notes of 50, 100, 200, 500 and 1000. At the time of going to press the exchange rate is NOK12.60 to £1 and NOK8.80 to $1 but this is obviously subject to fluctuation.

Norway still operates a restriction on the amount of money you can bring into or leave the country with. If you carry more than NOK25,000 on you, you are required to fill in a form from the national bank, F/2711, and give it to the customs. There are also restrictions on the value of goods that you can bring into the country if you leave for a short time, most of all on alcohol and tobacco.

TAXATION

Taxes in Norway are generally higher than in other European countries because of the high cost of financing the welfare state, social services and state subsidies. Taxes are levied at national, county (*fylke*) and local authority (*kommune*) level. Both individuals and corporations are subject to tax. Income tax is paid directly as a percentage of individual income and is deducted at source by the employer. Norway also operates a wealth tax (i.e. tax on commodities such as cars) which ranges upwards from 2.4% on capital wealth. Norway has a double taxation agreement with all EEA countries to prevent individual liability in two countries at the same time. Individuals should discuss their tax and national insurance contributions with their employer before accepting work. When you start work you will be issued with a tax deduction card; failure to produce a tax deduction card means that you will be taxed a maximum amount of 49.3%.

Any questions about tax should be directed to your local *likningskontor* (sometimes written *ligningskontor*) or tax office. There is a special office for foreign taxpayers in Sandnes. Information on taxes is posted in English on the website www.skatteetaten.no.

Income Tax

There are two classes of tax-payer. Class 1 includes single persons; Class 2 is for couples or partners. Couples may file jointly or separately, depending on which gives the lower tax liability. Expatriates with a non-resident spouse will only be placed in Class 2 if their spouse earns more than NOK60,000 (approx. £4,740/US$6,780) a year.

Income tax (*inntektsskatt*) on individuals is of two kinds. The first is on net ordinary income (*alminnelig inntekt*), which is all your income from whatever source, minus tax deductions. This currently stands at 28%, of which 21% consists of municipal tax and 7% is county tax. Residents of the Finnmark and Nord-Troms counties only pay 24.5%. A single Class 1 tax payer has a personal exemption of NOK30,100 (in 2002); couples, or anyone with a dependent, benefits from an exemption of NOK60,200. There are further exemptions for children. Contributions to a private pension fund are deductible up to NOK40,000. Personal expenses can be deducted up to a similar sum. Trade union membership fees are also deductible. Child benefit is tax-free.

There is another tax on your gross personal income (*personinntekt*), the total of your employment and pensions income; on this basis you pay 7.8% social security payments (*trygdeavgifter*) and a further 13.5% surtax (*toppskatt*) if your income exceeds NOK320,000. A higher rate of 19.5% is levied on income above NOK830,000. You are not liable for social security payments if your income is less than NOK23,000 per year.

Expatriate residents receive a 15% deduction on their ordinary income, before the personal exemption, if they work in Norway for less than four years. After four years they only receive the same exemption as Norwegian citizens. Anyone who stays in Norway for less than six months is not a resident; they pay the 28% rate of tax. Temporary workers cannot avoid paying tax.

Wealth Tax or *formuesskatt* is levied on your net worldwide assets if you are a resident in Norway. The commune wealth tax is levied at 0.7% on assets above NOK120,000 (approx. £9,480/US$13,560). The state wealth tax is levied at 0.2% (NOK120,000-540,000) and 0.4% (over NOK540,000) for Class 1 taxpayers.

Property Tax. Properties are given a *likningsverdi* or tax value, and tax is levied on this at 2.5% above a value of NOK80,000 (approx. £6,320)/US$9,040) and 5% above NOK451,000. There is no lower threshold on second homes. The *likningsverdi* generally does not exceed 30% of the market value of the house.

MVA (*merverdiavgift*) is a value added tax of 23% on all services and purchases with the exception of books, medical services, used cars, property and some other items. It is included in the price of goods in the shops.

Useful Addresses

Non-Resident Claims, Fitz Roy House, PO Box 46, Nottingham NG2 1BD; ☎0115-974 1919; fax 0115-974 1919; www.inlandrevenue.gov.uk.

Centre for Non-Residents (CNR), Residence Advice & Liabilities Unit 355, St John's House, Bootle, Merseyside L69 9BB; ☎0151-472 6202; fax 0151-472 6003.

Oslo Likningskontor og folkeregister, Hagegaten 23, 0630 Oslo; ☎815 444 55; fax 22 68 85 86; www.likningskontoret.oslo.no.

Sentralskattekontoret for utenlandssaker, Central Office for Foreign Tax Affairs (COFTA), Prinsensvei 1, 4315 Sandnes (visiting address); ☎51 96 96 00; fax 51 67 85 59; e-mail postkassesfu@skatteetaten.no. Postal address: PO Box 8031, 4068 Stavanger.

HEALTH INSURANCE AND HOSPITALS

A well-developed system of health and welfare programmes in Norway means that there is a very high standard of public health. Membership of the national health insurance scheme is compulsory for all people resident in Norway regardless of nationality; this applies to offshore workers as well. Resident here means that you intend to remain in Norway for more than a year, or have already been in Norway for a year. Employees of Norwegian companies have to be insured from the time of arrival in Norway. This ensures free medical care in hospital, compensation for doctor's fees, free medicine and a compensation allowance for lost earnings. Salaried employees must join an additional scheme which secures cash benefits during pregnancy or illness; this scheme is optional for the self-employed.

Under EEA regulation 1408/71, EEA nationals may apply to be exempted from social security payments while they remain in Norway; it is necessary to produce a certificate of coverage from the national insurance institution in your own country. Non-EEA citizens can do the same. The United States has a social security totalisation agreement with Norway. Applications are made to the National Insurance Office, Madla, PO Box 484, 4090 Hafrsfjord; ☎51 59 72 50.

Most hospitals are owned by the state, the counties or the municipalities; the municipalities generally deal with primary health care, the counties run the hospitals and mental health services. The state also runs some hospitals, including the *Rikshospitalet* (National Hospital). There is a growing number of private hospitals. The Norwegian Board of Health supervises health care in Norway, and is a part of the Norwegian Ministry of Social Affairs and Health.

The state spends a relatively large amount per head on health care; there are nonetheless shortages of trained staff, although there is no shortage of hospital beds. Other features of the Norwegian health care system include free family counselling, and free basic dental care for children under 18. Specialised dental care for under-18s will be refunded up to 75%.

Since 2001 you are expected to choose one general practitioner; you may change GP up to twice a year if you can find a doctor with free space. If you do not choose your physician, then you are responsible for finding one when you need one. You will also have to pay a fee. Admittance to hospital is usually arranged by a doctor. For further details about your health rights in Norway contact the Norwegian Board of Health. Private doctors are listed in the phone book under *leger*; the word *lækjarvak* indicates doctor on duty. To make an appointment with a doctor dial the free number 800 40 101; www.doctors.no.

Emergencies and Chemists

For medical emergencies dial 113 in Oslo. In other parts of the country dial the operator on 180 and ask for the local emergency medical help (*nødhjelp*).

For chemists look for *apotek* or *medisinsutsalgene* in the phone book. Most large cities have all-night pharmacies. In Oslo you will find one opposite the Oslo S central station: Jernbanetorgets 4b; ☎22 41 24 82. In Bergen Apoteket Nordstjernen near the bus station stays open till midnight; ☎55 21 83 84; e-mail nordstjernen.bergen@apotek.no. In Stavanger Løveapoteket, at Olav V gade 11, is open until 11pm Monday to Saturday, and until 8pm on Sundays; call 51 52 06 07; e-mail loeveap@online.no. St Olav's Apotek at Beddingen 4, Solsiden kjøpesenter, Trondheim is always open until midnight; ☎73 88 37 37. In some cities there is a rotating system of late night pharmacies in which case the schedule will be displayed on the chemist's door. Emergency dental treatment is available in Oslo outside office hours from Oslo Kommunale Tannlegevakt, Tøyen Senter, Kolstadgata 18; ☎22 67 30 00.

Useful Addresses

Helsedepartementet, Department of Health, Einar Gerhardsens plass 3, Postboks
8011 Dep, 0030 Oslo; ☎22 24 90 90; http://odin.dep.no/hd.
Norwegian Board of Health, Calmeyers Gate 1, 0183 Oslo; ☎22 24 90 90;
www.helsetilsyn.no.

The E111 and Private Health Insurance

Until such time as you join a health insurance scheme in Norway you will
need to make provision for medical costs. Private health insurance is advisable
to meet the cost of any health treatment that may be required. Expacare
(e-mail info@expacare.net or visit www.expacare.net) are specialists in expatriate
healthcare offering high quality health insurance cover for individuals and their
families, including group cover for five or more employees; cover is available for
expatriates of all nationalities worldwide.

It is possible to obtain refunds of some of the cost of urgently needed medical
treatment received in Norway, if you have a form E111 with you. The application
form is available in leaflet T6 *Health Advice for Travellers* from your post office. The
leaflet SA29 *Your social security insurance, benefits and health care rights in the European
Community, and in Iceland, Liechtenstein and Norway* is also available from the UK
Department of Work and Pensions on their website: www.dwp.gov.uk.

If you are already in Norway you can have your E111 sent to you by International
Services, Inland Revenue, National Insurance Contributions Office, Longbenton,
Newcastle upon Tyne NE98 1ZZ (☎0845-915 4811 *or* 44 191 225 4811 from
abroad; fax 0845-915 7800 *or* 44 191 225 7800 from abroad). Allow one month for
International Services to process your application. Details are also available on
the Inland Revenue website which can be found at www.inlandrevenue.gov.uk/
nic/intserv/osc.htm.

SOCIAL SECURITY AND UNEMPLOYMENT BENEFIT

The Norwegian social security system is funded by contributions from
employers, employees or self-employed workers, the government and
municipalities. Employers contribute up to 14.1% of an employee's gross salary.
The employee's contribution is up to 7.8%. Self-employed individuals contribute
10.7% of their income up to 12 times the basic allowance (NOK40,090 – approx.
£3,167/US$4,530), and then 7.8%.

The Norwegian social security system provides financial security for the
persons covered by the system in areas of pensions, disability allowances,
occupational injury, medical treatment, sickness benefits, maternity allowance,
single parent support and unemployment benefit. Non-residents are insured if
working for a Norwegian employer and are covered from the moment of starting
work regardless of the period of employment. Non-resident employees working
on the Norwegian Continental Shelf are also included in the National Insurance
Scheme. Those working on ships operating beyond the territorial borders may
be exempted from National Insurance payments, but have to be covered for
occupational injury.

Unemployment

If you become unemployed in Norway register with the nearest job centre (*Arbeidsformidling*) who will advise you on where and how to claim benefits. All EEA nationals will receive social security benefits on the same basis as Norwegian nationals if they are employed or self-employed in Norway.

If you have been receiving contributions-based unemployment benefit in your home country for at least four weeks you can transfer your benefit to another EEA country. This entitlement runs out after three months, however, so it is necessary to plan ahead if you want to do this. Your UK Employment Centre will take care of the arrangements. UK unemployment benefit will, of course, not go very far in a country as expensive as Norway.

Useful Addresses

Rikstrygdeverket (National Insurance Administration), Drammensveien 60, N-0241 Oslo; ☎22 92 70 00; e-mail rtv@trygdeetaten.no; www.trygdeetaten.no.

Arbeidsdirektoratet (Directorate of Labour), Postboks 8127 dep, 0032 Oslo; ☎23 35 24 00; e-mail aetat.apost@aetat.no; www.aetat.no.

Royal Ministry of Social Affairs, Einar Gerhardsens plass 3, Postboks 8019 Dep, 0030 Oslo; ☎22 24 90 90; e-mail postmottak@shd.dep.no; http://odin.dep.no/sos.

DWP Pensions and Overseas Benefits Directorate, Newcastle-upon-Tyne NE98 1BA; ☎0191-218 7777; www.dwp.gov.uk.

Federal Benefits Unit, American Embassy, Drammensveien 18, 0244 Oslo; ☎22 44 85 50; e-mail oslo@usa.no; www.usa.no.

LOCAL GOVERNMENT

Norway is divided into 19 counties, of which Oslo og Akershus forms one; the others are: Østfold, Hedmark, Oppland, Buskerud, Vestfold, Telemark, Aust-Agder, Vest-Agder, Rogaland, Hordaland, Sogne og Fjordane, Møre og Romsdal, Sør-Trøndelag, Nord-Trødelag, Nordland, Troms, Finnmark and Svalbard. The counties, or *fylker*, are divided into rural and urban municipalities. Councils are elected every four years, two years after the *Storting* elections, and tend to reflect the political divisions of the *Storting*. Each council elects a board of aldermen and a mayor. The governing bodies of towns also often employ councillors for local affairs such as finance, schools, social welfare and housing. Norwegians pay direct taxes to local as well as central government. Delegates for the *fylker* councils are elected by the municipalities but *fylke* governors, *fylkesmannen,* are elected by the Cabinet.

The counties have their own municipal department which runs county-wide services, such as the roads, health, schools and energy. There are 435 municipalities or *kommunene*, at the level of local government, with a municipal board, *kommunestyret*.

CRIME AND THE POLICE

Crime rates are very low in Norway and most law-breaking consists of driving offences. The streets of major cities are very safe compared with the rest of Europe and the main form of harassment is likely to be from drunks hassling for cigarettes although Vigeland Park in Oslo has a reputation for drug dealing and theft. Serious crime is very rare and even very small children are left to play outside by parents. Violence on TV and in cartoons is carefully monitored. Crime against foreigners is infrequent and more likely to come from other foreigners.

The further north you go the lower the crime rate gets and it is not unusual for people to leave their cars and houses unlocked. Generally the police are friendly, approachable and helpful. A police officer has the power to stop and search if he/she has reasonable grounds for suspicion. A person can be detained for up to 24 hours without charge but has a statutory right to see a solicitor. Drug violations carry very strict penalties. Drug dealing carries a maximum penalty of 21 years imprisonment – the same as for premeditated murder. In emergencies dial 112 for the police in Oslo and 180 for local emergency numbers outside of Oslo. The police have a website: www.politi.no.

The Legal System

Norwegian law is largely the product of the interaction of customary law and general civil law. In the courts, precedent is not binding except in decisions of the Supreme Court. Civil cases must, in most cases, be submitted to conciliation councils first and many issues are settled without the need for formal legal action. Appeals can be made against the decision of conciliation councils to the courts and there is also a formal system of courts of appeal. The final arbiter of legal decisions is the Supreme Court. Citizens' rights are upheld by an ombudsman who can act as an intermediary on their behalf in matters of public administration.

Foreign judgements cannot be enforced in Norway, but where the foreign court was deemed to be competent, the Norwegian court will base its decisions on the foreign judgement. In 1961 Great Britain and Norway agreed a convention which gave reciprocal recognition and enforcement of judgements in civil cases. This does not apply to family law, for decisions in the proceedings of the recovery of taxes, fines or other penalties.

For further details about the Norwegian legal system contact: Den Norske Advokaftorening (Kristian Augustsgate 9, 0164 Oslo 1; ☎22 03 50 50), or contact the local district governor (fylkesmann). In Oslo this is at Fylkesmannen i Oslo og Akershus, Tordenskioldsgaten 12, 0160 Oslo; ☎22 00 35 00; fax 22 00 35 35. If you require free legal assistance in Oslo, contact Oslo Kommune Fri Rettshjelp, Storgaten 19, 0184 Oslo; ☎22 42 52 60.

RELIGION

88% of Norwegians belong to the Evangelical Lutheran church. Whilst almost every village is graced by the distinctive white Lutheran chapel, active church attendance, particularly by the young, is low. There are many churches in Oslo including the American Lutheran Church which holds services in English, as does the Anglican Episcopalian Church of St Edmund's. Norway has a surprising mix of religious minorities which includes: Quakers, Jews, Baptists, Pentecostalists, Methodists, Catholics and, because of Asian immigration, Buddhists and Muslims.

Places of Worship

The following churches/synagogues have services in English. It is advisable to contact the church first as services may not be held every Sunday. All services are Protestant.

St Olaf's Church, Balestrand; ☎22 69 22 14; fax 22 69 21 63. June, July, August.

Engensentret Chapel, Baneveien, Bergen; ☎22 69 22 14; fax 22 69 21 63.

American Lutheran Church, Fritznersgate 15, Oslo; ☎22 44 35 84; fax 22 44 30 15; e-mail office@alcoslo.org.

St Edmunds, Møllergate 30, Oslo; ☎22 69 22 14; fax 22 69 21 63.

Bethel, Løkkeveien, Stavanger; ☎51 55 67 12.

Cathedral, Nidarosdomen, Trondheim; ☎22 69 22 14; fax 22 69 21 63.

Orthodox Synagogue, 15 Bergstien, 0172 Oslo; ☎22 69 65 70; www.dmt.oslo.no

Orthodox Synagogue, Arkitekt Christies gate 1B, Trondheim; www.dmt.trondheim.no.

SOCIAL LIFE

The Norwegians

Despite the reputation for Nordic reserve, Norwegians are usually friendly and helpful when approached. Whilst they do not as a rule make the first move, any move on your part is likely to be well received. Norwegians can show exceptional hospitality to foreigners way above and beyond the call of good manners. Don't be deceived by the serious exterior – whilst they don't go in for slapstick much, Norwegians often have a very dry sense of humour. Norwegians are generally gentle and shy but they also tend to be very independent in their views. Centuries of domination by Denmark have left Norway fiercely patriotic – criticise Norway to a Norwegian at your own peril.

Norwegians tend to describe themselves as simple people with simple tastes. While they are generally very well educated and read a great deal, there can also be a certain degree of naïvety, or diffidence in their contacts with outsiders. Honesty and straight talking are valued highly. They will not waste words on idle chit-chat. Like the other Scandinavians, Norwegians think carefully before they speak. They prefer not to feel under an obligation to someone else, as this goes against their sense of independence.

Manners and Customs

Handshaking is the norm when meeting strangers in Norway, but even casual acquaintances usually shake hands on meeting and parting. In Norway it is customary to introduce yourself by your full name. Norwegians set great store by politeness although this tends to be more out of pleasantness than formality. If you are invited to someone's home, a gift of flowers or chocolates is always acceptable. When drinking a toast or to someone's health (*skåling*) there is a delicate ritual of eye contact. Eye contact is made before drinking, then say *skål* (cheers), chink glasses, look each other in the eye again and drink. The same applies in large gatherings.

Culture

Given its small population and agricultural past, Norway has made a significant national and international cultural contribution. The 19th century in particular saw a blossoming of culture and talent; the end of the century produced such famous names as the dramatist Henrik Ibsen, the novelist and Nobel laureate Knut Hamsun, the expressionist painter Edvard Munch and the composer Edvard Grieg.

Norway has a powerful folk art culture based around isolated farming communities and this is particularly apparent in the works of Grieg, most notably his suite *Peer Gynt*, the text of which was written by Ibsen. National romanticism (sometimes referred to as Viking romanticism) went hand in hand with Norway's cultural revival at the turn of the 19th century when thoughts were turning towards independence from Sweden. Although the Vikings are universally known for their rape and pillage culture, their skills and craftsmanship in jewellery, boat-building and exploration are greatly admired by modern Norwegians.

Heavy-timbered houses with the traditional turf roofs are highly prized and protected as are handcrafted objects and furniture made from wood in local forests. Wooden objects are often decorated by the distinctive *rosemaling* or rose painting which features prominently in Norwegian folk art. The earliest surviving examples of the *rosemaling* art date back to the 1700s but it may well predate this by many centuries. The remote separate valleys often reveal a distinct local artistic style. The tradition of woodcarving survives into the present with modern day *hytter* or wooden holiday homes exhibiting intricate carving on the exterior.

Many Norwegians wear the national costume (the *bunad*) not just for fancy dress but as formal attire for events like weddings, making the *bunad* one of the most frequently worn national costumes in Europe.

The Great Outdoors

Exploring the wilds is a national pastime in Norway, which is hardly surprising in a nation which produced some of the world's most famous explorers. Amongst the earlier ones were Garðar Svarsson who discovered Iceland in the late ninth century, and Leif Eriksson who in about 1000 AD was the first European to set foot on the American continent. One could call the Vikings the first tourists. More recently Norway has produced the polar explorers Roald Amundsen and Fridtjof Nansen and the nautical explorer Thor Heyerdahl. Whilst most modern Norwegians do their exploring on a more modest scale, the Great Outdoors has a tremendous hold on the Norwegian national character. Enshrined in Norwegian Law is the public's right of way law (*Allemannsretten*) which guarantees the individual right to cross uncultivated land regardless of ownership. Landowners still have the right to control access where damage could be done by walkers. Norwegians in any case respect and protect the land and the whole country is imbued with a strong ecological awareness.

With vast tracts of Norway being wild, unspoilt and indescribably beautiful it is hardly surprising that one in four Norwegians lists outdoor recreation as their favourite pastime. Walking, mountain climbing and cross-country skiing are some of the favourites and are enjoyed by all sectors of the population from king to commoner. One-quarter of the population own a *hytte*, a wooden holiday home which, ideally, is situated in a remote valley, space being highly valued here. Many Norwegians also own their own boats. Sailing is a favourite summer pastime and both the late King Olav V and the present King Harald V hold Olympic medals for sailing. Messing about on the fjord may be an atavistic yearning for the Viking sea-going era but the boat is also a common feature of daily life for remote rural communities for fishing and crossing local rivers and fjords. Sport is also very popular and there are indoor and outdoor facilities nationwide. Cycling, canoeing, fishing, golf, horse-riding, rafting, skating and skiing are all popular.

Entertainment

Hardly surprisingly, the majority of Norway's night life is in Oslo. Cities outside Oslo are relatively small and quiet by European standards which makes the northern city of Tromsø claim to be the Paris of the North seem unduly pretentious. Although Oslo has tended to have a fairly low profile, the late 1980s saw Oslo blossom as a cosmopolitan city thanks to injections of cash from the oil boom. Money has been invested in the arts and Oslo has a thriving cultural life, many museums, a national theatre, 30 cinema screens and an active music life. Clubs and concerts are hosts to international and mainstream music makers. Bands can be seen at the Drammen Stadium; a new arena, the Forum, has been built near the central station to provide multicultural activities. It is advisable to book cinema places on Sunday night as this is the most popular time for cinema going.

Some clubs have a minimum age of 21 or 23 and in some it is as high as 26. There are bars, clubs and cafés throughout Oslo which range from the homely to the upmarket. The tourist information centre produces the *Oslo Guide* and *What's On in Oslo* which gives a run-down of what's available; it is advisable to consult listings in the paper as venues can open and close down fairly quickly.

Food and Drink

Food in Norway has traditionally been regarded more as a source of human fuel than as a source of titillation for the palate. Home-made Norwegian food still tends to reflect this and is simple and filling. Norway's is a largely carnivorous society and vegetarians may need to be particularly inventive when creating dishes other than those which are cheese-based. Typical Norwegian fare includes: *kjøttkaker* (meat cakes), *medisterkaker* (pork sausage patties) and *reinsdyrkaker* (reindeer meatballs). Lamb is also popular but inevitably the mainstay of the Norwegian diet is fish served in many varieties. Some fish dishes are an acquired taste, in particular *rakfisk* (fermented trout) which even native Norwegians may find hard to stomach.

Food is easy to come by throughout the country, including the far north, but is generally very expensive – a result of hefty government subsidies which encourage farmers to produce homegrown fare in a difficult environment. Typically, Norwegians eat a large breakfast, of bread, herrings, cold meat and cheese, a simple lunch of open sandwiches, and a hot meal at dinner. Dinner is eaten relatively early between four and six pm. Norwegians are great coffee drinkers; it is usual to serve coffee whenever people meet. You may also be bombarded with pastries – if you must refuse do so politely.

Attitudes to alcohol are fairly ambivalent in Norway. You can sometimes get the impression that the country is split between hardline would-be prohibitioners and potential candidates for Alcoholics Anonymous. Beer is sold in most grocery stores but the import of wines and spirits is a state monopoly; alcohol is sold in the chain of Vinmonopol shops. Laws regarding the sale of alcohol are decided at the *kommune*, or town and local council levels, and the availability of alcohol varies considerably throughout the country. Alcohol is widely available in Oslo and can be sold in some places into the early hours of the morning. Generally, the Vinmonopol is open from 10am-5pm Monday to Friday and from 9am-1pm on Saturdays. There is a widespread ban on drinking on Sundays. Home-distilling from sugar and potatoes is illegal though the law is not strictly observed. Alcohol is prohibitively expensive – about 50NOK (approx. £3.95/US$5.65) for half a litre of beer in a bar.

Eating and drinking out in Oslo (and all of Norway effectively) is a very expensive affair. International cuisine tends to be restricted to the restaurants of Oslo and the major cities.

Shopping

Most shops are open from 9am to 5pm on weekdays although on Thursdays there is usually an extended opening time until 7 or 8 pm. Large shopping centres, kiosks and suprmarkets also often have extended opening times. Private offices are open from 8am-4pm Monday to Friday and public offices from 8am-3.15 pm (in summer they close slightly earlier at 3pm). There is a range of typical Norwegian crafts for sale in almost every city and they include woollen knitwear (classic designs are snowflakes and reindeer), textiles, candlesticks, wooden ornaments and useful kitchen objects. Norwegian jewellery is distinctive – often made of silver and tending to favour Viking designs. Antique Norwegian rustic items may not be exported.

METRICATION

For information on the metric system including a conversion chart see under *Metrication* at the end of the *Daily Life* chapter in the section on Denmark.

PUBLIC HOLIDAYS

1 January	New Year's Day
Easter	Maundy Thursday, Good Friday, Easter Monday
1 May	Labour Day
17 May	Independence or Constitution Day
Ascension Day	
Whit Monday	
23 June	Midsummer Eve (Sankt Hans), a nationwide celebration with dancing and beach bonfires throughout the country
25 December	Christmas Day
26 December	Boxing Day

RETIREMENT

Norway is not a place to retire unless you have prior connections here. Anyone considering such a move needs to think carefully through the implications of living on a pension, and therefore probably on a reduced income, in a country where the basic cost of living is exceptionally high. As long as you are active and able to drive you should not experience any mobility problems but bear in mind that significant areas of Norway are covered in snow in winter and roads can become impassable. Most of the southern cities also experience some snow in winter and retirement age might not be quite the best time to take up skiing.

Set against this is the fact that most Norwegians speak excellent English (although if you are planning to retire there it's a good idea to acquire as much Norwegian as you can before taking up retirement). Health provision in Norway is excellent and elderly people are not treated as second class citizens or as a 'poor investment' by the health services. The average number of patients per doctor is just over 300. Norway enjoys some of the highest longevity rates in the world and elderly people tend to remain active. The environment in Norway should be excellent given the ecological consciousness of the nation but this is marred by acid rain from other countries (principally Britain) and the industrial effluent from the neighbouring former Soviet Union in the east. Before taking up permanent residence in Norway it is advisable to spend a trial period there, preferably including winter.

Residence Requirements

You can stay in Norway without working, if you are an EEA citizen, but you must be able to provide documents that you are receiving regular income to support yourself. Evidence that you have sufficient means can be provided in the form of bank account statements. The amount you receive must be at least the equivalent of a basic state pension in Norway – currently NOK88,032 (approx £6,950/US$9,950) per annum. You will also need to provide evidence of medical insurance from your own country or prove that you have taken out sufficient medical insurance for the duration of your stay in Norway.

Pensions

Since joining the European Economic Area, Norway has come into line with the rest of the EU as regards social security, insurance benefits and health care rights for nationals of the countries involved. If you are entitled to a state pension before leaving Britain you can have it paid to you in Norway but it will remain at British levels. If you move to Norway before retirement age and are still paying national insurance contributions to Britain you will qualify for a British state pension. If you are working for a Norwegian company or employer and have made a sufficient contribution to the Norwegian social security system you will be entitled to a Norwegian pension.

Pensions in Norway are relatively generous, especially if you have worked for some time there. Everyone who has made contributions for 40 years between the ages of 16 and 66 is entitled to the Basic Allowance or B.a., which in 2001 stood at NOK40,090 per annum for a single person. A special supplement (*særtillegg*) is added on to produce the minimum pension (*minnstepensjon*); this stood at NOK88,032 a year in 2001. A married couple receive NOK151,524 together. Individual pensions vary according to pension earning time and individual income. The normal age for the old-age pension in Norway is 67. If you continue working between the ages of 67 and 70 your pension may be reduced depending on how much you earn. Foreign residents can only qualify for pension payments once they have spent three years working in Norway.

A supplementary pension (*tilleggspensjon*) was introduced in 1967. Under this system any earnings over and above the B.a. can be counted towards 'pension points' (*pensjonspoeng*). The excess is divided by the B.a. to produce the points. Your 20 highest-earning years are averaged out to give a final points total (*sluttpoeng*) which is then used to calculate how much more pension you will receive above the basic amount. Because the system was only introduced in 1967, the full amount of *tilleggspensjon* will only start to be paid in 2007, since no one will have fulfilled 40 working years before then. There is of course nothing to prevent you from taking out a private pension plan as well.

The UK Department of Work and Pensions will advise on your pension rights. The website: www.pensionsguide.gov.uk will give you some idea of what you can expect to receive. You can also ask for a 'pension prediction' from the DWP two years before you retire. In Norway the Rikstrygdeverk will tell you what your rights are. Their website carries some useful information in Norwegian. The Ministry of Social Affairs has some information in English. Some general information for UK citizens is given in the DWP leaflet SA29: *Your Social Security insurance, benefits and health care rights in the European Community*; download from the website www.dwp.gov.uk.

Useful Addresses

Pensions and Overseas Benefits Directorate, Department for Work and Pensions, Tyneview Park, Whitley Rd, Benton, Newcastle-upon-Tyne NE98 1BA; 0191-218 7777; www.dwp.gov.uk.

Rikstrygdeverket, Drammensveien 60, Oslo; www.trygdeverket.no.

Royal Ministry of Social Affairs, Einar Gerhardsens plass 3, Postboks 8019 Dep, 0030 Oslo; ☎22 24 90 90; e-mail postmottak@shd.dep.no; http://odin.dep.no/sos.

Statens Pensjonskasse (State Pension Fund), PB5364 Majorstua, 0304 Oslo; ☎22 24 15 00; fax 22 24 15 01; www.spk.no.

Health

All employees of Norwegian firms automatically contribute to the national health insurance scheme. Nationals of the European Economic Area are entitled to use reciprocal health care arrangements in Norway (see 'Health' in the *Daily Life* chapter).

Entertainment and English Language Clubs

British television and satellite and cable TV are widely available in Norway. The English language NATO station is available all year round on 105.5 FM in Norway and English is available throughout the summer on 106.8 FM. You can also tune into the BBC radio World Service. For frequencies and times see www.bbc.co.uk/worldservice, or contact BBC On Air magazine, Bush House, Strand, London WC2B 4PH; www.bbconair.co.uk.

Embassies can supply names and addresses of expatriate clubs. The following are based mainly based in Oslo.

Useful Addresses

American Women's Club of Oslo, POB 3101 Elisenberg, 0207 Oslo; ☎22 29 71 95; e-mail President@AWCOslo.org; www.fawco.org.

Anglo-Norse Society, c/o British Embassy, Thomas Heftyesgate 8, 0244 Oslo; ☎22 14 70 17.

The British Council, Fridtjof Nansens Plass 5, 0160 Oslo; ☎22 39 61 90; fax 22 42 40 39; e-mail british.council@britishcouncil.no; www.britishcouncil.no.

The Caledonian Society, ☎55 99 61 83.

The International Forum, Postboks 1505 Vika, 0117 Oslo; ☎22 24 35 13.

Norway America Association, Raadhusgaten 23B, 0158 Oslo; ☎47 23 35 71 60; fax 47 23 35 71 75; e-mail namerika@online.no; www.noram.no.

Oslo Rugby Klubb, Hasleveien 10, 0571 Oslo; ☎22 37 95 30.

Petroleum Women's Club, Postboks 196, 1322 H vik; ☎22 52 14 60.

Scottish Country Dance Group, ☎22 22 08 92.

St Edmund's Guild (St Edmund's Church), ☎22 69 22 14.

Welsh Society, Postboks 63, 1555 Son; ☎64 95 93 85; e-mail: ows@c2i.net; http://home.c2i.net/oslo – welsh – society.

Women's Commonwealth Club, ☎22 14 90 06.

Wills and Inheritance

It is highly advisable to draw up a will before moving to a foreign country and to take expert legal advice. You should also seek legal advice on wills in Norway. Many lawyers in Norway speak English; the British Embassy website carries a list. There are strict rules about which heirs have priority. The rules will override any will made outside Norway.

Inheritance tax (*arveavgift*) is higher in Norway than the UK or US. The first NOK200,000 (approx. £15,800/US$22,600) is tax-free for everyone. Heirs in direct line pay 8% between NOK200,00 and 300,000, and 20% above. For others the amounts are 10% and 30%. There is no tax on inheritance from your spouse. Tax is levied at the same rate on gifts in the years prior to death.

If you live with someone, you can register your partnership with a notary. Registered partnership (*registrert partnerskap*) is much the same as marriage for legal purposes; it can only be dissolved by legal process. You are not allowed to enter into a partnership agreement if you are married to someone else. You should take legal advice if you intend to leave your assets to a registered partner. According to the law your partner should be treated the same as if they were your spouse.

SECTION II

WORKING IN NORWAY

EMPLOYMENT

PERMANENT WORK

TEMPORARY WORK

STARTING A BUSINESS

EMPLOYMENT

THE EMPLOYMENT SCENE

At a first glance the employment scene in Norway seems quite promising. Inflation currently stands at a mere 2.5%, and headline unemployment is only 3.5%. The state runs a budget surplus of 10% of GDP; the state finances depend very much on the current price of oil. Norway is dependent on specialist skills from abroad that cannot be supplied by the home labour market in order to exploit its oil and gas. Norway's oil reserves are expected to run out by 2020: they are quite small in comparison with some Middle Eastern countries. Its natural gas reserves will last a lot longer.

Despite its economic strength, Norway's decision in 1994 not to join the European Union caused some dismay in the business world. Following Norway's rejection of EU membership, the Norwegian Confederation of Business and Industry warned that the vote might lead to the loss of as many as 100,000 jobs, a prediction that proved quite unjustified. Norwegian industrialists warned that many manufacturers may consider moving to lower-cost countries in the EU. In reality, the opposite has happened; foreign investment has increased dramatically, as foreign entrepreneurs see Norway as an underdeveloped market with an increasingly wealthy consumer base.

In voting against the EU, Norway has placed its faith in its natural resources of gas and oil to see it through. Norway is to some extent riding a roller coaster as far as the North Sea oil and gas reserves are concerned; when prices are low, as they have been, then there is less money around to subsidise loss-making industries. The overheating effect caused by large oil revenues necessitates high interest rates, and consequently high prices.

Thirty-seven per cent of the labour force are employed in community, social and personal services. Nearly 15% work in mining, industry and electricity and water utilities. The retail trade and hotel and restaurant industry account for 18.5%, agriculture, forestry, hunting and fishing employ 4.1%, financing, real estate and business services 11.3% , building construction 6.5% and transport, storage and communications 7.4%. The main trend is away from primary industries, towards services and high-tech.

UK citizens can undertake both full-time and part-time work in Norway providing that their part-time work is sufficient to cover their living expenses.

Short-term jobs are often available because the Norwegians do not want to do them – this is particularly true of low-paid work such as farming. Menial jobs tend to be taken by Finns or other Nordics. One of the surprising features of the labour market is that although the employment service makes information available to foreign jobseekers, temporary work agencies tend to discourage applicants from non-Nordic countries, with the argument that they should learn to speak Norwegian first if they want to work in Norway. People with higher education and skills in areas where there is a labour shortage, on the other hand, will not be turned away.

Whilst there is no minimum wage, wages are usually considerably higher than in most of Europe, although the high Norwegian taxes and cost of living mean that what looks like well-remunerated employment may not be quite as profitable as you thought.

RESIDENCE AND WORK REGULATIONS

Nationals of the European Economic Area do not need to obtain a work permit to work in Norway and can stay in Norway for up to three months to look for work. For further details on work and residence regulations see Chapter Two, *Residence and Entry Regulations*.

Skills And Qualifications

To pursue professional careers abroad, authorisation, official approval or licences are often required. Since joining the EEA, Norway has come into line with the European Union regulations with regard to reciprocal recognition of professional qualifications. If you have had a professional training you would not therefore, normally, need to undergo supplementary training or examinations before taking up a career in Norway. Examples are medicine, nursing, dentistry, veterinary, law etc. There are fewer regulated professions in Norway than in the UK; each profession has its own national association.

For details of comparability of academic qualifications contact NAIC (The National Academic Information Centre: Postboks 8150 Dep., 0033 Oslo; ☎21 02 18 25; fax 21 02 18 02; e-mail NAIC@nnr.no; www.nnr.no/naic/). You can also get information on comparisons between British and Norwegian qualifications by contacting the Norwegian Central Government Educational Offices (*Statens Utdanningskontorer,* ☎22 92 77 00), or through the Royal Ministry of Education and Research (Akersgaten 42, Postboks 8119 Dep, 0032 Oslo; ☎22 34 90 90; http://odin.dep.no/ufd). The latter website has some information in English on comparability.

For the comparability of vocational qualifications such as catering, construction and agriculture contact the Comparability Coordinator, Employment Dept., Qualifications and Standards Branch (QSI), Room E454, Moorfoot, Sheffield SP1 4PQ; ☎0114-2594144. Anyone wanting to work on the Norwegian oil rigs (even if it is only as a refurbisher) will need to have an Offshore Safety Certificate. Those awarded by the Robert Gordon University (Aberdeen AB9 2PG) meet with Norwegian requirements and are the equivalent of the Norwegian *Leiro* offshore certificate.

SOURCES OF JOBS

NEWSPAPERS AND DIRECTORIES

Jobs in Norway are occasionally advertised in the UK and American press. *Overseas Jobs Express* (available by subscription only from Overseas Jobs Express, 20 New Road, Brighton, East Sussex BN1 1UF; ☎01273-699611; www.overseasjobsexpress.com) has adverts from agencies looking for workers in petrochemicals, engineering and IT. The *Oil & Gas Journal*, and other professional journals, are good places to look for postings.

Information on casual and summer jobs can be found in the publications *Work Your Way Around the World*, *The Au Pair and Nanny's Guide to Working Abroad*, *Summer Jobs Abroad* and *Teaching English Abroad* all available from Vacation Work Publications (see inside cover).

Norwegian Newspapers. You could try placing your own advertisement in one of the Norwegian dailies such as *Dagbladet,* although it would be just as effective to post your CV on a job website. Addresses of main newspapers are listed below.

If you can read Norwegian consult the daily national and regional papers which carry adverts for jobs. The major source for jobs is the daily *Aftenposten*. Regional papers which advertise jobs are *Bergens Tidende* in Bergen, *Adresseavisen* in Trondheim and *Stavanger Aftenbladet*. Vacancies in the public sector, as well as public tenders and other official notices, are advertised in the government journal *Norsk Lysingsblad* which appears five days a week. The *Teknisk Ukeblad* is a weekly for engineers and other technical staff where you can place an advertisement. *Benn's Press Directory*, available from most main reference libraries, has an exhaustive list of Norwegian newspapers, magazines and trade journals. Some newsagents in London stock Norwegian newspapers, or you can try to order a copy directly.

Adresseavisen, Industriv. 13, 7003 Trondheim; ☎07 200; fax 72 50 11 15; www.adressa.no.

Aftenposten, Postboks 1178 Sentrum, 0107 Oslo; ☎22 11 50 40; fax 22 86 40 39; www.aftenposten.no.

Bergens Tidende, Krinkelkroken 1, Postboks 7240, 5020 Bergen; ☎55 21 45 00; www.bergens-tidende.no.

Dagbladet, Akersgaten 49, 0107 Oslo; ☎22 31 06 00; fax 22 42 95 48; www.dagbladet.no.

Dagens Næringsliv, Grev Wedels plass 9, Postboks 1182 Sentrum, 0107 Oslo; ☎22 0 10 00; www.dn.no.

Dagsavisen, Møllergata 39, Oslo; ☎22 99 80 00; fax 22 99 82 54; www.dagsavisen.no.

Stavanger Aftenbladet, 4013 Stavanger; ☎51 50 00 00; fax 51 50 17 18; www.aftenposten.no.

Norsk Lysingsblad Postboks 177, 8501 Narvik; http://norsk.lysingsblad.no.

Teknisk Ukeblad, Postboks 5844 Majorstua, 0308 Oslo; e-mail resep@tekblad.no; www.sol.no/tu.

Verdens Gang, Akersgatan 55, Pb. 1185, Sentrum 0107 Oslo; ☎22 00 00 00; fax 22 42 67 80; www.vg.no.

INTERNET

The internet is becoming more and more important for job seekers. Apart from the official site www.aetat.no, there are many more sites that advertise job vacancies, or allow you to post your CV. The main jobsearch site is www.jobbtilbud.no. Other ones include www.finn.no, www.yahoo.no, www.agaton.net, and www.hjemmenett.no/jobb. The newspaper sites given above have job pages, especially *Adresseavisen*, *Aftenposten* and *Dagbladet*.

Not many jobs in Norway are advertised on the EURES website; the best time to look is in spring or early summer. See http://europa.eu.int/comm/employment. The website www.nordjobb.net carries numerous ads for summer jobs, but it is aimed at people who can speak at least one Scandinavian language well.

THE DIRECT APPROACH

A direct approach by letter, followed up with an e-mail or telephone call, may yield some results. This is likely to be most effective where a company needs seasonal workers – the ski resorts in winter for example or the youth hostels and hotels in summer. Needless to say one should make sure to apply at the right time of year, say three months before the season actually begins. The Norwegian Tourist Office can supply lists of resorts and hotels. Writing to or e-mailing companies where workers are needed is a feasible approach, although you may have to go to Norway for an interview. Information on sectors which require workers at the moment is given below.

CVs can be posted on some employment websites, e.g. www.jobbtilbud.no or www.aetat.no. CVs should be short and matter of fact. Trying a hard sell, or using hyperbolic language will not go down well.

NORWEGIAN STATE EMPLOYMENT SERVICE

The *Arbeidsformidling* (Norwegian State Employment Service) has a European division which can provide useful information for foreigners looking for work in Norway. There are five trained EURES officers in Oslo who are most likely to be sympathetic to foreign job seekers. If possible you should try to contact the Euroadviser, at Øvre Slottsgate 11, 0101 Oslo; ☎22 42 41 41; fax 22 42 44 38; www.aetat.no. A temporary work agency operates from the same address; you can phone them on 22 42 60 00, fax 22 42 10 08. The Employment Service operates a Green Line, or free telephone service providing information on vacancies throughout Norway, telephone 800 33 166. Job centres – *Arbeidsformidling* – have computer terminals where job seekers can look at vacancies themselves. In principle all job vacancies advertised in Norway are registered on the employment services database, which can be viewed on the website www.aetat.no. Other sites are given above.

To find the address of your nearest job centre in Norway look under *Arbeidskontor* in the Yellow Pages (www.gulesider.no). There are over 150 jobcentres in Norway which all provide free advice on regulations for EEA nationals seeking work, working and living conditions in Norway, job vacancies and unemployment benefit. You will be allowed to use the telephone to ring an employer free of charge and perhaps a computer. The opening hours are 9am-3pm.

NORWEGIAN TEMPORARY EMPLOYMENT AGENCIES

Private temping agencies are listed in the Norwegian Yellow Pages under *vikartjenester* or *vikarbyråer*; temping agencies are becoming more popular; all the main cities have them. Some foreign jobseekers have found them to be unhelpful to anyone who does not speak Norwegian, so you may need to be determined to find something. The main jobs offered are secretarial, accountancy and switchboard operators. All charge a fee for their services.

Useful Addresses

Adecco Norge, Karl Johans gate 25, 0158 Oslo; ☎22 94 10 00; fax 22 33 20 25; www.adecco.no.

Adecco Norge, Haugåsv. 8, 4016 Stavanger; 51 81 26 00.

Kelly Services Norge, Vika Atrium, Munkedamsv. 45, 0118 Oslo; ☎815 00 044; fax 22 42 00 72.

Kelly Services, Strandg. 18, 5013 Bergen; ☎815 00 044; fax 55 31 52 52.

Kosmo Vikarbyrå, Haslevei 28, 0571 Oslo; ☎22 87 17 37; 22 87 17 38; www.kosmo.no.

Manpower, Dronning Mauds gate 10, 0202 Oslo; ☎22 01 80 00; fax 22 83 52 00; www.manpower.no.

Manpower, Dronnigengs g. 23, 4610 Kristiansand S; ☎38 10 53 00; fax 38 07 06 23.

Manpower, Storg. 80-82, 9262 Tromsø; ☎77 60 68 00; fax 77 60 68 01.

JOB ORGANISATIONS IN THE UK

Jobcentres in the UK can put you in touch with EURES advisors who are trained to deal with enquiries about working in the EEA, which includes Norway. The Overseas Placing Unit (Rockingham House, 123 West Street, Sheffield S1 4ER; ☎0114-259 6051/2) produces the useful fact sheet *Working in Norway*. You can also try the Recruitment and Employment Confederation (36-38 Mortimer Street, London W1N 7RB; ☎020-7462 3260; www.rec.uk.com) which issues a list of employment agencies who are members.

EXECUTIVE RECRUITMENT

The following international executive recruitment firms have offices in Norway as well as the UK and US.

Horton International Norge, Sognsveien 75E, 0855 Oslo; ☎23 00 78 90.

Marlar International, Sommerogaten 17, 0255 Oslo; ☎22 55 20 00; fax 22 44 63 39; www.selectiongroup.no.
Ray & Berndtson, Sørkedalsveien 10d, 0369 Oslo; ☎23 36 99 99; fax 23 36 99 80.

PERMANENT WORK

INFORMATION TECHNOLOGY

There is a strong demand for English-speaking IT staff, and knowledge of Norwegian is not always necessary, at least to begin with. IT recruiters in the UK sometimes arrange jobs in Norway, or one can try contacting one of the agencies below:

Computer People International, 33 Regent St, London SW1Y 4NB; ☎020-7440 2000; www.computerpeople.com.
Computer People Inc., 2049 Century Park East, Suite 3390, Los Angeles, CA 90067; www.computerpeople.com.
Computer People Oslo/Data Vikar, Drammensveien 127, 0277 Oslo; ☎23 13 14 40; fax 23 13 14 50; www.computerpeople.no.
Elan IT ReSource Oslo, Dronning Maudsgate 15, Postboks 2584 Solli, 0203 Oslo; ☎22 01 83 00; fax 22 01 83 01; www.elanit.no.
IT Executivesearch, Eil Sundts g. 41, 0355 Oslo; ☎23 33 43 00; fax 23 33 43 01.
IT-Vikar, Brynsveien 16, 0667 Oslo; ☎22 07 07 50; fax 22 07 07 99; www.it-vikar.no.

MEDICINE AND NURSING

Norway is experiencing a shortage of medical staff. German doctors and dentists are sought after for temporary and long-term positions, partly because of a surplus of medical staff in Germany, and because they are able to learn Norwegian quickly. Nurses are recruited from all over the world; many come from Poland and the Phillipines. Nursing positions and technical posts are advertised on the National Hospital website, www.rikshospitalet.no. Some medical positions are advertised on the UK jobs and training website www.worktrain.gov.uk. If you belong to the Royal College of Nursing, then you can get help with finding a job in Norway. There are also recruitment agencies looking for medical staff.

Recruitment Agencies
Helsenor AS, Christian Krohgs g. 2, 0186 Oslo; ☎22 17 65 00; www.helsenor.no.
Henie Medisinsk Personal, Erich Mogensøns vei 38; ☎23 20 70 00; 23 24 61 62.
Medpower, Rosencrantz g., 0159 Oslo; ☎22 33 55 33; fax 22 33 55 34.
Olsten Helsetjenester, Grensen 9B, Postboks 815 Sentrum, 0104 Oslo; ☎22 40 12 00; fax 23 10 54 00.

Other Organisations

Helsedepartementet (Department of Health), Einar Gerhardsens plass 3, Postboks 8011 Dep, 0030 Oslo; ☎22 24 90 90; http://odin.dep.no/hd.

Norwegian Board of Health, Calmeyers Gate 1, 0183 Oslo; ☎22 24 90 90; www.helsetilsyn.no.

Norwegian Medical Association, Postboks 1152 Sentrum, 0107 Oslo; ☎23 10 90 00; fax 23 10 90 10; e-mail legeforeningen@legeforeningen.no; www.legeforeningen.no.

Rikshospitalet (National Hospital), 0027 Oslo; ☎23 07 00 00; www.rikshospitalet.no.

TEACHING AND LECTURING

Teaching English as a foreign language may be a passport to talking your way around the world but whether it will be your ticket to living and working in Norway is by no means certain. The Norwegian population generally has a very high level of English competence and whether dealing with manual workers or high fliers you will probably find you have no problem in making yourself understood. Consequently, the demand for English teachers in Norway is not particularly high and the outlook for TEFL teachers is not very promising. Teachers are expected to have a degree, and some kind of teaching qualification, as well as experience. Some training in teaching Business English or English for Special Purposes would be advantageous.

The Folk High Schools and similar organisations will employ teachers between September and June. There are also private language schools, which will generally require teachers on a part-time basis. These can be found under *språkundervisning* in the Yellow Pages.

International schools where teaching is done in English hire teachers abroad; see the list of schools in the *Setting Up Home* chapter. The Norwegian Ministry of Education and Research produces a useful leaflet: *Information for Foreign Teachers Seeking Positions in the Norwegian School System,* available free on request.

Specialists in English Language or literature (i.e. with postgraduate education up to doctorate level) could approach the English faculties of Norwegian Universities as posts are sometimes advertised in *The Times Higher Education Supplement* or *The Times Educational Supplement.* The New Red Cross Nordic United World College, which opened in 1995, has advertised for teachers in many disciplines (languages, history, geography, the sciences, art and design, economics and environmental science) in *The Times Educational Supplement.* The language of instruction is English.

The Norwegian School of Management BI is one of Norway's largest educational institutions; it employs 780 people and has about 350 faculty members. BI offers an 11-month MBA course, a MSc programme and a doctoral programme in English. BI is the nation's largest business school.

Private Language Schools

Berlitz, Akersgaten 16, 0158 Oslo; ☎22 33 10 30.

Det Internasjonale Språksenter, Dronningens gate 32, 0154 Oslo; fax 22 33 69 30; e-mail intsprak@online.no.
Oslo Business English School, Fossumhavene 32, 1343 Eiksmarka; ☎22 13 46 20.
Polaris Institute, Dronningen 1, Pb. A. Bygdøy, 0211 Oslo; ☎22 55 46 11; e-mail polaris.institute@online.no.

Adult Education

Arbeidernes Opplysningsforbund, Postboks 8703, Youngstorget, 0028 Oslo 1; ☎23 06 10 50; fax 23 06 12 70; aofnorge@aof.norge.telemax.no.
Folkeuniversitetet Oslo, Torggata 7, Postboks 496 Sentrum, 0105 Oslo; ☎815 00 380 or 22 47 60 00; fax 22 47 60 01; www.fu.oslo.no/oslo.
FU Asker, Lensmannslia 30, 1386 Asker; ☎66 98 99 00; www.aske.fu.no.
FU Bergen, St Jakobs plads 9, 5838 Bergen; ☎55 55 36 30.
FU Kristiansand, Markens g. 2, 4610 Kristiansand S; ☎38 12 21 00; www.funorge.no.
FU Stavanger, Fabrikkveien 8, 4033 Stavanger; ☎51 81 08 50; fax 51 81 08 51; www.fustavanger.no.
FU Tromsø, PB 248 Sentrum, 9253 Tromsø; ☎77 68 62 62; fax 77 06 52 10; e-mail folktro@online.no.
FU Trondheim, Olav Tryggvasons gata 5, 7011 Trondheim; ☎73 33 89 70; fax 73 53 81 95; www.fu.no/trondheim.

Tertiary Education Colleges

The Red Cross Nordic United World College, Haugland, 6968 Flekke; ☎57 73 70 00; fax 57 73 70 00; www.rcnuwc.uwc.org.
The Norwegian School of Management BI, Sandvika, Oslo; ☎67 55 70 00; fax 67 55 76 70; e-mail info@bi.no; www.bi.no.

For a list of International Schools in Norway see *Schools and Education* in the *Daily Life* chapter.

OIL, GAS AND TECHNICAL

Norway is among the world's major producers of oil and gas. The Norwegian oil industry is based in Stavanger and foreign nationals have traditionally filled many technical posts. Rewards are high as are professional standards. Only applicants with appropriate skills will be considered. Oil and gas companies need a wide variety of engineers and support staff; these are mostly employed through contractors. Petrochemical firms generally only recruit university graduates directly. Those wanting to work on the oil rigs should have taken an offshore survival course (see *Skills and Qualifications*) and many UK companies will require at least two years' experience on North Sea rigs before considering workers for overseas assignments. To begin a career in the oil industry, you should be aged between 21 and 28.

Norwegian heavy technology plant giants Kvaerner have diversified into many main areas of the Norwegian technical and petrochemical fields and are major recruiters of overseas foreign workers. Kvaerner offer contracts from between two weeks and four years. A married worker is entitled to a return flight to their home every two weeks and an accommodation allowance. A single worker receives less but is allowed some expenses. On contract work there are no paid holidays and most workers take holidays at the end of their contract. Wages are good – workers are given a net deal and typically a draughtsman can earn £15 per hour take home pay. Skilled engineers can earn as much as £50 per hour after tax.

For further information on the oil and gas industry consult *The Oil and Gas International Yearbook* available from most public libraries. *The Oil and Gas Journal* has job adverts. Jobs in petrochemicals and related fields are advertised on the internet; the site www.nettavisen.no is particularly useful, although most adverts are in Norwegian. British recruitment companies are listed on the site www.applegate.com. Multinational oil and marine engineering companies are listed at the end of this chapter, under Major Employers.

Engineering and Construction Companies

Kvaerner Recruitment Services, Gilbert Wakefield House, 67 Bewsey St, Warrington, Cheshire WA23 7JQ; ☎01925-659700; www.kvaerner.com.
W S Atkins Group Consultants, Woodcote Grove, Ashley Road, Epsom, Surrey KT18 5BW.
Mott MacDonald, Wellesley Road, Croydon CR9 2UL; www.mottmac.com.

Recruitment Consultants

Contracts Consultancy Ltd, 162-164 Upper Richmond Rd, Putney, London SW15 2SL; www.ccl.uk.com.
Overseas Technical Services Ltd, 100 College Road, Harrow HA1 1BQ; www.ots.co.uk.
Sherry Sherratt Technical Recruitment Ltd, PO Box 4529, London SW18 3XD; e-mail SSTR.LTD@pobox.com.
Team Moore Recruitment, Pennine House, Concord Way, Stockton-on-Tees, Cleveland TS18 3TL; www.team-moore.com.

Recruitment Companies in Norway

IMS AS, Otto Sverdrups vei 9, 1337 Sandvika; www.ims.no.
Raadhuset, Tevlingveien 18, 1081 Oslo; e-mail soeknad@raadhuset.no; www.raadhuset.no.
Raadhuset Rogaland AS, Petroleumsvn. 8, 4033 Stavanger; e-mail rogaland@raadhuset.no.
Techconsult AS, Møllendalsveien 61A, 5009 Bergen; e-mail post@techconsult.no; www.techconsult.no.
Techpower, Dronning Mauds gt. 15, 0202 Oslo; e-mail tp–oslo@techpower.no; www.techpower.no.
Techpower, Skagenkaien 35-37, 4002 Stavanger; tp–stavanger@techpower.no.

TEMPORARY WORK

FARMING

Norwegian farms are mainly small, family-run affairs and there is a considerable seasonal demand for extra labour. Work is varied and can range from haymaking, tending livestock, picking fruit and vegetables, driving tractors, milking, painting fences, maintenance and house work. Under Norwegian law all foreigners working on farms with domestic animals in Norway must go through a disinfection of both themselves and their clothes – you will be given further details on applying although it is apparently a fairly harmless procedure. Foreign workers usually live with the family who will probably speak good English. Most people experience the Norwegians as friendly, laid-back and very hospitable and you will probably be treated as if you were one of the family.

An average working day might be from 8am to 4pm, although bear in mind that some farmers may want you to do more, especially when harvesting or haymaking; the work will be physically demanding. There are a few agencies which can offer placements on Norwegian farms: Atlantis Youth Exchange operates a working guest programme where you will receive pocket money and board and lodging. Agricultural experience is preferred but is not essential. UK residents should go through Concordia; US residents through InterExchange.

The International Farm Experience programme is part of the National Federation of Young Farmers Club and offers placements of three to 12 months at any time of the year. To be offered a place on the programme you must have at least two years farming experience (one of these could be at an agricultural college), be aged 18-28, have a valid driving licence and intend to take up a career in agriculture or horticulture. Work is paid but wages are often only sufficient to cover costs and you will be taxed at local rates. Accommodation and food are free. IAEA in the USA operates a similar programme.

Casual farm labour in Norway is generally employed for fruit picking. The majority of harvesters are foreign – a reflection on the low wages which are paid for piece work. You could try contacting farms around Drammen in early July for the season. Beyond Trondheim the harvest is from mid-July to August. Crops include strawberries, raspberries, blueberries and potatoes and other vegetables. For accommodation you will probably have to take your own tent though you may see other Europeans, mainly Poles, who make for the Norwegian harvests and camp in their cars.

The Norwegian branch of WWOOF, APØG, produce a list of ecological farms in Norway which need volunteers. There is a charge of £15 or $20 for the list.

Useful Addresses

APØG, c/o Nøll, Langeveien 18, 5003 Bergen; e-mail organic@online.no.
Atlantis Youth Exchange, Kirkegata 32, 0153 Oslo; tel/fax 22 47 71 79; e-mail post@atlantis-u.no; www.atlantis-u.no.

Concordia Youth Services Volunteers, 20/22 Boundary Road, Hove, East Sussex BN3
    4ET.
Interexchange, 161 Sixth Ave, New York, NY 10013; ☎212-924-0446; fax 212-924-
    0575; www.interexchange.org.
The International Farm Experience Programme. National Agricultural Centre,
    Stoneleigh Park, Warwickshire CV6 2LG; ☎01203-696578.
The International Agricultural Exchange Association (Servicing Office) 1000 1st Avenue
    South, Great Falls, Montana 59401 United States of America; IAEA (Servicing
    Office), No. 206, 1505-17 Ave. S.W. Calgary, Alberta T2T OE2 Canada.

THE SKIING INDUSTRY

Ask a Norwegian if he's a skier and he'll probably tell you 'No, I'm a bank
manager/teacher/farmer...'. To most Norwegians skiing is almost as natural
as breathing and hardly worth a mention unless you are one of the country's
possessors of Winter Olympic medals. The saying goes that Norwegians are
born with skis on and this slight exaggeration implies, not without justification,
that they are on skis almost as soon as they can stand upright. Norwegian ski
resorts are comparatively uncommercialised and the ratio of skiers to ski slopes is
much lower than in the European Alps. The scenery is spectacular and there are
plenty of opportunities for cross-country skiing. Qualified ski instructors can try
contacting Norwegian winter ski resorts prior to the season. Although there is no
shortage of Norwegian instructors, many resorts also employ English-speaking
ones too.

Norwegian ski resorts may be far less congested than those of the Alps, but
there are still work opportunities in the ski season and foreigners have found
work in bars, hotels and cafeterias and also in snow clearing and DJ-ing. If you
get work you will probably find that it is only sufficient to cover your living costs
and to enable you to ski through the season. You should try to arrange work
in advance by writing to resorts, outlining your skills. The main skiing resorts
are: Oppdal, Trysil, Geilo, Voss, Gausdal and, of course, Lillehammer which was
home to the 1994 Winter Olympics. For a comprehensive list of Norwegian ski
resorts contact the Norwegian National Tourist Office (www.visitnorway.com),
or look at the website: www.skiscandinavia.com. For further details on working
in the skiing industry consult the book *Working in Ski Resorts,* by Vacation Work.

TRAVEL AND TOURISM

Tourism is a boom area and one of Norway's biggest earners. About 170,000
people are employed in the tourist industry and this figure looks set to
increase. Although you can go to Norway and look for work it is better to try to
arrange something in advance to save time, money and possible disappointment.
You can obtain a list of Norwegian hotels from the Norwegian tourist Office (see
above address). The majority of hotels are based in the south, and around the
beach resorts of the south coast and on the fjords.

The net monthly wage for an unskilled worker is about NOK9,000 (approx. £710/US$1,000) after deductions for board and lodging. Unless you have a particular skill or are able to speak the language you are unlikely to get anything more lucrative. The big advantage of hotel work is that food and accommodation will be provided. Several Norwegian youth hostels also employ unskilled domestic staff, providing board and lodging but little more than pocket money. Contact the headquarters at: Norske Vandrerhjem, Dronningens Gate 26, 0154 Oslo; ☎23 13 93 10; www.vandrerhjem.no.

AU PAIRS

The demand for au pairs in Norway is not huge but there are opportunities, particularly in the larger cities of Oslo and Bergen. The other cities of southern Norway are also worth trying to locate jobs in. Preference is given to au pairs who are prepared to work for 10 months or more, although some families will accept au pairs for shorter stays during the summer. Conditions laid down for au pairs by the Council of Europe are strictly observed in Norway and you will not normally be expected to work more than six hours a day. It is stipulated that au pairs come to Norway to learn Norwegian and to absorb Norwegian culture; some will go on to university in Norway. It is of course quite likely that your host family will speak good English.

You can do this kind of work if you are aged between 18 and 30. Boys are also eligible. Board, lodging and pocket money are provided. You should be paid a minimum of NOK2,800 (approx. £220/US$316) per month before tax and social security deductions. In practice you should look for a minimum of NOK4,000. To apply you should provide two references and a medical certificate obtained within the previous three months. It is generally advisable to apply to Norwegian agencies directly; foreign agencies cannot do much more than put you in touch with an agency in Norway. For further details on au pair work in Norway consult *The Au Pair and Nanny's Guide to Working Abroad,* published by Vacation Work (see inside back cover).

Useful Addresses

Adequate Assistance A/S, Gl. Gardermovei 5, Sand, 2050 Jessheim; ☎94 13 86 57; e-mail aa@adequate-assistance.com; www.adequate-assistance.com.
Atlantis Youth Exchange, Kirkegata 32, 0153 Oslo; tel/fax 22 47 71 79; e-mail post@atlantis-u.no; www.atlantis-u.no.
Inter Au Pair, Astubben 68, 0381 Oslo; ☎22 52 15 60.
Norintrex AuPair Bureau, Nordnesveien 62, 5005, Bergen; tel/fax 55 23 08 46.

VOLUNTARY WORK

There are few opportunities for voluntary work in Norway. International Dugnad is the Norwegian branch of the Service Civile International which promotes international peace through work projects. Volunteers should be 18 or over and be prepared to work a 35-40 hour week. Work camps take place between June and September and participants stay for two to four weeks. Food, accommodation and insurance are included but you will have to provide your own transport and there are no wages. Work could be on farms or in the community and is usually manual in nature.

The Norwegian Farm Guest Programme run by Atlantis Youth Exchange could be considered to be voluntary work although participants receive pocket money. WWOOF also comes under voluntary work. See under 'Farming' for details.

The British Trust for Conservation Volunteers arranges working holidays for two weeks in the summer in conjunction with the Norwegian Nansen Institute. Work involves construction of footpaths, conservation of old buildings and aspects of countryside maintenance. Volunteers should be aged over 18. Transport, board and lodging will be provided in Norway but you will have to provide your own fares and there is a cost of £250 for the trip. No wages are paid.

Useful Addresses

The British Trust for Conservation Volunteers, 36 St Mary's Street, Wallingford, Oxfordshire OX10 0EU; ☎01491-839766; e-mail information@btcv.org.uk; www.btcv.org.uk.

Fridtjof Nansen Institute, P.O. Box 326, 1326 Lysaker; www.fni.no.

International Dugnad, Nordahl Bruns gate 22, 0165 Oslo; ☎22 11 31 23; fax 22 20 71 19.

ASPECTS OF EMPLOYMENT

The Norwegian labour force is generally of a high quality, literate and hard working. With low unemployment has come a shortage of workers in all sectors, particularly of skilled workers such as engineers for the oil sector. Turnover rates in industry are generally quite low. Absenteeism for unskilled labour averages at 11% for women and 16.5% for men, in line with Scandinavian norms. The activity rate – people aged 16 to 66 in the labour force – stands at 80.6%, higher than Sweden and Denmark.

SALARIES

Surprisingly for a somewhat socialist country there is no national minimum wage in Norway. Base wages are fixed in collective bargaining agreements. In practice, a wage would rarely be less than the equivalent of £7 per hour. Wages in Norway are high relative to the rest of Scandinavia, but they are generally lower than those in the UK except for unskilled work. Payment for overtime is at an agreed rate of between 50%-100%. Most employers will provide group insurance benefits, a subsidised canteen and some employees receive a company car. In order to make a comparison, there are about NOK12 to the pound, and NOK9 to the dollar: a wage of NOX30,000 is worth approx. £2,370/US$3,390).

TABLE 12	SALARY LEVELS
Salary Levels in 2001/NOK per month	
Petroleum technician	36,158
Petroleum manager	53,191
Machine operator in petroleum industry	29,613
Bus driver	21,030
Clerk	20,923
Financial services manager	40,980
Industrial manager	39,006
Labourer	17,715
Nurse	21,649
Physician – chief	47,043
Physician	39,374
Restaurant worker	18,503
Schoolteacher – nursery	19,448
Schoolteacher – primary	23,930
Schoolteacher – upper secondary	26,804
Shopworker	20,000
Source: Norwegian Statistics Bureau.	

WORKING CONDITIONS

The Working Environment Act legislates on employment conditions and regulates employees' rights and duties and employers' obligations. Because of the Act employees have some say in their working environment and increased protection against dismissal. The average working week in Norway is 40 hours although administrative jobs tend to be 37.5 hours per week. Shift workers have slightly shorter working weeks. Overtime is limited by Norwegian law but a temporary exemption can be granted by the *Arbeidsdirektoratet* (Labour Directorate). All employees are entitled to four weeks plus one day of holidays each year and 10 days of legal holidays. Employees aged over 60 are entitled to five weeks holiday. Employees can take three consecutive weeks of holidays during the summer vacation. Workers receive 10.2% of their total compensation as holiday pay. Foreign employees on short-term contracts, particularly in the oil and gas fields, may not receive paid holidays; many choose to wait until the end of the contract before taking holidays.

DISMISSALS AND DISCRIMINATION

Employment can be terminated because of a company's situation, e.g. reduced production levels or because of an employee's behaviour, e.g. gross misconduct, incompetence, etc. Between two and six months notice are required depending on the length of service. The notice period with full pay usually eliminates the need for severance payments. Employees have the right to contest dismissals but in practice this rarely happens. If you feel that you are being unfairly treated at work you can contact the local office of the Directorate of Labour Inspection (*Arbeidstilsynet*) who will treat your case with confidentiality.

SOCIAL SECURITY

The 1966 Social Security Act in Norway requires everyone who works or resides in Norway to contribute to the social security programme. The basic contribution is 7.8% of gross income. You are also required to pay 3% of your income into the pension fund, up to an amount not exceeding a quarter of the Basic allowance (NOK40,090 – approx. £3,167/US$4,530). Foreigners are exempt from paying social security contributions if they are covered by a social security system in their home country and/or are a member of a country with which Norway has signed a social security agreement. Proof that you are covered in your home country has to be supplied. Application for exemption should be made before your employment commences.

Sickness Benefits. If your annual income is at least half of the Basic allowance (B.a.), which was NOK49,090 in 2002, and you have been with an employer for at least 14 days, then you can receive 100% of your pensionable income as cash benefit for up to 260 working days, in effect one year. The employer has to pay the cash benefit for the first 16 calendar days. Self-employed persons can also receive benefits at 65%, or 100% if they pay higher contributions.

Maternity Benefits. Maternity benefits are paid at the same rate as sickness benefit. Insured parents who have been in paid employment for six out of 10 months preceding the commencement of the period of paid leave are entitled to daily cash benefits in case of maternity for 42 weeks or 210 days. These can be extended for another 10 weeks, at a reduced rate of 80%.

Other Benefits. Child benefit is paid at a rate of from NOK12,000 (approx. £948/US$1,350) to NOK14,000 per child per year. Disability benefits are paid at rates in accordance with the degree of disability. They can only be paid to persons who have worked in Norway for at least three years.

TRADE UNIONS

The majority of workplaces in Norway have one or more trade unions. The relationship between unions and employers is generally good with unions taking an active part in company decisions. Most companies with between 50 and 200 employees have one-third labour representation on the board of directors. Although this is not compulsory, employees are entitled to request it. Companies with more than 200 employees elect a corporate assembly with a minimum of 12 members, the majority of whom are chosen at the annual shareholders meeting and the rest by fellow employees. The corporate assembly is the final decision-making body and elects the board of directors. Assembly meetings are held twice a year and decisions are made about major investments, modernisation and other issues affecting the labour force. Shop stewards are often part of committees for the hiring of workers so that unions are often involved in the hiring and laying off of workers.

Membership of a trade union is voluntary and the annual monthly membership fee is about 1% of the gross pay. Most trade unions provide collective insurance coverage. Unions are organised according to trade or craft under the umbrella of the Norwegian Confederation of Trade Unions (LO) (www.lo.no). Negotiations on working conditions and wages are usually conducted on an industry-wide basis between the Confederation of Norwegian Business and Industry and the LO. If agreement cannot be reached the matter is usually referred to arbitration.

WOMEN AT WORK

Norway claims to provide equal rights for workers regardless of gender, race, colour or religion. Norway's record generally on women's rights is good and this applies to the work place. Norwegian women are entitled to 10 months maternity leave on full pay. European regulations state that the minimum allowance should be 14 weeks. Inevitably the rich pickings for manual and technical labour in the oil and gas fields of the North Sea are still a male preserve.

The Norwegian Regional Development Fund (*Distriktenes Utbyggingsfond*) makes relatively high grants for projects which are aimed at employing women, particularly in business and industry and has special incentives for training women in these area.

ETIQUETTE IN THE WORKPLACE

Norwegians like state-of-the-art business frills; everyone uses mobile phones, and business cards and electronic diaries are prevalent. Beyond the frills they can be disarmingly honest – the used car salesman pitch is rare in Norway and you will probably be told of a product's shortcomings before getting down to the business of fixing a deal. Negotiating can be difficult: your Norwegian counterpart may state his final offer straight away; haggling has not really caught on here.

Norwegians place a high value on honesty, and delivering on your undertakings. Failure to deliver, or sharp practice, may end the relationship. It is a general custom not to accept gifts from business partners, since these are interpreted as inducements. Gifts may be refused or returned. Since everything is generally above board the atmosphere will probably be pleasantly relaxed.

Norwegians dress for business occasions as much as anywhere else although there is a tendency towards more casual dress in summer to take account of the better weather. Most people take their holidays from mid-June to the beginning of August so this is not the best time to do business. Liquid lunches are rare; given the very high price of alcohol this is probably a blessing. Traditionally the working day has been from 8am to 4pm, but in the service sector this is now tending to change to 9am to 5pm.

BUSINESS AND INDUSTRY REPORT

Owing to geographical factors, Norway was industrialised comparatively late by European standards. Historically, Norway has always been an agrarian country and until fairly recently the economy was dependent on farming and fishing. These sectors exercise less influence on the Norwegian economy than they used to, although psychologically the Norwegians are still closely tied to the land and the sea. Norway's decision not to join the European Union came largely from the fishing and farming communities. The idea of self-sufficiency is deep-rooted; the current influx of foreign workers is tending to change the mentality of the people so that the country comes more into line with the rest of Europe.

During the post-war years Norway experienced a marked development in manufacturing, and now ranks as one of the world's most modern nations whose products are accepted everywhere. Norway is particularly noted for its advanced technology and for its electrochemical and electrometallurgical industries. Norway is the largest producer of aluminium in Western Europe and one of the world's largest producers of ferrosilicon and metal silicon.

The oil and gas industry tends to dominate the economy, but it has also led to the growth of specialised support industries. Norway has traditionally been a shipbuilding nation, and now specialises in constructing oil rigs, pipelines and related equipment. Norway has also always had a significant wood and paper industry, although nowhere near as big as those of her neighbours, Sweden and Finland. The service sector is expanding rapidly; IT and telecoms are significant growth areas. Norwegian companies are acquiring foreign subsidiaries: Kvaerner has for example taken over parts of the British Trafalgar House group. Norway also has a significant presence in Asia and America. At the same time foreign investment is running at record levels, creating the potential for whole new industries to take off.

Norway is heavily dependent on foreign trade. Approximately 44% of the GNP comes from exports whilst imports account for 37%. Main imports include oil rigs, airplanes, ships, motor vehicles, metal ores, industrial material and equipment, clothing, iron and steel, office machines and petroleum-related products. Major exports include natural gas, petroleum and petroleum-related products, ships, oil platforms and fish. Norway's main trading partners are the United States, the UK, Sweden, Denmark, Germany, France and the Netherlands.

SHIPPING

Shipping has been a traditional mainstay of the Norwegian economy. Until 1973, Norwegian ships carried up to 10% of the world's tonnage and accounted for one-third of the country's foreign currency earnings. However shipping crises in the 1980s, high costs and strict personnel regulations led to many ship owners registering their ships abroad in order to stay competitive. Economic depression at the end of the 1980s and increased competition from low-cost Far-Eastern companies led to empty order books and closed ship yards in Norway as elsewhere in the world.

The introduction of the Norwegian International Ship Register in 1987 helped revitalise shipping operations and there has been a consequent increase in export revenues. Gross shipping freights accounted for 52 billion NOK (approx. £4/US$5.8 billion) of the 130 billion NOK earned abroad in the Norwegian service sector in 2000. Norway currently commands the third largest merchant fleet in the world (including Norwegian ships under foreign flags). The biggest success story is the rise of the shipbuilding division of Kvaerner, Norway's leading heavy engineering company, who have risen to become one of the world's top three shipbuilders. Kvaerner employs a total of 34,000 workers, and has bought up many of Europe's ailing ship yards, including yards in Scotland, East Germany and Finland.

FISHING

Norway's extensive coastline and poor soil meant that fishing traditionally played an important role in the Norwegian economy. Today, however, it contributes less than 1% of the GDP. Of the country's 25,000 fishermen, only about half list fishing as their sole occupation and the fishing industry forms the basis for a large and increasing fish-processing industry which offers seasonal employment to many farmers. The last few years have seen more and more resources being diverted from the traditional fisheries to fish farming with bred salmon and trout figuring increasingly on the export list. Norway exports about NOK30 billion in fish and fish products every year, about 6% of total exports. A large part of this is salted fish sold mainly to Greece, Spain and Portugal.

Employment opportunities in the fish industry are negligible. Fish-processing factories will take on foreigners, but will not employ anyone for less than a year. They employ a lot of Finnish workers who are willing to put with the working conditions.

OIL AND GAS

The petroleum industry in Norway is relatively young but it has been enormously successful. Norway proclaimed sovereignty over the Norwegian Continental Shelf in 1963 when the first oil and gas licences for exploration were allocated. In 1969, after four years of exploratory drilling, the first commercially important discovery of petroleum was made in the Ekofisk field. The first submarine pipeline was put into operation in 1975 when petroleum was first exported. By 1980 the export of oil and gas had come to rival the combined value of traditional commodity exports. In 1980 drilling began north of the 62nd parallel and in 1981 the first discoveries were made outside the coast of Norway. By 1987 17 fields were in production on the Norwegian Continental Shelf. Most of the reserves of the Norwegian Continental Shelf are in the North Sea (south of the 62nd parallel). Total reserves are estimated at 14 billion ton oil equivalents (toe), about 63% gas and 37% oil.

Oil and gas account for some 64% of all exports. Norway is the world's second biggest natural gas exporter after Russia. Very little gas is used in Norway itself, since most of the country's domestic energy comes from hydrothermal sources. Gas-fired power stations have only recently started operation.

Whilst the oil and gas discoveries have given a massive boost to the Norwegian economy, making it one of the world's richest nations, it has left Norway highly vulnerable to oil price swings. Norway experienced its deepest depression since the 1930s when oil prices slumped in 1986 from $40 to $10 a barrel, directly causing a reduction of 7% in the GDP. Everyone is aware that Norway has to invest in other industries so that the country can continue prosper when the oil runs out.

MINING, MINERALS AND CHEMICALS

Norway has a few ores, principally pyrites (giving copper and sulphur) and iron ore; small amounts of zinc, copper and lead are also mined. Southwestern Norway has Europe's largest deposit of ilmenite (titanium ore). Huge quantities of electric power are supplied by rivers; as well as supplying domestic need, they also drive industry. Half of Norway's hydroelectricity is used by the electrochemical and electrometallurgical plants which make Norway the world's largest exporter of iron-based alloys and metals. Norway is also a major exporter of aluminium, nickel, copper and zinc. The plant at Herøya is the world's second largest producer of magnesium. Other industries include silica, graphite and quartz. Metals account for 8% of exports, and chemicals for 5%.

Norway's biggest international industrial group, Norsk Hydro, centres some of its main activity on key industrial materials with an energy base and has more than 40 sections based throughout western Europe.

FARMING AND FORESTRY

About 5% of Norway's total area is agricultural land. Only 93,000 people work in agriculture now, a fall of 25% since 1990. There are about 64,000 farms. Farms are generally small and isolated. Only about one-third of the farms have more than 25 acres (10 hectares) and less than 1% have more than 125 acres. Farm labour is scarce and most farmers do the work themselves whilst taking on seasonal temporary labour. The country is more or less self-sufficient in animal products. Cereals are mostly imported. Farms are heavily subsidised by the government.

Forestry has a traditional role in the Norwegian economy and forms the basis for the wood-processing industry. Pulp and paper amount to about 3% of traditional commodity exports.

MANUFACTURING

Many Norwegian industries provide products used in gas and oil exploration, development and production. The decline in the shipping industry saw a move away from shipbuilding to the production of sophisticated equipment for off-shore exploration. About one-third of the employment in manufacturing is in the engineering industry. Norwegian civil engineers claim to be some of the best in the world and they have achieved some outstanding results in the transportation system with the unpromising material of Norwegian terrain, in terms of road building and surfacing, tunnelling and bridge building. Electrical equipment is a major Norwegian industry; electronics is a growth industry.

TOURISM

The travel industry has grown strongly in recent years, and is set to go on growing. About 7 out 10 Norwegians take their holidays in Norway. With the best scenery in Europe Norway has had no difficulty in projecting an attractive image. Tourism is very seasonal, with most visitors coming in the summer, or for skiing. The conference business is also doing well in Oslo. Norway's main disadvantage is its image as one of the world's most expensive countries.

Norway naturally attracts anyone interested in the environment. The Norwegians' insistence on hunting whales has made them unpopular in some quarters. Paradoxically Norway has been cashing in on the natural attractions of whales by offering 'whale safaris'.

REGIONAL EMPLOYMENT GUIDE

Inevitably, employment in Norway is influenced by the regional variations in population. The majority of the population live in the south with Oslo, Bergen, Trondheim and Stavanger forming the major urban areas. Most industry in Norway has developed along the coastline. The fjords of Vestlandet are home to the majority of Norway's smelting plants which were built here to capitalise on the great resources of hydroelectic power in the region. The interior, in particular the vast plains of Finnmark, have very little industry. Industry is spread out along the coastline up to Narvik, which is a major iron ore centre, and further north the city of Tromsø has a large fish processing industry.

Central Norway around the Trondheim Fjord forms the heart of Norway's agricultural region, being amongst the more fertile areas of Norway. This area also contains a large percentage of Norway's mining and forestry industry. The inland fjords of the Hardanger district are more sheltered and are the home of fruit-growing, especially in apples and cherries. The Sunnmøre district north of Bergen has many engineering firms. Most of the Norwegian furniture industry centers on the industrial town of Ålesund. The oil and gas industries operate primarily from the south-east coast of Norway; the hub of off-shore mining activity is Stavanger. Stavanger is also an expanding industrial centre and is historically linked to the canning and fishing industries. Whilst fishing is carried out throughout the Norwegian coastline, it tends to predominate around the cities of Molde and Kristiansund. The shipping industry is based mainly around the larger port towns of the southern tip of Norway. The tourist industry with the majority of hotels is based in the south.

DIRECTORY OF MAJOR EMPLOYERS

For information on Norwegian companies consult *Kompass Produkter* which should be available from your local library; it is more conveniently consulted on the CD-Rom Kompass Western Europe. The directory Bizkit lists companies on a national basis. For financial information on the largest Norwegian companies consult *Norges Største Bedrifter*; this is available in most main libraries and is published by Økonomisk Literatur AS, Langkaia 1, 0150 Oslo; ☎22 47 49 00; fax 22 47 49 01. Table 13 lists some of Norway's biggest employers by numbers of employees worldwide.

TABLE 13	NORWAY'S BIGGEST EMPLOYERS	
Aker RGI	19,800	Industrial conglomerate
Bergesen d.y. ASA	3,900	Shipping
Elkem	4,100	Metal products
Hakon Gruppen	12,000	Distribution
Jotun	4,100	Chemicals, petrochemicals
Kvaerner Group	34,000	Shipbuilding, engineering, construction, etc.
Norsk Hydro	17,700	Chemicals
Norske Skog	5,000	Paper, board, newsprint
SAS	29,000	Air transport
Selmer ASA	4,400	Civil and marine engineering
Statoil	17,000	Petrochemicals
Storebrand	4,100	Insurance, banking
Telenor	22,000	Telecoms, TV, radio
Veidekke	6,800	Construction
Wilh. Wilhelmsen	12,000	Shipping

Chemical Engineering

BASF Norge AS, Postboks 311, 1370 Asker; ☎02 90 46 60, fax 02 90 47 55.

Henkel Norden ABI, Postboks 6405, Etterstad 0604 Oslo; ☎23 37 15 20.

Norsk Hydro AS, Bygdøy allé 2, 0240 Oslo; ☎22 53 81 00; fax 22 53 27 25.

Civil and Marine Engineering

Halliburton A/S Gruppen, Elfiskveien 1, 4065 Stavanger; ☎51 83 70 00; fax 51 83 83 83.

Norsk Hydro ASA, Sandslivegen 90, 5020 Bergen; ☎55 99 50 00; fax 55 99 66 00.

Norske Conoco AS, Tangen 7, 4070 Randaberg; 51 41 60 00; fax 51 41 05 55.

Odfjell Drilling AS, Sandslimarka 63, 5863 Bergen; ☎55 99 89 00; fax 55 99 89 01.

Petroleum Geo-Services ASA, Stradveien 50E, 1325 Lysaker; ☎67 52 66 00; fax 67 53 68 63.

Schlumberger Oilfield Services, Hamrasletta, 4056 Tananger; ☎51 94 60 00.

Scientific Drilling Controls, Kokstadveien 40B, 5257 Kokstad; ☎55 98 21 00; fax 55 98 21 01.

Selmer ASA, St Olavs gata 25, 0107 Oslo; ☎22 03 06 00; fax 22 20 88 30.

Smedvig ASA, Finnestadveien 28, 4001 Stavanger; ☎51 50 99 00; fax 51 50 96 88.

Engines and Pumping Equipment

Fjord Instruments (Schlumberger) AS, Kvassnesveien, 5100 Isdalstø; ☎05 35 11 80, fax 05 35 13 37.

Norske Pumpe & Gregersen AS, Lilleakerveien 10, 0283 Oslo; ☎22 73 67 00; fax 22 73 67 80.

Norsk Hydro AS, Bygdøy allé 2, 0240 Oslo; ☎02 53 81 00; fax 22 53 27 25.

TUROteknikk AS, Postboks 225, 1301 Sandvika; ☎02 54 72 25, fax 02 54

40 77.

Ulstein Bergen AS, Hordvikneset 125, 5108 Hordvik; ☎55 53 60 00; fax 55 19 04 05.

Fish Processing

Nordica Foods AS, Øtrem, 6013 Ålesund; ☎70 17 69 69; fax 70 17 69 65.

Norfood Group AS, Kai 16, Brattøra,7010 Trondheim; ☎73 54 60 50; fax 73 54 60 60.

Norges Sildesalgslag, Postboks 307, 9483 Harstad; ☎77 05 96 00; fax 77 05 96 30.

Seabay Sjøvik AS, 6475 Midsund; ☎71 27 02 00; fax 71 27 02 01.

Forestry Products

3M Norge, Hvamveien 6, 2026 Skjetten; ☎63 84 75 00; 63 84 17 88.

Fjordtre Gruppen AS, 6797 Utvik; ☎57 87 67 00; 57 87 67 20.

Norske Skog, Oksenøyveien 80, 1326 Lysaker; ☎67 59 90 00; fax 67 59 91 81.

Norske Skog Flooring, Fiboveien 26, 4575 Lyngdal; ☎38 34 22 00; fax 38 34 37 44.

Metal Products

Elkem ASA, Hoffsveien 65B, 0303 Oslo; ☎22 45 01 00; fax 22 45 01 55.

Hydro Aluminium AluCoat AS, Kirkeveien 1, 3080 Holmestrand; ☎33 05 42 00; fax 33 05 34 20.

Norsk Stål, Nye Vakås, Postboks 123, 1378 Nesbru; ☎66 84 28 00; fax 66 84 28 50.

Office Equipment

Computer Associates Norway AS, Fornebuv. 7/9, 1327 Lysaker; ☎67 52 40 00; fax 67 52 40 01.

G & L Beijer Electronics AS, Teglverks-

veien 1, 3400 Lier; ☎32 24 30 00;
fax 32 84 85 77.

IBM AS, Rosenholmv. 25, 1411 Kol-
botn; ☎66 99 80 00; fax 66 99 82 42.

NCR Norge, Nydalsvn. 38, 0486 Oslo;
☎22 95 36 00; fax 22 95 26 01.

Petrochemicals

BASF AS, Leangbukta 40, 1372 Asker;
☎66 79 21 00; fax 66 90 47 55.

BP Amoco Norge, PB 197, Forus, 4065
Stavanger; ☎52 01 30 00.

Enterprise Oil Norge, Løkkev. 103, 4007
Stavanger; ☎51 84 30 00; fax 51 84
30 40.

Esso Norge AS, Drammensveien 149,
0277 Oslo; ☎22 66 30 30; fax 22
66 37 77.

Exxon Mobil, PO Box 66 Forus, 4064
Stavanger; ☎51 60 60 60.

Jotun AS, Hystadveien 167, 3235 Sandefjord; ☎33 45 70 00; fax 33 45
72 42.

Kvaerner Oil & Gas Field Development,
Professor Kohtsvei 5, 1326 Lysaker;
☎65 51 34 00.

Norsk Hydro ASA, Bygdøy Allé 2, 0257

Oslo; ☎22 53 81 00; fax 22 53 27 35.

A/S Norske Shell, Risavikvegen 180,
4098 Tananger; ☎51 69 30 00; fax
51 69 30 30.

Statoil ASA, 4025 Stavanger; ☎51 99
00 00, fax 51 99 00 50.

Shipping

Bergesen DY ASA, Drammensveien
106, 0204 Oslo; ☎22 12 05 05; fax
22 12 05 00.

Fjord Line AS, Skoltegrunnskaien, 5892
Bergen; ☎55 54 87 00; fax 55 54 86 25.

Hoegh Fleet Services AS, Wergelandsveien
7, 0203 Oslo; ☎22 86 97 00; 22 11
11 65.

Navion ASA, Verven 4, 4014 Stavanger;
☎51 44 27 00; fax 51 44 28 00.

Odfjell ASA, Conrad Mohrs veg 29,
5072 Bergen; ☎55 27 00 00; fax 55
28 47 41.

Star Shipping AS, Fortunen 1, 5809
Bergen; ☎55 23 96 00; fax 55 23
25 30.

Wilh. Wilhelmsen ASA, Strandveien 20,
1324 Lysaker; ☎67 58 40 00; fax 67
58 40 80.

STARTING A BUSINESS

About 24,000 new business start up every year. The average age of new entrepreneurs is between 30 and 39. The Norwegian economy is heavily dependent on international trade and has a favourable attitude towards foreign investment in most sectors. There are relatively few investment restrictions and investment is particularly encouraged in projects that help to develop the oil and gas resources and in areas of high technology. Co-operative ventures between national and international partners are also encouraged; since 1988 foreign investors can own up to one-third of a Norwegian industrial firm and up to 25% of the largest commercial banks.

PROCEDURES INVOLVED IN BUYING OR STARTING A NEW BUSINESS

Anyone contemplating starting a business in Norway should seek appropriate advice from the relevant sources. To establish a business in Norway, a foreign investor must obtain the relevant permits from the Ministry of Industry. Permits are usually readily granted. All business permits must include a clause which states that Norwegian labour and materials will be given preferential treatment but where there is a shortage of Norwegian skilled labour, foreign skilled labour may be used.

Where appropriate, a building permit must be obtained from the local authorities and permission given for altering or expanding premises when the development costs NOK25 million (approx. £2/US$2.8 million) or requires 100 man years or 100 employees. All new businesses should be registered at the Register of Companies (*Foretaksregisteret*) and firms must also register with the tax and social security offices.

Sources of Help

The Norwegian Government is particularly open to foreign investment and a number of sources can provide useful information for the prospective entrepreneur. The main agency that can help foreign entrepreneurs is the SND (*Statens Nærings- og Distriktsutviklingsfond*), which has offices all over the country. Through the website www.snd.no it is possible to access websites of other agencies.

The Ministry of Trade and Industry (NHD) has set up a website – www.bedin.no – which it calls the 'Enterprise and entrepreneur portal'. This is particularly useful as it has an English-language edition and again gives access to other important agencies. Bedin will answer questions by e-mail: narviktelefonene@vinn.no; you can also contact an adviser at the Narvik Business Hotline, on the free number 800 33 840. Note that free numbers will not work from abroad or from mobile phones.

The Central Office for Foreign Tax Affairs (COFTA) produces a detailed brochure telling you your obligations as an employer, with examples of forms in both English and Norwegian: *Guide for foreign employers and employees*. The whole text can be downloaded from the website www.skatteetaten.no. COFTA welcomes enquiries and will be happy to discuss your individual requirements.

All businesses have to be registered with the *Foretaksregister* in Brønnøysund (see below). If you have employees you will need to contact the National Insurance (*Trygdeverket*) office. Many communes or municipalities have a business department (*næringsetaten*) who will be ready to advise you. The *Bedriftenes Rådgivningstjeneste (BRT)* or Business Advice Service, exists to support small business entrepreneurs and has offices in each of the counties.

The Norwegian Trade Council is the national service organisation for all exporters of goods and services. The Council prepares market surveys with information about customs and import regulations, sales channels, current profit rates etc. The Trade Council is particularly involved in assisting in setting up trade links between Norwegian exporters and foreign firms, and has 38 missions in other countries. Lastly, the North Sea Commission Business Development Group has created the website www.SME365.com, to promote international business co-operation around the North Sea.

Useful Addresses

Development and Regional Fund (Statens nærings- og distriktsutviklingsfond), Post-boks 448 Sentrum, 0104 Oslo; ☎22 00 25 00, fax 22 33 34 49; e-mail snd@snd.no; www.snd.no.

The Central Office for Foreign Tax Affairs (Sentralskattekontoret for Utenlands-saker), Prinsens Vei 1, 4300 Sandnes; ☎51 67 80 88, fax 51 67 85 59; e-mail postkassesfu@skatteetaten.no.

Foretaksregisteret, 8901 Brønnøysund; ☎75 00 75 00; fax 75 00 75 05; e-mail firmapost@brreg.no; www.brreg.no.

Norwegian-American Chamber of Commerce, Drammensveien 20 C, Postbox 2604 Solli 0203 Oslo; ☎22 54 60 40; fax 22 54 67 20; e-mail amchamno@online.no; www.amcham.com.

Norwegian Chamber of Commerce, Post-boks 2900 Solli, 0230 Oslo; ☎22 54 17 00; fax 22 56 17 00.

Norwegian Information Service, 825 3rd Avenue 38th Floor, New York, NY 10022; ☎212 421 7333; fax 212 754 0883.

The Norwegian Trade Council, Dram-mensveien 40, N-0243 Oslo; ☎22 92 63 00, fax 22 92 64 00; www.ntc.no.

The Norwegian Trade Council (UK), Charles House, 5-11 Lower Regent Street, London SW1Y 4LR; ☎020-7389 8800; fax 020-7973 0189; www.ntclondon.com.

The Norwegian Trade Council (US), 800 Third Avenue, 23rd Floor, New York, NY 10022; ☎212-421-9210; fax 212-838-0374; www.ntcusa.org.

Raising Finance

If you are intending to reside in Norway you will find that British banks will not usually lend money for you to set up a business in Norway. Norwegian banks will lend money to foreign businesses in the form of short- or medium-term credit. For long-term credit you will normally have to apply to a commercial bank or to private investors. For all types of loans you will have to submit a detailed business plan with your loan application, including details of the business, the intended market and available collateral. You will also need to provide a loan repayment schedule with cash flow projections. Some lenders require audited financial statements. Major commercial banks are Den Norske Bank, Kommunalbanken, the Christiania Bank, and the Nordic Investment Bank.

Useful Addresses

Christiania Bank, Middelthunsgate 17, 0368 Oslo; ☎22 48 50 00; fax 22 48 47 90.
Nordisk Industrifond, ☎23 35 45 40; fax 23 35 45 45; e-mail info@nordicinnovation.net; www.nordisk-industrifond.no.
SND Invest, ☎22 00 29 00; fax 22 42 32 22; e-mail info@sndinvest.no; www.sndinvest.no.

Investment Incentives

The principal body for Government incentives is the Regional Development Fund (*Distriktenes Utbyggingsfond*) which gives loans, guarantees, grants and free advice to foreign companies investing in Norway.

Loans: may be given if all other means of financing have been exhausted. Loans are provided for investment in equipment, machinery and buildings although construction loans must be obtained from other credit institutions. Interest is charged at the prevailing rate and the period of repayment of loans on buildings does not usually exceed 25 years. In most cases repayment of the loan does not begin for one to three years and in some cases other terms can be negotiated.

Investment Grants: These are usually given with the intention of developing economic activity in business and of increasing employment in areas with low economic activity. Grants are not normally made for public administration, retail trade, agriculture and fishing. The largest grants are awarded for the establishment of a new business enterprise, the relocation, expansion or restructuring of an existing enterprise, or for upgrading existing technology within an enterprise. Relatively high rates of grants are paid for projects aimed at employing women.

Grants for the Development of Business and Industry: These are grants to encourage the development of new businesses and to strengthen existing ones. Grants may cover as much as 50% of the cost of the projects and projects in northern Norway attract the highest amount. Each case will be considered on its merit. Again, projects which increase the employment of women can lead to higher grants. Special regional support programmes include: applied information technology, marine biotechnology and management, organisation and administration.

Location Advice: The Regional Development Fund can advise on the location of establishing a business enterprise and has location registers for most of the country's municipalities. Information includes the availability of premises, manpower, communications and housing. For further details contact the SND.

Other sources of finance are the Norwegian Industrial Fund (*Industrifondet*) which grants loans for research and development and ordinary loans for manufacturing. The fund can also provide some grants for product development.

The Small Business Fund (*Småbedriftsfondet*) is a government owned credit institution which provides loans to companies outside the geographic range of the Regional Development Fund. For details of these schemes contact the Norwegian Trade Council (see above address).

Business Structures

There are four main types of companies in Norway:

○ **The Private Joint Stock Company** (*aksjeselskap* or AS), which is a company where no individual or group has personal liability for the obligations of the company.
○ **The Public Joint Stock Company** (*allmennaksjeselskap* or ASA), similar to the above, except that it is quoted on the stock market.
○ **The Limited Partnership** (*kommandittselskap* or KS) has one or more general partners who are liable to the full extent of their assets. Limited partners are only liable up to the specified amount of their investments.
○ **The General Partnership** (*ansvarlig selskap* or ANS) where each partner in the company is personally liable for debts incurred by the firm to the extent of their assets.

All new companies must be listed in the Register of Companies or *Foretaksregisteret* (see above) for which there is a registration fee and a filing fee for subsequent amendments to the original registration. The time required for processing a registration application is usually two weeks.

AS: To establish an AS a minimum share capital of NOK100,000 (approx. £7,900/US$11,300) is required. An AS should have at least one founder. The founder may be foreign but should be resident in Norway and have lived there during the two preceding years (exceptions may be made to this stipulation by the Ministry of Industry). If the share capital exceeds 3 million NOK the board of directors must have a minimum of three members. Employees have the right to be represented on the board of directors if there are more than 30 employees.

ASA: The initial capital requirement for an ASA is NOK1,000,000. The minimum number of directors is three. ASs and ASAs hold annual general meetings.

Branches: A branch of a foreign company is treated as a Norwegian corporation and is subject to the same tax requirements. The foreign company remains liable for the branch's debts and the branch must be registered in the Register of Companies (see above).

Sole Proprietorship: A sole proprietor has unlimited liability for the debts of their business. Sole proprietors engaging in trading activities or employing more than five persons have to register with Register of Companies.

Exporters

The Trade Partners UK Information Centre is worth a visit; it has useful information on Norway, including trade and telephone directories. The Centre's address is Kingsgate House, 66-74 Victoria Street, London SW1E 6SW. It is open from 9am to 8pm Monday to Thursday (last admission 7.30pm and 9am to 5.30pm on Fridays (last admission 5pm). Further information on the Centre's resources is available on the Trade Partners UK website at www.tradepartners.gov.uk, by telephone on 020-7215 5444/5; fax 020-7215 4231 or by e-mail; use the e-mail option on the website. The website also has a useful report on Norway.

IDEAS FOR NEW BUSINESSES

The British Department of Trade and Industry has identified the following areas as providing opportunities for British firms: offshore engineering for companies with experience of the UK Continental Shelf (although competition is fierce); the construction industry due to the building of the Gardermoen airport which includes an associated rail link and the construction of a major new university hospital at Gaustad. The demand for advanced capital equipment and for consumer goods such as home textiles and clothing is continuing to rise (very little clothing is produced in Norway and British fashion tends to be highly regarded) and concern over environmental issues and pollution in Norway makes it a very open market for environmentally friendly goods.

RUNNING A BUSINESS

Employing Staff

Contracts: Employment contracts should be written and drawn up according to Norwegian employment legislation. However, employees may not usually be dismissed without at least one month's notice unless there is a collective agreement or other written agreement stating otherwise. Managerial posts often require three months notice but this can be longer. The reasons for dismissal must be plausible and relate to the circumstances of the company or to the behaviour of the employee.

Paid Holidays: All employees are entitled to four weeks plus one day of holidays each year and 10 days of legal holidays. Employees aged over 60 are entitled to five weeks holiday. Employees can take three consecutive weeks of holidays during the summer vacation.

Labour Relations: Most companies with between 50 and 200 employees have one third labour representation on the board of directors. Although this is not compulsory, employees are entitled to request it. Companies with more than 200 employees elect a corporate assembly with a minimum of 12 members, the majority of whom are chosen at the annual shareholders meeting and the rest by fellow employees. The corporate assembly is the final decision-making body and elects the board of directors. Corporate assembly meetings are held twice a year and decisions are made about major investments, modernization and other issues affecting the labour force.

Social Security Contributions: Employers contribute a percentage of the employee's gross salary and benefits in social insurance contributions, on a sliding scale between 14.1% and 0%. In some branches, the 14.1% rate applies all over the country. Employees normally contribute 7.8% whilst self-employed individuals contribute 10.7% of their personal income up to 12 times the Basic allowance (NOK40,090 – approx. £3,167/US$4,530 in 2002), and then at 7.8%. The employer's contribution is levied on all salaries and benefits. Generally, a foreign employer must pay the social security contribution for employees working in Norway or on the Norwegian Continental Shelf.

Taxation

Norwegian regulations on tax are multiple and various and anyone considering working or doing business in Norway should try to familiarise themselves with them. For a very detailed overview consult the *Guide for Foreign Employers and Employees*, published by the Central Office for Foreign Tax Affairs (Postboks 8031, 4068 Stavanger; www.skatteetaten.no). PriceWaterhouse Coopers have published *Doing Business in Norway* on the web.

Employers are required to withhold taxes from salaries paid to employees. Both self-employed people and employees are obliged to make advance tax payments during the income year. Employees are issued with a tax deduction card from their local assessment office. If this card is not presented or is not issued the employer is obliged to withhold 50% of the employee's gross salary and should deposit the amount withheld with the tax authorities.

Resident Corporations: Resident companies are subject to taxes on worldwide income, excluding net income derived from property abroad. The corporate tax rate is 28%. Corporate taxes are payable during the year after the income year. The tax office can make an estimated preliminary tax assessment based on information from the company's previous year's income; this is paid in two instalments on 15 February and 15 April. The remainder is paid on 15 September and 15 November. The amount of the last two payments is based on the actual tax liability according to the taxpayer's return. Interest charges are levied if half of the total tax is not paid before 1 May.

Non-Resident Companies: Non-resident companies are taxed on income which can be attributed to Norwegian business activity. Usually non-resident companies are subject only to corporate tax if they trade in Norway through a branch firm. The branch will normally be taxed at the going corporate rate.

Partnerships and Joint Ventures: Partnerships, limited partnerships and joint ventures are taxed on a parity level with companies and corporations.

Self-employed: Income from self-employment is subject to the ordinary income tax (business income) at 28% and personal surtax of 13.5%. Personal income includes income from personal services, pensions, self-employment income and shareholder income. Additionally, employee social security contributions are computed according to personal income. Self-employed individuals receive an estimate of taxes to be paid during the income year from the assessment office. Estimated taxes are paid in equal instalments on the 15th of March, May, September and November.

Legal Advice

Anyone contemplating doing business in Norway should seek proper legal advice both for purchasing and setting up a business. You should use lawyers who are familiar with Norwegian law. The following firms deal in most areas of business law:

KPMG Consulting, Brynsveien 12, 0667 Oslo; ☎22 07 22 07.
PriceWaterhouse Coopers Advokatfirmaet, Karenslyst allé 12-14, 0277 Oslo; ☎23 16 00 00; www.pwcglobal.com.
Advokatfirmaet Steenstrup, Fridtjof Nansens pl. 5, 0160 Oslo; ☎22 40 56 00; www.steenstrup.no.

Accountancy and Auditing Advice

Financial statements must be presented annually in accordance with Norwegian law and should contain the necessary information for evaluating a company's financial position. A company should retain accounting records for up to 10 years after closure. Accounts may be kept abroad if most business is conducted out of Norway. All companies should keep the following records:

- A cash journal for receipts.
- A separate journal for all other entries.
- Ledgers for accounts which are payable and accounts which are receivable.
- A general ledger.
- A bound register which includes the balance sheets, income statements, the director's and auditor's reports and consolidated group accounts where applicable.

Annual accounts should include:

- A director's report (if the company has a board of directors).
- A balance sheet.
- An income statement.
- Notes for the financial statement.
- A cashflow analysis (for companies valued at more than NOK10 million.

Auditing Requirements Public and private joint stock companies (AS and ASA), as well as general and limited partnerships with a turnover higher than NOK5 million (approx. £395,000/US$565,000) or more than five partners must prepare annual financial statements and appoint an independent auditor. Sole proprietors with assets exceeding NOK20 million or with more than 20 employees must do the same.

To be appointed as an independent auditor in Norway the accountant must be either a Registered Auditor or a State Authorised Public Accountant. The auditor's Report should be free of any restrictions imposed by the company.

Useful Addresses

Ernst and Young: Tullinsgaten 2, PB 6834 St Olavs Pl. 0130 Oslo; ☎22 03 60 00; www.ey.no.

PriceWaterhouse Coopers, Karenslyst allé 12, 0245 Oslo; ☎23 16 00 00; www.pwcglobal.com

Norwegian Federation of Authorised Accountants, Postboks 99, Sentrum, 0101 Oslo; ☎23 35 69 00; fax 23 35 69 20; e-mail post@narf.no; www.narf.no.

Norwegian Institute of Public Accountants, Pilestredet 75 D, PO Box 5864 Majorstuen, 0308 Oslo; ☎23 36 52 00; fax 22 69 05 55; e-mail Firmapost.dnr@revisornett .no; www.revisornett.no.

Sweden

SECTION I

LIVING IN SWEDEN

GENERAL INTRODUCTION

RESIDENCE AND ENTRY REGULATIONS

SETTING UP HOME

DAILY LIFE

RETIREMENT

GENERAL INTRODUCTION

DESTINATION SWEDEN

Mention Sweden and the following might spring to mind: pine trees, saunas, wooden houses, Abba and au pairs. Sweden conjures up images of a squeaky clean environment of wide open spaces, glittering lakes, mysterious forests and a pine fresh atmosphere. At first glance there is something almost disarmingly pure about Sweden; this is a country which has stayed neutral for nearly 200 years, is the birthplace of the founder of the Nobel Peace Prize, runs one of the world's most advanced cradle to grave welfare states, and has an environment as fresh as its numerous pine trees. A less superficial look at Sweden, however, reveals some contradictions in all this: despite Swedish neutrality the country is a major arms exporter, and the founder of the Nobel Peace Prize, Alfred Nobel, was also the inventor of dynamite. This is also the country that practised forcible sterilisation of the handicapped for 40 years from 1935 to 1975. On the plus side, Sweden takes in more refugees than any other country in Europe, and does much to promote peace around the world.

Contradictions tend to be a feature of Swedish life but this does not detract from the enchanting beauty of the country and the enlightened social concern. Despite being geographically rather removed from the rest of western Europe, Sweden has made a significant contribution to the diplomacy for world peace, to the arts, and not least to safer motoring in the form of Volvos and Saabs. Membership of the EU has not brought the hoped-for economic advantages; Sweden is not doing as well as its neighbour Norway which voted to stay outside the Union. On the other hand, there are no longer any barriers to working in here for British and other EU citizens, so this is a good time to look at the opportunities Sweden has to offer.

PROS AND CONS OF MOVING TO SWEDEN

Although not always considered part of mainstream Europe, Sweden is certainly more advanced industrially and socially than many nations, and the locals enjoy a very high standard of living. Despite the country's nonpareil welfare state and social equality there is a downside. Funding the 'Swedish Model' costs an arm and a leg in taxes and welfare contributions and the general cost of living generally ranks as one of the highest in the Europe.

Those going to Sweden for the first time are often amazed at the spaciousness of the country. Cities are small and towns and villages are spread out thinly across a land dominated by pine trees and lakes. While the country is undoubtedly beautiful the predominance of two or three tree species and lakes everywhere can become a bit tedious, and outside the main cities there are limited sources of entertainment.

As a northern country Sweden experiences very long hours of daylight in summer and very long nights in winter; within the Arctic Circle daylight hours in winter can be reduced to three per day and are accompanied by extremely low temperatures. Set against this is the beautiful light and shade on the forests and lakes in summer. The coastline has numerous beaches and small islands and these are ideal for swimming and picnics on long summer days when temperatures can be surprisingly warm.

Pros
O   Beautiful country.
O   Excellent welfare state.
O   High standard of living.
O   Small population.
O   Most people speak English.

Cons
O   Housing is very expensive in big cities.
O   Long hours of cold and darkness in winter.
O   Limited entertainment resources.
O   High cost of living.
O   High unemployment levels.

Opinions on the Swedish character tend to be divided and the Swedes themselves are fiercely opposed to national stereotyping, but generally, like the other Nords, Swedish people are reserved and it usually takes a few drinks to bring some of them out of themselves. Perhaps it is the long dark winters which contribute to the heavy alcohol consumption and a tendency towards melancholia, known as *svårmod*. Nonetheless, many Swedes have a very dry sense of humour and are helpful and friendly when approached and the majority speak excellent English.

POLITICAL AND ECONOMIC STRUCTURE

Background

In modern times Sweden has played a relatively low-key role in European economic and political affairs, which has changed somewhat with the accession to the EU. Since 1814 Sweden has remained staunchly neutral (including during both World Wars) and for a long time stayed out of the European Community. Sweden does not particularly seek a high profile in international affairs, but inevitably its role in the EU will bring it more into the limelight.

Not that much is known about the earliest inhabitants of Sweden, or Scandinavia, for that matter. Nomadic herders probably first roamed across Sweden in about 6,000 BC and by 3,000 BC had begun to create settlements. The early Swedish settlers were traders in fur and amber, but trade was disrupted by a deteriorating climate around the time of the birth of Christ. The sixth century saw the rise of the small kingdom of the Svear tribe, who gave Sweden its present-day name of Sverige. The eighth century marks the beginning of the Viking era and there is some evidence to suggest that the Swedish Vikings were amongst the first to begin raids, turning eastwards towards the Baltic and on towards the Byzantine Empire. The era marked the heyday of paganism when nine human sacrifices were offered annually at Uppsala north of Stockholm. The Vikings established a parliament or *Thing* which operated in each province and was elected by free men. Christianity was slow to gain a foothold in Sweden; in 1008 King Olof Skättonung was converted, and by 1130 Uppsala had changed from being a pagan site of worship to a centre for Christianity.

The Middle Ages mostly saw interminable power struggles between different rulers. The country enjoyed a period of stability and progress under the rule of Magnus Ladulås from 1275 to 1290, during whose reign the first stone churches were built and scholars sent abroad to study at foreign universities. This was also a time when Sweden expanded its hold over Finland. Trade flourished under the German Hanseatic League and a trading centre was established at Visby on the Swedish island of Gotland. The Black Death arrived in 1350 and wiped out about one-third of the population. There was another brief period of stability when Norway, Denmark and Sweden were united at Kalmar in 1397 under Erik of Pomerania, son of Queen Margrethe of Denmark. The Kalmar Union was a troubled one and Sweden seceded in 1523 when Gustav Ericsson founded the Swedish Vasa dynasty. The 17th century saw Sweden's age of greatness under Gustavus Adolphus when Sweden became the dominant military power. Denmark waged war on Sweden in the hope of resurrecting the Kalmar Union, but was defeated in the Thirty Years War (1618-1648). In 1660 at the Peace of Copenhagen the present-day boundaries between Denmark and Sweden were agreed.

The imperial ambitions of Gustavus Adolphus' descendant Charles XII eventually led to disaster, with an unsuccessful invasion of Russia and the loss of Sweden's eastern territories. While the 18th century was generally an unstable period politically, with more defeats by Russia, several figures emerged whose names are still household words, notably the philosopher Swedenborg, the scientist Celsius, and the botanist Linnaeus.

Recent History

Sweden stayed out of the Napoleonic Wars to start with, but eventually joined in on the British side. Finland was finally lost to Russia in 1809. Rather paradoxically, one of Napoleon's generals was asked to become king in 1810, founding the Bernadotte dynasty that rules today. In 1814 Sweden attacked Denmark, forcing her to surrender Norway. By the Treaty of Kiel in 1814 a union was established between Norway and Sweden which lasted until 1905.

Industrialisation was slow to start and poor rural areas saw mass migration to America. The late 19th century saw the rise of trade unionism and in 1889 the

Social Democratic Party was founded. Sweden maintained neutrality throughout World War I but suffered economic hardship because of blockades. In 1929 the first Social Democratic government came into office; this party came to dominate Swedish politics in the 20th century. Sweden claimed neutrality again during World War II, but was obliged to allow German troops passage through to Finland and Norway, something that created lasting ill-feeling with the Norwegians, but not so much with the Finns, who were allies of the Germans until 1944.

The years between 1946 and 1950 might justly be called the great age of social reform in Sweden. The Social Democrats introduced comprehensive laws that were to form the basis of the welfare state; Sweden steered its famous 'Middle Way' during the Cold War by adopting the best political and economic aspects of both socialism and capitalism. By means of tax reorganisation there was a wider and more even distribution of wealth, but plans for the nationalisation of industry were not enforced.

In the latter half of the 20th century Sweden became increasingly integrated into international political and economic affairs. In 1952 the Nordic Council was founded between the Scandinavian countries to promote co-operation between the Nordic parliaments. In 1971 Sweden declared its intention not to seek membership of the European Community on the grounds that it wished to preserve its neutrality. In 1995 Sweden got round this by adopting observer status in the Western European Union (the defence arm of the EU). An estimated 70% of Swedes are still currently opposed to abandoning their traditional neutrality. Sweden hit the world headlines in 1986 following the inexplicable assassination of the Swedish Prime Minister, Olof Palme; the matter is still under investigation. He was succeeded by Ingvar Carlsson. In 1991 the Conservatives held a brief three-year term in office, but the Social Democrats were returned to office again in 1994, the same year in which Sweden voted to join the European Community. 1994 was marked by the tragic sinking of the ferry Estonia, when 852 passengers lost their lives in the Baltic Sea.

Recently, Sweden held the presidency of the EU for the first half of 2001. In other respects this is a country that stays out of the headlines. If it were not for its tennis players and export trade in football managers its profile would be virtually invisible.

Economy

Sweden ranks at 21 on the world scale of Gross National Product per capita, but about 56% of GDP passes through the public sector, including payments of welfare benefits. As a result welfare contributions are some of the steepest in the world. Since 1983 state involvement in the distribution of national income has, however, lessened and the majority of enterprises are privately owned. Sweden is highly dependent on international trade and exports account for about 30% of GDP. Although formerly most of Sweden's exports were in the form of raw materials or semi-manufactured products (steel, pulp and cut wood), today finished goods dominate the market, in particular cars and telecommunications equipment. Major imports are engineering products, chemicals, textiles and imported foodstuffs include coffee, tea, fruit and fish.

Most of Sweden's major industrial companies are multinationals; because industry has tended to invest more abroad than at home, some firms (among them Volvo and Electrolux) employ more cheap foreign labour than native Swedes. About 800,000 workers are employed in private industry but half that number again work abroad.

The traditional industries of agriculture, forestry and fishing declined in the second part of the 20th century, while industry and manufacturing have developed. However, the biggest growth area has been in services and administration, in particular in the public sector. Sweden is well-endowed with natural resources, including wood, hydroelectric power and metallic ores, which are the historical backbone of Sweden's industrial economy. 50% of electricity comes from hydroelectric sources and 45% from nuclear sources, making Sweden one of the highest users of nuclear power per capita in the world. Following a 1980 referendum Sweden is aiming to eliminate the use of nuclear power by 2010. Northern Sweden has large mineral resources and the state-owned company Luossavaara Kirunavaara at Kiruna in Lapland manages about 90% of the total production capacity of the iron ore deposits. Parts of Nordland have a wide range of metal mines including zinc, gold, copper and lead.

Farming. Just under 6% of Sweden is cultivated for farming; the most profitable agricultural land is in southern Sweden. In the south, potatoes, vegetables, sugar beet, oilseeds, wheat and barley are the main crops, while in the north, up to the Arctic Circle, hay and potatoes are dominant. Generally, animal products are more important than arable products and dairy cows are found throughout Sweden. Pig farming and poultry tend to be concentrated more in the far south. Swedish farms have some of the world's highest yields. About 2% of the population are employed in the agricultural sector, which accounts for about 1% of the gross domestic product.

Forestry. Approximately 55% of land in Sweden is covered by forest, with the main trees being spruce and pine. 50% of Swedish forest land is in private ownership with the remainder being divided evenly between company and public ownership. Since the 19th century forestry in Sweden has been conducted on a sustained-yield basis which is very strictly enforced. The average growing time for a new tree is 70 years in the south and 140 years in the north. Forestry work was once a winter occupation for farmers but today it is carried out all year round by professional foresters. About 37,000 people are employed in the forestry industry. Sweden is one of the main world exporters of wood products and manufactures a wide variety of them including pulp and paper, furniture and prefabricated houses.

Fishing. Fishing plays only a small part in the Swedish economy, with an annual catch of about 340,000 tonnes. The centre for the fish market and the major fishing harbour is Gothenburg. Major fish products are salmon, herring, cod, plaice and mackerel.

Manufacturing. Sweden's main manufacturing industry is engineering, in particular the transport industry. The aerospace and automotive industries have major plants in south-central Sweden; the big names are Volvo in Gothenburg and Saab-Scania in Trollhättan. Other main products are communication equipment and metal, plastic and glass products. Both the pharmaceutical and biotechnology industries are growing in Sweden as is the petrochemical industry based around Stenungsund. Before the 1980s petrochemicals accounted for 25% of the value of Sweden's total imports but now account for less than 5%. Whilst the construction and food-processing industries in Sweden continue to play a part in the economy, the textile and shoe industries have declined because of competition from cheap imports.

The economy did well between 1997 and 2000; a global economic slowdown from 2001 has seen unemployment rising again, but with new high-tech industries developing there is a good chance that the economy will at least remain stable, even if it does not grow very much. Whether Sweden joins in with the euro will have a considerable bearing on her future prosperity.

Government

Sweden has a multi-party democratic system and a constitutional monarchy. The monarch (currently King Carl XVI Gustaf)) has only a ceremonial role and political power rests with the *Riksdag* (Parliament). The Swedish Constitution was revised in 1975 and is based on four basic laws: the Instrument of Government, the Act of Succession, the Freedom of the Press Act and the Riksdag Act. The main principles are representative democracy, popular sovereignty and parliamentarianism. The Prime Minister is appointed by the Speaker of the Riksdag but must be approved for office through a vote of Parliament. The cabinet is appointed by the Prime Minister and is responsible for all government decisions. There are at present 13 ministries, which are relatively small; administration and the implementation of legislation are dealt with by central administrative agencies.

The Riksdag is a unicameral parliament which is elected every four years (three years prior to 1995), usually in September. The 349 members of the Riksdag are elected by proportional representation. The voting age is 18 and turnout is usually very high, averaging 90%. The role of the ombudsman is very important in Swedish affairs and a Parliamentary Ombudsman monitors and investigates suspected cases of abuses of authority by civil servants. The majority of government documents are open to inspection by the press and the public at any time.

The five main political parties are split into two blocs with the Social Democrats and the Left Party (formerly the Communist Party) representing the socialists, and the Conservatives, the Centre and the Liberals representing the more right-wing group. In addition, there is now an up-and-coming Green Environment Party in Sweden. There is a quota rule in Swedish politics which excludes parties with less than 4% of the national vote or less than 12% of the votes in at least one electoral district. By far the most dominant party of the 20th century was the Social Democratic Party. Closely allied with the trade unions, the party was in power from 1932 to 1976 (with a brief loss of power in 1936) and from 1982 to 1991. In 1991 the Conservative Party came to power under Carl Bildt, coinciding with Sweden's worst economic crisis since the 1930s, but in 1994 the Social Democrats under the former Prime Minister Ingvar Carlsson were re-elected; he was replaced by Göran Persson in 1996. The Social Democrats who founded Sweden's 'cradle to grave' social welfare state were forced to make welfare cutbacks in the hope of reviving the Swedish economy.

Better economic management in the late 1990s has resulted in large budget surpluses, but has not solved the problem of high unemployment. Membership of the European Union has not brought the benefits that were expected. Consequently, in the 1998 elections the Social Democrats lost heavily, while the anti-Brussels Left and Green parties made big gains. A coalition of the Social Democrats, with the Left Party and the Green Party as junior coalition partners, has been in power for four years. The current government is pursuing a policy of cutting taxes, while spending more on health and education. The question of whether to join the euro has been shelved for the time being. If the euro is successful then a referendum could be held, although there are considerable doubts about whether the electorate would want to join. Göran Persson was still in office in 2002. New elections are due in September 2002.

Northern Sweden is home to the five Swedish Lapp or Sami communities. Like the Norwegian Lapps, the Swedish Lapps have their own parliament which meets at Gällivare within the Arctic Circle. The rights of the Lapps have been recognised by statute since 1650. The younger Lapps are struggling to maintain their unique cultural and racial identity and are finding support from the nation's Greens.

GEOGRAPHICAL INFORMATION

Sweden occupies the eastern sector of the Scandinavian peninsula and covers a total area of 173,732 sq miles/449,964 sq km. At twice the size of the United Kingdom, Sweden is Europe's fourth largest country, stretching 1,000 miles/ 1,600 km from north to south and averaging 250 miles/400 km from west to east. About half of the land is covered in forests interspersed with nearly 100,000 lakes and numerous rivers. The eastern coastline is studded with thousands of tiny, wooded islands which have remarkably similar shapes due to the action of glacial ice. Sweden shares most of its western border (1,000 miles/1,600km) with Norway and in the far north shares a small border with Finland. Sweden is separated from Denmark by a mere 10 miles at the narrowest point in the Oresund strait leading into the Baltic Sea. There is now a bridge/tunnel link between Denmark and Sweden. The creation of the so-called Oresund region, it is hoped, will bring greater prosperity to both Copenhagen and the Malmö area; the results have yet to be seen on the Swedish side.

Sweden lies on northerly latitudes (the same as Alaska) and about 15% of the country is above the Arctic Circle. It is divided into three traditional regions: Norrland in the north covers about three-fifths of the country and is primarily an area of mountain and forests. Svealand in central Sweden contains lowland in the east and highlands in the west; and Götaland in the south contains the Småland highlands and the rich fertile plains of Skåne. The Lapps or Sami in the north do not recognise national boundaries and move freely between Norway, Sweden, Finland and Russia. One-fifth of the country, particularly the southwest, is covered by peat and bog land. In addition to the three traditional regions, Sweden is divided into 24 Län or counties. The Scandinavian mountains between Norway and Sweden form a natural physical border and are the source of Sweden's chief rivers, most of which flow southeastwards towards the Gulf of Bothnia or the Baltic Sea. The longest of these is the Klar-Göta River which rises in Norway and flows for 447 miles to the North Sea. Many of the rivers, except in the far north where they are protected, are a source of the nation's hydroelectric power.

Population

The present population of Sweden is approximately 8.9 million, giving it one of the lowest population densities in Europe. The average number of inhabitants per square kilometre is 21 although in northern Sweden the average can be as low as one person per square kilometre. 70% of the country has a density of six inhabitants or less per square kilometre although in Stockholm the average is 3,655. The annual rate of population increase declined during the 1980s, but the trend has been slightly upwards in the early 1990s. The increase is accounted for mainly by increased immigration levels; Sweden has approximately 1 million immigrants of whom 60% are Finnish. Sweden has two minority groups of indigenous peoples: the Lapp population of about 15,000 who are scattered throughout Sweden's northern interior, and the Finnish-speaking people of the northeast along the Finnish border.

Until 1870 fewer than 10% of the Swedish population lived in urban areas. Economic growth after World War II led to a dramatic migration from the countryside to the towns and cities resulting in a depopulation of rural Sweden. There is a very big demographic divide between the north and south with over 90% of the population living in the south of the country, and 90% of these in cities and urban areas. The majority, 1.5 million, live in the capital Stockholm, while 734,000 live in Gothenburg and 480,000 in Malmö in the south.

Climate

Despite being on the same latitude as parts of Greenland, Sweden enjoys a relatively mild climate thanks to the southwest Atlantic winds warmed by the North Atlantic currents. High-pressure systems to the east create sunny summers but cold winters; there are periodic shifts in climate because of the interaction between the Atlantic currents and high-pressure systems. The northern interior is particularly cold in winter, experiencing up to eight months of snowfall with temperatures falling as low as -20°F to -40°F/-30° to -50°C. Between November and May the Gulf of Bothnia freezes over. In southern Sweden temperatures are milder in winter with irregular snowfall. Coastal waters rarely freeze in the south.

Rainfall varies from 28 inches/700mm on the east coast to 40 inches/1000mm on the western slopes of southern Sweden. There is rainfall throughout the year but the wettest period is from late summer to autumn.

TABLE 14   TEMPERATURES IN DEGREES CELSIUS

	January	June	August	October
Jokkmokk	–10.1	13.4	14.1	–0.3
Lund	–2.5	15.9	20.9	7.4
Stockholm	–1.5	16.2	21.3	5.1
Växjö	–3.8	15.5	19.7	4.8

Figures supplied by the Swedish Travel & Tourism Council.

REGIONAL GUIDE

Information Facilities

Sweden has few tourist offices abroad. Where there is none, you should go to the nearest Swedish Embassy for information. There is a considerable amount of information in English on the internet about Sweden. Some websites end in .nu rather than .se. NU stands for Nordic Union.

Swedish Travel & Tourism Council, 11 Montagu Place, London W1H 2AL; ☎020-7870 5600; fax 020-7724 5872; e-mail info@swetourism.org.uk; www.visit-sweden.com.

Scandinavian Tourist Board, 655 3rd Ave, New York, NY 10017; ☎212-885-9700; www.visit-sweden.com.

Sweden is usually divided into three regions: Norrland, Svealand and Götaland. Because of the low population density, the country can be divided into the following fairly large areas:

Stockholm and Environs

Stockholm is the most beautiful of the Nordic capitals and one of the most beautiful in Europe. Built on 14 small islands, Stockholm is a spacious city of parkland, water, old buildings and new state-of-the-art architecture. The old quarter, Gamla Stan, with its medieval twisting streets and waterside walks contrasts with the glass and steel skyscrapers of the modern ciy. With over 50 museums and galleries Stockholm is a city of culture but also contains a strong rural element in its many parks and lakes. For a relatively small city Stockholm has a varied and lively nightlife. Stockholm is now thought of by many as Europe's trendiest city; it is easy to get around, compact and has just about everything that anyone could want. It is a very expensive city, however, and some of the locals seem to be out to fleece foreigners: there are even entrance fees to some of the better restaurants. Parking is also hugely difficult.

Most Stockholmers live in high-rise apartments in the surrounding forested suburbs and commute to the centre via the efficient transport infrastructure. The city is clean and safe and pollution is kept to a minimum. Out at sea Stockholm is the archipelago comprising hundreds of tiny islands with beaches which are popular tourist resorts in summer. An hour away from Stockholm to the north is the cathedral and university town of Uppsala which is regarded as the country's religious and historical centre. Just north of Uppsala is the ancient pagan settlement of Gamla Uppsala with royal burial grounds dating back to the sixth century, making it a kind of Swedish Stonehenge.

All the information services are conveniently located at Sweden House in Hamngatan; this houses the Stockholm Information Service and Tourist Office, the Swedish Institute, and the Sweden Bookshop. The Information Service publishes the monthly *What's On in Stockholm.* For hotel reservations go to the Hotellcentralen in the Central Station.

Stockholm Information Service, Sweden House Tourist Centre, Hamngatan 27, Kungsträdgården, Stockholm; ☎08 789 24 90; fax 08 789 24 91; e-mail info@stoinfo.se; www.stockholmtown.com.

Hotellcentrallen, Central Station, Stockholm; ☎08-789 24 90; fax 08-791 86 66; e-mail hotels@stoinfo.se. For hotel bookings and tourist information.
Uppsala Tourism AB, Fyris Torg 8, 75310 Uppsala; ☎018 27 48 00; fax 018 13 28 95; e-mail tb@utkab.se; www.res.till.Uppland.nu.

The South East, Gotland and Öland

The whole of southern Sweden is called Götaland, after the tribe who occupied it in earlier times. Stockholm is a forested region containing the two counties of Östergötland and Småland. The centre of Småland is home to the delightfully named 'Crystal Kingdom' which is based around the town of Växjö. The Crystal Kingdom refers to the local glassblowing factories for which the region is famous.

Gotland and Öland are Sweden's only two major islands. Öland is connected to the mainland at Kalmar by bridge and is a very popular tourist attraction in summer. The island bears a surprising resemblance to the Netherlands, having flat green countryside and over 400 windmills. Wooden cottages, castles, fortresses and burial mounds give it an historic charm which keeps the tourists coming. Gotland is also a popular tourist resort frequented by Stockholmers in search of a good time. The capital Visby was an early Viking Settlement and was the hub of the Swedish traders in the Hanseatic League in the 12th century.

Gotlands Turistförening, Hamngatan 4, Visby; ☎0498 20 17 00; fax 0498 20 17 17; e-mail info@gotlandinfo.com; www.gotlandinfo.com.
Turism i Kronoberg, Stationshuset, Norra Järnvägsgatan, 352 30 Växjö; ☎0470 74 25 70; fax 0470 478 14.
Smålands Turistråd, Box 1027, 551 11 Jönköping; ☎036 19 95 70; fax 036 71 43 01; info@visit-smaland.com; www.visit-smaland.com.
Ölands Turist AB, Möllstorp, Box 74, 386 21 Färjestaden; ☎0485 56 06 00; fax 0485 56 06 05.

The Southwest and Göteborg (Gothenburg)

The south of Sweden contains extensive forests and two of the largest lakes: Lake Vänern and Lake Vättern. The landscape is relatively flat and is more similar to that of Denmark which is just a stretch of water away. The coastal beaches make it a popular holiday resort for the Swedes and the area is also graced by attractive old towns and cities of which the principal one is Göteborg, known in English as Gothenburg. Gothenburg is the second largest city in Sweden with a population of over 500,000. It has traditionally been a ship-building city, has a fishing harbour and is the landing point for the ferry from Newcastle.

Beyond the inelegance of the shipyards it is one of Sweden's most attractive cities. South of Gothenburg are the three provinces of Halland, Skåne and Blekinge. They are rather different in character from the rest of Sweden, several centuries of being under Danish rule setting them apart. Skåne in particular has a distinctive dialect and customs and there is even an independence movement within the province. The port town of Helsingborg is literally only a few minutes ferry ride away from the Danish port town of Helsingør. The region is generally flat and contains some of Sweden's most fertile farming country.

Gothenburg Turistbyrå, Kungsportsplatsen 2, 411 10 Göteborg; ☎031 61 25 00; fax

031 61 25 01; e-mail turistinfo@gbg-co.se; www.goteborg.com.
Malmö Tourist Office, Central Station, 211 20 Malmö; ☎040 34 12 00; fax 040 34 12 09; e-mail malmo.turism@malmo.se.
Skånes Turistråd, Skiffervägen 34, 224 78 Lund; ☎046 12 43 50; fax 046 12 23 72; www.skanetur.se.

The East Coast

North of Uppsala, the east coast forms the edge of the Gulf of Bothnia, a narrow corridor of water that separates Sweden from Finland and stretches up to Haparanda on the Finnish border. Towns are small and spaced out on the coast and depend mainly on fishing for their livelihood. The principal coastal towns are Gävle, Sundsvall, Umeå and Luleå although none of them is particularly big. Umeå and Luleå are modern manufacturing centres, but Gävle, Hudiksvall and Skelllefteå retain some of Sweden's heritage in the form of old wooden buildings. The area enjoys clean beaches and crystal-clear water.
Mitt Sverige Turism, Norra Kyrkogatan 15, 871 32 Härnösand; ☎0611 55 77 50; fax 0611 221 07; www.mittsverigeturism.se.
Västerbottens Turistbyrå, Rennmarkstorget 15, 903 26 Umeå; ☎090 16 16 16; fax 090 16 34 39; www.vasterbotten.se.

Central and Northern Sweden

From north of Lake Vänern through the Arctic Circle to the north Norwegian border you get the picture postcard image of Sweden. The area is characterised by rural counties with tiny populations living amongst forests and lakes with reindeer for the local wildlife. The central province of Dalarna is known as the 'Folklore District' and is a place of forests, mountains, lakes and painted wooden farmhouses. It is the favoured site for the midsummer celebrations and home to traditional Swedish naïve religious paintings. The traditional region of Norrland stretches from the northern border 620 miles/1000 miles south and is a vast tract of wide open spaces. More than 30% of the area is virtually uninhabited but the far north above the Arctic Circle is home to the Swedish Laplanders. Although once nomadic reindeer herders, the majority of Lapps now have permanent homes. Technology and the modern world have encroached on the traditional way of life and even helicopters may be used to round up the reindeer these days.

The northernmost Swedish city is Kiruna, home to the nation's huge iron ore mines. Kiruna has the world's largest underground iron mine at 310 miles/500 km long. Spread over an area half the size of Switzerland, Kiruna is sometimes called the 'world's biggest city' although the population is small; it is also home to the Laplander museum. Also of note in northern Sweden are the towns of Gällivare, another iron ore mining town, and Jokkmokk the Lapp cultural centre and host to the great 400-year-old Lapp winter market in February. Norrland is characterised by mountainous ranges to the west, forests and moorlands in the centre, and wild rugged coastline to the east. However, Sweden's excellent transport system means that it is relatively accessible. There are two main national parks in northern Sweden, the most stunning being Sarek which is Sweden's highest mountain area with over 90 peaks and home to Arctic animals like elk, bear, wolverine, lynx and the Arctic fox. Slightly less impressive is the Muddas National Park which is less mountainous and more forested.

Jämtland Härjedalen Turism, Rådhusgatan 44, 831 82 Östersund; ☎063 10 44 05; fax 063 10 93 35; e-mail info@jhtf.se; fax www.upplevjamtland.se.

Jokkmokk Turistbyrå, Stortorget 4, Jokkmokk; ☎0971 121 40; e-mail jokkmokk.turistbyra@jokkmokk.se.

Kiruna Turistbyrå, Folketshus, Kiruna; 0980 188 80; www.lappland.se.

GETTING TO SWEDEN

Air

Both British Airways and Scandinavian Air Systems (SAS) operate regular daily flights between London and Stockholm. The cheapest flights are run by Ryanair. Check the website regularly to find the best deals. Note that routes can change.

There are a few direct flights from the US to Stockholm. SAS flies from Chicago and New York to Stockholm. Delta Air Lines from New York to Stockholm, and American Airlines from Chicago to Stockholm. It is also possible to fly Icelandair to Stockholm with a stopover in Reykjavík.

Useful Addresses

British Airways, ☎0845-773 3377; www.britishairways.com. London to Stockholm/Gothenburg.

Finnair, ☎0870-599 77 11; www.finnair.com. London/Manchester to Stockholm.

Maersk Air Ltd, (see BA). Birmingham to Stockholm.

Ryanair, ☎0541-569569; www.ryanair.com. London to Stockholm/Kristianstad/ Malmö.

Skyways, (see SAS) Manchester to Stockholm.

SAS, 0845-60 727 727; www.scandinavian.net. London to Stockholm/ Gothenburg.

Ferries

Scandinavian ferries tend to set the comfort standards for ferries anywhere in the world. At the moment there is just one ferry from the UK to Sweden, run by DFDS Seaways from Newcastle to Gothenburg, via Kristiansand in Norway. The journey takes 26 hours and runs twice a week. Call 0870-533 3000; or see www.dfdsseaways.com.

Rail and Coach

It is feasible to take a train now from England to Sweden; it would take about 30 hours to get from London to Malmö, via Brussels, Cologne, Hamburg and Copenhagen. If you had an Interrail Pass and were stopping off on the way this might be a reasonable way to travel. Otherwise taking a plane would be far cheaper. If you are coming from a neighbouring country, then you should certainly consider using the Scanrail Pass, which allows five days travel out of 15 days (or 10 days in a month or 21 consecutive days) in Denmark, Sweden, Norway and Finland, and represents one of the few good deals one is likely to find in this rather expensive part of the world. In the UK you can buy it from German Rail. It can also be bought from travel agents. In the USA, look at the websites www.europebytrain.com, or www.raileurope.com for details on how to book.

There is a coach service five days a week from London to Stockholm via Malmö and Gothenburg; the whole journey takes about 36 hours. Eurolines runs services all over Europe; if you were touring around Europe, then taking a coach might be an option worth looking at. Eurolines will send a copy of their complete timetable on request.

Useful Addresses

German Rail, ☎08702-435 363; e-mail sales@deutsche-bahn.co.uk.

Eurolines (UK), 4 Cardiff Rd, Luton, Beds LU1 1PP; ☎08705-143219; e-mail welcome@eurolines.co.uk; www.eurolines.co.uk. London to Stockholm.

RESIDENCE AND ENTRY REGULATIONS

THE CURRENT POSITION

Before Sweden joined the European Union, gaining a work permit was a complicated process for EU citizens. These days we have most of the same rights to live and work in Sweden as native Swedes. For non-EEA nationals the situation is much the same as it was before.

EU NATIONALS

Residence Permits

Citizens of the European Union and the EEA can stay in Sweden for up to three months without a residence permit; they should be able to support themselves financially during this period. Those wishing to extend their stay beyond three months must apply for a residence permit (*uppehållstillstånd*). This is done through the local office of the *Migrationsverk* (Immigration Authority). The addresses and other useful information are listed on the website www.migrationsverket.se. You will need to present a passport (or identity card for citizens of Belgium, France, Italy, Luxembourg, the Netherlands, Germany or Austria) and proof of employment. Once you have shown that you have employment for at least 12 months, a residence permit is usually granted for five years. If your employment is expected to last less than 12 months the permit will be for the period of your employment.

The *Migrationsverk* suggests that you should apply for a residence permit before you enter Sweden, so that you can be given a national registration number as soon as you arrive. Your permit has to be valid for a year at least in this case.

Family Members

The following family members of EEA/EU nationals working in Sweden are entitled to enter the country and apply for a residence permit:

O   Husband/wife or partner.
O   Children under 21 or disabled dependent children.
O   Dependent parents.

Family members can obtain a work permit by producing the following documents:
O   Passport or identity card.
O   A certificate confirming the relationship.
O   For dependants, a certificate confirming dependency.

Those entitled to live in Sweden are also entitled to work without a work permit. Partners of a citizen of an EEA/EU country who come from a country outside the EEA/EU must have been granted a residence permit before arrival in Sweden.

Entering to Work – EU Nationals

Sweden is subject to the European Union regulations concerning the free movement of labour. EU nationals can enter Sweden with the intention of looking for work and do not need to have an offer of employment or a work permit before entering the country. You can start work straight away while your application for a residence permit is being processed; you can also apply for the residence permit in your home country at a Swedish embassy or consulate (see above).

EU nationals have the same rights as Swedish citizens as regards pay, working conditions, access to housing, vocational training, social security and trade union membership. Families and dependants have similar rights.

When entering Sweden to work you need to obtain a national registration number (*personnummer*) which consists of your birthdate and a four-digit code. Registration numbers are issued by the tax authorities; to find your local tax office look up *lokala skattemyndigheten* in the pink pages of the phone book. The main one in Stockholm is Skattehuset, at 76 Götagatan on Södermalm (☎0771-778 778). You should take your residence permit and passport/identity card with you. The tax office will also issue you with a tax card (*skattsedel*) which gives the appropriate level of taxes to be deducted from your pay.

Entering to Start a Business

EU citizens are free to enter Sweden for up to three months with the intention of setting up a business. They may run their own business in Sweden on the same conditions as Swedish citizens. This also applies to agencies, branches and subsidiaries. All businesses must be registered with the Registrar of Companies and you should include a certificate of registration from the Registrar of Companies or the Swedish Patent and Registration Office when you apply for a residence permit. See *Starting a Business* chapter.

Students

Students who are members of the European Union and European Economic

Area are entitled to a residence permit for the duration of their studies in Sweden but must have adequate means of financial support. A student may work while studying and partners and dependents will be granted a residence permit for the duration of the student's studies provided that they have adequate means of support. Residence permits for students are usually granted for one year at a time and this is renewable. If the period of study is shorter, students should take out comprehensive sickness insurance.

Pensioners

Pensioners from EEA and EU countries and family members will be given a residence permit if they can prove that they have adequate means of support: the equivalent after a tax of the national basic Swedish pension: some SEK4,700 (approx. £320/US$455) a month. See *Retirement* chapter.

Residence Only

Citizens of the EEA/EU will be granted a residence permit to live in Sweden without working if they have adequate means of financial support and will not have to rely on the social welfare system. Proof will be required in the form of bank deposits or through another party guaranteeing the livelihood of the applicant and his/her family. The authorities have the right to deport anyone who is likely to become a public charge.

NON-EEA NATIONALS

Entry

US, Canadian, Australian and New Zealand citizens can enter Sweden for up to three months without a visa but must have a valid passport. They are given the Schengen visa on arrival. On a few occasions, it must be said, planeloads of Americans have arrived in Stockholm and been let into the country without having their passports checked, however it is still necessary to have your passport stamped, otherwise you would not be able to prove how long you have been in Sweden. Border controls between the Nordic countries have not been entirely abolished; there is always the chance of one's status being checked, particularly in the northern areas or coming off ferries.

Sweden signed up to the Schengen agreement in March 2001, whereby anyone with a Schengen visa can spend 90 days out of six months in Sweden, or in the Schengen area as a whole. While most nationals of foreign countries are not required to have a visa to enter Sweden, they should check with the Swedish embassy in their own country first.

Work Permits for Non-EEA Nationals

Non-members of the European Union still have to face stringent regulations regarding the employment of foreigners in Sweden. Sweden does not need many foreign workers; only if no EEA citizen can be found can a job be offered to a non-EEA citizen.

In practice you have to secure a job first and have a firm written offer of employment before you can apply for your work permit. The offer of employment should include details of working hours, pay, length of employment and accommodation arrangements. Once you have been made a firm offer of employment you should contact the nearest Swedish embassy or consulate for a work permit. It is quite common for the embassies to interview you regarding your application. If you are entering Sweden to start a business with self-employed status then you only need to apply for a residence permit.

The Swedish National Labour Markets Board (AMS) usually considers the work permit application and will assess the current state of the Swedish labour market when making a decision. If a work permit is granted it will usually limit you to a specific employer, a specific job and a specific length of stay in Sweden. Work permits are rarely granted for longer than one year at a time, but these can be renewed if the circumstances under which they were given still apply.

Useful Addresses

Aliens Appeals Board, Utlänningsnämnden, Box 45102, 104 30 Stockholm; ☎08-728 46 00.

Migrationsverket (Head office), 601 70 Norrköping; ☎011-15 66 04; fax 011-15 63 35; e-mail migrationsverket@migrationsverket.se; www.migrationsverket.se.

Migrationsverket (Gothenburg), Streteredsvägen 90, 428 80 Kållered; ☎031-774 61 00; fax 031-795 53 30.

Migrationsverket (Malmö), Östra Farmvägen 5, Malmö; ☎040-28 40 00; fax 040-18 52 28.

Migrationsverket (Stockholm), Pyramidvägen 2A, Solna; ☎08-470 97 00; fax 08-470 99 30.

Ministry of Foreign Affairs, Gustav Adolfstorg, Box 16121, 103 39 Stockholm; ☎08-405 10 00; www.utrikes.regeringen.se.

Swedish Embassy, 11 Montagu Place, London W1H 2AL; ☎020-7917 6400; fax 020-7724 4174; e-mail embassy@swednet.org.uk; www.swednet.org.uk.

Swedish Embassy, 1501 M St, NW, Suite 900, Washington DC, 20005-1702; ☎202-467-2600; fax 202-467-2699; e-mail ambassaden.washington@foreign.ministry.se.

British Embassy, Skarpögatan 6-8, Stockholm; ☎08-671 3000; e-mail britishembassy@telia.com.

United States Embassy, Dag Hammarskjölds väg 31, 115 89 Stockholm; ☎08-783 5300; fax 08-665 3303; www.usemb.se.

SETTING UP HOME

Long-term foreign residents in Sweden will sooner or later want to buy a property, given the very high rental costs in the cities. Swedish property firms and newspapers with property adverts can now be viewed on the internet, so it is much easier to know what is available before you go to Sweden. Loans for mortgages can only be obtained from Swedish banks. European Union citizens have the same rights of access to housing as Swedish citizens.

HOW DO THE SWEDES LIVE?

The standard of housing is very high in Sweden and Sweden's housing policy is based on giving everyone the opportunity to own their own home at a reasonable price. In the mid-1960s the Swedish parliament introduced the 'million programme' whereby more than 1 million flats were built over a period of 10 years. In 1984 the government embarked on a programme of updating and improving all dwellings which lacked proper fittings and conveniences and also sought to adapt flats for energy conservation and for the use of the elderly and disabled and to install lifts. Another programme was started in 1993, but since then the level of new building has gone down to not much more than 15,000 per year. It is supposed to pick up, and by 2005 the annual number of starts should be 29,000. The building industry collapsed because of the 1993 recession, and tax changes made building new houses much more expensive. Building properties to rent is not attractive because of the strict rent controls. About 80% of building companies went out of business between 1993 and 2002. The standard of housing is nonetheless very high; the problem is actually finding a place to live.

The average number of dwellings per thousand inhabitants is 470, only second to France. Because 40% of all households consist of one person, and another 30% of just two, there is actually a housing shortage where one would not expect one. There are several reasons for the low occupancy rate: it is rare in Sweden for more than two generations to live together and Swedish housing policy seeks to help the elderly continue to live in their own homes for as long as they wish. Most elderly people live in one- or two-person households. It is also usual for grown-up children to find their own accommodation relatively quickly when they leave home, although this is becoming more difficult in metropolitan areas.

With a small population and so much empty space the Swedes can afford to be generous when it comes to living area. Government policy laid down in the 1960s states that dwellings should be sufficiently large for no more than two persons to occupy the same room, excluding the kitchen and living room, and just under 100% of houses and flats conform to this standard. The average living space per person is 47 square metres with approximately two rooms per inhabitant. Most people in major towns live in apartments and about 2.2 million dwellings are in blocks of flats. Sweden has a large number of big country houses, especially in the southern provinces and the area around Lake Mälaren in particular has a large number of castles and manors dating from the 16th to 18th century. In central Sweden traditional painted wooden farmhouses are preserved as part of Sweden's heritage.

More than 70% of the population live in towns or cities, and over 22% own a second vacation home in the countryside. 65% of dwellings are owner-occupied. About 30% of the population live in the largest cities of Stockholm, Gothenburg and Malmö. 40% of the population live in towns of at least 2,000 inhabitants and 30% are on farms or in small village communities. Housing generally is of a very high standard and Swedish cities are noted for being carefully and tastefully planned. About 40% of the population live in subsidised housing.

Where to Look for Accommodation

If you are arranging to work abroad before moving to Sweden you should consult your prospective employer as regards accommodation. Finding accommodation for foreign workers is a particular problem in Stockholm. Valuable properties in central Stockholm are often only rented out to companies who will pay over the odds to house their foreign employees. On the open market you are only likely to find somewhere a long way from the centre of town on one of the many commuter lines. If you are being hired to go to work in Sweden, then you should find out if your employer is going to provide accommodation or help you find it.

The usual means of finding accommodation is through the newspapers, on the internet, or by word of mouth. Travellers' hostels in the main cities are another possible source of leads. The largest circulation dailies which carry listings are: *Expressen* (Stockholm), *Svenska Dagbladet* (Stockholm), *Göteborgs-Posten* (Gothenburg) and *Sydsvenska Dagbladet* (Malmö). The best internet sites are www.hemnet.se, www.bostad.se, www.svebo.se and www.maklarsamfundet.se. Svenska Bostäder, based in Stockholm, is the largest municipal rental company in Sweden; see www.svebo.se.

Types Of Tenure

There are three kinds of tenure in Sweden: ownership, tenant-ownership and rental. About 17% of housing units are tenant-owned, 49% are rented, and 34% owner-occupied. Tenant-owners are members of a non-profit making organisation which provides its members with accommodation (usually flats). Members make an initial capital investment in the property (typically from SEK500,000 (approx. £34,000/US$48,500) to SEK600,000 for three and four room flats) and then pay monthly charges to cover the cost of the organisation's loan and capital expenditure. Tenant-owners are usually responsible for their own maintenance. A co-operative usually has a residents' council – *bostadsrätt* – where decisions are made about the running of the co-op, and anti-social tenants dealt with.

There are both for-profit and non-profit housing co-operatives. Municipalities own the stock in many non-profit co-operatives. The type of housing should be qualified as public housing rather than social housing; it is not reserved for any particular income bracket. Some organisations determine the price you are allowed to ask for your property if you want to sell, but generally it is a free market. There is a black market in contracts for co-op property; it is also common for owners to illegally exchange a smaller property for a bigger one so that they finally end up with a big villa.

In Stockholm there is a 10-year waiting list for public housing, so there is not much chance for foreigners to get into this system. Elsewhere you have a much better chance of being allowed to buy into a co-operative.

Finance

Raising finance for a mortgage in Sweden may be impossible if you are not intending to reside there for a long period of time. Mortgages are arranged with banks as well as with specialised mortgage lenders. and you will need to discuss your individual needs with the finance company or bank. The main mortgage bank is Stadshypotek; see www.stadshypotek.se or call 020-75 00 31 for more information.

Taxation

A tax reduction of 25% of interest outgoings is allowed for interest expenses on owner-occupied houses and tenant-owned homes. As from 2001 property tax is levied at 1% of the assessed value of apartments and houses. This represents a reduction in tax from 1.5% payable in 1998. If you only occupy the property for part of the year you pay in proportion to the annual amount. For the residential part of newly built properties no real estate tax is levied for the first five years, and for the following five it is paid at half the usual rate. A general assessment takes place every other year; if the property has undergone material changes then a special assessment is carried out. The assessment is designed in such a way that the value generally equals 75% of the market value. Capital gains tax of 30% is levied on half the profits from the sale of owner-occupied and tenant-owner property. Full capital gains tax is levied on income from renting out properties, where this does not constitute business income.

RENTING PROPERTY

About 40% of Sweden's dwellings are rented and almost all rented dwellings carrying tenancy rights are to be found in blocks of flats. Standards regarding the cost of renting property are carefully monitored in Swedish housing property under the utility value provisions legislation. This ensures that the rent for a flat may not be significantly higher than that of another flat in the same area which is of roughly the same value. In public housing (usually flats), the rent is set by negotiation between the corporation and the tenant organisation. Public housing rents usually include the cost of maintenance, management and capital expenditure. In privately owned property in 90% of cases the rent is set by negotiations between the landlord and a tenant organisation; costs incurred by the landlord are not normally taken into account.

Usually tenants enjoy right of tenure and in some cases may transfer their rented flat to another person when they move on. In the past the costs of rent in the private and public sector were comparable, but there is now more of a variation between the two sectors. Nonetheless, Sweden's rental system is generally favourable towards tenants and tenants' rights are respected.

The availability of rented accommodation varies throughout the country. Finding rented accommodation in Stockholm is difficult but rather easier in Gothenburg and Malmö; most vacant apartments will be found in the suburbs. You can advertise for rented accommodation in local and regional papers or go through municipal and private housing companies (look under *bostadsföretag* in the yellow pages). To find a sub-let apartment through an agency look in the yellow pages under *bostadsförmedling*. Agencies charge a fee for this service. Sub-let apartments can be found in newspaper adverts and are comparatively easy to find. About 7-12% of apartments are sub-let illegally; the tenants move to a cheaper place and add on 60% or more to the original rent; the added-on rent is known as *överhyra*. The practice is particularly common with apartments close to Stockholm city centre. There are of course risks in sub-letting illegally; rental agencies are not necessarily aware that an apartment is being sub-let without the owner's permission.

Monthly rentals for apartments and houses are highest in the more desirable area near the centre of Stockholm, such as Danderyd, Lidingö and Solna. There are also areas which one might want to avoid, in particular Rinkeby. For central Stockholm one can typically expect to pay SEK4,700 (approx. £320/US$455) for 75 sq.m. (big enough for two people); and SEK8,000 for 120 sq.m. Rental for flats built or renovated in the past five years is about 20% higher than the average.

2 RK/rum och kök	2 rooms and kitchen
1 KV/rum och kokvrå	1 room and kitchenette
andrahandslägenhet	sub-let apartment
bytesrum	room to exchange
hiss	lift (elevator)
hyra	rent
möblerad	furnished
omöblerad	unfurnished
sovrum	bedroom
tvättinrättning	laundry

Given the problems with finding rented accommodation on the open market, it is perhaps not surprising that the largest non-governmental organisation in Sweden is the *Hyresgästernasriksförbund* (Union of Tenants) which has 560,000 members. If you are interested in housing, as the Swedes evidently are, then it is well worth getting hold of this organisation's excellent publications, in particular *Vår Bostad* (Our House) the most popular magazine in Sweden.

Housing policy in Sweden is directed by the National Board of Housing, Building and Planning (*Boverket*). Credit guarantees for development come under the National Housing Credit Guarantee Board (*Statens Bostadskreditnänd*). The Ministry of Finance also issues information in English on house-building, e.g. *Housing and Housing Policy in Sweden*.

Useful Addresses

The Swedish Union of Tenants Association, Norrlandsgatan 7, S-103 92 Stockholm; ☎08-791 02 00; fax 08 20 53 24; e-mail info.forbundet@hyresgasterna.se; www.hyresgasterna.se.
Boverket, www.boverket.se.
Ministry of Finance, www.finans.regeringen.se.
Statens Bostadseditnänd, www.bkn.se/english.html.

PURCHASING PROPERTY

If you can afford to buy property in Sweden you should find the purchasing procedure relatively straightforward. Real estate brokers (the equivalent of estate agents) can be found through the daily papers or in the yellow pages under *fastighetsmäklare*. The two leading nationwide housing associations are HSB and Riksbyggen. A lot of property is advertised on the *Dagens Nyheter* website: www.dn.se.

For more details about real estate brokers in Sweden and for a list of local brokers look at the Swedish Association of Real Estate Brokers' website, www.maklarsamfundet.se, or contact Mäklarsamfundet, Svärdvägen 25A, 182 33 Danderyd; ☎08-544 96 550. Table 14 gives approximate figures for property prices at the start of 2002 in SEK: as a basis for comparison, SEK500,000 is worth approx £34,000/US$485,000.

TABLE 14	PROPERTY PRICES IN SEK		
Area	1-bed flat	2-bed flat	3-bed house
Stockholm Centre	1,300,000	2,250,000	3,800,000
Greater Stockholm	810,000	1,350,000	1,900,000
Göteborg	450,000	680,000	1,500,000
Malmö	310,000	460,000	1,000,000

Mortgages

Banks and mortgage institutions will lend up to 90% of the market value of a property. Interest rates stood at 4.8 to 5.4% in 2002, for floating (*rörlig*) rates. The website www.comboloan.se has a ready reckoner for mortgage costs, which will show all the offers available and work out your monthly mortgage costs after your 25% interest deduction.

UTILITIES

There are high standards of heating and insulation in Sweden which, given the climate, is probably a good thing. In apartment blocks it is usual for there to be laundry facilities in the basement for general use, although the amount of time you can spend using them is fiercely regulated by elderly ladies employed as laundry attendants.

The electrical current in Sweden is 220 volts A/C, 50 cycles; American equipment may not work properly unless it can be switched to 50 cycles. Transformers must be able to handle the wattage of the equipment.

Utility companies are either private or owned by the municipality. Some companies will also supply broadband internet and telephone services. Gas is not available everywhere in Sweden. The following are some of the main companies:

Göteborg Energi Nät, Johan Willins g. 3, Box 53, 401 20 Göteborg; ☎020-62 62 62; fax 031-15 63 40; www.goteborgenergi.se.

Sydkraft, Carl Gustafs väg 1, 205 09 Malmö; ☎400-25 50 00; www.sydkraft.se.

Vattenfall Customer Service, Box 10702, 121 29 Stockholm; ☎020-82 00 00; fax 08-725 05 01; e-mail kundservice@vattenfall.se.

Installing a Telephone

Your first telephone has to be installed by the state-owned Telia. The basic service, called a Telia Bas Abonnemang, costs SEK975 (approx. £66/US$95) for the initial connection, plus SEK125 per month rental. Rental charges are paid quarterly in advance.

Telephone directories are available on the internet. The Gula Sidorna (Yellow Pages) are on www.gulasidorna.se, and the White Pages on http://privatpersoner.gulasidorna.se.

For mobile phones, try the following numbers: Comviq/Tele2: 0200-22 20 40; Telia/Dof: 903-50; Europolitan: 020-22 22 22.

RELOCATORS

The task of relocators is to help employees of foreign companies to settle in quickly when posted abroad. Their services are not cheap, but they save employers a lot of money by ensuring that transfers are done as smoothly as possible. Services range from helping with immigration formalities, finding accommodation, looking at schools, to being on the end of a phone for 24 hours a day in case of emergencies. There are just a few relocators in Sweden:

Europatria, Box 10142; 100 55 Stockholm; 08-545 895 40; fax 08-545 895 49; info@europatria.com; www.europatria.com.

RelocSweden, Kopenhamnsvägen 112, 217 71 Malmö; ☎40 98 23 73; e-mail info@relocsweden.com.

SAS Relocation Services, Dept WK-H, 195 87 Stockholm; ☎87 97 55 86; e-mail sas.relocation@sas.se.

REMOVALS

Moving house to somewhere as far away as Sweden is inevitably going to be expensive. If you can leave the job to a removals company then it may not be that different from moving in the UK. The process could be a lot simpler if you could reduce your possessions to the contents of a car boot but this is not always practical, particularly if you are moving abroad for a long period. Even though Sweden is the home of pine furniture the price of setting up a home from scratch will be high and you may not particularly like the Ikea look anyway.

Moving goods to Sweden from the UK could cost several thousand pounds. It is not even worth using a removals company unless you have at least six cubic metres of goods to move. You would be better off using your car. If you are going to use a removals company, then go for an experienced removals company with international experience. The British Association of Removers produces a useful leaflet for anyone thinking about moving overseas, and can also give names of companies that do removals to Sweden. Send a SAE to the address below.

Useful Addresses

BAR, 3 Churchill Court, 58 Station Road, North Harrow, Middlesex HA2 7SA; ☎020-8861 3331; fax 020-8861 3332; e-mail info@bar.co.uk; www.barmovers.com.

Crown Relocations, 5252 Argosy Drive, Huntington Beach, CA 92469, USA; ☎714-898-0961; e-mail general.ususa@crownpacific.com.

Household Goods Forwarders Association of America, www.hhgfaa.org.

EXPORTING A UK-REGISTERED CAR

If you plan to take your car out of the UK for more than 12 months, you must notify its export to the Driver and Vehicle Licence Agency in Swansea; they will send you a certificate V561 for registering abroad. If you are going abroad for less than a year, you need to take the registration document with you, or apply for a temporary certificate of registration from the DVLA. See website www.dvla.co.uk for further information.

Importing a Car

EU citizens may import a car as part of their removal goods (flyttsaker), as long as it is at least six months old. Your car does not have to be brought into Sweden at the same time as your other household goods; goods can be brought in over a 12-month period. You should bring the original invoice, and the registration and insurance documents with you. As soon as you have passed through customs you need to have your vehicle inspected at a Bilprovningsstation, and apply for provisional or full registration. The car will be inspected to make sure that it conforms to EU regulations on emission controls. Older cars may need to have a catalyst installed.

The customs authorities automatically notify the National Road Administration that you have brought a foreign-registered car into the country. Even tourists are only allowed to drive in Sweden in a foreign-registered car for one week. The inspection stations are listed on the website www.bilprovningen.se. To book an inspection call 0771-600 600, or call the customer service on 0711-600 800.

For non-EU citizens, it is also possible to bring your car in as part of your household goods, as long as you have been resident outside the EU for 12 months. You must be able to prove that you have owned the car for 12 months; you are not allowed to sell, rent or lend out the car for one year after import. Cars can only be imported by someone who has permission to stay in Sweden for at least three months, and who already has their *personnummer.* The car has to be inspected to see that it conforms to EU norms, at one of the ten *Bilprovningsstationer* that can carry out a *Komponentkontroll* (listed on the website).

If for some reason you cannot bring the car in as part of household goods, the taxes are very heavy, basically 10% import duty, plus 25% VAT on the car's value and the shipping costs. In this case it is probably not worth importing a car into the country.

Useful Addresses

Bilprovning (Vehicle Inspection Company), ☎0771-600 800 or 08-759 21 00; e-mail kundtjanst@bilprovningen.se; www.bilprovningen.se.
Bilregistret (Vehicle Register), ☎077-114 15 16.
Tullverket (Swedish Customs), ☎0771-520 520; e-mail huvudkontoret@tullverket.se; www.tullverket.se.
Vägverket (National Road Administration), ☎0243-750 00; e-mail vagverket@vv.se; www.vv.se.

IMPORTING PETS

Regulations for importing a dog or cat to Sweden are strict. Cats and dogs can be imported from a rabies-free country (UK, Ireland, Norway, Iceland, Australia, New Zealand, Mauritius, Hawaii) without going into quarantine, as long as you comply with the conditions for obtaining an import licence, which is issued by the Animal Disease Control Division of the National Board of Agriculture (*Statens Jordbruksverk*), based in Jököping. Vaccination against rabies, and other diseases, treatment for tapeworm, as well as having a microchip implanted or a tattoo are part of the requirements. The animal has to have remained in a rabies-free country for six months, or since birth, before departure; transit through a country where rabies is present means four months quarantine, unless you can ship the animal in a sealed container.

Your nominated veterinarian is required to obtain the Veterinary Health Certificate form from the Board of Agriculture. You will be issued with an import licence which allows you to import up to 10 cats and dogs during one year. If your pet has a microchip implant you are required to supply your own microchip reader; some customs stations have equipment to read microchips but there is no guarantee that they will have the right equipment. You can contact the customs service on 0771-520 520 to see if a customs station has microchip reading equipment.

If you bring in a cat or dog from any other country apart from the ones listed above then it has to go into quarantine for four months. Quarantine facilities for cats and dogs are available in Linköping, and for dogs only in Vallentuna. Pets from abroad can only be brought in at a manned customs station. All dogs and cats will be examined by a vet on arrival in Sweden, and given further treatments where required. The *Jordbruksverk* will be happy to give you any information you need (see below).

If you intend to bring your pet back with you from Sweden to the UK, or you acquire a pet in Sweden and wish to bring it back with you, it may no longer be necessary to put your animal into quarantine, as long as you follow the right procedures. For information on the Pets Travel Scheme look at the UK Department of the Environment, Food and Rural Affairs website: www.defra.gov.uk, or call 0870-241 1710. In general, DEFRA does not give information on exporting animals from the UK, only on importing them.

Useful Addresses

Animal Disease Control Division, National Board of Agriculture, Vallgatan 8, 551 82 Jönköping; ☎036-15 50 00; fax 036-15 50 05; e-mail jordbruksverket@sjv.se.

Djurskyddsförening, Göteborg (Gothenburg Animal Protection Society), Mölndalsv. 6, 435 42 Mölnlycke; ☎031-88 88 80.

Djurskyddsförening, Svenska (Swedish Animal Protection Society), Erik Dahlbergsg. 28, Box 10081, 100 55 Stockholm; ☎08-783 03 68; www.djurskydd.org.

Tullverket (Swedish Customs), ☎0771-520 520; www.tullverket.se.

DAILY LIFE

Sweden is one of the most efficient states in Europe and life in Sweden has a justifiable reputation for running smoothly. Red tape is kept to a minimum – passports can be issued in ten minutes providing the applicant has the necessary information, registering a car under another name takes two weeks, the results of blood tests are usually given on the same day, divorces take one or two months (there is a compulsory six-month trial separation if children are involved), a phone can be installed in five days although cancellation takes only one hour, marriages can take place within a day, providing there is no hindrance, and birth registration forms are completed and sent off by the hospital without you having to raise a finger. If all that sounds too good to be true, it gets better – even the trains run on time. Nonetheless, moving to any foreign country necessarily involves upheaval and a period of getting to grips with new customs and a new way of life. Whilst some initial disorientation is inevitable, what follows is an overview which may help you deal with some of the basic day-to-day realities which influence life in Sweden.

THE LANGUAGE

Like most of their Scandinavian cousins, the Swedes have an impressive facility for acquiring foreign languages. Their perfectionist bent means they usually speak English better than other foreign learners. English is taught in Swedish schools between the ages of 5 and 18; children can also take German and French later on. You should have no trouble making yourself understood amongst all sectors of the population (with the possible exception of the very young and the elderly). The influence of British and American television means that many Swedes hear English spoken daily and they will inevitably listen to the words in English rather than relying on the subtitles.

The Swedish language is a north Germanic language and shares similarities with Norwegian, Danish and Icelandic but there has also been a Finnish, French and English influence. Regional dialects in Sweden are gradually being eroded through the influences of education and the mass media. Spoken Swedish is most noted for its tone or pitch which gives it a distinctive singsong sound. There are three letters of the alphabet which are peculiar to Sweden: Å, Ö and Å; all come after the letter Z in the alphabet. Swedish is the most widely spoken of the Scandinavian languages (an estimated 17.5 million people speak it world-wide) and it is understood by most people in Norway and Denmark.

Those wanting to learn Swedish will find books and tapes readily available and may find that it is on offer at local evening classes. Both the Berlitz Language Schools and Linguarama offer courses in Swedish (see below) in different parts of Britain, and Linguaphone offer a course of tapes/compact discs and books for home-study. Facilities for studying Swedish in the USA are shown on the University of Minnesota website: http://carla.acad.umn.edu/lctl/access.html under *Course Offerings for Less Commonly Taught Languages*. Free online Swedish dictionaries are available at: www.yourdictionary.com.

There is extensive provision for learning Swedish in Sweden and if you want to take advantage of it you should contact *Skolverket* in Sweden (for address see below). Students who wish to study at a Swedish university can arrange for an examination through the municipal adult education scheme or can take the Swedish Language Test for Academic Purposes. Details of this can be obtained through embassies or through the Institute for English-speaking Students in Sweden (see below). Immigrants or refugees are entitled to free Swedish classes for three hours a day. These are available throughout Sweden and are run by the SFI (*Svenska För Invandrare*). You can be taken on to a SFI course as long as you have a fixed address in Sweden and some ID.

Useful Addresses

The Berlitz School of Languages, 321 Oxford Street, London W1A 3BZ; ☎020-7408 2474; www.berlitz.com.

Linguaphone, 111 Upper Richmond Rd, London SW15 2TJ; ☎020-8333 4898; www.linguaphone.co.uk, www.linguaphone.com/usa.

Linguarama, Oceanic House, 89 High Street, Alton, Hants GU34 1LG; ☎01420-80899; www.linguarama.com.

Svenska För Invandrare Mottagningen, Magnus Ladulåsg. 63 BV,118 27 Stockholm; ☎08-508 334 40; fax 08-508 334 60.

Skolverket, 106 20 Stockholm; ☎08-723 32 00; e-mail skolverket@skolverket.se; www.skolverket.se.

SCHOOLS AND EDUCATION

Educational policy comes under the National Agency for Education (*Skolverket*). State education is free. Recently there has been an increase in the number of independent schools, particularly catering for religious minorities. Parents are free to choose a school outside their municipality, or to send the children to an independent school. All schools have to be approved by the National Agency for Education. The number of private or independent schools has increased in recent years. Independent schools receive municipal grants depending on the number of pupils. Around 2% of pupils attend such schools.

Primary and Secondary Education

Compulsory primary education was introduced into Sweden as early as 1842.

Swedish children attend a compulsory 10 years of comprehensive school (*grundskola*) from the age of six (before 1997 it was from the age of seven). Until 1995 the comprehensive school system was divided into three stages of three years each: lower, middle and upper. Now that these divisions have been done away with pupils are evaluated in the fifth and ninth grades. About 90% of all children continue from the comprehensive school to the upper secondary school (*gymnasieskola*). In the upper secondary school the curriculum is divided into university- and vocationally-oriented programmes which take place over three years. In recent years this curriculum has been revised and is now aimed at being more knowledge-oriented; vocational courses which used to take two years now take three. Books and lunches are provided free.

Children are entitled to enter upper secondary school up to the age of 20. After that they have to go into the adult education system; if they succeed then they are entitled to go to university.

Higher Education

Sweden has 13 major universities; the oldest at Uppsala was founded in 1477. Higher education is available at 30 locations. About 35% of those completing upper secondary school continue directly on to some form of higher education although the government is trying to increase this figure. Course fees are paid for by the state throughout the higher education system up to doctorate level, although most students pay for their own board and lodging and books. Government grants and loans for education are widely available and no one is excluded because of lack of money. Sweden has a good record on research, particularly in science and technology and a large proportion of research funds come from business. About 40,000 young adults a year attend long-term courses, and another 150,000 short-term courses, at one of Sweden's 147 Folk High Schools.

The National Schools for Adults (SSV) run courses for adults who are not able to attend a school near where they live. The tuition is mainly by distance learning, with tutored instruction from time to time. There are National Schools for Adults in Norrköping and Härnosand.

Foreign Students

The Swedish authorities encourage international exchanges. The University of Stockholm runs a graduate programme in social sciences for students already enrolled on a master's or doctoral programme in an accredited university. EU citizens can get grants to study in Sweden through the Erasmus scheme. Students are required to show sufficient funds to support themselves, currently SEK6,000 (approx. £408/US$580) a month. In the EU the Eurydice programme provides information on academic programmes in Sweden.

Americans can follow summer programmes at Swedish universities. The programmes are listed on the American-Scandinavian Foundation website. The Swedish Institute produces several leaflets in English, such as *Study in Sweden: A Guide for Foreign Students, Masters Degree Programs,* and *A Student Handbook for Visiting Students and Researchers,* available from the Swedish Information Service in the USA, or the Swedish Institute in Stockholm.

Useful Addresses

American-Scandinavian Foundation, Scandinavia House, 58 Park Avenue, New York, NY 10016; ☎212-879-9779; e-mail info@amscan.org; www.amscan.org.

Erasmus UK, Socrates Erasmus Council, R&D Building, The University, Canterbury, Kent CT2 7PD; ☎01227-762712; fax 01227 762711; erasmus@ukc.ac.uk; www.erasmus.ac.uk.

Eurydice, Eurydice unit for England, Wales & Northern Ireland, National Foundation for Educational Research, The Mere, Upton Park, Slough, Berkshire SL1 2DQ; ☎01753-574123; fax 01753-531458; e-mail eurydice@nfer.ac.uk; www.nfer.ac.uk/eurydice.

International Graduate Programme (IGP), Stockholm University, 106 91 Stockholm; ☎016-34 66; e-mail info@igp.su.se; http://www.igp.su.se.

The Swedish Information Service, One Dag Hammarskjold Plaza, 45th Floor, New York, NY 10017-2201; ☎212-583-2550; e-mail swedinfo@ix.netcom.com.

The Swedish Institute, Sweden House, Hamngatan 27, Kungsträdgården, Stockholm; www.si.se.

Adult Education

About a quarter of the adult population in Sweden has a higher education. Continuing and adult education play an important part in Swedish life. An average of one in three adults is engaged in some kind of educational programme available at folk high schools, on courses run by government and employment agencies, or through one of the 11 nationwide adult education associations. Adult education receives subsidies from central and local government and is usually affiliated with a special interest organisation or a political party.

Study circles are very popular in Swedish adult education – these are run as informal gatherings of adults with a common educational interests and attract government funding. Radio and television courses are available for people who are unable to attend education centres. For further details contact the Folk High School Information Centre (Box 740, 101 35 Stockholm; ☎08-796 00 50; fax 08-21 88 26; e-mail fin@folkbildning.se; www.folkbildning.se; visiting address is Västmannagatan 1).

International Education

A number of English-speaking schools cater for children whose parents have temporarily moved to Sweden. International schools offer the International Baccalaureate (IB), an international curriculum that qualifies students to enter universities in any country. Some schools offer the Swedish upper secondary curriculum taught in English; tests in English are substituted for the Swedish state examinations. The curriculum is often designed to ensure proficiency in both languages; some Swedish schools have an international section that offers the IB. The children of foreigners who attend Swedish schools are entitled to lessons in both their own native language at school and extra Swedish tuition. If you want information about state schools you should contact the education authority (Skolverket). The internet site has a search engine which allows you to look for courses and schools in your area. Contact Skolverket, Kungsgatan 53, 106 20 Stockholm; ☎08-723 32 00; www.skolverket.se/kursinfo.

For general information about schools in Europe contact the European Council of International Schools, 21 Lavant Street, Petersfield, Hampshire GU32 3EL; ☎01730-268244; www.ecis.org. For information about the International Baccalaureate in Sweden contact The Associate Regional Director for Europe, International Baccalaureate Nordic Countries, Johannesgatan 18, 11138 Stockholm; ☎08-24 00 51; fax 08-24 00 52; e-mail IBSW@ibo.org.

Useful Addresses

Stockholm

British International Primary School of Stockholm, Östra Valhallavägen 17, 182 62 Djursholm, Stockholm; ☎08-755 23 75; fax 08-755 26 35; www.britishprimaryschool.se (3-11). Offers the UK national curriculum.

Engelska Skolan Norr, Roslagstullbacken 4, 114 22 Stockholm; ☎08-441 8580; fax 08-673 29 15; e-mail info@engelskanorr.com; www.engelskanorr.com (6-16). Modified Swedish curriculum. English and Swedish medium.

Engelska Skolan Söder, Lingvägen 123; 122 45 Enskede; ☎08-505 533 00; fax 08-505 533 11; e-mail info@engelska.se; www.engelska.se (12-19). Swedish national curriculum. English and Swedish medium.

International School in Nacka, Brantvägen 1, Box 4003, 133 04 Saltsjöbaden; ☎08-718 83 00; fax 08-718 83 02; www.isn.nacka.se (12-20). Swedish national curriculum; IB.

International School of Stockholm, Johannesgatan 18, 111 38 Stockholm; ☎08-412 40 00; fax 08-412 40 01; e-mail admin@intsch.se; www.intsch.se (4-15). Offers the US and UK national curriculum.

Kungsholmen's Gymnasium, Hantverkargatan 67-69, Box 12601, 112 92 Stockholm; ☎08-508 380 00; fax 08-508 380 01; www.kun.edu.stockholm.se

(15-19). Swedish national curriculum and IB.

Montessoriförskolan Bellmanskällan, The Secret Garden, Brådstupsvägen 9, 129 39 Hägersten; ☎08-97 32 05; fax 08-97 30 27 (3-5).

Sigtunaskolan Humanistiska Laroverket, International Section, PO Box 508, 193 28 Sigtuna; ☎08-592 571 00; fax 08-592 572 50; e-mail info@sshl.se; www.sshl.se (13-19). Offers the Swedish national curriculum and IB. Has boarding facilities.

The Tanto School, Flintbacken 20, 118 42 Stockholm; ☎08-669 71 71; fax 08-643 09 94; www.tantoschool.org (6-12). English national curriculum.

Gothenburg

Hvitfeldtska Gymnasiet, International Section, Rektorsgatan 2, 411 33 Göteborg; ☎031-778 64 52/4; fax 031-81 17 97; e-mail agneta.santesson@educ.goteborg.se; www.hvitfeldt.educ.goteborg.se (16-20). Offers Swedish Natural Science curriculum and IB.

English School in Gothenburg, Redegatan 2, 426 77 Västra Frölunda; tel/fax 031-29 80 24; www.theenglishschool.se (3-16). English and Swedish curriculum.

The International Preschool, Allmänna vägen 13, 414 60 Göteborg; ☎031-42 33 35.

MEDIA AND COMMUNICATIONS

Newspapers and Magazines

Swedes are avid newspaper readers and the average newspaper circulation is 534 per 1,000 people. The most popular daily is *Expressen* with a daily circulation of 566,000, followed by the independent liberal newspaper *Dagens Nyheter*, with 400,000, and the conservative *Svenska Dagbladet* with 220,000. In Gothenburg the most popular paper is the liberal *Göteborg-Posten* (circulation 187,000) and in Malmö it is *Sydsvenska Dagbladet* (circulation 148,000). The main business paper is *Dagens Industri*. Apart from the national newspapers Sweden has a wide selection of regional papers and popular, trade and organisational magazines. Magazines published by the trade union organisations reach a wide readership and play an important role in public debate.

Traditionally Swedish papers have been linked to political parties and this is still true to some extent – a number of papers are party owned – but in Sweden priority is given to critical monitoring of people in power. The Freedom of the Press Act guarantees the protection of anonymous sources, gives journalists freedom of access to public documents and establishes procedures in trials involving freedom of the press issues, making it very difficult to win damages against journalists. A press ombudsman supervises the adherence to ethical standards within the press. On top of that there are state subsidies for the press.

British newspapers are available in Stockholm and a wide selection of foreign publications can be found at the Press Centre (*Gallerian*: Hamngatan, Sveavägen 52, Stockholm) and at the Central Station. The annex to the main public library in Stockholm at Odengatan 59, has a good selection of foreign newspapers; it is also open on Sunday afternoons. The following are the websites of Sweden's main daily newspapers:

Expressen, www.expressen.se.
Dagens Industri, www.di.se.
Dagens Nyheter, www.dn.se.
Svenska Dagbladet, www.svd.se.
Göteborgs-Posten, www.gp.se.
Sydsvenska Dagbladet, www.sydsvenskan.se.

Television and Radio

Radio and Television in Sweden come under the umbrella of the Swedish Broadcasting Corporation which was modelled on the BBC. The main TV channels are TV1 and TV2, which do not show advertising. There are also satellite and cable channels, the Nordic channel TV3 which is also available in Denmark and Norway, and also TV5. Private companies can broadcast TV via satellite and cable to a large proportion of Swedish households. The Swedish Broadcasting Company is mainly financed by household licences, but now it runs a commercial channel, TV4, with English programming. There are many imported foreign programmes on Swedish TV and you can usually tune into a familiar English or American soap opera even inside the Arctic Circle.

Swedish radio has expanded in recent years. Radio Sweden International has an impressive range of foreign language broadcasts on 1179KHz. Check the website www.sr.se/rs for times of broadcasts. Radio Stockholm International broadcasts on 89.6FM in the Stockholm area. You can also tune into the BBC World Service on 9410KMHz (www.bbc.co.uk/worldservice). Radio Bandit blasted onto the Swedish airwaves in 1994. Bandit is an all-English commercial radio station owned by Americans; tune in on 105.5.FM.

The Postal System

The Swedish postal system is highly efficient. Post offices in Sweden are usually open Monday to Friday from 9.30am to 6pm and from 10am to 1pm on Saturdays. The post office at the Central Station in Stockholm is open Monday to Friday 7am to 10pm and on Saturdays and Sundays from 10am to 7pm. The main post office in Stockholm at Drottninggaten 53 is open Monday to Friday from 8am to 6.30pm and on Saturday from 10am to 2pm. For questions about postal services in Sweden call the free number 020-23 22 21 or e-mail kundtjanst@posten.se.

Post boxes in Sweden are yellow or blue. The blue ones are for local post.

Telephones

Post offices generally do not have telephone facilities but there are a few *Telebutik* telephone offices including the Telecenter at the Central Station in Stockholm which is open daily from 8am to 9pm. There are three methods of payment for public phone calls: money (currently accepts 1 SEK and 5 SEK), *Telefonkort* (Telephone card) and credit card. *Telefonkorten* can be bought from *Telebutiker* and hospitals. Pay phones are widely available in Sweden; red pay phones have replaced the old green ones. A local call currently costs a minimum of SEK2.

To call abroad dial 00 followed by the country code. To call Sweden from abroad dial 00 46. For directory enquiries in Sweden call 118 118 and for other foreign enquiries call 118 119.

Emergency Numbers

In an emergency call 112 for the police, fire brigade or ambulance. The number is free and you will not need coins for a call box. In the case of serious illness or death, Radio Sweden can broadcast urgent messages in emergencies. See www.sr.se. In a Swedish telephone directory the letters ä, ö and å come after the letter Z. The letters V and W are treated as the same at the beginnings of names.

CARS AND MOTORING

Roads

Roads in Sweden are well maintained; away from cities and towns can often be empty for many miles at a stretch. Sweden's 49,600 miles/80,000km of roads vary in type: four-lane motorways on the busiest stretches, *motorled* or conventional two-lane roads, and *grus* or gravel roads, which tend to be rather more off the beaten track. The motorway network is fairly small and where the motorways run out the *motorleder* take over. Effectively the *motorleder* are two-lane main roads with hard shoulders. The hard shoulders are used as additional lanes in the event of overtaking (the driver being overtaken moves onto it).

The E04 Arctic Highway is Sweden's main route. It starts in Helsingborg in the south-west, runs via Jönköping and Norrköping to Stockholm, then through Uppsala and along the coast right up to Haparanda on the Finnish border. Driving west from Stockholm, the E18 provides a direct route to Oslo and neighbouring Norway. Sweden's south coast is served by a good network of major and minor roads, reflecting the greater size of the population in the south. Further north roads become progressively fewer and large tracts of land are not served by road although all towns and cities can be reached.

Petrol is available throughout Sweden although you should stock up on a full tank if you are covering long distances, particularly in the north, and as a precaution it's a good idea to carry a can of spare fuel. Fuel is very expensive in Sweden; the price of diesel is the second highest in Europe. The majority of petrol stations are self-service: this is indicated by the sign *Tanka Själv*; many have automatic pumps (*Sedel Automat*) which can be used 24 hours a day. Automatic pumps are usually slightly cheaper. Payment is generally with a credit card. The sign *Konto* on a pump indicates that it is for local account holders.

Weather

Not surprisingly, many roads in the north become impassable in winter. Studded tyres and snow chains are compulsory for mountainous and difficult terrain. Studded tyres can only be used when there is snow; the dates for starting and stopping with studded tyres are announced in the media. The *Vagverk* (Swedish National Road Administration) posts weather information on its website. You can also have a special receiver installed in your car which allows you to receive radio-transmitted messages on weather conditions, known as the Traffic Message Channel. The service operates 24 hours a day and is free of charge.

Breakdowns and Accidents

Sweden has a relatively low rate of accidents considering the driving conditions. The death toll of around 590 a year is considered too high, and the government has embarked on an ambitious campaign to eliminate road deaths altogether. Swedes are excessively careful drivers; there is a law that obliges drivers to stop if a pedestrian appears to be about to cross the road at a pedestrian crossing.

Traffic policy, maintenance of roads, and the application of regulations are all in the hands of the *Vägverket*. The major motoring organisation is *Motormännens Riksförbund* and their breakdown service is called *M Väghjälp*. There are numerous other local breakdown organisations. The website www.hjalpportalen.se lists every conceivable breakdown and emergency assistance organisation, for all conceivable accidents and 'unpleasant happenings' as they put it.

When there is an accident in Sweden it is mandatory to exchange names and addresses with the other party involved even in the case of non-serious accidents. The main hazards to look out for on Swedish roads are wild animals wandering on to the road – mainly reindeer in the north and elk in the north and further south. They can be particularly hard to spot in bad light and at twilight. As elk can weigh as much as 120 stone both you, and your car, will know if you collide with one.

Elk are involved in one-fifth of Swedish road accidents. For emergencies, ring your breakdown organisation or the police (112). You do not have to inform the police if an accident is not serious.

Useful Addresses

Motormännensriksförbund, Sveavägen 159, 104 35 Stockholm; ☎08-690 38 00; fax 08-690 38 24; www.motormannen.se.

M Väghjälp (Breakdown Service), ☎020-21 11 11 (enquiries), 020-91 11 11 (breakdowns); www.motormannen.se.

Vagverket, Röda vägen 1, 781 87 Borlänge; ☎0243-75 000; e-mail vagverket@vv.se; www.vv.se.

Inspections and Road Tax

Vehicles have to be inspected at intervals at a *Bilprovningsstation*; *Bilprovningen,* the Vehicle Inspection Company, is 52% owned by the state, and the rest by motoring organisations and private companies. The first inspection for new cars is after three years, then again after two years, and then annually thereafter. The time for inspection occurs within a five-month period, which depends on the final number on your licence plate. You will be notified by the National Road Administration when your inspection is due. Addresses of *Bilprovningsstationer* are given on the website: www.bilprovningen.se, as is an explanation of the whole inspection system.

You will be notified by the *Vägverk* when your vehicle tax *(fordonsskatt)* is due. Once you have paid up, you will receive a coloured sticker to put in your window. For lighter cars up to 900 kg you pay 585 kronor (approx. £40/US$56) per year; then an extra SEK149 for each additional 100 kg. Diesel vehicles are taxed much more heavily.

Bilprovningen, Customer Service, Box 508, 162 15 Vällingby; ☎0771-600 800; www.bilprovningen.se.

Vehicle Tax Office (Fordonskatteenhet), 701 87 Örebro; ☎019-674 50 00; fax 019-674 51 80; e-mail fordon@skm18.rsv.se.

Driving Regulations

Speed limits in Sweden are: 110kph/68mph on motorways, between 90kph/56mph and 70 kph/43mph on other roads, and 50kph/31mph in built up areas. In the summer (mid-June to mid-August) speed limits on motorways are dropped to 90kph on most routes. Driving on motorways forms part of the Swedish driving test.

Driving is on the right in Sweden and the main rule is to give way to traffic coming from the right unless the road signs indicate otherwise. Drivers of right-hand drive cars should adjust their headlights so that the beam sweeps to the right. Dipped headlights are obligatory both by day and by night. US cars need to have their indicator lights changed from amber to plain; speed indicators must show kph as well as or instead of mph. The driver and all passengers must use seat belts.

Parking: This is a vexed subject, particulary in Stockholm, where the regulations are enforced with draconian efficiency. The parking signs have a language all their own, which one could hardly do justice to in a paragraph. Where parking is payable you will see the word *Avgift* on a blue background, with the times of day when you have to pay, e.g. 9-22. The times in brackets refer to the days before Sundays and holidays; in red means Sundays and holidays are also not free. A more tricky one is a yellow sign with a day of the week and 0-6, meaning that the street is cleaned or cleared of snow between midnight and 6am. A *lastzon* is for unloading lorries. There are fines ranging from SEK425 to SEK700 for parking offences. For more information see the website www.gfk.stockholm.se.

Drink-Driving

Drink-driving regulations in Sweden are the toughest in the world and the best policy is simply not to drink and drive. The police have the power to stop drivers at any time to take a breathalyser test. The legal limit is a mere 20mg/100ml – less than one can of beer. Random breath tests are routine and if you are over the limit (a mere 0.02% of the blood alcohol content) you can expect fines, loss of licence and sometimes imprisonment. Driving with a blood alcohol level over 1.5% can lead to one year's imprisonment. Driving under the influence of drugs incurs comparable punishments. The regulations are applied to foreigners and Swedes alike; pleading ignorance of the law will not get you off.

Driving Licences

British and other EU licences (*förarbevis*) are valid in Sweden for as long as they are valid in one's home country. You can also exchange your licence for a Swedish one if you want. If your foreign licence is near its expiry date you need to contact the Driving Standards and Licencing Division to arrange to get a Swedish licence.

Holders of most other licences have to take a Swedish driving test within a year of arrival in Sweden. The only exceptions are licences issued in Switzerland and Japan which can be exchanged within the first year of becoming resident in Sweden.

Useful Address

Vagverket, Driving Standards and Licencing Division, ☎0243-750 00; e-mail vagverket@vv.se; www.vv.se.

Insurance

All vehicles registered abroad must carry international liability insurance and an accident report form. These are available from motoring organisations. You can, if need be, buy temporary insurance cover at the border. You should join the *Motormännens Riksforbund* if you are going to stay in Sweden. Insurance companies are listed under *försäkring* in the phone book.

Useful Addresses

Automobile Association (AA), Overseas Department, PO Box 2AA, Newcastle-upon-Tyne, NE99 2AA; ☎0870-606 1615; www.theaa.com.
RAC Motoring Services, Travel Services, PO Box 1500, Bristol BS99 1LH; ☎0800-550055; www.rac.co.uk.

Motormännens Riksförbund, Sveavägen 159, 104 35 Stockholm; ☎08-690 38 00; fax 08-690 38 24; www.motormannen.se.

TRANSPORT

Rail

The Swedish State Railway Company (Statens Järnvägar or SJ) operates one of Europe's most efficient, punctual and scenic train services. Bookings can be made through German Rail in London. The website – www.sj.se – allows you to plan your journey; it is worth bearing in mind that many remote places have only a few trains a day. Not all the trains are run by SJ; some local services (*läntrafik)* are run by the counties. One service from Stockholm to Narvik in the north is run by *Tägkompaniet* (www.tagplus.se).

Swedish trains have been substantially upgraded in recent years and innovations include sleeping cars with en-suite toilets and showers, family coaches with play areas for children and even cinema coaches for trains travelling to the north of Sweden. The Rolls Royce of the Swedish railway system is the X2000 high speed train, can take you from Stockholm to Gothenburg in three hours at speeds of 125 mph. There is a supplement for travelling on the X2000, but there are facilities included such as newspapers, headphones and telephones. Many trains require reservations, particularly on long journeys, and these can usually be made up to the time of departure. There are frequent departures of the Inter Nord trains which travel between the three Scandinavian capitals of Stockholm, Copenhagen and Oslo. These travel both day and night and have restaurant cars and cafeterias. Since the opening of the Øresund bridge and tunnel there are through trains from Copenhagen to various destinations in Sweden.

One of the few good deals in this part of the world is the Scanrail Pass, which allows unlimited travel on five days out of 15 in the Nordic countries, and other formulas, and includes discounts on some ferries and tourist attractions. It can be bought in advance in the UK from German Rail. In the USA it can be bought via travel agents; look at the website www.raileurope.com. Rail tickets for Sweden can be bought through Sweden Booking, an organisation based in Visby on the island of Gotland.

Useful Addresses

German Rail (UK), ☎08702-43 53 63; e-mail sales@deutsche-bahn.co.uk. *Sweden Booking,* ☎0498-20 33 80; fax 0498-20 33 90; e-mail info@swedenbooking.com; www.swedenbooking.com.

Domestic Flights

Internal air travel can save a considerable amount of travelling time in Sweden, particularly in the north where towns are far apart. The main agent for internal flights is SAS Scandinavian Airlines. If you book a return flight with SAS from the UK or USA, you can get a Visit Scandinavia Air Pass which consists of discount coupons for flights within Denmark, Norway, Sweden and Finland. With these coupons you can take internal flights for around $75 to $145; you can buy a maximum of eight coupons at a time, and they have to be used up within three months.

There are other good deals you can buy in Sweden itself, notably off-peak fares and 'micro-fares', which are return flights, which can knock up to 60% off the price, but they have to be booked two weeks in advance. Contact SAS on 020-727 555, or see the website www.scandinavian.net.

Boats and Ferries

There are frequent ferry services to neighbouring countries. Ferry trips have been traditionally popular as they are an opportunity to drink cheap alcohol. Prices from Stockholm to Finland can be extraordinarily cheap. The ferries to Denmark are loaded with people making the trip to stock up on cheap alcohol. There is also a thriving trade in taking the empties back.

There are plenty of ferry crossings to neighbouring countries. Scandinavian Ferry lines operate the ferry route from Elsinor in Denmark to Helsingborg in Sweden. This crossing should take 25 minutes but it is very busy and can take up to an hour. The following is a selection of services between Sweden and neighbouring countries (courtesy of the Swedish Travel and Tourism Council). Almost all run at least once a day; some may not run in bad weather.

The archipelago off Sweden's coastline has given rise to almost an armada of local boat services and there are ferry services from the mainland to the islands throughout the coastal regions. For further details and for sailings along Sweden's Göta Canal which links the Baltic Sea with the North Sea contact Norwegian State Railways (see above for address).

Useful Addresses

DFDS Seaways, 0870-533 3000 (UK), 031-650 650; www.dfdsseaways.com. Helsingborg to Oslo (Norway).

Estline, 08-667 00 01; www.estline.ee. Stockholm to Tallinn (Estonia).

Lisco Line, 08-667 52 35; www.shipping.lt. Stockholm to Klaipeda (Lithuania).

Mono Line, 08-667 52 35; www.shipping.lt. Stockholm to Riga (Latvia).

Polferries, 08-520 181 01; info@polferries.se. Ystad to Swinoujscie (Poland); Nynäshamn to Gdansk (Poland).

Scandlines, ☎042-18 61 00; www.scandlines.se. Helsingborg to Copenhagen; Helsingborg to Helsingör (Denmark); Malmö to Copenhagen.

Scandlines Hansa Ferry, ☎042-18 61 00; www.scandlines.se. Trelleborg to Sassnitz (Germany); Trelleborg to Rostock (Germany); Ystad to Sassnitz (Germany).

Stena Line, ☎0870-570 7070 (UK); www.stenaline.co.uk. Gothenburg to Frederikshavn (Denmark); Gothenburg to Kiel (Germany); Karlskrona to Gdynia (Poland)

Silja Line, ☎08-22 21 40; www.silja.com. Gothenburg to Frederikshavn (Denmark); Stockholm to Mariehamn-Turku-Helsinki (Finland).

Viking Line, 08-452 4000; www.vikingline.se. Stockholm to Mariehamn-Turku-Helsinki (Finland).

Buses and Public Transport

There is a network of express bus services which link towns and cities in southern and central Sweden. There are also regular services from Stockholm to the north. The main operator is Swebus Express: call 08-655 00 90; www.swebus.se.

Most Swedish towns and cities have a reliable and relatively cheap public transport system and in some cities buses operate 24 hours a day. Bus services are the mainstay of urban transport but Gothenburg and Norrköping also have trams, and Stockholm is serviced by a comprehensive underground called the *Tunnelbana* which is centred on T-Centralen station. Transport in Stockholm is operated by *Storstockholms Lokaltrafik* (☎08-600 10 00; www.sl.se). A ticket on the Stockholm public transport system, and other cities, allows you to ride for an hour on the *Tunnelbana* and buses. A multi-ride ticket will save you at least 40% on a single ticket.

BANKS AND FINANCE

Swedish banks operate on a similar system to the British one; opening a bank account should be a relatively straightforward affair but you will need to obtain a personal identity number from the tax office first (see *Residence and Entry Regulations*). Cheques are not used much in Sweden; most transfers are done by bank-giro. The Swedish post office also operates a post-giro system; the major Swedish bank Nordbanken provides its banking service through the post office as well as through its other branches.

Opening hours in banks are generally from 9.30am to 3pm Monday to Friday and also between 4pm and 5.30pm on Thursdays; branches in larger cities may stay open until 5.30pm. Banks are closed on Saturdays. Major credit cards are accepted throughout Sweden.

The Currency

The Swedish currency is the Swedish Krona (plural Kronor) which is usually abbreviated to Kr in shops or SEK to differentiate it from the Norwegian and Danish Krone and the Icelandic króna. The Swedish Krona divides into 100 öre. Coins are issued in values of 50 öre and in 1, 5 and 10 kronor. Bank notes are printed in values of 20, 50, 100, 500, 1,000 and 10,000 kronor. At the time of going to press there were nearly SEK15 to the pound sterling, and SEK10 to the dollar.

There are no limits on the amounts of Swedish or foreign currency which can be imported into Sweden, but currently not more than SEK6,000 in Swedish notes and currency may be exported.

TAXATION

If you intend to move to Sweden for more than six months, it is essential to inform the authorities in your home country of your intentions. Foreigners who work in Sweden for more than six months are taxed on the same basis as Swedish residents; they are required to file a tax return and to pay taxes on their worldwide income. If you remain for less than six months you can apply to be taxed at a flat rate 25% on your earnings, but you will still have to file a special tax return by May in the year following the income year. If your employer is a foreign company then you will pay your taxes in your home country.

The Swedish tax system includes numerous direct and indirect taxes and charges. Taxes in Sweden are very high. In 2002 the overall tax burden was about 52% of the GDP, making it the highest in the world. Sweden underwent major tax reforms which came into effect in 1991 and 1992. Effectively the tax reforms abolished national income tax for the majority, making employees liable only for local (municipal) income tax. Marginal income tax has been reduced to a maximum of 50%. It is estimated that someone earning £20,000 a year pays 37% of their income in tax; their employer pays out another 33% in social security contributions.

When you start your employment in Sweden you will receive an A-tax card; your employer deducts the Preliminary A-tax from your salary. At the end of the year you fill in a tax return; you will receive a notice of assessment by the beginning of the following September. The different kinds of taxes and the rules that apply to foreigners are explained in various brochures supplied by the Tax Authority, which can also be downloaded from their website; there is also an explanation in Swedish of how to fill in a tax return.

Statlig Inkomstskatt: Basic state income tax is levied at SEK200 (approx. £13/US$19) on your taxable income (*beskattningsbara förvärvsinkomst*). Tax is levied at 20% on income over SEK252,000 (approx. £17,100/US$24,400) and at 25% over SEK390,400 (the limits are subject to indexation). There is a basic exemption (*grundavdrag*) ranging between SEK10,000 and SEK19,500 (also subject to revision); if you spend less than a year in Sweden, the exemption is proportional to the number of months you are in Sweden.

Kommunal Inkomstskatt: Municipal income tax rates vary between 26% and 35%. If you or your company are not registered in a municipality the rate is 25% paid into a central fund.

Inkomstskatt på Kapitalinkomst: Capital Gains Tax, is payable at 30%, regardless of your other income. Gains from the sale of a private dwelling are taxed on 50% of the profit, but this tax may be deferred if you buy another property or become a tenant-owner within a year of the sale.

Förmögenhetsskatt: A wealth tax of 1.5% is charged on your assets over SEK1,000,000. If you are married or cohabit with someone for most of the year then the limit is raised to SEK1,500,000 on your incomes as a couple. The tax is on your net assets; if your debts exceed your assets, then you can ask for a tax reduction.

Fastighetsskatt: Property Tax is charged at 1% on private properties based on a notional market value.

Kyrkoavgift: You may choose to pay Church Tax at around 1% of your taxable income if you are a member of a recognised church. In addition you can make contributions to your burial costs (*begravningsavgift*) at around 0.24% of your income.

MOMS: Value Added Tax is paid at 25% on most goods and services. Food, hotels, campsites and passenger transport is taxed at 12%; newspapers and some cultural goods and services are taxed at 6%.

Foreign Key Personnel. Since 2001 a tax relief scheme has been in operation for foreign key personnel, defined as personnel with skills that are difficult or impossible to find in Sweden. Naturally this concerns highly paid staff such as executives or researchers. Such foreigners will be taxed on only 75% of their income for the first three years they are in Sweden. Income includes all kinds of benefits and perks. There is also a 25% reduction on the basis on which social security contributions are calculated.

Useful Addresses

Non-Resident Claims, Fitz Roy House, PO Box 46, Nottingham NG2 1BD; ☎0115-974 1919; fax 0115-974 1919; www.inlandrevenue.gov.uk.

Centre for Non-Residents (CNR), Residence Advice & Liabilities Unit 355, St. John's House, Bootle, Merseyside L69 9BB; ☎0151-472 6202; fax 0151-472 6003.

Riksskatteverket, Swedish Tax Authority, Solnastrandveien 10, 171 94 Solna; ☎020-567 000; e-mail rsv@rsv.se; www.rsv.se.

Skattehuset, Götgatan 76, Södermalm, Stockholm; 0771-778 778.

HEALTH INSURANCE AND HOSPITALS

B ritish and EU citizens working and living in Sweden are entitled to health care in Sweden on the same terms as Swedish citizens. All Swedes are covered by the national health insurance system, which provides medical care, medicines, hospitalisation and some dental services either free of charge or at a small cost.

Medical Care

About 9% of the GDP goes on health care and health care in Sweden is generally of a very high standard. Since the 1980s there has been a move away from the infrastructure of big hospitals towards decentralising health care as much as possible. Responsibility for health care, both in-patient and out-patient, lies with the 23 county councils and three large municipalities. When you receive your personal number, you should go to the local *vårdcentral* (municipal clinic) to register with a doctor of your choice. There are about 27,000 doctors in Sweden of whom 5% are in private practice. When registering with or calling a doctor you should check that they are affiliated to the *Försäkringskassa* (Swedish National Health Service) or you may end up paying for a private practitioner. Virtually all doctors and staff will speak English.

Sweden does not have a general practitioner system. You go to the local clinic (*vårdcentral*) or casualty department (*akutmottagning*), with your passport and E111.

The charge is up to SEK300 (approx. £20/US$29) for a visit, and SEK80 a night if you stay in hospital. If you need any medicines you should obtain a prescription from the doctor and take it to a pharmacy or *Apotek*. You will have to pay the full cost of medicines up to SEK400, and a proportion of the excess, up to a maximum of SEK1,300 in one year.

Those who want to cover themselves for the full costs of medical treatment and possibly for private medical treatment are advised to take out private medical insurance. Expacare (e-mail info@expacare.net or visit www.expacare.net) are specialists in expatriate healthcare offering high quality health insurance cover for individuals and their families, including group cover for five or more employees; cover is available for expatriates of all nationalities worldwide. Anyone from outside the EU would be well advised to make sure that they have medical insurance; the full cost of medical treatment can be ruinous.

Emergencies

If there is an emergency you should go to the casualty department (*akutmottagning*) of the nearest major hospital but otherwise you should consult the local health clinic. In more remote districts where there is no hospital go to the local clinic. Ambulances can be called free on 112. The fee for a visit to an *akutmottagning* is currently SEK300 (approx. £20/US$29).

Dentists

There is a set fee for dental services of SEK700 (approx. £48/US$68) per hour. Only under-19s receive free treatment. Between 20 and 29 dental treatment is partly subsidised; over 30 you pay the full cost. Dental surgeries are indicated by the word *tandläkare*. Main cities operate an emergency out of hours dentist service.

Useful Numbers

Ambulance/Fire/Rescue/Police/Poison/Doctors on Duty: 112
Health information line: ☎08-320 100 (Stockholm); see under *läkare* in other areas.
Anti-poison services: ☎08-33 12 31
Information on medicines/chemists: 020-66 77 66
Aids Information (freephone): 020 78 44 40
Emergency dental services: Stockholm: 08-545 512 20; Gothenburg: 031-80 78 00; Malmö: 0709-10 14 10.

The E111

UK residents intending to go to Sweden to look for work, or on holiday, should obtain an E111 from the post office or the Inland Revenue before they leave. The E111 enables you to receive urgent medical treatment abroad free of charge; it is valid for three months and will cover you until you are on the population register in Sweden. The application form for the E111 can be found in the leaflet T6, *Advice for Travellers*. Allow one month for it to be processed.

If you are already in Sweden you can have your E111 sent to you from International Services, Inland Revenue, National Insurance Contributions Office, Longbenton, Newcastle upon Tyne NE98 1ZZ (☎0845-915 4811 *or* 44 191 225 4811 from abroad; fax 0845-915 7800 *or* 44 191 225 7800 from abroad). Allow one month for your application to be processed. Details are also available on the Inland Revenue website: www.inlandrevenue.gov.uk/nic/intserv/osc.htm. The leaflet SA29 *Your social security insurance, benefits and health care rights in the European Community, and in Iceland, Liechtenstein and Norway* can be downloaded from the Department of Work and Pensions website: www.dwp.gov.uk or ordered from your local Employment Centre.

The Swedish authority responsible for giving information on health care benefits is: *Riksförsäkringsverket* (RFV), Adolf Fredriks Kyrkog. 8, 103 51 Stockholm; ☎08-786 90 00, fax 08-411 27 89; rfv@rfv.se; www.rfv.se.

SOCIAL SECURITY AND UNEMPLOYMENT BENEFIT

Social security is something of a way of life in Sweden which might have some claim to be the original welfare state. The overall aims of the welfare system are to distribute income more evenly over each individual's life cycle, to narrow the gaps between social classes and to provide a good standard of living for everyone. 25% of private expenditure comes from social security benefits. There is of course criticism of the perceived Big Brother welfare state; many problems are blamed on the Soviet-style social engineering of the past. There is a general feeling that the welfare state is not what it was; some people now experience genuine hardship, which would not have happened 10 years ago. The former communist party has gained in influence recently, and there are moves to try to increase benefits again.

Under EU regulations, member nationals are entitled to the same social security rights in Sweden as the Swedes. When you start work in Sweden you will contribute to the social security system and you will therefore have right to the benefits. US citizens, and anyone coming from a country with which Sweden has a totalisation agreement, may apply to be exempted from social security payments. Contributions are paid entirely by the employer, except for the pension contribution. An application for exemption should be made before you start work if possible.

Maternity Benefits

You can start to claim maternity cash benefit from 60 days before the expected confinement, up to 10 days before. Parents' cash benefit is paid for 360 days from childbirth at 80% of previous income, and for an additional 90 days at SEK60 a day. The benefit can be taken up at any time until the child is 8, by either parent. There are tax-free child allowances for every child up to the age of 16; families with three or more children receive an additional payment. Parents get up to 60 days leave per year to look after sick children and are paid at about 80% of their normal wage. Foreign residents qualify for these benefits once they have paid into the social security system for 240 days.

Day-care centres and pre-school child care are widely available and day-centres typically stay open between 6am and 6.30pm. Eighty per cent of children between 3 and 6 are in childcare, and 40% of 0- to 2-year olds. The state funds up to 90% of the cost of pre-school care. For local details look up *barnomsorg* in the green pages of the local telephone directory. Responsibility for social welfare services rests primarily with the municipalities.

Sickness Benefit

All employees in Sweden are entitled to cash benefits during periods of illness. The social security system pays 80% of a person's normal income when they are sick. From 1992 employers were made responsible for the first two weeks of sick pay, partly as a way of combatting high levels of absenteeism. There is no compensation for the first day of absence from work. From the 14th day sickness allowance is paid by the social insurance office. Freelance and self-employed workers receive sickness cash benefit from the social insurance office from the start. A medical certificate is required from the seventh day of absence, and a more detailed certificate has to be produced after the 29th day.

Unemployment

Most working people in Sweden have unemployment insurance through their trade unions, and pay contributions of about 1% of their monthly salary. Unemployment insurance funds connected with the unions (*akassorna*) are open to all; workers who do not pay voluntary contributions into an insurance fund, receive a basic benefit from the *arbetsmarknadskasse*. The basic sum is SEK270 (approx. £18/US$26) a day for 300 days, paid for five days a week. If you have paid into an insurance scheme, you receive 80% of your previous earnings up to SEK680 a day for 100 days, and then SEK580 for 200 days. There are conditions attached to these benefits; you cannot qualify for the basic payment until you have worked an average 70 hours a month for six out of the previous 12 months. For the higher payment you have to have been a member for at least 12 months. If you have voluntarily left your job or been dismissed for misconduct, or refuse to take employment that is offered to you, then you will be suspended from the system for 20 to 60 benefit days.

If you become unemployed you should register with your nearest local employment office which will advise you about labour market schemes and claiming unemployment benefit. If you are coming from the UK you may be asked to bring an E301 form stating your periods of employment and unemployment before you moved to Sweden. It is possibly to transfer one's unemployment benefit from the UK to Sweden, as long as you do so within the first three months of becoming unemployed. Your employment centre will give you the necessary forms.

Useful Addresses

DWP Pensions and Overseas Benefits Directorate, Newcastle-upon-Tyne NE98 1BA; ☎0191-218 7777; www.dwp.gov.uk.
Federal Benefits Unit, US Embassy, Strandvägen 101, 115 89 Stockholm; ☎08-783 53 00.

National Social Insurance Board (Riksförsäkringsverket RFV), 103 51 Stockholm; ☎08-786 90 00; www.rfv.se. The visiting address is Adolf Fredriks Kyrkogata 8.

LOCAL GOVERNMENT

Sweden is divided into 286 *Kommuner* (municipalities) each with an elected assembly and the right to levy income taxes. *Kommuner* deal with matters concerning schools and social and public housing services. Elections for the *Kommuner* coincide with national elections, held every four years. Since 1976 immigrants who have been resident in Sweden for three years are entitled to vote in the *Kommuner* elections.

Between the national and municipal governments are the County Councils. Sweden is divided into 24 *län* or counties whose principal responsibility is to administer regional transport, public health and the medical services. County governors and county administrative boards are elected by the national government.

CRIME AND THE POLICE

As with the rest of Scandinavia, crime in Sweden is fairly low. In the unlikely event of crime call the police free on 112 and ask for *polislarm*. The police headquarters in Stockholm are located on Norra Agnegatan 33-37; ☎08-401 01 00. Non-emergency numbers are: Gothenburg 031-739 20 00 and Malmö 040-20 10 00. If you are arrested you should inform the nearest embassy or consul immediately. A person can be detained for six, and in some cases, 12 hours without orders from a prosecutor. After orders from a prosecutor they can be held for another day and sometimes longer. At this stage they have the right to contact a solicitor and a court must decide whether the person is to be detained or set free. You are entitled to legal representation.

About 15,000 people are sent to prison each year and the most common offence is drink-driving. This is a reflection on the stringent penalties, rather than on the fact that Swedes are more prone to drinking and driving than other nationalities. Between 25 and 50% of those currently serving prison sentences are there for drug-related offences. Drug abuse is less prevalent amongst the young in Sweden than in other European countries, because of the severe penalties. Anyone who is found guilty of possessing drugs is required to go on a re-education programme or face a heavier punishment. Prisoners are allowed conjugal visits once a month, as long as they behave themselves.

The Judicial System

Courts are organised on three levels : Local courts (*Tingsrätter*) courts of appeal (*Hovrätter*) and the Supreme Court (*Högsta domstolen*). All criminal and civil cases start in the local courts and may subsequently be taken to the courts of appeal. Only cases involving issues of major interest are taken to the Supreme Court. The equivalent of jury members in Swedish courts are lay assessors who work with legally trained judges and also participate in decisions on sentencing. There are also administrative courts in Sweden which deal with cases involving taxes, social insurance etc. You can turn to any lawyer for one hour of discounted legal advice. Look up *advokatbyråer* in the yellow pages. There is an extensive legal aid system for those who cannot afford legal costs.

RELIGION

Eighty-five per cent of the Swedish population belong to the Lutheran Church. All Swedish citizens are automatically registered in the Church at birth, providing that one parent is a member. Even though only about 5% of the population actually attend church and religion is generally considered to be far less important in Sweden than in many other countries, few people actually bother to opt out of the Church. An annual subscription to the Church is automatically deducted in taxes; the Church also derives revenue from its ownership of land and forests.

There are many other smaller denominations in Sweden, the largest of which is the Pentecostal Movement with over 100,000 followers. Immigrants have swelled the ranks of non-Christian groups which include 50,000 Moslems, 2,000 Buddhists and 2,000 Hindus.

There are English-language church services in Sweden in various locations. Churches are a meeting point for expatriates. The following are Anglican/ Episcopalian unless otherwise stated.

Church of St Peter and St Sigfrid, Strandvägen 76, 115 27 Stockholm; ☎ 08-663 82 48; e-mail anglican.church@telia.com; www.stockholmanglicans.net.

Ecumenical Church of Stockholm, St Jacob, Västra Trädgårdsgatan 2, 111 53 Stockholm; ☎ 08-723 30 00.

Gothenburg Anglican Chaplaincy, Norra Liden 15, 411 18 Göteborg; ☎ 031-711 19 15.

St Andrew's Church, Hvitfeldtsplatsen 2, 411 20 Göteborg; ☎ 031-13 95 37.

Sta Eugenia Catholic Church, Kungsträdgårdsgatan 12, 111 47 Stockholm; ☎ 08-679 57 70.

SOCIAL LIFE

Anyone who is a fan of Ingmar Bergman may have gained an image of the Swedes as rather complicated people. The Swedes are generally quite reserved, although easy-going. Whilst they have their gloomy side, they can also be surprisingly cheerful and uninhibited. For foreigners Sweden is an easy country to live in, since it is so well-organised. The locals do, however, expect outsiders to conform to the rules. Most people go out of their way to be friendly and helpful to foreign visitors. Some elements of the population have strong prejudices against immigrants, however, and there is a small neo-Nazi movement.

Angry displays are rare in Sweden and there is some statistical evidence to suggest that aggressive behaviour and loud confrontations in the home and the workplace occur less in Sweden than in many other countries. One foreign psychotherapist who has practised in Sweden for over 20 years has opined that the Swedes' almost pathological dislike of confrontation, termed *undfallenhet,* or 'giving way to other people', has much to do with the complexities of the Swedish psyche. No one wants to fall out with you, or become an *uvän* or 'non-friend', which may give one an unrealistic feeling of being more popular than one really is.

Sweden is a famously liberal country (at least from the outside), which is credited with inventing blue movies and massage parlours, although there is very little evidence of these things these days. The inhabitants have an uncomplicated attitude towards sex; one writer rather unfortunately called them 'great outdoor lovers'.

Social engineering has been tried here on a vast scale, which is a reflection of a typically Swedish obsession with security or *trygghet;* Ingmar Bergman called the socialist state a 'monstrosity of cosiness'. Other Scandinavians tend to criticise the Swedes for their excessive respect for authority, a trait which was already well established in the Viking era. It is certainly significant that the best-known literary figure to come out of Sweden is Pippi Longstocking (by Astrid Lindgren), a girl who engages in all sorts of anarchic and scandalous behaviour. Ingmar Bergman's last film *Fanny and Alexander,* in which he summed up his own personal creed, concerns the battle of a family of actors trying to get back their children from a tyrannical Lutheran bishop, with the help of two Jewish brothers.

Entertainment And Culture

Cultural activities reach all parts of the country through travelling theatre, concerts and exhibitions. The country's cultural institutions are state subsidised. There are over 300 museums throughout Sweden and each municipality has its own public library which is free of charge. Stockholm is home to symphony orchestras and the national opera and theatre. Famous contributors to Swedish culture include classic writers such as August Strindberg and the more homely Astrid Lindgren, the children's author most famous for the Pippi Longstocking series. Additionally, film-maker Ingmar Bergman and composer Wilhelm Stenhammar are revered internationally.

Whilst there are night clubs and concerts in Stockholm, Sweden's nightlife is decidedly low-key with many people preferring to go to an evening class. Jazz is fairly popular, but the old-fashioned dance band is rather more in evidence than heavy metal bands; pubbing and clubbing is popular with those in their late teens and early 20s. Like their Norwegian cousins, Swedes are great nature lovers and right of public access to the countryside is upheld in the *Allemansrätt,* which translates literally as 'every man's right'.

Second homes in the country are common in Sweden and outdoor sport is also popular, particularly cross-country ski-ing, football and orienteering. Sports organisations receive extensive subsidies from the state although facilities are much better in the south than in the north.

A more surprising aspect of Swedish life is the hunting of wild animals. Every year some 200,000 reindeer and elk are shot by private citizens, and the meat taken home for the freezer. The numbers of these animals would otherwise get out of control; evidently the authorities do not wish to be seen to be cruel to wild animals. About 80 species ranging from squirrels to beers to wolves (which are virtually extinct anyway) can be legally hunted, and almost anyone can get a licence.

SHOPPING

The main Swedish cities have indoor shopping malls complete with fountains and cafés. Urban centres usually have the ubiquitous department stores of Åhlens and Domus and the popular clothing chain of Hennes & Mauritz. H&M have branches in the UK and other European countries.

Usual shopping hours on weekdays are 9am to 6pm and 9am to between 1pm and 4pm on Saturdays, but in practice many shops will stay open longer. Some shops in the big cities open on Sunday afternoons between 12pm and 4pm.

Food and Drink

In general Sweden does not really have a 'foodie' culture; if you are looking for sophisticated French cuisine this may not be the best country for you. More unusual vegetables such as asparagus are unobtainable outside the big cities; the produce in the supermarkets is of an acceptable if not exceptional quality.

Sweden is home to the designer sandwich or *Smörgås*, an elaborate work of art on bread. Probably the only well-known Swedish food export is the *Smörgåsbord* (literally sandwich table) – a large buffet affair usually served at lunchtime and washed down with beer. One inevitably ends up eating a lot of fish in endless permutations. There is also game (mainly elk or *älg* and reindeer or *ren*). Breakfast usually consists of coffee and two or three kinds of bread, cheese and meat. Lunch, eaten between noon and 2 pm is often the main meal of the day in Sweden. It is usually *husmanskost* (home cooking) and tends to be filling fare such as meat and potatoes with salad. Dinner is usually a fairly light meal. Coffee and cakes are a popular snack.

Sweden's policies on alcohol have been very restrictive until recently; a reminder of the days when alcoholism was such a problem that rationing had to be introduced. Wine, spirits and beer for the moment can only be bought through the state-controlled shops known as *Systembolaget*, which open from Monday to Friday. Because of EU regulations, the laws on the production and retailing of alcohol will have to be relaxed; there is some concern that this will lead to more drunkenness, but there is no doubt that attitudes towards alcohol are changing, and most likely there is not going to be a major problem.

METRICATION

For information on the metric system including a conversion chart see under *Metrication* at the end of the *Daily Life* chapter in the section on Denmark.

PUBLIC HOLIDAYS

1 January	New Year's Day
6 January	Epiphany
Good Friday, Easter Sunday and Easter Monday	
1 May	Labour Day
Whit Sunday and Whit Monday	
Midsummer Day (approx 21-23 June but varies)	
1 November	All Saints' Day
25 December	Christmas Day
26 December	Boxing Day
31 December	New Year's Eve

RETIREMENT

S weden has one of the best records in the world in terms of caring for its senior citizens but there has been concern in recent years over the increasing number of elderly people placing a heavy burden on the medical and welfare system. A growing percentage (currently 21%) of the population is over 65. By the year 2050 some 10% of the population will be over 80. This is due to the fact that Sweden shares with the rest of Scandinavia some of the highest longevity rates in the western world.

To choose to retire to Sweden is not particularly common – both the weather and the high cost of living tend to militate against it. Nonetheless, retired people can expect to enjoy a high standard of living and social care. Many elderly people in Sweden are able to stay in their own homes thanks to an extensive system of home help services. Every municipality employs workers who help the elderly, as necessary, with cleaning, shopping, cooking and personal care. Pensioners pay for this service according to their means. Other benefits for pensioners include housing allowances, home adaptation grants and on-call warden services where needed. You can get further information about retiring in Sweden by contacting the *Pensionärernas Riksorganisation*, Adolf Fredriks Kyrkogatan 12, Stockholm; ☎ 08-701 67 00; e-mail info@pro.se; www.pro.se. This organisation has some 385,000 members and is the main pensioners' organisation in Sweden.

Residence Requirements

Since 1 January 1992 pensioners from EU states have been free to live wherever they wish in the European Union provided that they have adequate means of support. Sweden's membership of the EU in 1995 has brought it into line with regulations on these matters. Currently, the Swedish regulations state that a pensioner from any EEA country and his/her family members will be granted a residence permit if they can show that they have adequate means of support which is at least the equivalent of a basic Swedish pension after tax, about SEK80,000 (approx. £5,440/US$7,760) Additionally they must be able to prove that they have enough assets after tax to cover their housing costs. Proof will be required in the form of bank statements etc.

Pensions

If you become entitled to a state pension before leaving the UK you can arrange to have it paid to you in Sweden although you should bear in mind that it will be linked to British levels. People who have moved to Sweden before retirement, but have continued to pay British national insurance contributions will qualify for a British pension, but if they have paid into the Swedish welfare system they will be entitled to a Swedish pension. You can get some idea of how much your British state pension is going to be by looking at the website www.pensionguide.gov.uk. To claim a combined British and Swedish pension the Swedish and British authorities exchange records and calculate how much is payable to you from each country. For further details consult the DWP leaflet SA29 *Your Social Security, Health Care and Pension Rights in the European Community*, available on the website www.dwp.gov.uk.

The pension system is going through a major revamp in Sweden at the moment. Because of the rapidly ageing population the authorities have increased the contributions that are payable. In the past there was the national basic pension (*folkpension*) and the national supplementary pension (ATP). The basic pension was calculated on the basis of your 15 highest earning years out of 30 working years. The new system takes the whole 40 working years into account and links the amount of contributions with the final pension amount. As well as paying 16% of your income into the pension fund, everyone is required to pay 2.5% of their income into a Premium Pension fund of their own choice. There is no formal retirement age; as long as you go on working you can make contributions to the pension fund. You can start to draw pension from the age of 61, at 25, 50, 75 or 100%, and you can go on working while you draw your pension. Pensions are still taxable, but pensioners enjoy higher tax exemptions than others.

The basic pension is nominally about SEK37,000 (approx. £2,516/US$3,589) a year; in the case of those who have not paid enough contributions, the figure is increased to around SEK90,000, but it would be very difficult to live on this amount of money.

Anyone born after 1954 will be entirely in the new system. Those born between 1938 and 1953 will receive pensions in both systems, while those born before will be entirely in the old system. For further details about pension rights in Sweden contact the National Social Insurance Board, www.rfv.se.

Clubs and Societies

The number of fellow English-speaking expatriates is relatively small in Sweden; unless you speak the language opportunities for entertainment may be limited. The main pensioners' grouping in Sweden is the *Pensionärens Riksorganisation* (see above). Your embassy can help to put you in touch with English-speaking organisations. The following lists a few English-speaking clubs. More are listed on the British Embassy website (www.britishembassy.com):

American Women's Club of Sweden, Box 12054, 102 22 Stockholm; e-mail awcsweden@fawco.org; www.awc.nu.

American Women's Club of Gothenburg, Box 2018, 429 11 Särjö; e-mail webwoman@awcgothenburg.com; www.awcgothenburg.com.

American Women's Club of Malmö, Box 17005, 200 10 Malmö; e-mail awcmalmo@awcmalmo.com; www.awcmalmo.com.

British & Commonwealth Association, Box 550, 101 30 Stockholm; ☎08-767 19 18; e-mail bca–stockholm@hotmail.com.

British Business Club, Kullbäckstorpsvägen 15, 435 42 Mölnlycke; ☎031-88 31 93.

English Theatre Company AB, Nybrogatan 35, 114 39 Stockholm; ☎08-662 41 33; fax 08-660 1159.

Stockholm Exiles RFC, Jäntansvägen 4, 132 35 Soltsjö-Boo (Rugby Union).

Swedish-British Society, Strandvägen 57, 115 26 Stockholm; ☎08-678 73 33; fax 08-678 73 33.

Wills and Death

Swedish inheritance taxes (*arvsskatt*) are far higher than in the UK or US. Residents are taxed on their worldwide estate, so it is important to plan ahead if you want your heirs to benefit. Heirs are classified into three categories: Class 1 covers spouses, registered partners, and cohabitants; children, grandchildren, and other descendants; partners of children, and surviving partners of children; Class 3 concerns juridical persons, such as churches, municipalities and other public bodies; Class 2 covers anyone who does not fall into Class 1 or 3. Within Class 1 tax is levied at 10% on the first SEK300,000 (approx. £20,400/US$29,100), then 20% up to SEK600,000, and 30% on the remainder. Taxes on the other two classes are even higher.

A will made in the UK may be taken into account, insofar as it does not conflict with Swedish law. The Swedish system does not give you the freedom to disinherit family members. The only practical way to safeguard your assets is to put your property and other assets in the names of family members at the start. There is the risk that if they predecease you then you have to pay inheritance tax on your own assets. Starting an offshore company is an even better way, but only really relevant to someone who is very wealthy, and already quite old.

SECTION II

EMPLOYMENT

THE EMPLOYMENT SCENE

Sweden operated government programmes to combat unemployment as far back as the outbreak of World War I. Then as now they were aimed at finding jobs for everybody and providing incentives for occupational mobility. The presiding ethos of Swedish labour market policy is the activation principle, or work-for-all, which gives priority to ensuring that everyone who can be is employed, and that unemployed people should be placed in labour market programmes. Because of the rapidly ageing population, it is government policy to increase the participation rate as much as possible. Sweden spends over 2% of GNP on labour market schemes, by far the highest amount anywhere. These are offered by the *Arbetsmarknadsstyrelse* (AMS), or Employment Service, the main instrument of government labour market policies.

Sweden experienced its greatest economic boom between 1940 and 1970. Between 1991 and 1994 there was a severe recession. The Swedes had grown used to unemployment levels of 2%; by 1995 unemployment it had risen to 10.7%. Joining the EU in 1995 brought no obvious benefits for the economy. 1998 to 2001 were good years for the economy, but 2002 has again seen a rise in unemployment up to 5%. Sweden is certainly not clamouring for foreign workers at the present; it also has a growing immigrant population, many of whom are unemployed. For EU citizens job opportunities are mainly in short-term work, and in sectors which require highly qualified personnel.

Over the past 100 years Sweden has evolved from being a largely agrarian country into a modern, efficient and technologically advanced nation. Only 2% of the population now work in agriculture and fishing, 60% work in services, 19.1% in manufacturing and mining and 5.4% in construction. The labour force participation rate is 79%; 80% of men are employed and 77% of women. In the last decades growth in employment has mainly been in the public sector; a quarter of the labour force, 1 million workers, are employed by local government. In the private sector, the main increase in employment has been in IT services, with 210,000 workers.

RESIDENCE AND WORK REGULATIONS

Sweden's membership of the European Economic Area and subsequent membership of the European Union effectively removes barriers for nationals of member states who want to look for work in Sweden. A work permit is no longer required and citizens of the EEA and EU countries can enter Sweden with the intention of looking for work and should be given equal rights as regards employment as Swedish citizens. Some kinds of work, e.g. those connected with national security such as the army, will remain open only to Swedes. Anyone who wishes to stay in Sweden for more than three months must apply for a residence permit (see Chapter Two, *Residence and Entry Regulations*).

Skills and Qualifications

For an opinion on the comparability of your qualifications with those in Sweden, contact the National Agency of Higher Education (*Högskoleverket*), Box 7851, 103 99 Stockholm; ☎08-453 70 41; fax 08-453 71 40; www.hsv.se. You can try asking your UK Employment Centre to do this for you, which will save you having to pay a charge. You should be aware that it is not easy to directly compare British qualifications with Swedish ones. Graduates are usually expected to have a degree which is directly relevant to the job for which they are applying. For vocational training such as catering, construction and agriculture contact the Comparability Coordinator of the Employment Department (TS1E 1, Moorfoot (Room E603), Sheffield S1 4PQ; ☎0114-259 4144) who can provide a fact sheet to aid comparability of skills.

If you have experience but no formal qualifications, it is possible to obtain a European Community Certificate of Experience. For EU citizens in the UK this is issued by the DTI. Since the Certificate costs £80 to process, you should first make sure that your type of work experience is covered by an EC directive by asking the authorities in Sweden or the DTI, who will try to send you a copy of the relevant directive, together with an application form and any available literature. There is an enquiry line on 020-7215 4004 (fax 020-7215 4489), or you can write to: Certificates of Experience Unit, Department of Trade & Industry, Kingsgate House, 66-74 Victoria Street, London SW1E 6SW.

SOURCES OF JOBS

NEWSPAPERS AND DIRECTORIES

Adverts for Swedish jobs in the foreign press are rare and looking there is probably not the best method of finding work in Sweden. However *Overseas Jobs Express* (available on subscription only from Overseas Jobs Express, 20 New Road, Brighton, East Sussex BN1 1UF; ☎01273-699611; www.overseasjobsexpress .com) has a substantial variety of job adverts from around the world and you may well see something for Sweden. More information on temporary jobs can be found in the *Directory of Summer Jobs Abroad, Teaching English Abroad,* and *The Au Pair and Nanny's Guide to Working Abroad,* from Vacation Work, www.vacationwork.co.uk.

Swedish Newspapers

The morning daily *Dagens Nyheter* has the biggest number of adverts for job vacancies. *Svenska Dagbladet* and *Dagens Industri* concentrate mainly on business. In Sweden, Sunday is the most important day for publishing job advertisements. You may consider taking out a subscription. It is possible to order copies using the internet. Further details can be found on the websites:

Dagens Industri, www.di.se.

Dagens Nyheter, www.dn.se.

Svenska Dagbladet, www.svd.se.

Platsjournalen and *Nytt Jobb* are two publicly financed magazines containing vacancies and information about the Swedish labour market. They can be found in all the Employment Centres in Sweden.

Advertising in Newspapers.

You can advertise in Swedish newspapers for employment, although this is not a particularly common practice in Sweden. For *Dagens Nyheter* contact the UK advertising rep: Powers Turner Group (100 Rochester Row, London SW1P 1JP; ☎020-7630 9966; www.publicitas.com). For *Sydsvenska Dagbladet* and *Göteborgs Posten* contact Crane Media Partners (20-28 Dalling Rd, London W6 0JB; ☎020-8237 8601), and for *Dagens Industri* contact David Todd Associates Ltd (32/33 Skylines, Limeharbour, Docklands, London E14 9TS; ☎020-7538 5811; www.davidtoddassociates.co.uk).

Professional Journals and Magazines

You can find a comprehensive list of UK trade magazines which may contain adverts for jobs abroad in media directories such as *Benn's Press Directory: UK* which is available in most reference libraries. *Benn's Press Directory: International* contains a comprehensive list of Swedish trade journals and magazines, for example *Civilingenjören* for graduate engineers, or *Computer Sweden.* Adverts are usually in Swedish, but not always. You can also look in *Ulrich's Periodicals Directory* for a bigger selection of journals.

INTERNET

The web is becoming more and more important for finding jobs in Sweden. The Swedish employment service can give advice on which are the best sites. These are just a selection:

General sites: http://jobb.ams.se; www.jobshop.se; www.jobline.se; www.topjobs.se; www.jobfinder.se; www.stepstone.se.

IT, engineers, economists: www.academicsearch.se.

Graphic design, and related: www.avd55.gf.se/mapp/grafikformedling.se.

Engineers: www.cf.se/o.o.i.s/1132.

Executives, project leaders, specialised staff: www.alumni.se.

Executives, specialist staff: www.intersearch.se.

EMPLOYMENT ORGANISATIONS

The Swedish State Employment Service

The Swedish labour market comes under the aegis of the *Arbedsmarknadsstyrelse*, or Employment Service, which carries out government labour policies. About 90% of all job vacancies in Sweden are reported to the Employment Service. The Labour Market Administration (*Arbetsmarknadsverket*) has about 380 employment offices (*Arbetsförmedlingar*) throughout Sweden which deal with about 35% of all vacancies. The *Arbetsförmedlingar* offer placements and job counselling services. There are adverts for temporary work; see the website http://jobb.ams.se under *vikariebanken*; there is also a section for jobseekers to post an ad; see *jobbsökande*. Other facilities include the weekly employment magazines *Platsjournalen,* which has county-wide editions, and the more specialised *Nytt Jobb,* which comes in several versions (see below for explanation). Every employment office has access to a computer terminal with a list of vacancies (*platsautomaten*) and up-to-date information about jobs. This database can be accessed on the internet at: www.umu.se/af.

TABLE 15 VERSIONS OF *NYTT JOBB* (NEW JOB)

○ *Nytt Jobb Värd Omsorg*	Medical and Care Professions, Social Work
○ *Nytt Jobb Teknik Data*	IT, Technical, Architects, Electronics, Engineering
○ *Nytt Jobb Ekonomi Administration*	Economists, Administrative, Sales and Marketing, Secretaries
○ *Nytt Jobb Undervisning Kultur*	Librarians, Translators, Teachers, Lecturers
○ *Nytt Jobb Utland*	Abroad (i.e. outside Sweden)

Information about new vacancies can be sent to your home address. You do not have to be registered at an employment office to find out about vacancies and to use the facilities but you must be registered if you want to claim unemployment benefit. The main employment office is in Stockholm (*Arbetsförmedlingen,* Sveavägen 24-26, Box 7763, 103 96 Stockholm; ☎08-406 57 00; fax 08-406 57 01; www.ams.se/city-stockholm), but for regional employment office details look under *arbetsförmedlingen* in the telephone directory. The office at Sveavägen has English-speaking staff; on Thursday afternoons there is an international jobs office open upstairs.

When you register with the employment office you will be required to specify the kind of job you are looking for and you will often be expected to narrow your choice down to one specific type of work. After 100 days you will be expected to accept work in other fields. If you become part of the long-term unemployed you will be asked to go on a reactivation programme which lasts six months, which includes some training. At any one time about 5% of the workforce are on some kind of labour market programme.

Private Swedish Agencies

Private job agencies have been allowed to operate in Sweden since July 1993, and are becoming more common. There are two types of agencies apart from public offices: private agencies which supply mostly office staff, and union agencies which deal mainly with salaried personnel such as engineers. To find an agency look under *arbetsförmedlingar* in the yellow pages of the local telephone directory. Manpower has 44 branches, Adecco 23.

Useful Addresses

Adecco, Drottningholmsv. 22, 102 24 Stockholm; ☎08-598 980 00; www.adecco.se.
Kelly Services, Apelbergsg. 57 3tr, 103 61 Stockholm; ☎08-546 511 00.
Manpower, Vegag. 14, 113 82 Stockholm; ☎08-736 19 00; www.manpower.se.
Manpower, N. Hamng. 32, 404 23 Göteborg; ☎031-61 72 00.
Manpower, Skeppsbron. 3, 201 23 Malmö; ☎040-660 63 00.

UK Employment Organisations

The Recruitment and Employment Confederation (36-38 Mortimer Street, London W1N 7RB; ☎020-7462 3260; www.rec.uk.com) issues a list of employment agencies who are members; some agencies have contacts with Scandinavia, or may send people out there.

The *EURES and Euroadviser Network*: You can contact UK employment centres for information and advice on working in Sweden. The British branch of EURES is based at the Overseas Placing Unit (OPU) of the Employment Service in Sheffield (Rockingham House, 123 West Street, Sheffield S1 4ER; ☎0114-259 6051/2). Most UK Employment Service offices have computer access to the vacancies held at Sheffield. Vacancies are listed on the EURES network: http://europa.eu.int/comm/employment. Many jobs are seasonal; employers are looking to fill posts quickly. The system works best for qualified graduates.

THE APPLICATION PROCEDURE

Finding a job via personal contacts and through word of mouth is fairly common in Sweden. Speculative applications are also quite common, but it is usual to make a telephone call first and talk to the personnel officer or someone in middle to senior management. CVs can be sent by e-mail. CVs should be realistic and to the point; exaggerating your abilities will go down like a lead balloon. It is not the practice to give names of referees in CVs. You may well expect to be asked how you would feel about living in a country with high taxation and a testing climate; it is not only a question of wanting a job, but also whether you have positive reasons for wanting to live in Sweden.

PERMANENT WORK

The demand for permanent employees from other countries has in some respects increased over the years. Sweden is expanding its IT and pharmaceutical industries, and needs specialist foreign workers in these areas. Unskilled jobs are more seasonal, but there is certainly scope for foreigners to work here.

MEDICAL

There is a demand for all kinds of medical staff: doctors, nurses, dentists, physiotherapists, occupational therapists etc. The authorities state that openings for foreign personnel are limited, mainly because of the language barrier. For more information contact the National Board of Health and Welfare (RT-enheten, 106 30 Stockholm; ☎08-783 30 00, fax 08-783 30 06; e-mail socialstyrelsen@sos.se). When you contact the board you will be sent a form which you should complete and return with proof of your qualifications.

TEACHING

Teaching English

There are fewer opportunities for teaching English as a foreign language in Sweden than in other parts of Europe, notably the south, because standards of English in Sweden are generally very high. Nonetheless, attending adult evening classes is a way of life in Sweden and many Swedes like to have the opportunity to practise their English in a group gathering. Since 1955 the Folk University of Sweden has placed British teachers in a network of adult education centres for one academic year. Centres are extra-mural departments of the Universities of Stockholm, Uppsala, Gothenburg, Lund and Umeå and there are branches in many other small towns, including in the far north. Students are varied, ranging from the unemployed to business people, and from housewives to pensioners.

The Folk Universities hire teachers aged between 22 and 40, preferably with a teaching qualification, and guarantee the number of hours you will work over a nine month period. Wages are not particularly high (between £14 and £18 per class) although you should earn enough to live on and the work is not particularly onerous, consisting of 45-minute lessons usually spread over four evenings. Those prepared to work in the far north will receive favourable consideration and the absence of a TEFL qualification may be waived if you can convince them that you are prepared to stick it out. You may be able to find freelance teaching work when in Sweden to supplement your income and extend your stay in Sweden by arranging another teaching job before the first one has expired.

Another alternative is to try ringing around colleges of further education and commercial language schools. Addresses can be obtained from the National Agency for Higher Education (address below) or look under *språk* in the yellow pages. You will be in a stronger position if you can offer Business English to corporate clients. Business English attracts higher wages of about £30 per hour. Terms begin in September and January and you should time your application to coincide with these.

Other Teaching Jobs

Qualified primary and secondary school teachers who want to teach abroad English or international schools abroad should contact the European Council of International Schools (ECIS) or WES Worldwide. Teachers should have a minimum of two years teaching experience. See 'Education' in *Daily Life* chapter for a list of British and international schools in Sweden.

Useful Addresses

ECIS, 21 Lavant Street, Petersfield, Hampshire GU32 3EL; ☎01730-268244; www.ecis.org.

The National Agency for Higher Education (Verket för högskoleservice, VHS), Box 45503, 104 30 Stockholm; ☎8 728 36 00, fax 8 34 27 25.

The Folk High School Information Centre, Box 740, 101 35 Stockholm; ☎08-796 00 50, fax 08-21 88 26; e-mail fin@folkbildning.se; www.folkbildning.se.

Folkuniversitetet – förbundskansliet, Eriksbergsgatan 1A, Box 26152, 100 41 Stockholm; ☎08-679 29 50; fax 08-678 15 44; info@folkuniversitetet.se; www.folkuniversitetet.se.

World-wide Education Service Ltd, Canada House, 272 Field End Road, Eastcote, Middlesex HA4 9NA; ☎020-8582 0317; fax 020-8429 4838; e-mail wes@wesworldwide.com; www.wesworldwide.com.

INFORMATION AND COMMUNICATION TECHNOLOGY

The IT sector is rapidly expanding; Sweden wants to be the IT centre of Scandinavia, although it faces stiff competition from the Finns, who are doing rather better than the Swedes in this area. IT employment is heavily concentrated in the areas of Stockholm and Linköping; it is estimated that 10% of employees in the Stockholm area are in IT-related jobs.

L.M. Ericsson is a famous name in communications technology, although it has fallen back to third place after Nokia and Siemens in mobile phones. Some agencies in the UK and possibly the US can arrange IT jobs in Sweden. The best source of IT jobs within Sweden are the web pages of *Computer Sweden,* the main computer magazine: http://csjobb.idg.se. This site lists numerous employers, and also gives detailed information on pay levels. For UK/US-based recruitment companies see listings under Norway and Denmark.

Useful Addresses

ElanIT, Drottninggatan 86, 111 83 Stockholm; ☎08-508 954 40; e-mail info.stock@elanit.se.

ElanIT, Kalendegatan 26, 203 11 Malmö; ☎040-665 61 40; e-mail info.malmo@elanit.se.

ElanIT, Norra Hamngatan 32, 404 23 Göteborg; ☎031-61 72 30; e-mail info.gote@elanit.se.

TMP Worldwide, Finlandsg. 12, 164 74 KISTA, 08-506 007 00; fax 08-506 007 99.

TEMPORARY WORK

AU PAIR AND DOMESTIC WORK

Perhaps better known for providing au pairs than for looking for them, Sweden's demand for domestic help is not particularly high. This is mainly because child care provision is extensive and available to all sectors of society. There is some demand for domestic employees in Sweden, although this is mainly amongst the wealthier sectors of the population who are to be found in the large houses in southern Sweden. For au pair agencies placing people in Sweden see addresses below. The employment service is also involved in helping to find au pair positions; look for the *Arbetsförmedling* in your area or look at the website: www.ams.se. The American-Scandinavian Foundation can assist with work permits for US residents.

To work as an au pair you must have a residence permit and a work permit; only the former is necessary for EU citizens. You must be aged between 18 and 30, and interested in studying Swedish. A permit is granted for the period that you are employed, up to a maximum of 12 months. The Swedish Migration Board has an information sheet: *Facts About Work Permits for Au Pair Employment* on its website: www.migrationsverket.se.

If you enter into a formal agreement to work as a domestic or au pair within a household you will be covered by the 1970 Act on domestic work which states that you should not normally work more than 40 hours per week and you cannot be expected to do more than 48 hours overtime within a four week period or more than 300 hours during a calendar year. Your employer must keep a record of your overtime and pay you accordingly either in wages or time off in lieu. You are entitled to 36 hours of continuous time off every week and usually this will be at weekends. Employees who are under 18 may not work more than 10 hours during a 24-hour period.

Domestic employees are entitled to a written contract. Au pairs have to earn at least SEK3,500 (approx. £235/US$340) a month in pocket money in order to get a work permit; qualified nannies can earn between £100 and £200 a week. If the contract is indefinite, one month's notice is required from either side. You will have the right to a written reference when you leave.

Useful Addresses

American-Scandinavian Foundation, Scandinavia House, 58 Park Avenue, New York, NY 10016; ☎212-879-9779; e-mail info@amscan.org; www.amscan.org.
Aupair Center of Sweden KB, Nedre Langvinkelsgatan 36, 252 34 Helsingborg; e-mail aupair@aupaircenter.com; www.aupaircenter.com.
Au Pair World Agency, Kaflegatan 6, 461 40 Trollhättan; ☎0520-138 13; fax 0520-311 89; e-mail InterTeamTHN@swipnet.se; www.interteam.se.
Swede Au Pair, Nämndemansvägen 32, 643 32 Vingåker; e-mail swedeaupair@swipnet.se; www.azeaupair.nu.

FARM WORK

Just over 2% of the Swedish population work in agriculture and horticulture. The main types of agriculture are arable, pigs, mixed and dairy and horticulture, including tree nurseries, greenhouse produce and vegetables. The International Farm Experience Programme can arrange placements on Swedish farms for young farmers and horticulturalists. To qualify for a place on the programme you should be aged 18-28, have had two years experience of farming (one of which could be at college), have a valid driving licence and intend to make a career in agriculture or horticulture. Placements are for between three and 12 months all year and as far as possible the work is matched with individual interests. Participants live in with the farming family and receive board and lodging and a basic wage of SEK3,500 (approx. £235/US$340) after tax.

If you are interested in working on an organic farm but are not actually training to be a farmer, you may be taken on by the WWOOF programme (Willing Workers on Organic Farms). See below for a contact.

Useful Addresses

The International Farm Experience Programme, National Agricultural Centre, Stoneleigh Park, Warwickshire CV6 2LG; ☎01203-696578.
The International Agricultural Exchange Association (Servicing Office) 1000 1st Avenue South, Great Falls, Montana 59401, United States of America; IAEA (Servicing Office), No. 206, 1505-17 Ave. S.W. Calgary, Alberta T2T OE2 Canada.
WWOOF Sweden, c/o Andreas Hedren, Palstorp Hunna, 340 30 Vislanda; ☎0470-75 43 75; www.wwoof.org.

HOTEL AND CATERING

It is possible to go to Sweden to look for work in the hotel and catering trade. You may also find adverts on the EURES website in the spring (see above). A fair number of jobs for bartenders, cooks, waiters and other staff can be found in the weekly *Platsjournalen* available from the *Arbetsförmedlingar*. If you decide to do an on-the-spot job hunt you should contact the nearest employment office which can provide up-to-date details of the latest vacancies but it is also feasible to tout around the hotels themselves.

Most hotel work will be found in the holiday resorts around the south coast, particularly around Orebo, Are, and Linköping. Of the main cities, Stockholm and Gothenburg have the largest number of hotels. The average wage is about £1,200 a month for an average working week of 40 hours. Much of this type of work is seasonal and accommodation is usually provided which should help towards the Swedish high cost of living. An alternative is to write to hotels prior to the season, stating your interests and any relevant qualifications. A list can be obtained from the Swedish Travel & Tourism Council, 11 Montagu Place, London W1H 2AL; ☎020-7870 5600; fax 020-7724 5872; e-mail info@swetourism.org.uk; www.visit-sweden.com.

Sweden is served by an extensive coastline and 46 ferries regularly travel to and from Sweden's 25 ports. In the past foreigners have found jobs working aboard the cruisers and ferries plying across the Gulf of Bothnia to Finland and the Baltic States. Additionally there are the ferries which take tourists island-hopping around the archipelago off Stockholm; there is the Göta Kanal tourist route which links the Baltic with the North Sea via Sweden's two largest lakes, Vänern and Vättern. As well as catering, some of the ships need staff for entertainment such as DJ-ing. Whilst there is no formal procedure of application, you could enquire about jobs on board at the Swedish job centres, or approach the shipping company directly. You can obtain addresses of ship companies from the Stockholm Information Service, Sweden House Tourist Centre, Hamngatan 27, Kungsträdgården, Stockholm; ☎08-789 24 90; fax 08-789 24 91; e-mail info@stoinfo.se.

VOLUNTARY WORK

There are a few opportunities for voluntary work in Sweden. *Internationella Arbetslag*, the Swedish branch of Service Civil International, recruits volunteers to take part in international work camps in Sweden. Work varies from manual labour to social activities and there are usually study themes attached to the work camps. Work camps last for two weeks between June and September. Applicants should be over 18 and be prepared to work hard for 35-40 hours a week. Food and accommodation are provided but you will have to pay your own fares and insurance. You should apply through your local branch of Service Civil International; in the UK this is IVS; see www.sciint.org; in the US, www.sci-ivs.org.

Foreningen Staffansgarden is a community for adults with learning disabilities which takes on between five and 10 volunteers a year to work in the community. Work is varied and covers all aspects of daily life including cooking, cleaning and farming. The minimum age limit is 19 and the minimum length of stay six months; preference is given to applicants who can stay for one year. Board and accommodation are provided in the first six months and a small wage is paid thereafter.

Useful Addresses

International Arbetslag (IAL), Barnängsgatan 23, 116 41 Stockholm.
Foreningen Staffansgården, Box 66, Furugatan 1, 820 60 Delsbo; ☎0653-168 50; fax 0653-109 68.

ASPECTS OF EMPLOYMENT

SALARIES

There is no statutory minimum wage in Sweden and wages are usually fixed by collective agreements or by individual agreements between the employer and employee. Blue collar workers are normally paid according to hours worked on a fortnightly or weekly basis whilst white collar workers are usually paid a fixed monthly salary. Wages are not automatically adjusted to the cost of living although changes in the cost of living are taken in to account when collective agreements are made. Detailed lists of salary levels can be found on the Sweden Statistics website: www.scb.se; you will need to know the exact Swedish word for the type of job you are looking at.

TABLE 16 PRIVATE SECTOR MONTHLY EARNINGS		
Bank manager	SEK58,700	approx £3,990/US$5,690
Computer programmer	SEK25,000	approx. £1,700/US$2,420
Clerical Worker	SEK17,400	approx. £1,180/US$1,680
Industrial worker (paper and pulp)	SEK21,000	approx. £1,420/US$
Managing director	SEK75,000	approx. £5,100/US$7,250
Production manager	SEK26,800	approx. £1,820/US$2,600
Sales director	SEK52,500	approx. £3,570/US$5,090
Shop assistant	SEK18,900	approx. £1,280/US$1,800
Waiter	SEK16,100	approx. £1,094/US$1,560

TABLE 17 PUBLIC SECTOR MONTHLY EARNINGS		
Bus/tram driver	SEK18,100	approx. £1,230/US$1,750
Secondary school teacher	SEK26,000	approx. £1,760/US$2,500
Primary school teacher	SEK21,000	approx. £1,420/US$2,020
Cook	SEK16,500	approx. £1,120/US$1,600
Electrician	SEK19,500	approx. £1,320/US$1,890
Engineer	SEK33,000	approx. £2,240/US$3,200

Mine worker	SEK19,000	approx. £1,290/US$1,840
Nurse	SEK20,600	approx.£1,400/US$2,000
Physician	SEK42,000	approx. £2,850/US$4,070
Social Worker	SEK21,000	approx. £1,420/US$2,020

As a general rule, Swedish salaries are lower than those in the UK and the other wealthier EU countries, except for unskilled work, by a considerable margin, once taxation has been taken into account. Managing directors and top executives earn about a third of what they would earn in the United States. At other levels net pay is about 40% of US levels. Pay is about 60% of UK levels, after tax. This is not a country to get rich quick; generally people come here because they like the lifestyle and the social philosophy.

You can expect to pay between 31% and 45% of your salary in tax and pension contributions. If you are in a high earning bracket you could pay half of your salary, but no more. For this you get one of the world's best social security systems, however, you may not feel particularly wealthy at the end of the month. Tables 16 and 17 give monthly earnings in the private and public sectors in Swedish Kronor (2002 figures).

WORKING CONDITIONS

The average working week in Sweden is officially defined as 40 hours; in practice it is 37 hours. Employees are entitled to at least 36 hours of leisure time in a seven-day period, usually at weekends. Employees are entitled to have a break during working hours and should not work more than five hours in a row. There may be exemptions to this, for example in the case of those who work at sea or in road transport. Working conditions are monitored by the National Board of Occupational Safety and Health and the implementation of laws governing working conditions are supervised by Labour Inspectorates. Salaried employees often have shorter working days in the summer. Employees are entitled to at least 25 days paid holiday per year and in addition there are 13 public holidays. At least four weeks of continuous leave can be taken during the period between June and August unless there is a collective agreement to the contrary. There is no legislation regarding work on Sunday, but generally most employees do not work at the weekend.

CONTRACTS

Verbal or even tacit contracts are legally binding in Sweden, but it is still advisable to get a written one. The employer is legally obliged to inform you in writing within a month of your start of employment about rules and conditions for employment. The information must give the name and address of your employer, the details of your work assignment, the duration of employment, period of notice, rights to paid vacation, working hours and any relevant collective agreements. Under the 1982 Act on Security of Employment employees can only be dismissed on objective grounds (unless there is a statement in the contract that states otherwise, e.g. temporary employment). Objective grounds include serious breach of rules, non-authorised absence from work, crime in the workplace and an inability to co-operate at work. Non-objective grounds include sickness, pregnancy, minor offences and crimes not related to the workplace.

Employees have the right to a minimum of one month's notice from the employer in the event of dismissals and employers have a similar expectation from employees. The period of notice increases with length of service and the age of the employee. Regulations regarding unfair dismissal are very comprehensive and you should approach your union representative if you feel you have been unfairly treated or make use of the ombudsman system which is prevalent throughout the country.

Part-time

There are no specific rules about part-time employment in Sweden, but part-time contracts are as legally binding as any other kind of contract and employees who work part-time are entitled to the same rights and duties as other employees. Part-time work is quite common; about a quarter of workers work less than 35 hours a week. Women do more part-time work than men.

Private Employment Agency Workers

Those employed by private employment agencies are entitled to the same rights and duties as all other employees. The employment agency is classed as your employer. If you have voluntarily left an employment and are taken on by an employment agency you may not be leased out to your former employer for at least six months after you have left that employer.

ETIQUETTE IN THE WORKPLACE

Many Swedes hate notions of nationalism and national character, believing that this is only a step away from racial stereotyping, nonetheless it will not be appreciated if you criticise Sweden or the Swedes to their face. Generally matters are conducted along smooth lines and fuss is kept to a minimum. Interview studies have revealed that in the workplace loud confrontations are less frequent than in many other countries and politeness and respect are the norm amongst all sectors of the workplace. Less of a distinction is made between workers and management in Sweden than, say, in Britain or the US. A strong history of trade unionism means that worker's opinions are represented and listened to when important decisions are being made and bosses frequently consult with their employees; the preferred leadership style is consultative.

The furniture designers Ikea in particular have operated on egalitarian principles where all employees are encouraged to contribute to company development and where top executives fly economy class, giving it a rather Swedish Body Shop image. Attitudes in Sweden tend to emphasise the importance of the group rather than the individual. Whilst it is normal for Swedes to work hard during working hours it is recognised that people have duties towards their families and other groups so there is an annual limitation on overtime (about 200 hours a year).

In general, handshaking is *de rigueur* when doing business; the majority of Swedish business men and women will not deafen you with hype – their disarming honesty can take a bit of getting used to. A Swedish business meeting will usually start on time and the small talk that is customary in many countries is usually by-passed.

TRADE UNIONS

Trade unions were first formed in Sweden in the 19th century and are an important feature of Swedish labour relations. The central organisation for the workers is the Swedish Trade Union Confederation or LO and for employers it is the Confederation of Swedish Enterprise, formerly known as the Swedish Employers Confederation or SAF. There are a number of other unions representing professional and white collar workers of which the most important are the Confederation of Salaried Employees (for white collar employees) and the Confederation of Professional Associations (mainly for university-educated white collar employees).

The LO is the largest confederation in Sweden representing almost 85% of blue collar workers and comprising 21 trade unions nationwide. The LO and SAF came to a joint agreement in 1938 whereby the interests of workers and employers should be protected. The agreement has undergone some modification since but labour relations in Sweden are on the whole good. About 90% of employees belong to a union. Labour and employer organisations are hierarchically structured at local, regional and central levels As well as overseeing working conditions they form an important political power base in Swedish society.

Useful addresses

The Trade Union Confederation (LO), Barnhusgatan 18, 105 53 Stockholm; ☎08-796 25 00; www.lo.se.

Confederation of Swedish Enterprise (Svenskt Näringsliv), Storgatan 19, 114 82 Stockholm; ☎08-553 430 00; e-mail info@svensktnaringsliv.se; www.svensktnaringsliv.se.

Confederation of Professional Employees (TCO), Linnégatan 14, Stockholm; ☎08-782 91 00; www.tco.se.

Confederation of Professional Associations (SACO), Box 2206, 103 15 Stockholm; ☎8 613 48 00; www.saco.se.

WOMEN IN WORK

The number of women with paid jobs is now equal to the number of men. 85% of mothers with pre-school children work and this is made possible through extensive child care facilities. Women are working longer hours now than they used to because of the increased provision of child-care services. About

60% of employed women work full-time. There are still fairly traditional divides between male and female occupational choices – 90% of all engineers, architects, electricians and mechanics are men; women predominate in areas such as clerical work, pre-school teaching, secretarial work, kitchen work and nursing. Whilst women enjoy a relatively good representation at middle management levels they are under-represented at higher levels and very few women hold top leadership positions in companies and trade unions. Politically women are relatively prominent in elected bodies such as Parliament and the municipal and county councils. 40% of Members of Parliament are women, even though there is no law that obliges political parties to have women-only shortlists.

BUSINESS AND INDUSTRY REPORT

Sweden has to a large extent recovered from the devastating recession of 1991-1997. GDP per head has, however, only returned to where it was in 1990, so that the country is actually now at only 21 in the scale of wealthiest countries. Most new employment has come through the state sector. Sweden now hopes to capitalise on its highly educated workforce, and push ahead with the creation of a 'knowledge-based' society. It is considered a particularly favourable location for research and development, thanks to the close co-operation of the academic world and industry. Investment in industry is strong, with increased foreign ownership the main theme.

In most respects the economy is now on a very sound footing, and while taxes may not come down much, Sweden is facing up to the challenges of an increasingly ageing population much better than many other EU countries. Much depends on how the global economy develops from 2002 onwards; the economy is very export-oriented and thus easily blown off course by recessions elsewhere. Public finances are generally much healthier than they were before 1997, thanks to better economic management. Inflation stands at a relatively low 1.5%; the state had a budget surplus of 4.1% of GDP in 2001. The public debt has come down to 48% of GDP.

Sweden's entry into the European Economic Area in 1994 followed by entry into the European Union in 1995 has given a boost to trade and industry by increasing trade opportunities, reducing red tape and removing tariff restrictions. The abolition of restrictions on cross-border acquisitions and overseas investments led to some notable investments by Sweden including Stena's acquisition of British Sealink Ferries and Svenska Cellulosa's purchase of the German conglomerate Feldmühle G. Nobel, although the proposed merger between Swedish Volvo and French Renault proved to be abortive. Some major Swedish companies have come under foreign ownership. Saab's automotive side is now part of General Motors, and Volvo's car production company is part of Ford.

The Swedish economy is heavily dependent on foreign trade; Western Europe and North America are the main Swedish export markets. The biggest trading partners are Germany, the UK, the USA and the Nordic countries of Denmark,

Norway and Finland. Sweden's main sources of imports are the UK and Germany. Major imports include machinery and equipment for industry, office machinery, petroleum and petroleum products, and iron and steel. Principal exports include road vehicles, medical and pharmaceutical products and industrial machinery.

The following section provides a guide to some of the most important Swedish industries.

ENGINEERING

Engineering forms a significant sector of Swedish industry. About 385,000 people are employed in engineering; engineering products make up 56% of exports. The industry is mainly concentrated in southern and central Sweden and includes several of Sweden's largest industrial companies including Asea. In 1988 Asea linked with Switzerland's Brown Boveri to form the world's largest electrotechnology group, ABB. Another giant is SKF which is a world leader in all kinds of bearings; SKF employs 150 British managers at a senior level. Electrolux has become a household name in white goods and is amongst the world's largest producers. After the motor industry, mechanical engineering is the most important sub-sector of Swedish engineering, followed by electrical products (telecommunications and household appliances) and metal goods. Telecommunications account for 40% of Sweden's electrical industry; the giant Ericsson has been particularly popular with foreign investors. Medical electronics is also a growth area.

THE AUTOMOTIVE INDUSTRY

The automotive industry is the most important sub-sector of engineering and is dominated by the two Swedish giants, Volvo and Saab-Scania. The automotive industry contributes 13% of total Swedish exports, some SEK100 (approx. £6.8/US$9.7) billion a year.

Volvo has made a remarkable come-back since the company experienced its highest ever losses between 1988 and 1993 when car sales fell from 340,000 to 125,000; sales were up to 422,000 by 2001. In the late 1990s Volvo became hugely profitable again. Efficiency has been sharply improved in the process with the number of hours taken to produce a car reduced from 70 to 40. Volvo had to abandon an attempt to merge with Renault, although it has retained Renault's trucks section. The car production company, Volvo Cars, was sold to the Ford Motor Company in 1999, while the trucks and buses section remains in the Volvo Group. Volvo is now the world's third largest manufacturer of trucks; about one in five of trucks sold in the western world are produced by Volvo and Scania.

Saab also went through extensive restructuring; it is a far smaller company than Volvo, producing about 133,000 cars a year. In 1989 the US-owned General Motors and Saab-Scania signed an agreement spinning off the Saab division into a new company Saab Automobile AB, with Saab Scania and GM each owning 50%. The signs for both Saab and Volvo are good although their shared traditional selling points – environmental friendliness and safety – are fast being caught up with by competitors.

Both Volvo and Saab-Scania also produce heavy engines and aircraft components.

ARMS INDUSTRY

Despite a long history of neutrality, Sweden has the Nordic region's largest defence industry. With a population the same size as Los Angeles, Sweden ranks as a major producer of defence technology. The defence industry is undergoing extensive restructuring and reductions following the end of the Cold War and there has been a move towards co-operation amongst the four Nordic countries of Sweden, Denmark, Norway and Finland in the production of defence equipment. It is expected that Sweden's contribution will be largely in the field of artillery. Car giants Saab have produced fourth generation aircraft of which the most recent is the JAS 39 Gripen fighter plane. Sweden's main armaments company, Bofors, is now part of the US United Defense group; employment has fallen to a mere 550; it functions as a development and assembly company, with the main focus on long-range artillery systems.

CHEMICALS

About 75,000 employees work in the chemical industry. In total, the chemical industry (including rubber and plastic products) accounts for 11% of Sweden's industrial output. The most important sector of the industry is pharmaceuticals which employs 18,000 people, and accounts for 5% of Sweden's exports. Overall, 90% of production is exported. Pharmaceuticals is dominated by two giant companies, AstraZeneca and Pharmacia. Pharmacia is now based in America, with 59,000 employees, of whom 5,000 work in Sweden. AstraZeneca has its headquarters in London; globally it has 50,000 employees, with 11,000 in Sweden.

Many specialised biotechnology companies have sprung up around the main university research centres of Lund, Malmö, Gothenburg, Stockholm and Umeå. Most are very small R&D outfits, developing products to be sold to larger companies. Pharmacia and AstraZeneca are also involved in biotech research; APBiotech, jointly owned by the British-based Nycomed Amersham and Pharmacia, is one of the world's leading suppliers of biotechnology systems, and products and services for research into genes and proteins, and the development of drugs. Pharmacia Corporation was itself formed from a merger of Pharmacia with Upjohn and Monsanto. Agrobiotechnology is dominated by two medium-sized companies, Novartis Seed and Svalöf Weibull. Other important areas are diagnostics and medical technology.

MINING AND STEEL

Mining is a centuries old tradition in Sweden but has declined in importance since the mid-1970s. The mining industry employs about 10,000 people and exports 52% of its products, accounting for about 1% of the total industrial value. The major mining company is the state-owned LKAB, which operates the giant Kiruna and Malmberget mines. Sweden has around 2% of the world's iron ore reserves; Kiruna produces 22 million metric tonnes of ores a year. The mine extends deep underground, with a total of 310 miles of tunnels. Sweden also produces large quantities of copper, lead, zinc, silver, gold and other non-ferrous metals which are mined in northern Sweden, principally from mines owned by Boliden (a subsidiary of Trelleborg).

With its large engineering industry, Sweden is amongst the world's largest per capita steel consumers. 24,000 people work in the steel industry which exports about 80% of its products and accounts for 4% of the country's total industrial value. Approximately 65% of production is in the form of speciality steels. The steel industry has undergone extensive restructuring and modernising. In 1991 Avesta merged with British Stainless Steel to form Avesta Sheffield; in 2001 it merged with the Finnish Outokumpu Steel to create AvestaPolarit. The other major specialty steel producers are Sandvik Steel, Ovako Steel and Uddenholm Tooling. The main ordinary steel producers are SSAB and Fundia AB.

FORESTRY AND PAPER PRODUCTS

Sweden's forests have traditionally been the foundation of her wealth, along with her metal-working industry. Just over half of all woodland is in private ownership; only 3% is owned by the state. Thanks to good management, the amount of growing stock has actually increased by 60% since the 1920s. There are some 48 paper mills, of which 15 use recycled fibre. About 70% of paper and packaging used in Sweden is recycled, a very high percentage in international terms. Sweden is also a world leader in the manufacture of logging and paper-making plant.

Exports of pulp, paper and paperboard products are the third largest in the world; the European Union forms 80% of the export market. About 45,000 employees work in the paper industry, which exports 70% of its production and accounts for 8% of the total industrial value.

The Swedish pulp and paper industry has undergone numerous mergers and has made large investments in the EU through the acquisition of Feldmühle and Reedpack by Stora Enso and SCA. Ten per cent of all paper production within the EU is manufactured by Swedish subsidiaries; the pulp and paper giants are Stora Enso, SCA and Holmen. As far as timber goes, the main producers are SCA/Scaninge, Assidomän, Stora Enso Timber and Sodra Timber. Sweden is the world's second largest exporter of sawn coniferous wood products.

Furniture producers Ikea have become as much a symbol of Sweden as Abba and Volvo; the company which started as a mail order business is now the biggest furniture group in the world with 65,000 employees in 25 countries. Described as 'cheap without the nasty', Ikea has stayed ahead by marketing furniture at prices 20-30% lower than its competitors. Fitted kitchens are another Swedish speciality; Nobia is one of the world's main manufacturers.

REGIONAL EMPLOYMENT GUIDE

Sweden is a large country with a small population of whom 90% live in the south and 85% in cities and urban areas. Consequently there is an inevitable divide between employment opportunities in the north and south. What follows is a general round-up of major work areas:

Fishing is concentrated largely around the south coast with Gothenburg as the leading fish harbour and fish market. The pulp and paper industry developed originally around the mouths of rivers around Lake Vänern and the Gulf of Bothnia although new plants have been built around the coasts of southern Sweden. Historically the metal industry has been dependent on water power and forest land (which gives charcoal fuel) which determined the location of iron mills. Oxelösund and Luleå on the coast are home to modern iron and steel mills. The main plants of the automotive and aerospace industries are situated in south-central Sweden. Volvo has its headquarters in Gothenburg and Saab-Scania in Trollhättan whilst heavy vehicles are produced in Södertälje and aircraft in Linköping. Electrics and the electronics industry are based mainly around Stockholm and Västerås. The forested areas of Southern Sweden are home to small plastic, metal and glass-processing plants. The petrochemical industry is based at Stenungsund on the west coast and the pharmaceutical and biotechnology companies are located near the leading university research centres in Lund, Uppsala, Umeä and Stockholm.

DIRECTORY OF MAJOR EMPLOYERS

For a full and detailed list of British owned subsidiaries operating in Sweden contact The Swedish Trade Council (Box 5513, 114 85 Stockholm; ☎ 08-783 87 00. *Kompass Sweden,* lists a lot of (but not all) Swedish companies, with precise details of subsidiaries, turnover etc. It can be more conveniently consulted on a CD-Rom at Tradepartners UK, and other business information centres (see *Starting a Business* section). *Major Companies of Scandinavia* (publ. Graham & Whiteside), lists the main companies in alphabetical order. *Europe's 15,000 Largest Companies* lists the top 50 firms in order of turnover. Dun & Bradstreet's *Who Owns Whom,* gives British and American companies with Swedish subsidiaries.

Company	Employees	Type of Company
ABB (Asea Brown Boveri)	19,500	Power transmission
Apoteket	10,000	Pharmaceuticals
Axel Johnson	13,000	Retail distribution
AB Electrolux	92,910	Consumer appliances
Ericsson	103,000	Telecoms
Kooperativa Förbundet	18,000	Retailing
Nordea	38,000	Banking
Pharmacia	61,000	Pharmaceuticals
Saab Automobile	10,100	Automotive
Scania AB	39,000	Trucks
Svedala Industri AB	11,200	Mining equipment
Skanska AB	39,000	Construction
AB SKF	40,300	Bearings
Svenska Cellulosa Aktiebolaget	37,600	Forestry products
Trelleborg AB	12,500	Engineering
AB Volvo	76,000	Automotive
Volvo Lastvagnar	23,700	Trucks
Volvo Personvagnar	29,000	Automobiles

MAJOR EMPLOYERS

Automotive

Autoliv Sverige AB, Vellentinsv., 447 37 Vårgårda.

Bilia AB, N. Långebergsg. 3, 421 32 Västra Frölunda.

SAAB Automobile, 461 80 Trollhättan.

Scania AB, 151 87 Södertälje.

Trelleborg Automotive, Järnsvägsg. 24, Horda, 33018 Jönköping.

AB Volvo, 405 08 Göteborg.

Volvo Bussar AB, 405 08 Göteborg.

Volvo Lastvagnar AB, Gropegårdsg., 417 15 Göteborg.

Volvo Penta AB, Dept 40000 Z1.3, 405 08 Göteborg.

Volvo Personvagnar (Components), Olofström, 293 80 Blekinge.

Volvo Personvagnar AB, 405 31 Göteborg.

Forestry

Assi Domän AB Forestry, 880 30 Näsåker.

Göteborgs List & Träindustri AB, Långavallsg 2, 424 57 Angered.

Jarl-Trä AB, Kalvamo, 361 93 Broakula.

Mellanskog Industri AB, Box 127, 751 04 Uppsala.

Niab AB, Box 117, 330 27 Hestra.

SCA, Stureplan 3, 103 97 Stockholm.

Skogsägarna Norrskog Ek Förening, Kontorsv. 2, 872 31 Kramfors.

Stora Enso Tiber AB, Lingheds Sågverk, 790 25 Linghed.

Tarkett AB, 372 81 Ronneby.

Furniture and Interiors

Bjärnums Möbelfabriker Hokus Pokus AB, Box 22, 280 20 Bjärnum.

Hyllteknik AB, Box 73, 432 22 Alvesta.

Ikea AB, Box 700, 343 81 Älmhult.

Kinnarps, 521 88 Kinnarp.

Nobia AB, Box 70376, 107 24 Stockholm.

TUVE Möbler AB, 147 82 Tumba.

Information and Communications Technology

Cap Gemini Ernst & Young, Gustavs-lundsv. 131, 161 51 Bromma.
Compaq Computer, Allén 6A, 172 89 Sundbyberg.
Ericsson Infotech AB, Lagergrens g. 2, 652 26 Karlstad.
Ericsson Software Technology, Ölandsg. 1, Karlskrona.
Hewlett Packard Sverige, Skalholtsg. 9, 164 40 Kista.
IBM Svenska, Oddeg. 5, 164 40 Kista.
Microsoft, Finlandsg. 30, 164 74 Kista.
Oracle Svenska, Färög. 7, 164 40 Kista.
Telefonaktiebolaget LM Ericsson, Telefonv. 30, 126 25 Stockholm.

Industrial Machinery

Atlas Copco Compressor, Marcusplatsen 1A, 131 34 Nacka.
Cardo, Roskildev. 1, 211 47 Malmö.
Ferm AB, Harpsundsv 166, 124 59 Bandhagan.
ITT Flygt AB, Svetsarv. 12, 171 41 Solna.
SKF Sverige AB, 415 50 Göteborg.
Svenska Klöckner, Drottningg. 22, 411 14 Göteborg.
Volvo Penta AB, Gropegårdsg., 405 08 Göteborg.
Zander and Ingeström AB, Dalv. 4, Solna.

Metal Products

AB SKF, 415 50 Göteborg.

AvestaPolarit, Box 16377, 103 27 Stockholm.
Ovako Steel, Hornsg. 1, 415 50 Göteborg.
Sandvik AB, 811 81 Sandvik.
SSAB Svenskt Stål, Birger Jarlsg. 58, 114 29 Stockholm.
Stena Metall, Fiskhamnsg. 8, 414 58 Göteborg.
Uddeholm Tooling, Aminog. 25, 341 53 Mölndal.

Pulp and Paper

Holmen Paper AB, Vattengränden 2, 602 22 Norrköping.
MoDo Paper AB, 891 20 Örnsköldsvik.
Stora Enso Hylte AB, 314 81 Hyltebruk.
Svenska Cellulose AB, Stureplan 3, 111 45 Stockholm.
Tumba Bruk AB, 147 82 Tumba.

Pharmaceutical Products

AstraZeneca AB, 151 85 Södertälje.
Aventis Pharma, Box 47604, 117 94 Stockholm.
Glaxo Wellcome, Aminog. 27, 431 53 Mölndal.
Hoechst Norden, Göteborgsv. 91B, 431 37 Mölndal.
Merck Sharp & Dohme, Box 7125, 192 07 Sollentuna.
Nobel Biocare, Box 5190, 402 26 Göteborg.
Pfizer AB, Nytorpsv. 36, 183 53 Täby.
Pharmacia AB, Lindhagensg. 133, 112 87 Stockholm.

STARTING A BUSINESS

The Swedish government's attitude towards foreign investment and ownership is favourable. Sweden's traditional position as a neutral nation enjoying good relations with other countries is complemented by a heavy emphasis on foreign trade.

Sweden has always had a high level of dependence on foreign trade and direct investments abroad by Swedish companies have grown at an astounding rate since the 1970s. A very high number of Swedes work abroad – about 500,000 in 2002 – and of these, 55% work in the EU countries and 18% in North America. The vast majority are employed in subsidiaries of Swedish manufacturing companies. An important result of the rise in Swedish corporate capital spending abroad is an increased access to foreign markets generally.

Foreign direct investments in Sweden have increased many times over in the past decade. The Nordic countries, France, the Netherlands, the United Kingdom, Germany and the United States are the major countries with investing in Sweden. Sweden's accession to the European Economic Area followed by membership of the European Union in 1995 made it easier for foreign companies to acquire Swedish businesses, hence Volvo and Saab's car-making concerns came under foreign ownership. About 40% of shares on the Swedish stock exhange are in foreign hands.

Sweden is an advanced industrial nation whose workforce is generally well-educated; the majority speak good English. Absenteeism is, however, a serious problem, although this is not unique in Scandinavia. The communications and transport infrastructure is well developed. In summary, the main market advantages for British investors include historical trade links, good communications, an English-speaking workforce and cultural compatibility. Market inhibitors include geographical remoteness, a small domestic market and the very high costs of labour.

PROCEDURES INVOLVED IN BUYING OR STARTING A NEW BUSINESS

Preparation from Scratch

Anyone contemplating starting or buying a business in Sweden should seek appropriate help from expert sources (see addresses below). Fact sheets on Swedish industry and on its various branches can be obtained from the Swedish Institute which acts as an information service for Sweden. The Institute can also provide general up-to-date information on the Swedish economy, foreign policy and the labour market. Some of this information is disseminated through the internet.

The Invest in Sweden Agency can provide information about the process of setting up a business in Sweden; see the website www.isa.se. Local Chambers of Commerce can also help. The Swedish Chamber of Commerce in London has a very useful yearbook, with addresses and information on setting up a business. Information on Swedish tax laws for business purposes can be obtained from the National Tax Board (*Riksskatteverket* – RSV). Details on Swedish business can be obtained from the Swedish Trade Council, which is the national service organisation for all exporters of goods and services and has missions in many countries. The Council can provide information about customs and imports regulations and is particularly involved in setting up trade links between Swedish exporters and foreign firms. For those intending to employ staff, the trade union of employers, the Confederation of Swedish Employers, runs its own information department.

Useful Addresses

British-Swedish Chamber of Commerce, Jakobs Torg 3, 4th Floor, Stockholm; ☎08-506 126 17; fax 08-506 129 15; www.bscc.swednet.net.

Invest in Sweden Agency, Box 90, 101 21 Stockholm; ☎08-402 78 00; fax 08-402 78 78; www.isa.se.

National Swedish Organisation of Small Businesses, Sergelgatan 1, 106 67 Stockholm; ☎08-406 17 00; fax 08-24 55 26; www.fr.se.

National Tax Board, Tritonvägen 21, 171 94 Solna; ☎08-764 80 00; www.rsv.se.

Swedish-American Chambers of Commerce, 119 Oronoco St, Alexandria, VA 22314; ☎703-836 6560; www.sacc-usa.org.

Swedish Chamber of Commerce for the United Kingdom, Sweden House, 5 Upper Montagu St, London W1H 2AG; ☎020-7224 8001; fax 020-7224 8884; www.swedish-chamber.org.uk.

The Swedish Trade Council, Box 5513, 114 85 Stockholm; ☎08-783 87 00; www.swedishtrade.se.

The Swedish Trade Council, 73 Welbeck Street, London W1M 8AN; ☎020-7935 9601; fax 020-7935 4130; www.swedishtrade.com/uk.

Registration

All new businesses in Sweden must be registered with the Register of Companies (*Bolagsregistret*). The purchasers of the new business must provide the company's name, registered address, the company's fiscal year-end, the number and nominal values of the shares (where appropriate), any restrictions on their transfer and the names and addresses of the directors and the auditor. Formation of a limited company usually takes one month and there is a registration fee of about SEK1,500 (approx £102/US$145). The company should also register with the tax office and social security office and where appropriate with the Patent and Registration Office (*Patent-och Registreringsverket*).

Useful Addresses

Register of Companies, 851 81 Sundsvall; ☎060-18 40 00.
The Patent and Registration Office, Trade Marks Department, Box 5055, 102 42 Stockholm; ☎08-782 25 00; www.prv.se.

Regional Trade Associations

Sweden has 12 local Chambers of Commerce which are run as independent private organisations representing industry and commerce in their areas. About 10,000 companies are members; the chambers assist with internal Swedish matters and promote trade between Sweden and other countries. The Swedish Trade Council promotes exports through the commercial departments of Swedish embassies abroad and through its own offices. The Council acts in cooperation with other Swedish export organisations and helps foreign companies who want to trade with Sweden. The Federation of Swedish Industries is a private federation of 1,300 companies. The Federation promotes trade and imports and has a special foreign trade department.

Useful Addresses

The Swedish Trade Council, Box 5513, 114 85 Stockholm; ☎08-783 87 00; www.swedishtrade.se.
Swedish Trade Council, 259-269 Old Marylebone Road London NW1 5RA, ☎020-7616 4070; fax 020-7616 4099; unitedkingdom@swedishtrade.se.
Federation of Swedish Chambers of Commerce, Box 16050, 103 21 Stockholm; ☎08-555 100 00; e-mail shf@chamber.se; www.cci.se.
Federation of Swedish Industries, Box 5501, 114 85 Stockholm; ☎08-783 80 00; www.industriforbundet.se.

Choosing an Area

When you have decided on a business idea and carried out the appropriate market research you will need to consider where to locate your business. As the Regional Employment Guide in the previous chapter indicated, the overwhelming majority of the population and businesses are to be found in the south and this will probably influence your choice of location to a very large degree. Whilst costs in the north may be generally lower it should be borne in mind that the population is much smaller and therefore labour supplies may be scarce. A certain remoteness in the north would also pose an increase in transport costs. However, there are more financial incentives on offer to businesses choosing to locate in rural areas where the economy is weaker. The Regional Development Fund (see ALMI below) can provide advice for those considering locating a business away from major urban areas.

Raising Finance

If you intend to reside in Sweden you will find it difficult to raise finance with a British bank, but Swedish banks will lend money to foreign businesses. The

Swedish banks have undergone a number of changes in recent years including the elimination of several regulatory restraints with a view to becoming more competitive in the international environment following Sweden's membership of the EU. One result has been an increasing number of commercial banks which are the leading source of short-term finance and about one-half of their loans are made to businesses. Because of the importance of foreign trade to Sweden, Swedish banks have a reputation for efficiency in handling foreign currency transactions. Other sources of credit include the National Pensions Fund whose assets exceed the combined assets of all commercial banks and which can provide long-term financing to companies. Insurance companies also have significant influence in capital markets.

Useful Addresses

Alfred Berg, Box 70447, 107 25 Stockholm; 08-723 58 00 or 0771-33 44 55; www.alfredberg.se.
Alfred Berg, 250 Bishopsgate, London EC2M 4AA; ☎020-7678 2700.
Handelsbanken UK, Trinity Tower, 9 Thomas More St, London E1W 1GE; fax 020-7578 8004; www.handelsbanken.se.
HSBC Bank, V. Trädgårdsg. 17, Box 7615, 103 94 Stockholm; ☎08-454 54 00.
Stadshypotek AB, Box 53, 701 41 Írebro; ☎020-75 00 31; www.stadshypotek.se.
Skandinaviska Enskilda Banken AB, Stureplan 2, 106 40 Stockholm; ☎08-679 58 95; www.seb.se.

Investment Incentives

The main sources for grants and financial aid for foreign investors are the Regional Development Funds (*Utvecklingsfonder*) now under the ALMI organisation, and the Swedish National Board for Industrial and Technical Development (NUTEK). However, Sweden's entry into the EU has meant that grants and aid have been reduced in order to comply with EU regulations.

Useful Addresses

ALMI Stockholm, Tegelbacken 4, 111 52 Stockholm; ☎08-4402 09 00; e-mail info.stockholm@almi.se; www.almi.se.
ALMI Väst, Box 8794, 402 76 Göteborg; ☎031-779 79 00; e-mail info.vast@almi.se.
NUTEK, Liljeholmsvägen 32, 113 99 Stockholm; ☎08 681 91 00; www.nutek.se.
Ministry of Industry and Commerce, Fredsgatan 8, 103 33 Stockholm; ☎08-405 10 00; www.naring.regeringen.se.

Business Structures

Companies: Limited liability companies (*aktiebolag* or AB) are used by the vast majority of business enterprises in Sweden. ABs are either private or public; there are about 300,000 ABs, but only 1,300 public ABs. A limited liability company is classed as a separate legal entity and is also considered to be a separate entity for tax purposes. Initial share capital in a private AB must be a minimum of SEK100,000 (approx. £6,800/US$9,700); in a public AB it is SEK500,000. ABs are the only form of limited liability company in Sweden. In the case of a private AB, you can attract share capital by making an offer by mail to up to 200 people; over this number you may only contact people who have already shown an interest in your company. Only one auditor is required for an AB, or you can appoint an accounting firm, who then appoint one auditor.

Partnerships: There are two types of partnerships: the *handelsbolag* (HB) and the *kommanditbolag* (KB). Partners in an HB have unlimited liability, whereas in a KB one or more partners has unlimited liability. Profits and losses of a partnership are divided among partners according to their agreement or according to the Partnership Act. Individuals are taxed on their shares of the net income but, for the purposes of VAT, the partnership constitutes a separate entity.

Non-trading partnership: The simplest form of company is an *enkelt bolag* or non-trading partnership. The company is not a legal entity in itself; the partners merely agree to conduct business jointly, and are liable for all the debts that may arise from the company. Non-trading partnerships are often used for joint ventures. A limited liability company is taxed directly but partnerships are not directly taxed; individual partners are taxed on their share of the profit.

Trusts: A trust (*stiftelse*) is formed when the founder appoints separate and independent property for a particular use. The tax authorities recognise three types of trust: privileged, family and others. Only a privileged trust is exempt from tax; more than 80% of its activities must benefit the public and it must use over 80% of its income over a five-year period as evidence that it is active.

Branches of Foreign Companies: A parent company operating within its country of origin may apply to form a branch company in Sweden. Branches are generally subject to the same rules as companies resident and domiciled in Sweden. Branches should maintain separate books, appoint a manager who is domiciled in Sweden and appoint an auditor who is a certified public accountant in Sweden.

IDEAS FOR NEW BUSINESSES

The UK Department of Trade and Industry identifies the following consumer goods as areas of opportunity for potential traders in Sweden: clothing, furniture (particularly reproduction) and foodstuffs. Clothing has especial potential because the Swedish manufacture of home-made clothes and shoes has declined due to heavy competition from abroad and British fashions are particularly favoured. Other areas which the DTI is exploring include automotive components and accessories and the food and drink sector. Another area of potential is in establishing language schools specialising in Business English as there is a big demand for this. Areas such as Gothenburg which have a large English-speaking expatriate community offer potential for the establishment of typically English/Irish pubs and eating places although food and alcohol costs may make this a rather expensive proposition. There is a high level of environmental concern in Sweden which may provide openings for the selling of environmentally friendly products.

Exporters

The Trade Partners UK Information Centre is well worth a visit; the Centre has useful information on Sweden, including trade and telephone directories. The Centre's address is Kingsgate House, 66-74 Victoria Street, London SW1E 6SW. It is open from 09.00 to 20.00 Monday to Thursday (last admission 19.30) and 09.00 to 17.30 on Fridays (last admission 17.00). Further information on the Centre's resources is available on the Trade Partners UK website at www.tradepartners.g ov.uk, by telephone on 020-7215 5444/5; fax 020-7215 4231 or by e-mail; use the e-mail option on the website. The website also has a useful report on Sweden.

RUNNING A BUSINESS

Employing Staff

Contracts: The important point to remember about contracts in Sweden is that even a tacit agreement can be considered legally binding. In practice many employment contracts are verbal although it is in everyone's interest to have a written contractual agreement drawn up. According to European Community directives employers are obliged to inform the employee in writing about the terms of the employment within a month from the beginning of the employment. This information should include the following:

- Name and address of employer and employee and the date on which the employment starts and the place of work.
- The employees duties and the nature of the position (i.e. open-ended or fixed-term contract).
- Notice period or date of termination of the contract.
- Methods and amount of payment.
- Hours of work and holiday.
- Any applicable collective agreement.
- Conditions for work abroad if the job abroad lasts more than one month.

The employer must give the employee one month's notice of any changes to the above conditions.

Under the 1982 Security of Employment Act it is possible to employ staff for a probationary period of not more than 12 months. Employment can be terminated before the end of the probationary period by both parties without the need to give a reason. In other cases, employees may only be dismissed on objective grounds, e.g. gross misconduct. The employer is obliged to consult and inform the employee and the relevant trade union in connection with a termination of an employment contract. The employee and trade union may challenge the dismissal through the courts. An employee may not be dismissed on grounds of pregnancy or sickness. Both the employer and the employee are entitled to a minimum of one month's notice and this period increases with length of service.

Trade Unions: About 90% of the labour force belong to a union. The central organisation for the workers is the Swedish Trade Union Confederation or LO; for employers it is the Confederation of Swedish Enterprise (*Svenskt Näringsliv*). The right to strike is guaranteed in the Swedish constitution unless it is forbidden by collective agreement. A strike does not terminate the employment contract but only suspends it for the duration of the action. In practice strikes are rare because of negotiation procedures which are built into the system.

Labour Relations: According to the 1976 Co-Determination Act, employees have far-reaching rights as regards representation, information and negotiation while the employer also has rights to negotiate with the trade union. The 1987 Board Representation for Employees in Private Enterprises Act states that in private enterprises employing more than 25 people employees can have two representatives on the board of directors. In companies employing more than 1,000 people, three employee representatives may be appointed. The representatives enjoy the same standing as the other members of the board. An employee involved in a work dispute has the right to assistance from her/his trade union; employees who are not members of a trade union have to find legal assistance elsewhere. The disciplinary powers of employers are fairly circumscribed by the Co-determination Act. An employee cannot incur any other penalty than damages for a breach of discipline; the burden of proof rests with the employer. An employee may only be dismissed for gross misconduct.

Employee Training: The 1974 Employee's Right to Educational Leave Act entitles every employee to leave of absence from employment for educational purposes. The Act applies to both public and private sector employees but does not entitle the employee to paid leave and nor does the Act cover purely private studies. The Act does not place any restriction on the duration of leave but the employer may be able to defer the leave for up to six months by negotiation. The Act is currently undergoing revision and some of the statutory provisions can be modified by collective agreement.

Wages and Salaries: There is no minimum wage in Sweden and wages are fixed by collective agreements or by individual agreements between employers and employees. Amendment of remuneration can only be done through collective agreements and the employer is obliged to inform the employees in writing of any amendments one month in advance.

Taxation and Social Security Contributions

Direct Taxes: These include national income tax which is levied on companies based on the results of their annual accounts with some adjustments made for tax purposes and individual income tax.

Individual Income Tax: Individual income tax is a local tax levied at a flat rate of on average 29%, and a national income tax which is levied on those in higher income brackets (see under *Daily Life*, Taxation for further details). Payment is withheld at source by the employer. Amounts withheld are paid to the authorities in the following month.

Corporate Income Tax: Corporate income tax is currently 30% and this is levied on all corporate income including interest, royalties and domestic and foreign dividends. For most companies the income year is the calendar year; income years ending on 30 April, 30 June and 31 August are permitted. A company should normally file a preliminary return before 1 December of the year before the income year.

Capital Gains Tax: Capital Gains Tax is a uniform 30%. The gain on sales of stock is fully taxable irrespective of the period of ownership. A gain on the sale of real property is taxed as income for business.

Social Security: The employer is responsible for all social security contributions, which add up to about 33% of the employee's salary. Pension contributions are, however, split between the employer and the employee. Both pay 8% of salary to the main pension scheme, and another 1.25% each to the Premium Pension scheme, adding up to 18.5% in total. There is a ceiling on the amount of pension contributions you have to pay. Self-employed people pay their own social security contributions at around 31% of income.

Legal Advice

Anyone contemplating doing business in Sweden should take specialist legal advice, preferably from a lawyer who is familiar with Swedish business law. The following English-speaking law firms specialise in Swedish business law:

Useful Addresses

Gärde Styrbjörn Advokatbyrå, Box 5208, Nybrogatan 34, 102 45 Stockholm; ☎08-587 240 00; fax 08-587 240 01; e-mail info@stockholm.garde.se.
Advokatfirman LJB, PO Box 465, 58105 Linköping; ☎013-12 30 40; e-mail lilaw@advljb.se; www.advljb.se.
Herslow and Holme HB, Södra Tullgatan 3, Box 4307, 203 14 Malmö; ☎040-10 14 60; fax 040-97 42 10.

Accountancy and Auditing Advice

Swedish law requires that under the Accounting Act of 1976 companies, partnerships and sole proprietors must comply with the following requirements:

- Account for all transactions and prepare accounts in a systematic and chronological order with appropriate supporting documents.
- Prepare annual reports.
- Retain all accounting material in Sweden for 10 years.

A company's annual report must be filed with the Registrar of Public Companies within one month of the company's AGM. It must be signed by the director and certify that the annual report and appropriation of profit were approved by the shareholders at the annual meeting.

Financial Reporting: The usual financial year is 12 months. Under the Accounting Act a business must prepare a financial statement at the end of each financial year. The statement should include a balance sheet and a statement of earnings with appropriate notes.

Audit Requirements: The annual reports of every limited liability company must be audited. The auditor must appoint at least one certified public accountant. The auditor's report must include the following:

○ Approval of the balance sheet and statement of earnings.
○ Approval of the board's proposed allocation of earnings for the distribution of dividends.
○ A discharge of responsibility for the members of the board with respect to their administration of the company for the fiscal year.

Swedish auditors are also required to express an opinion on the director's and chief executive's administration.

Useful Addresses

Ernst and Young, Box 3143, Adolf Fredriks Kyrkogata 2, 103 62 Stockholm; ☎08-520 590 00; www.ey.com.
The Association of Authorised Public Accountants, Nortullsgatan 6, Box 6417, 113 82 Stockholm; ☎08-506 112 00; www.far.se.
The Swedish Accounting Standards Board, Box 7831, 103 98 Stockholm; ☎08-787 80 28; www.bfn.se.

Personal Case Histories

DENMARK

JULIAN ISHERWOOD

Julian Isherwood is 49, and runs the radio station Banns Radio International at Banns.com from Copenhagen. He first came to Denmark in 1976 after marrying a Dane. With his natural talent for languages – he took a degree in Russian at London University – he set about learning Danish by working in a kindergarten. Since then he has had a varied career as a journalist covering all of Scandinavia, as well as setting up his own companies.

How did you manage to find a job?
I realised that I would have to learn Danish and I did this by working in a kindergarten; after nine months my Danish was good enough to land a job with *Politiken*, a leading Danish newspaper, as a features and picture editor. While I was at *Politiken* I became a stringer for UPI (an international news agency). Then after three years I went on to the Danish broadcasting corporation, Danmarks Radio, where I had a daily five-minute slot in English.

How did your career develop?
I was already established as a correspondent for UPI, and then had the good fortune to be asked to commentate on a boxing match being held in Copenhagen for the African Service of the BBC. I had another lucky break when I was asked to report on the Karlskrona incident, when a Russian submarine ran aground off Sweden, so I was then covering the whole of Scandinavia. Further work followed for *Time* and the *Daily Telegraph*. I also got into financial reporting with Knight Ridder and other firms, while still working for UPI. Eventually I set up a translation company, and then in 1996, Banns.com, which I now hope to expand to cover Norway, Sweden and Finland.

How easy was it to set up a business?
It is easy enough to set up a business here, but it is absolutely necessary to have a good accountant, whether you are Danish or not, because the rules are so complicated. Accountants are not that expensive here, and they know a lot about

the workings of the law; lawyers on the other hand are expensive. Without an accountant you will have problems keeping your business going.

Is it easy to find accommodation?
Accommodation is expensive; as a foreigner you need to have a steady income to be able to get a mortgage. Denmark has an odd system in that you usually have to take over several mortgages from previous owners, because the mortgage stays with the property. Every time someone takes over the property they take out a mortgage because they can't pay the full price, and so you end up paying off several loans.

How do you find the social life?
Although a lot of Danes speak good English, it is essential to learn Danish if you want to get to know people well. The Danes appear open on the surface, but they are actually quite difficult to get to know, and basically conservative. There are lots of pubs and clubs these days, where you might hit lucky. Fortunately Danish women like meeting foreigners. Otherwise it's best to join a health club or sports club; or support a football team, because the Danes are footballing fanatics.

How do you manage with the climate?
I must admit that I would find it hard to cope with the climate if I couldn't get away sometimes. The winters can be depressing, it's dark when you go to work, and dark when you come home. Denmark sometimes has a very good summer, but only every four or five years. Fortunately I love sailing, and the west coast is ideal, the sea being very dramatic. The other thing of course is that Denmark is very flat and windy. I do miss mountains and hills, but I make up for it by going to Norway and Iceland

FINLAND

NIC MEPHAM

Nic is 34 and has been in Finland since 1997. He lives in the town of Kajaani in central northern Finland, and works as a creative consultant in a brand design agency.

Have you learned to speak Finnish?
People say I have, but I don't think so myself. I still feel like a child learning the language (a 34-year-old Brit going on five-year-old Finn). Even my children put me to shame. In a way being English was an advantage at first, but has become a little bit of a handicap now. Almost everyone wants to, or is able to speak English here and typically they are good at it.

I might have learned Finnish faster if English hadn't been my first language. My work situation is also unusual as I use English with my customers, colleagues and other contacts so I have little or no use for Finnish in my daily working life.

It becomes an issue at the hospital, banks, police station, shopping and official organisations. If I expect difficulties I take my secret weapon with me – my wife at the other end of a GSM phone!

As a tip, it is better to get an intensive course in your own country before trying here once you are working. You can get courses in every language but Finnish it seems. There is a lot for those looking for work, but the assumption seems to be that if you have a job you won't need to learn Finnish. I have found it all quite frustrating and have resigned myself to absorbing the language naturally by watching and listening to my family, friends, TV etc.

How do you find the social life?
I think there are around three Brits living in Kajaani the town I live in. Since I live 'up north' I guess there is a similar sprinkling around these parts and then the remainder of migrants are down around Helsinki. My wife is Finnish, we don't have so many friends here, but we have a young family and this precludes socialising much. My wife's relatives are many and so I have grown to know a lot of Finns as well as my colleagues at work and my customers.

Was it difficult to find work?
I can only sing the praises of Finland. I really love living here. I work as an idea man and creative consultant for a small but respected branding and design agency. I got the job because I was a native English-speaking designer and could project manage overseas clients and improve my colleagues' conversational English. Small talk isn't really a Finnish habit.

I had travelled a lot though Europe previous to coming here because of my last occupation in a creative language theatre company; I had no luck getting a job in the UK in my newly studied profession as a graphic designer (too much competition). I met my future wife (women are one of Finland's finer exports) and she took me home as a souvenir, so it was a small step for me to consider working abroad. I then took the option of being paid unemployment benefit from the UK while I looked for work in Finland. You should have seen the faces there when I waltzed into the office and announced 'there must be an advertising agency or creative company here who would kill for a native English speaker'. Suddenly I had something really unique on my CV. 'But you don't speak Finnish, this region has the highest unemployment in the whole of Finland – are you mad?'

Imagine their surprise when I hauled a top job just two weeks later. I have had a lot of good fortune. Perhaps I owe some of it to the refreshingly honest and open-minded approach of the Finns and the progressive thinking which abounds here. Like everywhere there are all the normal frustrations and gripes, not to mention personality, cultural differences and language issues, but life goes on. I miss things in Britain but these are easily replaced with other delights here. Nature and space come top of the list and then you have the peculiar sense of reassuring safety. The country is damn dangerous if you consider the extremes of weather and the chances of a collision with a wild animal on the road or drowning in one of the many lakes. Even though we have the huge border with Russia it just adds flavour to the whole rather than any nervous anxiety.

How do you find the Finns?
There are so few people here and mostly keep themselves to themselves. In

my opinion the term 'taciturn' I have heard used is a very unfair description. It shoots from the hip and judges the book by its cover. In my experience Finns are sensitive, serious and don't suffer fools easily. You just have to work at it and meet-in-the middle culturally. They are committed and honest and care deeply about what they do. They contemplate and then they act. They don't waste words and don't waste time. First impressions can leave you feeling it is a cold response, but it is often the exact opposite. At least that is my opinion.

Necessity has been and still is the mother of invention here and Finns are experts at this, so it is no surprise that brilliant design and superb technology leaps out of the woodwork (wood being quite the appropriate analogy) everywhere. They are still a down-to-earth society and don't pretend to be what they are not. They would rather say nothing than make I fool of themselves. Don't underestimate a Finn ever, they can be razor sharp and painfully direct! I don't find it complicated to live here and that is what I like.

NORWAY

IAN BRYCESON

Ian Bryceson is 52, has Tanzanian and Irish nationality, and has been living in Norway for 20 years. He is now a researcher in marine and coastal ecology at the Agricultural University of Norway in Ås, just south of Oslo, and also a lecturer at the University of Bergen. He lives south of Oslo and is married to a Dane.

Is Norwegian bureaucracy easy to deal with?
As I had an academic competency that was in demand in Norway the authorities were willing to give me a residence permit. What was difficult was the alien police in Oslo, who were sometimes quite unpleasant and awkward. I found later on that the police are often much friendlier in countryside stations outside Oslo.

How easy was it to get work?
I had little difficulty in finding work, as I had a higher education in a field where I was needed. It's a paradox that Norway needs more workers, but discourages them from coming. I first came here as a post-doctoral fellow at the University of Oslo. After that I worked in the private sector, and then for NORAD, the Norwegian aid organisation. Since 1993 I have had a part-time position as adjunct professor in Bergen. Most of my work is now with Noragric, the Agricultural University of Norway.

Was it easy to find accommodation?
Housing is expensive here, but of a higher quality than in Britain. When I first arrived I expected the university to help, but I was left to my own devices. I was lucky to find a place to sublet from some Norwegians who were going abroad. I left Oslo as soon as I could; housing is much cheaper outside Oslo, and people are generally much friendlier in the countryside. Houses here are often made of wood, because they are actually easier to insulate than stone houses, and therefore

easier to heat. The only problem is that wooden houses don't last as long, so you have to replace the walls after some decades.

How did you find the social life and the Norwegians?

To start with most of my friends were other foreigners at the university. It takes time to get to know people. The Norwegians are reserved, but you can make good friendships after some time. They generally appreciate it if you take the initiative. One has to remember that the population is very spread out; there aren't really even villages as such, like in England, and going out to pubs and restaurants is more of a recent development. You are more likely to meet people if you join a club, or get involved in sports. If you have children at school you will meet other parents. There is a very big difference between town and country here; outside Oslo the people have held on to their traditions more, and it's a lot friendlier. Many Norwegians are sceptical about centralised power, which is why they are not all keen to join the European Union. However, there has been something of a change in the political climate here in the last 20 years: there is generally less concern with social equality, there is more of a difference between rich and poor than there was, and more of a culture of competition. The Norwegian Labour Party has rather got cut off from its ideals.

Have you been accepted in Norway?

As a white Tanzanian I'm in an unusual position; a lot of my friends are Africans and other people from the Third World, and they do experience problems here because of their race. In the beginning when I said I was from Tanzania, people would ask me when I was leaving: they were not that pleased when I said I was staying. Once I had learned to speak Norwegian things improved. The problem with racism in Norway is growing, though it is perhaps not as bad here as in some European countries, but the anti-immigrant party is in decline right now.

SWEDEN

CHRIS FOWLER

Chris Fowler is 47, British, and Professor of Pharmacology at Umeå University on the north-east coast of Sweden. He is married to a Swede, and has two children.

How did you first get work in Sweden?

After finishing my doctorate at Cambridge, I got a post-doc position in Sweden, in 1978, and stayed for two years. After spells in Ireland and France, I returned to Sweden to work for Astra Zeneca and stayed with them for 13 years. I got my present position in 1995.

How easy was it to learn the language?

It took me a year to learn Swedish. Although the Swedes say it's a difficult language, it isn't in my opinion, because it has very regular rules. Many Swedes speak very good English, however I found that the ones who spoke less good English were quite happy to speak Swedish with me, as they didn't want to be shown up in front of their colleagues. My superiors on the other hand would usually speak English with me.

How is the bureaucracy?
It's better than it was. I find I can fill in my tax return in half an hour. Residence permits are quite simple, unless you're from outside the EU. Running a business is more difficult, but that is more to do with the level of taxation rather than the organisation.

What about the taxes?
It is true that taxes are relatively high in Sweden, but you have to consider what you get in return. You don't have to pay for private health insurance; everything is taken care of. The way I see it is that paying taxes is a matter of solidarity with the less well-off. There is a belief that it's difficult to get foreigners to come to work in Sweden, because of the high taxes. Generally you wouldn't target people who were looking to make a fast buck. People come here for the quality of life rather than to make a lot of money in a hurry.

How did you find Swedish accommodation?
Housing is expensive, although not as much as in Britain, but of a very high standard. Stockholm is the most difficult to place to find accommodation; university towns are also difficult. If you live out in the countryside then you can find very cheap houses.

How did you find the social life?
The Swedes can be a bit reserved to start with, but once you get to know them you may soon know them much better than British people. It's not true to say that all Swedes are inhibited; there are some who will explode straight away if they get angry, and others who won't. Social life tends to revolve around study groups. When I first came here there were hardly any pubs or places to meet people, but there a lot more now. In the past Swedes were more binge drinkers, but these days the idea of having a beer after work is becoming more usual.

The Swedes are interested in meeting foreigners. If you have children you will meet other parents at the school. It's a good idea to join a sports club or some other kind of society. In general I would say that, at least as far as Brits are concerned, they either love it or hate it.

How is the climate?
Some people do find the long winters difficult. The worst time is in April and early May, when you know that it's spring elsewhere, and you're still waiting for it to arrive. I like it here in the winter, when there's snow outside and a blue sky. It very much depends on the individual how they feel about the climate.